For Karen and Chase

Get the eBook FREE!

(PDF, ePub, Kindle, and liveBook all included)

We believe that once you buy a book from us, you should be able to read it in any format we have available. To get electronic versions of this book at no additional cost to you, purchase and then register this book at the Manning website.

Go to https://www.manning.com/freebook and follow the instructions to complete your pBook registration.

That's it!
Thanks from Manning!

WEB DESIGN
PLAYGROUND

WEB DESIGN PLAYGROUND

PLAYGROUND

HTML + CSS THE INTERACTIVE WAY

Paul McFedries

MANNING
Shelter Island

Manning Publications Co.
20 Baldwin Road
PO Box 761
Shelter Island, NY 11964

Development editor: Karen Miller
Technical development editors: Doug Sparling and Helen Sparling
Review editor: Aleksandar Dragosavljević
Production editor: Deirdre Hiam
Copyeditor: Kathy Simpson
Proofreader: Michelle Melani
Technical proofreader: Louis Lazaris
Typesetting: Happenstance Type-O-Rama
Cover designer: Monica Kamsvaag

ISBN 9781617294402
Printed in the United States of America

Contents

Preface xi
Acknowledgments xiii
About This Book xv
About the Author xix

PART 1 GETTING STARTED WITH HTML AND CSS

Chapter 1 Getting to Know HTML and CSS 3
What Is HTML? 4
What Is CSS? 7
What Can't You Do with HTML and CSS? 10
How HTML and CSS Create the Web 10
Introducing the Web Design Playground 11
Adding HTML Tag Attributes 15
Some Helpful Features of the Playground 19

Chapter 2 Building Your First Web Page 21
Getting Your Web Page off the Ground 22
Learning the Most Common Text Elements 26

Chapter 3 Adding Structure to Your Page 37
HTML Elements for Structuring Page Text 38
Organizing Text Into Lists 44

Chapter 4 Formatting Your Web Page 51
Styling Text 52
Working with Text Styles 57
Styling Paragraphs 60
Working with Colors 64

Chapter 5 Project: Creating a Personal Home Page 69
What You'll Be Building 70
Sketching the Layout 70
Choosing Typefaces 71
Choosing a Color Scheme 71
Building the Page 72
From Here 81

PART 2 WORKING WITH IMAGES AND STYLES

Chapter 6 Adding Images and Other Media 85
Understanding Image File Formats 87
Getting Graphics 88
Inserting an HTML5 Figure 89
Setting Up an Image as a Link 90
Using an Image as a Custom Bullet 91
Aligning Images and Text 92
Controlling the Background Repeat 95
Setting the Background Position 96
Adding a Hero Image 97
The Background Shorthand Property 99
Optimizing Images 99
Adding Video and Audio to the Page 100

Chapter 7 Learning More About Styles 109
Adding Styles to a Page 110
Units of Measurement in CSS 119

Chapter 8 Floating and Positioning Elements 121
Understanding the Default Page Flow 122

Chapter 9 Styling Sizes, Borders, and Margins 139
The Anatomy of an Element Box 140
Watch Out for Collapsing Margins! 152

Chapter 10 Project: Creating a Landing Page 155
What You'll Be Building 156
Sketching the Layout 156
Choosing Typefaces 157
Choosing a Color Scheme 158
Building the Page 159
From Here 178

PART 3 LAYING OUT A WEB PAGE

Chapter 11 Learning Page Layout Basics 183
The Holy-Grail Layout 184
Understanding Web Page Layout Methods 185
Learning the HTML5 Semantic Page Elements 186
Creating Page Layouts with Floats 191
Creating Page Layouts with Inline Blocks 196

Chapter 12 Creating Page Layouts with Flexbox **203**

Understanding Flexbox *204*

Chapter 13 Designing Responsive Web Pages **229**

Creating a Responsive Layout *233*

Chapter 14 Making Your Images and Typography
Responsive **251**

Making Images Responsive *252*

Making Typography Responsive *257*

Gallery of Responsive Sites *263*

Chapter 15 Project: Creating a Photo Gallery **269**

What You'll Be Building *270*

Getting Your Photos Ready *270*

Sketching the Layout *270*

Choosing Typefaces *271*

Choosing the Colors *272*

Building the Page *272*

Adding a Few Tricks *281*

From Here *286*

PART 4 MAKING YOUR WEB PAGES SHINE

Chapter 16 More HTML Elements for Web Designers **289**

More about Links *298*

Inserting Special Characters *302*

Using the HTML5 Entity Browser *303*

Adding Comments *304*

Chapter 17 Adding a Splash of Color
to Your Web Designs **305**

Understanding Colors *306*

Adding Colors with CSS *309*

Choosing Harmonious Colors *317*

Using the Color Scheme Calculator *318*

Color Scheme Gallery *320*

Applying a Color Gradient *322*

Chapter 18 Enhancing Page Text with Typography **331**

Specifying the Typeface *332*

Working with Text Styles *340*

Web Typography Gallery *346*

Chapter 19 Learning Advanced CSS Selectors **349**

Working with ID Selectors 350

Web Page Genealogy: Parents, Descendants, and Siblings 352

Working with Contextual Selectors 353

Taking Things up a Notch by Combining Selectors 359

Resetting CSS with the Universal Selector 362

Styles: What a Tangled Web Page They Weave 363

Chapter 20 Project: Creating a Portfolio Page **371**

What You'll Be Building 372

Sketching the Layout 372

Choosing Typefaces 373

Choosing a Color Scheme 375

Building the Page 376

From Here 392

Appendix From Playground to Web:
Getting Your Pages Online 395

Index 407

Preface

In today's world, lots of people crave the experience of expressing themselves online. They can do that through fixed-format media such as Facebook, Twitter, and Instagram, but for many people, these sites are too restrictive. Instead, they prefer to build their own presence on the web, and the way to do that with the maximum amount of freedom and creativity is to learn HTML and CSS.

In programming circles, many people believe that the best way to learn how to code is by coding. Reading about the language is fine and necessary, but if you really want to learn the language, you must use it. My own belief is that the best way to learn to code is to *play* with code. For HTML and CSS, this means two things:

- In standard HTML/CSS teaching, you're given some code—a tag, say, or a template—and are told how it works. In *playful* HTML/CSS teaching, you're given some code and encouraged to play with it: change the font size, expand the padding, apply colors, and so on.

- In standard HTML/CSS teaching, you're given simple or trivial examples, such as the classic Hello World! demonstration. In *playful* HTML/CSS teaching, you're given substantive, useful projects to build from scratch and customize to suit your needs.

This spirit of playfulness and experiment pervades *Web Design Playground*, and I encourage you to view HTML and CSS as tools for creativity and expression.

Acknowledgments

The English essayist Joseph Addison once described an editor as someone who "rides in the whirlwind and directs the storm." I don't know if that's true for editors in some of the more sedate publishing nooks (novels and cookbooks and such), but I think it applies perfectly to the rigors of computer-book editing. Why? Well, the computer industry (and the web in particular) is so exacting that even the teensiest authorial (or editorial) lapse could result in a book that sows confusion and consternation rather than certainty and delight.

The good folks at Manning Publications minimize book blunders by subjecting each manuscript to a barrage of reviews, not only by editorial specialists, but also by a team of dedicated outsiders (in a process I call "gang reviewing"). Instead of a process in which single-digit numbers of eyeballs look at the manuscript, a Manning book is scrutinized by dozens, so you get a book that contains accurate and relevant information and a book that has passed muster with some of the sharpest eyes and ears in the business. My name may be the only one that appears on the cover, but tons of people had a big role in creating what you now hold in your hands. Those reviewers were Conor Redmond, Eric Cantuba, Itai Polatnick, Jose San Leandro, Liam Kemp, Nitin Ainani, Prabhuti Prakash, Richard Fieldsend, Sachin Kumar, Scott Dierbeck, Sebastian Maier, Shawn Eion Smith, Thomas Overby Hansen, Vasile Boris, and Zoheb Ainapore. Of those I worked with directly, I'd like to extend warm thanks to publisher Marjan Bace, acquisitions editor Brian Sawyer, development editor Karen Miller, editorial director Bert Bates, development manager Rebecca Rinehart, designer Monica Kamsvaag, review editor Aleksandar Dragosavljević, MEAP coordinator Matko Hrvatin, assistant acquisitions editor Nicole Butterfield, technical editors Doug Sparling and Helen Sparling, technical proofreader Louis Lazaris, copyeditor Kathy Simpson, proofreader Michelle Melani, production editor Deirdre Hiam, design editor Janet Vail, and quality reviewer Barbara Mirecki.

The members of the editorial team aren't the only people who had their fingers in this publishing pie. Flip back a few pages, and you'll find a list of other professionals who worked long and hard to produce this book. I tip my authorial hat to all of them. I'd also like to thank all the people who took the time to review the early manuscripts of the book and to offer comments and suggestions. Your couple of cents' worth was very much appreciated.

Finally, I'd be remiss if I didn't extend a hearty and heartfelt thanks to my agent, Carole Jelen, whose hard work made this project possible and whose breathtaking knowledge of the technical-publishing industry fills me with awe and makes me grateful every day to have Carole working on my behalf.

About This Book

In this book, I teach you how to create beautiful web pages in no time flat. I understand that the very idea of trying to create something that looks as good as what you see on the web sounds like an intimidating challenge. However, it's my goal in this book to show you that it's quite straightforward and that *anyone* can build an attractive and sophisticated web page with his or her bare hands. I even try to have—gasp!—a little irreverent fun as I go along.

You'll also be happy to know that this book doesn't assume that you have any experience in web design, HTML, or CSS. You start from scratch and slowly build your knowledge until, before you know it, you have your very own tract of web real estate. All the information is presented in short, easy-to-digest chunks that you can skim to find the information you want. The online Web Design Playground (https://webdesignplayground.io) also offers instruction and exercises that you can work through to hone your knowledge.

I'm assuming that you have a life away from your computer screen, so *Web Design Playground* is set up so that you don't have to read it from cover to cover. If you want to know how to add an image to your web page, for example, turn to the chapter that covers working with images (that would be Chapter 6). Beginners, however, will want to read at least chapters 1 through 4 before moving on to more esoteric topics. To make things easier to find, the following section gives you a summary of the book's 20 chapters (and one appendix).

Road Map

Chapter 1 introduces you to HTML and CSS. You learn about the benefits and limitations of these essential web design technologies, and you learn how HTML tags and CSS properties work. You also get a brief introduction to the book's companion website, the Web Design Playground.

Chapter 2 takes you on a journey to build your first web page. You learn how to set up the basic structure of a page and then add a title and some text. From there, you learn how to mark up important and emphasized text, quote text, add headings, and create links.

Chapter 3 shows you how to add some structure to a web page by giving you the HTML tags that divide page text into paragraphs, add line breaks, organize page text into separate chunks, and create inline containers for styling words and phrases. You also get the lowdown on building numbered and bulleted lists.

Chapter 4 shifts back to CSS and shows you how to format text by applying a typeface, a type size, and bold and italic styling. You also learn how to align and indent paragraphs and how to apply colors to the page text and background.

Chapter 5 covers the first project of the book. In this case, you gather the HTML and CSS knowledge from chapters 1 through 4 and use it to build a personal home page for yourself.

Chapter 6 shows you how to augment your web pages with nontext elements. Most of the chapter covers images, such as photos and illustrations, but you also learn how to add video and audio files.

Chapter 7 furthers your CSS education by showing you the three ways you can add styles to a page. You also learn how to wield class selectors, which are among the most useful and powerful CSS techniques. I also introduce you to the various measurement units you can use in your CSS rules.

Chapter 8 gives you the tools you need to take charge of your page elements by taking them out of the default page flow used by the web browser. You learn how to float elements on the page and also how to position elements relative to other elements or to the browser window itself.

Chapter 9 introduces you to one of the most powerful concepts in all of CSS: the box model. You learn what the box model is all about, and you use it to set an element's width and height, add padding around an element's content, and augment an element with a border and a margin.

Chapter 10 takes you through the book's second project, which is a landing page for a product or service. You run through the full page-building process, from sketching the design to choosing the typefaces and colors to building the page structure and content.

Chapter 11 gets you started on the all-important topic of web page layout. I introduce you to HTML5's semantic page layout tags—including `<header>`, `<article>`, and `<footer>`—and show you how to create page layouts by using both floated elements and inline blocks.

Chapter 12 gives you a complete tutorial on using the powerful, popular flexbox layout technology. You learn what flexbox is and what it can do; you learn the fundamentals of the technology; and then you put flexbox to work creating a standard web page layout.

Chapter 13 introduces responsive web pages, one of the hottest topics in modern web design. You learn techniques that enable you to structure your web pages so that they adapt to changing device screens, from giant desktop monitors to tiny smartphone screens.

Chapter 14 continues your education in responsive web design by showing you how to configure your images and your page typography to respond to screen size. This chapter also includes a gallery of sites that do the responsive thing right so you can see how the pros do it.

Chapter 15 covers the book's third project, which is an attractive, sophisticated photo gallery. You sketch the layout, choose font and colors, and then build the page step-by-step.

Chapter 16 takes you on a tour of many more HTML tags that will come in handy during your web design career. You also learn how to use more-sophisticated linking techniques, add special characters (ones that aren't readily accessible via the keyboard), and make your page source code easier to understand with comments.

Chapter 17 is all about color, and you learn some color theory; you also learn how colors work in CSS, and the various techniques that you can use to apply a color. This chapter gives you some pointers on choosing a harmonious color scheme for your pages. Finally, you learn how to apply a color gradient to a page element.

Chapter 18 focuses on web page typography. You learn more about how to apply a typeface, including using third-party fonts (such as those from the Google Fonts collection) and how to host your own fonts. You also learn how to apply small caps and set the line height for easier reading.

Chapter 19 presents several advanced but vitally important CSS concepts. You learn lots more about CSS selectors, and you get some background on three crucial CSS ideas: inheritance, the cascade, and specificity.

Chapter 20 presents the book's fourth and final project: a website for showing off your personal portfolio. After building the basic structure, you learn how to add site navigation, portfolio images, contact info, and more.

The appendix is devoted to getting your web code online. You learn the various ways you can get your code from the Web Design Playground to your computer. From there, I talk about how to choose a web hosting provider and how to obtain a domain name. I close by showing you how to upload and validate your files.

Code

To encourage play and experimentation, the book has a companion website called the Web Design Playground (located at https://webdesignplayground.io). The site lets you type your HTML and CSS code in the editors provided, and the browser's rendering of that code appears automatically in the Results window.

The Web Design Playground also gives you access to all the book's example files, which you can customize and play with as your creativity takes you. To facilitate experimentation and to reinforce the overall sense of play, the book's tutorial chapters also offer numerous hands-on exercises that direct you to use the Playground to modify the provided code in various ways. This helps you not only learn the material, but also see the range of what's possible.

The Playground has an extensive help system to show you how everything works, but you can find the basics in Chapter 1. Instructions for getting the code from the Playground to your computer are provided for you in the appendix.

About the Author

PAUL McFEDRIES has been a professional technical writer for more than 25 years. He has nearly 100 books to his credit, which collectively have sold more than 4 million copies worldwide. When he's not writing books, Paul is building web pages, which he's been doing since 1996. Paul has hand-coded many sites, including his web home (https://mcfedries.com); Word Spy (https://wordspy.com); WebDev Workshop (https://webdev.mcfedries.com); and this book's companion site, Web Design Playground (https://webdesignplayground.io).

Part 1

Getting Started with HTML and CSS

This book begins at the beginning by defining HTML and CSS, introducing you to tags and properties, and showing you what you can (and can't) do with these web design technologies. With Chapter 1's brief but necessary introduction out of the way, in Chapter 2 you dive in and create your first web page, complete with formatted text, headings, and links. The rest of Part 1 builds on this foundation by showing you how to add structure to your page (Chapter 3) and how to style typefaces, paragraphs, and colors (Chapter 4). Chapter 5 brings everything together with a project that shows you how to build a personal home page to show off to the world.

Chapter 1

Getting to Know HTML and CSS

This chapter covers

- Viewing the fundamentals of HTML and CSS
- Introducing the Web Design Playground
- Learning how to construct HTML tags and CSS properties

When a jazz musician creates an improvisation, no matter how intricate, she plays by using combinations of seven musical notes (A through G). When an artist creates a picture, no matter how detailed, he paints by using combinations of three primary colors (red, yellow, and blue). When poets create verse, no matter how inventive, they write by using words that are combinations of the 26 letters of the alphabet. These examples show that creativity and play don't require elaborate resources or complex raw materials. Imagination and curiosity combined with a few building blocks are all you need to express yourself in almost any art, including the art of web page design. As you learn in this chapter and throughout this book, HTML and CSS provide those building blocks. And although there are more of those blocks than there are musical notes, primary colors, or even letters of the alphabet, there aren't too many, but more than enough to let you express yourself on an exciting modern canvas: the web.

What Is HTML?

The hardest thing about HTML by far is its name. *HTML* stands for *Hypertext Markup Language*, which sounds about as inviting as a tax audit. But it becomes a lot less intimidating when you break down its terms.

I'll begin with *hypertext*. A *link*, as I'm sure you know, is a special word or phrase (or even an image) in a web page that "points" to another web page. When you click one of these links, your browser transports you to the other page immediately. The folks who invented the web used the geeky term *hypertext link* for this special text. (The prefix *hyper* means *beyond*.) Because these hypertext links are the distinguishing features of the web, pages are often known as hypertext documents. So *HTML* has *hypertext* in it because you use it to create these hypertext documents. (It would be just as accurate to call this language WPML, or Web Page Markup Language.)

My dictionary defines *markup* as (among other things) "detailed stylistic instructions written on a manuscript that is to be typeset." For the purposes of this chapter, I can rephrase this definition as follows: "detailed stylistic instructions typed in a text document that is to be published on the World Wide Web." That's HTML in a nutshell. It has a few simple alphabetic codes—called *tags*—for detailing things such as herding text into paragraphs, creating bulleted lists, inserting images, and (of course) defining links. You type these tags in the appropriate places in an ordinary text document, and the web browser handles the dirty work of translating—or *rendering*—the tags. The result? Your page is displayed the way you want automatically.

The word *language* may be the most intimidating because it seems to imply that HTML is a programming language. Fortunately, you can rest assured that HTML has nothing to do with computer programming. Rather, HTML is a "language" in the sense that it has a small collection of words that you use to specify how you want your text to appear—as a heading or as a numbered list, for example.

In short, playing with HTML means inserting a few codes strategically between stretches of regular text in such a way that you end up with an honest-to-goodness web page. As far-fetched as this may sound to you now, you'll create a working web page by the end of this chapter, and by the end of this book, you'll have created several impressive HTML projects.

What Can You Do with HTML?

When you add HTML to a document, you're essentially giving the web browser a series of instructions that specify how you want the page to be laid out within the browser window. You use HTML to specify, in its succinct way, the overall structure of the page and to let the browser know what you want each part of the page to be. You use HTML to supply instructions similar to the following:

- Use this line as the main heading of the page.

- Treat these lines as subheadings.

- Make this chunk of text a separate paragraph.
- Turn these five consecutive items into a bulleted list.
- Convert these six consecutive steps to a numbered list.
- Make this phrase a link.

These instructions likely seem a bit abstract to you now, so I'll show you a concrete example of HTML in action.

From Plain Text to HTML: An Example

Figure 1.1 shows a plain-text document displayed in a web browser. As you can see, except for the occasional line break, the browser displays a wall of unformatted, unwrapped text. This text is extremely difficult to read, and it's exceptionally hard to extract meaning from the text because it's almost entirely undifferentiated.

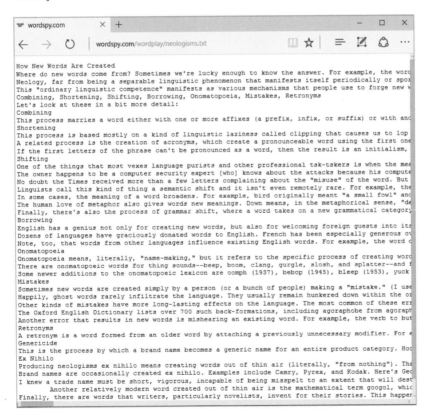

▶ Figure 1.1
The browser can display plain-text files, but they're awfully hard to read.

HTML rides to the rescue, not only providing the means to make plain text more readable, but also allowing you to display the text in a way that your readers will find meaningful. Figure 1.2 shows the text from Figure 1.1 with some HTML applied.

▶ Figure 1.2 With some HTML applied, the text from Figure 1.1 becomes easier to read, navigate, and understand.

Here, I've used headings to display both the article title at the top and a section title near the bottom. Notice that the section title is rendered in a type size that's slightly smaller than the main title, making the article hierarchy immediately clear. I also used HTML to add an image for visual interest. To help put the *H* in this page's HTML, I set up two of the words as links to (in this case) other sites. Although you see a bit later in this chapter that text formatting usually is the domain of CSS, you can also use HTML to add a bit of formatting flourish to your pages, such as the italics I added here. I also set up a quotation, which the browser renders indented from the regular text, and I added italics to that quotation for added differentiation. Finally, I used HTML to set up a bulleted list.

Now that you know what HTML can do, it's time to take a closer look at how you tell the browser what you want your page to look like.

What Is CSS?

When you build a house, one of the early jobs is framing, which involves putting up the basic structure for the floors, walls, and roof. That foundational framing is what you're doing when you add HTML to your page: You specify what you want to appear on the page, what you want the page's various items to be (such as a heading, paragraph, or list), and the order in which you want these items to appear.

But as a house isn't a home without finishing touches such as molding, paint, and flooring, your document isn't a modern example of a web page until you've used CSS to add some finishing work. *CSS* stands for *Cascading Style Sheets*, and as is the case with HTML, its name is more complicated than what it does. I'll break down the words, although in this case, I'll address them slightly out of order for simplicity's sake.

First, a *style* is an instruction to the browser to modify how it displays something on the page. (That something could be a word, a paragraph, or every instance of a particular HTML element.) These modifications usually are formatting-related, such as changing the typeface or the text color, but you can also use styles to control page layout and even to create animated effects. If you've ever used styles in a word processing program, you already have a good idea of what web page styles can do.

Okay, so what's a *sheet*? In the early days of publishing, firms maintained manuals that defined their preferred formatting for typefaces, headings, pulled quotes, and so on. This formatting was known as *house styles*, and the manual was called a *style sheet*. In web design, a style sheet performs essentially the same duties. It's a collection of styles that get applied to a particular web page.

To understand the *cascading* part of CSS, you need to know that, in the same way that water running down a hill can take different routes to the bottom, styles can take different routes before they get applied to an element. Some styles come from the web browser; some styles come from the user (if the user configures her browser to use a different default type size, for example); and some styles come from your style sheets. When these styles overlap, the web browser uses a complex algorithm to decide which style gets applied, and that algorithm is called the *cascade*.

You use CSS, in other words, to define how your page looks. It may seem that you use CSS only to add "eye candy" to a page, and it's certainly true that CSS offers you the tools to make only trivial or frivolous modifications. *How* your page looks, however, is every bit as important as *what* your page contains, because few people will bother to read text that's formatted poorly or incoherently.

BEWARE

The idea of the cascade is by far the most complex and convoluted aspect of CSS. I get into it later in the book (see Chapter 19), but for now, I highly recommend that you transfer it to a mental back burner until you get that far.

A Note about the Separation of Structure and Presentation

While you're trying to wrap your head around the differences between HTML and CSS, let me offer a key distinction. Although I'm generalizing somewhat, here's the basic difference between the two:

- HTML defines the overall structure of the web page.
- CSS defines the visual presentation of the web page.

Some overlap exists here (HTML can affect the presentation of the page, for example, and CSS can affect the layout), but for the most part, HTML and CSS enable you to separate structure and presentation, respectively. This distinction is important because when you keep these two aspects of a web page separate, your page will be easier to build, easier to maintain, and easier to customize.

What Can You Do with CSS?

When you add CSS to a document, you're telling the web browser how you want specific elements to look. Each style is a kind of formatting instruction to the browser. You can use these instructions in a wide variety of ways that are similar to the following examples:

- Display all the links in red text.
- Use a specific font for all the headings.
- Create a bit of extra space around this paragraph.
- Add a shadow to this photo.
- Use lowercase Roman numerals for all numbered lists.
- Always display this section of text on the far-right side of the window.
- Rotate this drawing by 45 degrees.

I'll make this list more concrete by showing you an example.

From Structure to Presentation: A CSS Example

Earlier in this chapter, I took a plain-text document (Figure 1.1) and applied a bit of HTML to give it some structure and improve its readability (Figure 1.2). In Figure 1.3, I've applied a few styles to make the page look a bit nicer.

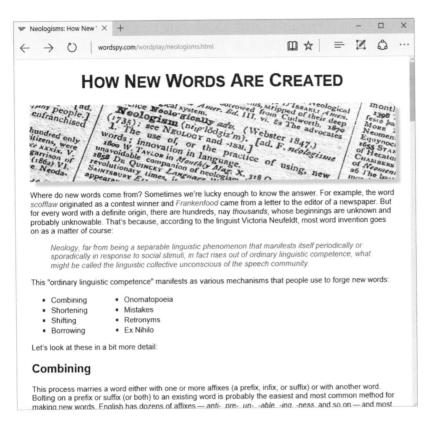

▶ Figure 1.3
The example web page with
a few styles applied

Here's a summary of the major styles changes I made:

- Displayed the title in a larger text size, centered and in small caps
- Added a shadow to the photo
- Made all the text slightly smaller
- Removed the underline from the links
- Displayed the quotation in lighter-color text
- Converted the bullets to a two-column list
- Increased the side margins

What Can't You Do with HTML and CSS?

Earlier, I mentioned that HTML isn't a programming language, so it's fairly straightforward to learn and to deploy it in your web pages, which is good news. The bad news is that HTML can't handle many higher-level operations *because* it's not a programming language. The list of what you can't do with HTML alone is quite long, but I'll mention the following because one or more of them may be on your to-do list:

- Get data from a server database or other remote address
- Process data submitted through a form
- Handle user accounts, logins, and passwords
- Add, hide, or remove web page elements on-the-fly

Performing tasks like these requires a programming language such as JavaScript or PHP, which are well beyond the scope of this book.

How HTML and CSS Create the Web

One of the most extraordinary facts about the web is that (with the exception of extra features such as images, videos, and sounds), its pages are composed of nothing but text. That's right—almost everything you see as you surf the web was created by stringing together the letters, numbers, and symbols that you can tap on your keyboard.

That idea is a mysterious one, to say the least, so I'll give you a quick look at how it works. Figure 1.4 shows the process.

The following steps explain the process in detail:

1 You use a text editor or similar software to create your HTML and CSS files.

2 You upload your HTML and CSS files to an online service called a *web hosting provider*, which runs a web server.

 When you sign up for an account, the hosting provider issues you a unique address, such as www.yourdomain.com. So if you upload a file named index.html, the address of that page is www.yourdomain.com/index.html.

3 A site visitor uses her web browser to type the address of your page.

4 The web browser uses that address to request your page from the web server.

5 After making sure that the address is correct, the web server sends the page to the user's web browser.

6 The web browser interprets the page's HTML tags and CSS properties through a process called *rendering*, and the rendered code appears on the user's device.

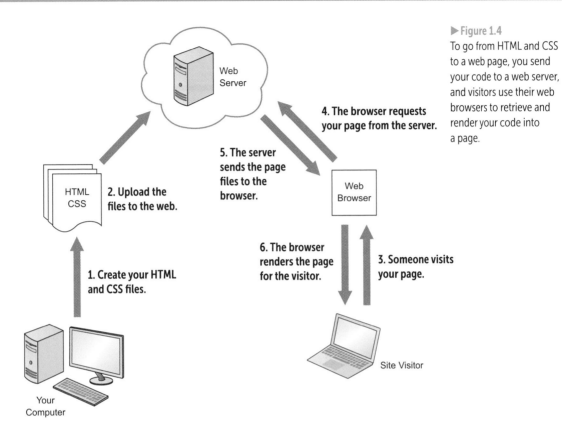

► Figure 1.4
To go from HTML and CSS to a web page, you send your code to a web server, and visitors use their web browsers to retrieve and render your code into a page.

As you can see, the fact that the web is made of simple stuff doesn't mean that getting that stuff on the web is a simple matter. In fact, the procedure is a bit convoluted, especially when you're starting. That's why I devote appendix A to the process.

Introducing the Web Design Playground

Right now, though, you're probably itching to start playing around with HTML and CSS and seeing what these fascinating technologies can do. I don't blame you. One of this book's core ideas is that the best way to learn HTML and CSS is to have fun playing with your new knowledge, trying out different tags and properties, and experimenting with different values. To help you do all that with the least amount of fuss, I've built an online tool called the Web Design Playground, shown in Figure 1.5, which you can access at https://webdesignplayground.io/.

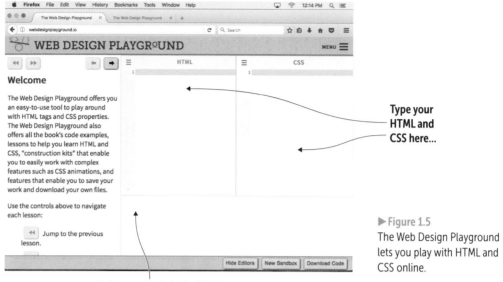

Type your HTML and CSS here...

...and what your code looks like in the web browser appears here.

▶ Figure 1.5
The Web Design Playground lets you play with HTML and CSS online.

You can use this site to try out HTML tags and CSS properties, load the book's example files, run through lessons that help you learn a topic, access various "construction kits" for experimenting with features, save your work, and even download the resulting file to your computer. The next few sections provide the details.

Playing with HTML and CSS

The main purpose of the Web Design Playground is to provide an easy-to-use tool for playing around with HTML tags and CSS properties. Here's how it works:

1   In the Web Design Playground, use the HTML Editor to type the HTML tags you want to try.

    If a tag requires one or more attributes, be sure to add them as well.

2   Use the CSS Editor to type the CSS property definitions you want to use.

3   Examine the Results box, which displays what your HTML and CSS will look like in a web browser.

4   Repeat steps 1–3 to fix any problems or perform further experiments.

Loading the Lesson Files

This book contains a ton of HTML and CSS code. As a general rule, you'll learn these subjects in a deeper way if you type the examples by hand (which gives you what I call a "fingertip feel" for the code). I understand, however, that you're a busy person who may not have the time to type each example. To help you, the Web Design Playground includes a menu that links to every lesson from the book. When you select a lesson, you see an introduction followed by one or more examples and then by one or more activities that help you learn the lesson material. In each case, the code appears automatically, and you can play around with it as you see fit.

Here are the steps to follow to load a lesson:

1 In the Web Design Playground, click Menu at the right end of the toolbar. A menu of the site's links appears.

The Book Lessons section contains an item for each chapter in the book.

2 Click the chapter that contains the lesson you're looking for.

3 In the submenu that appears, click the lesson you want to play with.

The lesson introduction appears.

4 Click the Next Page button.

The lesson example's HTML tags and text appear in the HTML Editor, and the example's CSS code appears in the CSS Editor.

5 Click Next Page to work through the activities for the lesson.

6 To jump to another lesson in the same chapter, click the drop-down menu above the Previous Page and Next Page buttons, and then click the lesson you want to see.

Preserving Your Work

You'll spend most of your time in the Web Design Playground performing experiments and trying out this book's exercises. Occasionally, however, you'll create some code that you want to save. The Web Design Playground gives you two ways to do that:

- *Copy some code.* To copy code for use elsewhere, use the HTML Editor or the CSS Editor to select the code you want to copy; click the editor's Menu icon; and then click Copy to Clipboard.

- *Download your work.* Click Menu, and below the Sandbox heading, click Download Code. This command saves the HTML and CSS and separate files, which are stored in a zip archive and downloaded to your web browser's default downloads folder.

Now that you know what you can do with HTML and CSS and how to use the Web Design Playground, you're ready to use the Playground to understand how to work with HTML tags and CSS properties.

Lesson 1.1: *Introducing HTML Tags*
Covers: HTML tags

➡ **Online:** wdpg.io/1-1-0

PLAY

The addresses that appear here and elsewhere in this chapter refer to locations in the Web Design Playground, this book's companion online site. See "Introducing the Web Design Playground" earlier in this chapter.

HTML works its magic through short codes called *tags*. Each tag consists of three parts:

- An opening left angle bracket (<), also known as the *less-than sign*.
- The name of the element you want to use. Element names are short alphanumeric codes such as p for a paragraph, em for emphasis, and h1 for a first-level heading.
- A closing right angle bracket (>), also known as the *greater-than sign*.

Angle brackets

`<h1>`

Element name

▶ Figure 1.6
The structure of a typical HTML tag

In most cases, the tag tells the browser to start laying out the page according to the element you specified. If you add the <em> tag, for example, you're telling the browser to display the text that follows in italics. (em is short for *emphasis*.) You also have to tell the browser when you want it to stop displaying the text with that element, so you need to add a companion called the *closing tag*. (The original tag is the *opening tag*.) The closing tag is the same as the opening tag except that it requires a forward slash before the element name. A closing tag consists of the following four parts:

- An opening left angle bracket (<)
- A forward slash (/)
- The name of the element
- A closing right angle bracket (>)

MASTER

Throughout this book, I use the word element *to refer to a specific item of HTML, such as p or em, and the word* tag *to refer to the element and its surrounding angle brackets, such as <p> or <em>.*

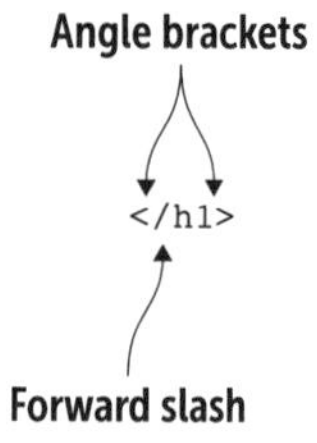

Angle brackets

`</h1>`

Forward slash

▶ Figure 1.7
The structure of the closing tag for the h1 element

Figure 1.7 shows the closing tag for an h1 element. Together, the opening and closing tags create a kind of container to which you add some text (or even other elements); the browser displays the text according to the element that you specify in the tags. In Figure 1.1 earlier in this chapter, the text *How New Words Are Created* appears at the top of the file. To turn that text into the article's main heading as shown in Figure 1.2, I applied the <h1> tag, which displays the text as a first-level heading. The following example shows how I did it.

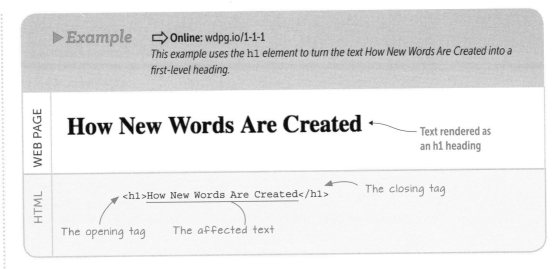

▶ *Example* ⇨ **Online:** wdpg.io/1-1-1
This example uses the h1 *element to turn the text How New Words Are Created into a first-level heading.*

WEB PAGE

How New Words Are Created ◄— Text rendered as an h1 heading

HTML

```
<h1>How New Words Are Created</h1>
```
The closing tag

The opening tag   The affected text

By adding a few characters, you're telling the browser to do a whole bunch of things to the text:

- Display the text in its own paragraph.
- Add a bit of vertical space above and below the text.
- Format the text as bold.
- Format the text larger than the regular-page text to make clear that the text is a heading.

You learn more about headings in Chapter 2, but you can see that this deceptively simple code lets you do many things without much work. That's the magic of HTML.

Adding HTML Tag Attributes

Many HTML elements require no embellishment: You add the tag to the page, and the browser does the rest. A few tags, however, do require extra information before the web browser can process them correctly. You use the `<img>` tag, for example, to insert a picture into a web page, but you need to tell the web browser where your image is located. Similarly, to create a link, you use the `<a>` tag, but again, the web browser needs more info. In this case, it needs to know *what* you want to link to (such as the address of another website).

You supply these and similar extra bits of data to the browser by adding one or more attributes to the tag. An *attribute* is a name-value pair in which the name tells the browser the specific attribute and the value assigns it the particular setting you want to use.

MASTER

Although most HTML elements have both an opening and a closing tag, not all of them do. The element that you use to insert an image, for example (see Chapter 6), doesn't require a closing tag. These tags are known as self-closing tags.

PLAY

The text in Figure 1.1 has several single-word paragraphs that are intended to be headings. Line 7, for example, consists of the text Combining. Given what you've learned about applying a first-level heading to the article title, apply a second-level heading to the Combining text.
⇨ Online: wdpg.io/1-1-3

When you're writing a link, for example, you specify the link address by adding the `href` attribute and setting its value to the address you want to use. Figure 1.8 shows an example.

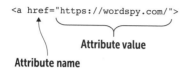

▶ Figure 1.8

You can use attributes to specify extra data for some HTML elements, such as the link address for an `<a>` tag.

Here, the `href` (short for *hypertext reference*) attribute is assigned the value `https://wordspy.com/`, which is the address the user will be taken to if she clicks this link. Notice that the attribute value is surrounded by double quotation marks. These quotation marks are optional, but using them makes your code easier to read and maintain.

When combined with attributes, HTML can do some useful, powerful things. But HTML isn't the only web page tool you get to play with. In many ways, CSS is far more powerful and fun than HTML, and you begin learning how it works in the next section.

Lesson 1.2: *Introducing CSS Properties*
Covers: CSS properties

⇨ **Online:** wdpg.io.com/1-2-0/

CSS consists of a large collection of items called *properties* that control aspects of your page such as the text color, the font size, and the margins that surround an object. For each property you want to use, you assign a value, and that property-value pair (also known as a *declaration*) is the instruction that the browser carries out.

You have multiple ways to define a style, as you see in Chapter 7. For now, I'll go through the two most common methods. Figure 1.9 shows the general form of the first method.

▶ Figure 1.9
The syntax to use for defining CSS properties

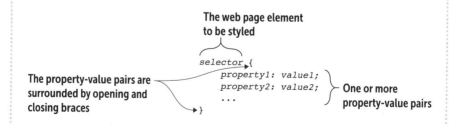

From Figure 1.9, you see that defining a style consists of the following five parts:

- A reference to the web page element or elements to which you want the style applied. This reference is known as a *selector* because you use it to choose which page elements you want the browser to style.

- An opening left brace ({).

- The name of the property you want to apply. Property names are short alphabetic codes such as `color` for the text color, `font-size` for the text size, and `margin` for the margin size. The property name is always followed by a colon (`:`) and then a space for readability.

- The value you want to assign to the property, as well as the unit you want to use, if necessary. To specify a text size in pixels, for example, you add `px` to the value. The value is always followed by a semicolon (`;`).

- A closing right brace (}).

Taken together, these five parts comprise a style *rule*. The following example shows the style rule I used to tell the browser to set the font size for the main (h1) heading in Figure 1.2.

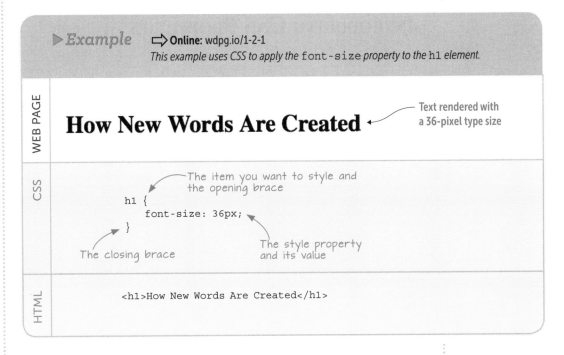

▶ *Example* ⇨ **Online: wdpg.io/1-2-1**
This example uses CSS to apply the `font-size` property to the h1 element.

WEB PAGE

How New Words Are Created ←

Text rendered with a 36-pixel type size

CSS

The item you want to style and the opening brace

```
h1 {
    font-size: 36px;
}
```

The closing brace

The style property and its value

HTML

```
<h1>How New Words Are Created</h1>
```

PLAY

How would you format a web page's second-level headings with a font size of 30 pixels? ⇨ Online: wdpg.io/1-2-2

The style begins by referencing the h1 HTML element, which tells the browser to apply what follows to every <h1> tag in the current web page. After the opening brace ({), the next line specifies the property-value pair: font-size: 36px;. This line instructs the web browser to display every instance of h1 text at a font size of 36 pixels. Finally, the closing brace (}) completes the style rule.

Here, you see one of the great advantages of using styles. If your page has a dozen h1 headings, this rule applies to them all, which gives the page a consistent look. Even better, if you decided that a size of 48px would look nicer for your headings, you'd have to change the value only once in the style rule, and that change would get reflected automatically in all your h1 headings.

Note that you're not restricted to a single declaration in your style definitions. As you can see in the following example, you can add multiple declarations as needed.

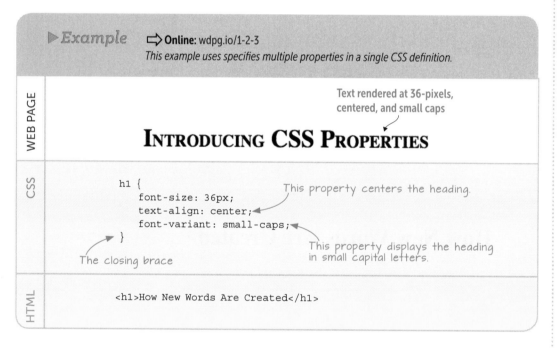

▶ *Example*   ⇨ **Online:** wdpg.io/1-2-3
This example uses specifies multiple properties in a single CSS definition.

WEB PAGE

Text rendered at 36-pixels, centered, and small caps

INTRODUCING CSS PROPERTIES

CSS

```
h1 {
    font-size: 36px;
    text-align: center;
    font-variant: small-caps;
}
```

This property centers the heading.

This property displays the heading in small capital letters.

The closing brace

HTML

```
<h1>How New Words Are Created</h1>
```

Here, I've added the declarations text-align: center; to center the heading and font-variant: small-caps; to display the heading in small capital letters.

I mentioned earlier that you have another way to specify a style. You can insert the declaration directly into an HTML element by using the `style` attribute:

```
<element style="property1: value1; property2: value2; etc.">
```

Here's an example:

```
<h1 style="font-size: 36px; text-align: center">
```

When you use this method, your styles apply only to the HTML element in which they're declared. I talk more about this method in Chapter 7.

CSS is slightly more complicated than HTML, but with that complication comes immense power and expressiveness. As you see throughout the rest of this book, CSS is your royal road to creating fantastic, fun web pages.

When your HTML structure is festooned with CSS formatting, you can create beautiful web pages that are a pleasure to read and navigate.

Some Helpful Features of the Playground

Now that you know what HTML tags and CSS properties look like, you can return to the Web Design Playground and run through a few features that are designed to help you enter your tags and properties correctly:

- The HTML tags and CSS property names and values appear in colors that are different from the regular text. These colors help you differentiate between code and noncode.

- In the HTML box, when the text cursor is inside a tag, the editor automatically highlights both that tag and its companion tag. In Figure 1.10, you see that when I have the cursor in the opening `<p>` tag (which is the tag for creating a paragraph—see Chapter 2), the editor highlights that tag as well as its closing `</p>` tag. This highlighting gives you a visual indicator that you've closed your tags.

Menu

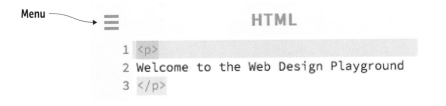

- The CSS editor has a similar feature: When the cursor is immediately to the left or right of a brace, the editor highlights the companion brace. This highlighting helps you make sure to enter both the opening and closing braces when you define a style.

MASTER

In this section's examples, I used four spaces to indent the declarations. This indentation isn't required, but it makes CSS much easier to read, so it's a good idea to get into the habit of indenting your properties.

PLAY

How would you format a web page's second-level headings with a font size of 30 pixels and right alignment?
⇨ Online: wdpg.io/1-2-4

▶ Figure 1.10
The Web Design Playground's HTML editor highlights both the opening and closing tags when the cursor is inside one of them.

- You can adjust the relative sizes of the editors by dragging the vertical border that separates the editors.

- The Web Design Playground can do a limited amount of error checking if you click an editor's Menu icon (pointed out in Figure 1.10) and then click Display Errors. If the editor detects something wrong, you see a red error indicator in the margin to the left of the line that has the problem. Hovering the mouse pointer over that icon displays the error message. If you forget the forward slash in a closing tag, for example, you see the error `Tag must be paired`, as shown in Figure 1.11.

▶ Figure 1.11
If the Web Design Playground detects a problem, an error icon appears in the margin to the left of the code, and hovering the mouse over the icon displays the error message.

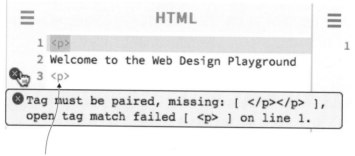

The closing tag's forward slash is missing.

Summary

- HTML defines the structure of your web page, whereas CSS defines the presentation.

- An *HTML tag* is a short code surrounded by angle brackets— such as `<h1>` or `<p>`—that applies an effect or inserts an object. Most tags also require a closing tag, such as `</h1>` or `</p>`.

- A *CSS property* is a name-value pair, and a CSS definition (or rule) is one or more properties surrounded by braces ({ and }) applied to a specified element (such as a tag name).

- To see this book's lessons and to play around with HTML and CSS code, use this book's companion website, the Web Design Playground: https://webdesignplayground.io/.

Chapter 2

Building Your First Web Page

Whatever you can do, or dream you can do, begin it. Boldness has genius, power, and magic in it! —William Hutchinson Murray

This chapter covers

- Learning the basic page structure and elements
- Learning the most common text elements and styles
- Creating links

Many of the modern technologies that we have to learn—whether it's building spreadsheets with Microsoft Excel, enhancing images with Adobe Photoshop, or maintaining a music collection with Apple's iTunes—require us to master complex features bristling with settings and plagued by unintuitive interfaces. So it's with great pleasure that we come across technologies such as HTML and CSS that have no complicated tools, settings, or interfaces to figure out. In fact, they have no interfaces at all. They're mere text—a blissfully simple symphony of letters and numbers and symbols. They're simple, yes, but not unsophisticated. With HTML tags and CSS properties, you can build a web page that reflects who you are, that shows off your creativity, and announces to the world, "Yes, I built this!"

That's why, after the brief introduction in Chapter 1, you get your HTML and CSS education off to a proper start by building your first web page. You learn the underlying structure that's common to all pages, as well as all the standard text elements, and you learn how to add headings and links. If you've got something to say, in this chapter you learn how to say it with HTML and CSS.

Getting Your Web Page off the Ground

This book's goal is to help you create your own web pages and thus lay claim to a little chunk of personal cyberspace real estate: a home page away from home, if you will. Before you can live in this humble abode, however, you have to pour the concrete that serves as the foundation for the rest of your digital domicile. In this section, I show you a few HTML basics that constitute the underlying structure of all web pages.

Lesson 2.1: **Laying Down the Basic Page Structure**
Covers: Page-structure elements

> ➡ **Online:** wdpg.io.com/2-1-0

All your web page projects, from the simplest page to the most sophisticated business site, begin with the same basic structure, which I outline in Listing 2.1.

MASTER

Here, I've used four spaces to indent the tags when they fall inside other tags. This indentation isn't strictly necessary, but it's a good idea; indentation makes your code easier to read and troubleshoot because you can more readily see each pair of opening and closing tags.

▶**Listing 2.1**
A Basic HTML Structure for Starting Any Web Page Project

```
<!DOCTYPE html>              #1
<html lang="en">             #2
    <head>                   #3
        <meta charset="utf-8">   #4
        <title></title>     #5
        <style></style>     #6
    </head>                 #3
    <body>                  #7
    </body>                 #7
</html>                     #2
```

No doubt this code looks a little intimidating to you. I apologize for that complication, but it's a necessary one that's baked into the way web pages are built. Fortunately, I can soften the blow somewhat by offering you two bits of good news:

- This code is by far the most complex you'll see in this chapter, so if you can muddle through the next few paragraphs, the sailing the rest of the way will be much easier.

- When you work in the Web Design Playground, you don't even *see* the code in Listing 2.1, because the Playground hides it behind the scenes. (You're welcome.)

The structure begins with `<!DOCTYPE html>` right at the top (#1), and this line tells the web browser which version of HTML you're using. This declaration tells the browser that you're using HTML5, which is the latest version and the version you learn in this book. The next part of the structure consists of the `<html>` tag and its closing `</html>` tag (#2), which together define the overall container for the rest of the page's HTML and CSS. The `<html>` tag includes the `lang="en"` attribute, which tells the web browser that the primary language of the page is English.

The rest of the structure is divided into two sections: the header and the body.

The header section is defined by the `<head>` tag and its closing `</head>` tag (#3). The header section acts like an introduction to the page because web browsers use the header to glean various types of information about the page. One important bit of data is the character set used by the page, which is what the `<meta>` tag is doing (#4). You also use the head section to define the page title (#5), which I talk about in the next section. Most important for this book, the `<style>` tag and its closing `</style>` tag (#6) are where you enter your style definitions.

The body section is defined by the `<body>` tag and its closing `</body>` tag (#7), and this section is where you'll enter most of your HTML tags. The text and tags that you type in the body section are what appear in the web browser.

PLAY

You can copy and paste the basic web page structure from the Web Design Playground.
⇨ Online: wdpg.io/2-1-0

REMEMBER

In the Web Design Playground, I've deliberately hidden elements such as `<!DOCTYPE>`, `<html>`, `<head>`, `<style>`, and `<body>` because (at least in the Playground) you don't work with these elements directly. When you type tags in the HTML Editor, the Playground adds them between the `<body>` and `</body>` tags behind the scenes. Similarly, when you type styles in the CSS Editor, the Playground adds them between the `<style>` and `</style>` tags in the background.

Lesson 2.2: *Adding a Title*

Covers: The `<title>` tag

⇨ Online: wdpg.io/2-2-0

You may be tempted to think of the page title as the text that appears at the top of the page. In HTML, however, the page title is what appears on the web browser's title bar (or the page's tab, if you're using tabbed browsing), as shown in the following example.

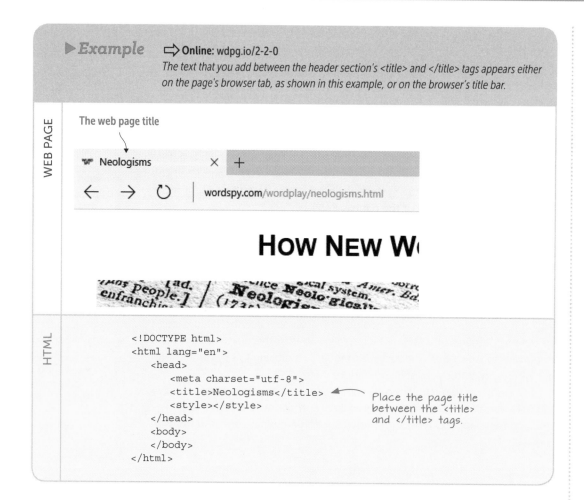

▶ *Example*   ⇨ **Online:** wdpg.io/2-2-0
The text that you add between the header section's <title> and </title> tags appears either on the page's browser tab, as shown in this example, or on the browser's title bar.

WEB PAGE

The web page title

🦋 Neologisms   ×   +

← → ↻ | wordspy.com/wordplay/neologisms.html

HOW NEW W

HTML

```
<!DOCTYPE html>
<html lang="en">
    <head>
        <meta charset="utf-8">
        <title>Neologisms</title>
        <style></style>
    </head>
    <body>
    </body>
</html>
```

Place the page title between the <title> and </title> tags.

Here are a few things to keep in mind when thinking of a title for your page:

- Make sure that your title reflects what the page is about.

- Make the title unique with respect to your other pages.

- Because a longish title often gets truncated when it's displayed in the narrow confines of a browser tab, put a truly descriptive word or two at the beginning of the title.

- Use a title that makes sense when someone views it out of context. A person who really likes your page may bookmark it, and the browser displays the page title in the bookmarks list, so it's important that the title makes sense when that person looks at the bookmarks later.

Lesson 2.3: **Adding Some Text**
Covers: Adding web page text

⇨ **Online:** wdpg.io/2-3-0

If you tried to load a page containing only the basic structure from Listing 1.1, you wouldn't see anything in the browser. Although the browser uses the tags in the header section internally, including displaying the title in the browser's current tab or title bar, the browser's content area displays only the tags and text that you place between the <body> and </body> tags.

❝ *Ultimately, users visit your website for its content. Everything else is just the backdrop. —Jakob Nielsen*

In the example below, I added the text Hello HTML World! to the body section.

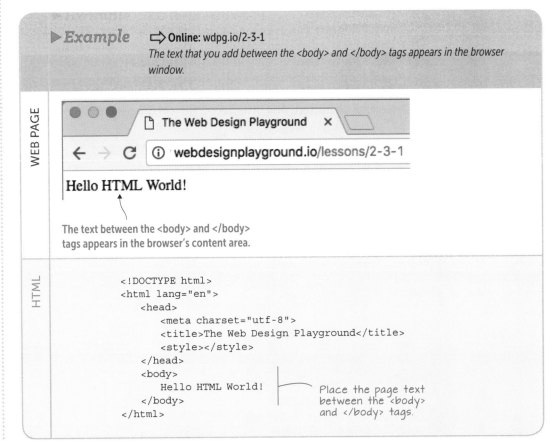

▶ *Example*   ⇨ **Online:** wdpg.io/2-3-1
The text that you add between the <body> and </body> tags appears in the browser window.

WEB PAGE

🗋 The Web Design Playground   ✕

← → C   ⓘ **webdesignplayground.io**/lessons/2-3-1

Hello HTML World!

The text between the <body> and </body> tags appears in the browser's content area.

HTML

```
<!DOCTYPE html>
<html lang="en">
    <head>
        <meta charset="utf-8">
        <title>The Web Design Playground</title>
        <style></style>
    </head>
    <body>
        Hello HTML World!
    </body>
</html>
```

Place the page text between the <body> and </body> tags.

Here are a few things you should know about adding text to a web page:

- If you're working in the Web Design Playground, remember that the HTML Editor assumes that what you type in that box will be inserted between the `<body>` and `</body>` tags, so you don't need to enter them.

- You may think that you can line things up and create some interesting effects by stringing together two or more spaces. Alas, no, that effect won't work. Web browsers chew up all those extra spaces and spit them out into the nether regions of cyberspace. Why? Well, the philosophy of the web is that you can use only HTML tags to structure a document and CSS to style it. So a run of multiple spaces—*whitespace*, as it's called—is ignored.

- Tabs also fall under the rubric of whitespace. You can enter tabs all day long, but the browser ignores them.

- Other things that browsers like to ignore are carriage returns. It may sound reasonable that pressing Enter or Return starts a new paragraph, but that's not so in the HTML world. I talk more about this topic in the next section.

- Earlier, I mentioned that web pages consist only of the characters that you can peck out on your keyboard. Does that mean you're out of luck if you need to use characters that *don't* appear on the keyboard, such as the copyright symbol or an em dash? Luckily, you're not. HTML has special codes for these kinds of characters, and I talk about them in Chapter 16.

Learning the Most Common Text Elements

Having great content is essential for any web page, and as you've seen so far in this chapter, you can get started on a web page by typing some text. But content is only the beginning. Figure 2.1 shows an example of a text-only web page.

How New Words Are Created Where do new words come from? Sometimes we're lucky enough to know the answer. For example, the word scofflaw originated as a contest winner and Frankenfood came from a letter to the editor of a newspaper. But for every word with a definite origin, there are hundreds, nay thousands whose beginnings are unknown and probably unknowable. That's because, according to the linguist Victoria Neufeldt (writing in her book A Civil But Untrammelled Tongue), most word invention goes on as a matter of course: Neology, far from being a separable linguistic phenomenon that manifests itself periodically or sporadically in response to social stimuli, in fact rises out of ordinary linguistic competence, what might be called the linguistic collective unconscious of the speech community. This "ordinary linguistic competence" manifests as various mechanisms that people use to forge new words.

▶ Figure 2.1 A web page with nothing but text

> *Content precedes design. Design in the absence of content is not design, it's decoration.* —Jeffrey Zeldman

What you're seeing in Figure 2.1 is a page in which the text isn't adorned with any HTML elements. Yes, you can read the page, but would you really want to? I didn't think so. The page as it stands is fundamentally unappealing because it's a bunch of undifferentiated text, which makes it both difficult to read and dull to look at. By contrast, check out the revised version of the page shown in Figure 2.2.

How New Words Are Created

Where do new words come from? Sometimes we're lucky enough to know the answer. For example, the word <u>scofflaw</u> originated as a contest winner and <u>Frankenfood</u> came from a letter to the editor of a newspaper. But for every word with a definite origin, there are hundreds, nay *thousands*, whose beginnings are unknown and probably unknowable. That's because, according to the linguist Victoria Neufeldt (writing in her book *A Civil But Untrammelled Tongue*), **most word invention goes on as a matter of course**:

> Neology, far from being a separable linguistic phenomenon that manifests itself periodically or sporadically in response to social stimuli, in fact rises out of ordinary linguistic competence, what might be called the linguistic collective unconscious of the speech community.

This "ordinary linguistic competence" manifests as various mechanisms that people use to forge new words.

▶ Figure 2.2 The web page from Figure 2.1 with some basic HTML text elements added

Ah, that's better! Now the page is easy to read and reasonably nice to look at. The difference is that in this version, I used some basic HTML text elements to redisplay the text in a form that's readable and understandable. You'll learn how I did that as you read this chapter. In the next section, you learn how to use the HTML required to mark text as important.

Lesson 2.4: **Marking Important Text**
Covers: The `strong` element

⇨ **Online:** wdpg.io/2-4-0

In your web page, you may have a word, phrase, or sentence that you want to be sure that the reader sees because it's important. This text may be a vital instruction, a crucial condition, or a similarly significant passage that needs to stand out from the regular text because you don't want the reader to miss it. In HTML, you mark text as important by using the `strong` element:

```
<strong>important text goes here</strong>
```

All browsers render the text between the `<strong>` and `</strong>` tags in a bold font. The following example shows some web page text with an important passage displayed in bold and the HTML markup used with the text.

MASTER

All web browsers define a default style for every text element, such as bold for text marked up with the `strong` *element. You don't have to stick with the browser styling, however, because in all cases you can augment or override the defaults by using your own styles. You get into this topic big-time in Chapter 4.*

KI 896 0109

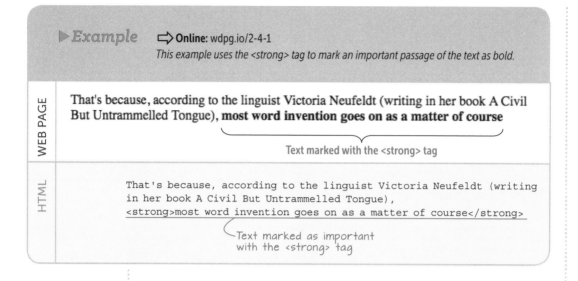

▶*Example*   ⇨ **Online:** wdpg.io/2-4-1
This example uses the <strong> tag to mark an important passage of the text as bold.

WEB PAGE

That's because, according to the linguist Victoria Neufeldt (writing in her book A Civil But Untrammelled Tongue), **most word invention goes on as a matter of course**

Text marked with the <strong> tag

HTML

```
That's because, according to the linguist Victoria Neufeldt (writing
in her book A Civil But Untrammelled Tongue),
<strong>most word invention goes on as a matter of course</strong>
```

Text marked as important with the <strong> tag

Lesson 2.5: *Formatting Keywords*
Covers: The b element

PLAY

To learn more about the strong *element, try the exercises on the Web Design Playground.*
⇨ Online: wdpg.io/2-4-2

USE IT

Other candidates for web page keywords include the name of a person (such as the infamous "boldface names" that appear in celebrity gossip columns) and the first few words or the opening sentence of an article.

PLAY

How would you mark up an article so that its lede sentence appears in bold? ⇨ *Online:* wdpg.io/2-5-2

⇨ **Online:** wdpg.io/2-5-0

In some cases, you want to draw attention to a word or phrase not because it's important per se, but because the text in question plays a role that makes it different from regular text. That text could be a product name, a company name, or an interface element such as the text associated with a check box or command button. Again, the text you're working with isn't crucial—it's different in some way—so you want it to look different from the regular page text.

Each of these items indicates a keyword (or keyphrase) that has meaning beyond the regular page text, and in HTML5, this type of semantic item is marked up with the b element:

    <b>*keyword*</b>

Web browsers render the text between the <b> and </b> tags in a bold font. At this point, I imagine you scratching your head and wondering what the difference is between the strong element and the b element, because both render as bold text. That's a fair point, and I'll admit that the difference is a subtle one. I should say that it's a *semantic* one because HTML5 uses these two separate elements to differentiate between important text and keywords. In the future, I hope, screen readers and similar assistive technologies for disabled readers will use this semantic difference to alert the visitor in some way that this text is important and that text is a keyword.

The following example shows some web page text with a keyword displayed in bold and the HTML markup used with the text.

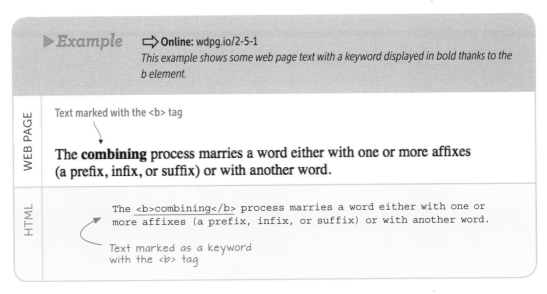

▶ *Example*   ⇨ **Online:** wdpg.io/2-5-1
This example shows some web page text with a keyword displayed in bold thanks to the b element.

WEB PAGE

Text marked with the <b> tag

The combining process marries a word either with one or more affixes (a prefix, infix, or suffix) or with another word.

HTML

```
The <b>combining</b> process marries a word either with one or
more affixes (a prefix, infix, or suffix) or with another word.
```

Text marked as a keyword
with the <b> tag

Lesson 2.6: **Emphasizing Text**
Covers: The em element

⇨ **Online:** wdpg.io/2-6-0

It's often important to add emphasis to certain words or phrases in a page. This emphasis tells the reader to read or say this text with added stress. Consider the following sentence:

```
Verdana is a sans-serif typeface.
```

Now read the same sentence with emphasis (expressed in italics) added to the word *sans*:

```
Verdana is a sans-serif typeface.
```

The meaning of the sentence and how you read the sentence change with the addition of the emphasis (in this case, to stress the fact that Verdana isn't a serif typeface).

In HTML5, this type of semantic item is marked up with the em (for emphasis) element:

```
<em>text</em>
```

FAQ

What's the difference between the strong *element and the* em *element? You use* strong *when the text in question is inherently crucial for the reader; you use* em *when the text in question requires an enhanced stress to get a point across.*

Web browsers render the text between the <em> and </em> tags in italics. The following example shows a web page with emphasized text displayed in italics, as well as the HTML markup that creates the effect.

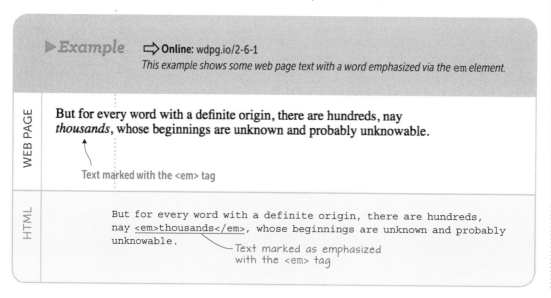

▶ *Example*   ⇨ **Online:** wdpg.io/2-6-1
This example shows some web page text with a word emphasized via the em element.

WEB PAGE

But for every word with a definite origin, there are hundreds, nay *thousands*, whose beginnings are unknown and probably unknowable.

Text marked with the <em> tag

HTML

```
But for every word with a definite origin, there are hundreds,
nay <em>thousands</em>, whose beginnings are unknown and probably
unknowable.
```
Text marked as emphasized with the <em> tag

Lesson 2.7: *Formatting Alternative Text*
Covers: The i element

PLAY

You can nest text-level elements within other text-level elements for extra effect. You can mark up a sentence as important by using the strong *element, and within that sentence, you can mark up a word with emphasis by using the* em *element.*
⇨ Online: wdpg.io/2-6-3

USE IT

Other examples of alternative text include publication names, technical terms, foreign words and phrases, and a person's thoughts.

⇨ **Online:** wdpg.io/2-7-0

It's common in prose to need markup for a word or phrase to indicate that it has a voice, mood, or role that's different from that of the regular text. Common examples of alternative text are book and movie titles. In HTML5, this type of semantic text is marked up with the i (for italics) element:

```
<i>text</i>
```

Web browsers render such text in italics. The i element may seem to be precisely the same as the em element, but there's a significant semantic difference: em adds stress to enhance the emphatic nature of the affected text, whereas i tells the reader that the text is to be interpreted in an alternative way to the regular text. Again, this subtle difference is potentially useful in terms of accessibility; a screen reader would (at least in theory) emphasize em text and let the user know about alternative text marked up with the i element.

The following example shows a web page with alternative text displayed in italics, as well as the HTML markup that does the job.

▶ *Example* ⟹ **Online:** wdpg.io/2-7-1
This example shows some web page text with a book title formatted as alternative text using the i element.

WEB PAGE

> That's because, according to the linguist Victoria Neufeldt (writing in her book *A Civil But Untrammelled Tongue*), most word invention goes on as a matter of course:

Text marked with the <i> tag

HTML

```
That's because, according to the linguist Victoria Neufeldt
(writing in her book <i>A Civil But Untrammelled Tongue</i>), most
word invention goes on as a matter of course:
```
Text marked as alternative with the <i> tag

Lesson 2.8: *Quoting Text*
Covers: The q and blockquote elements

⟹ **Online:** wdpg.io/2-8-0

Many web pages include quotes from other works, which could be web pages, people, books, magazines, or any written source. To ensure that your readers don't think that the quoted material is your own (which could lead to charges of plagiarism), you should mark up the text as a quotation. How you do this depends on the length of the quotation.

A short quotation should appear inline with your regular page text. You mark up this text as a quotation by using the q element:

```
<q cite="url">quotation</q>
```

Most web browsers display text marked up with the q element the same way as the regular page text but surrounded by double quotation marks. If your quotation comes from another web page, you can include the optional cite attribute and set its value to the URL of the web page.

A longer quotation should appear on its own for readability. You mark up a longer quotation by using the blockquote element:

```
<blockquote>
Long quotation
</blockquote>
```

PLAY

To get familiar with the i element, try the exercises on the Web Design Playground. ⟹ **Online:** wdpg.io/2-7-2

PLAY

To get familiar with the q and blockquote *elements, try the exercises on the Web Design Playground.*
⇨ Online: wdpg.io/2-8-2

The web browser displays text marked up with the blockquote element in a separate paragraph that's indented slightly from the left and right margins of the containing element.

The following example shows some web page text that includes a short quotation inline with the regular text and a longer quotation separated from the regular text, as well as the HTML markup.

▶ *Example* ⇨ **Online:** wdpg.io/2-8-1

This example shows some web page text with both a short quotation inline with the regular text and a longer quotation separated from the regular text.

WEB PAGE

That's because, according to the linguist Victoria Neufeldt (writing in her book *A Civil But Untrammelled Tongue*), **most word invention goes on as a matter of course:**

Longer, separated quotation marked with the <blockquote> tag

> Neology, far from being a separable linguistic phenomenon that manifests itself periodically or sporadically in response to social stimuli, in fact rises out of ordinary linguistic competence, what might be called the linguistic collective unconscious of the speech community.

This "ordinary linguistic competence" manifests as various mechanisms that people use to forge new words:

Shorter, inline quotation marked with the <q> tag

HTML

```
That&rsquo;s because, according to the linguist Victoria Neufeldt
(writing in her book <i>A Civil But Untrammelled Tongue</i>),
<strong>most word invention goes on as a matter of course</
strong>:
<blockquote>
Neology, far from being a separable linguistic phenomenon that
manifests itself periodically or sporadically in response
to social stimuli, in fact rises out of ordinary linguistic
competence, what might be called the linguistic collective
unconscious of the speech community.
</blockquote>
This <q>ordinary linguistic competence</q> manifests as various
mechanisms that people use to forge new words:
```

Text marked as a longer quotation with the <blockquote> tag

Text marked as a short quotation with the <q> tag

Lesson 2.9: **Working with Headings**

Covers: The `h1` through `h6` elements

⇨ **Online:** wdpg.io/2-9-0

A *heading* is a word or phrase that appears immediately before a section of text and is used to name or briefly describe the contents of that text. Almost all web pages have a main heading at or near the top of the page that serves as the title of the content. (Don't confuse this heading with the text between the `<title>` and `</title>` tags in the page's `<head>` section. The main heading appears in the page itself, whereas the text within the `title` element appears only on the browser tab.)

Besides the title heading, many web page contents are divided into several sections, each of which has its own heading. These sections may be further divided into subsections with, again, each subsection having a heading, and so on. Taken together, the title, section headings, and subsection headings form an outline that neatly summarizes the structure and hierarchy of the web page.

❝ *Well-written, thoughtful headings interspersed in the text act as an informal outline or table of contents for a page.* —Steve Krug

In HTML, you mark up your page's heading text by using the various heading elements, which run from `h1` for the highest level of your page hierarchy (usually, the page's main title) to `h2` for the section headings, `h3` for the subsection headings, and all the way down to `h6` for the lowest-level headings. The web browser displays each heading in its own block, formats the text as bold, and (as you see in the example that follows) adjusts the text size depending on the element used: `h1` is the largest; `h6` is the smallest.

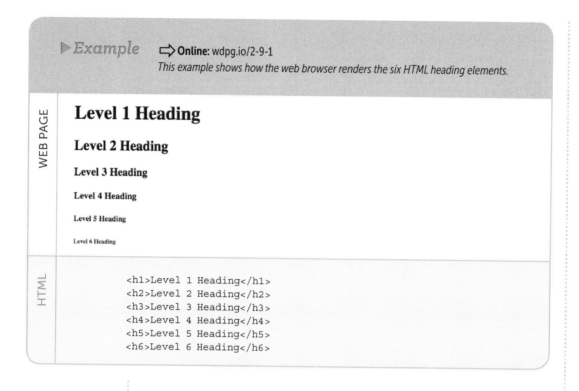

▶ *Example*   ⇨ **Online:** wdpg.io/2-9-1
This example shows how the web browser renders the six HTML heading elements.

WEB PAGE

Level 1 Heading

Level 2 Heading

Level 3 Heading

Level 4 Heading

Level 5 Heading

Level 6 Heading

HTML

```
<h1>Level 1 Heading</h1>
<h2>Level 2 Heading</h2>
<h3>Level 3 Heading</h3>
<h4>Level 4 Heading</h4>
<h5>Level 5 Heading</h5>
<h6>Level 6 Heading</h6>
```

Although HTML5 offers other ways to create semantic page divisions (see Chapter 11), using heading elements is an easy, common way to tell the browser and the reader how your web page text is organized, as shown in the following example, which includes the heading from the web page you saw earlier.

▶ *Example*   ⇨ **Online:** wdpg.io/2-9-2
This example shows how the web browser renders the h1 *heading element.*

WEB PAGE

How New Words Are Created ← `<h1>` heading

HTML

```
<h1>How New Words Are Created</h1>
```
← `<h1>` heading

Lesson 2.10: *Crafting Links*
Covers: The a element

⇨ **Online: wdpg.io/2-10-0**

I mentioned in Chapter 1 that one of the defining characteristics of HTML (in fact, the *H* in *HTML*) is *hypertext*: links to pages on your own site or to sites anywhere on the web. In fact, it's a rare page that doesn't include at least a few links, so you need to know how to craft hypertext by using HTML.

The HTML tags that you use to create a link are <a> and its corresponding </a> closing tag. The a element is a little different from most of the other elements you've seen in this chapter, because you don't use it by itself. Instead, you insert the address—often called the *URL* (short for *Uniform Resource Locator*)—of your link into it. Figure 2.3 shows how this element works:

The <a> tag takes the href attribute, which stands for *hypertext reference*. Set this attribute equal to the URL of the web page you want to use for the link, enclosed in double (or single) quotation marks. Most link addresses are one of the following:

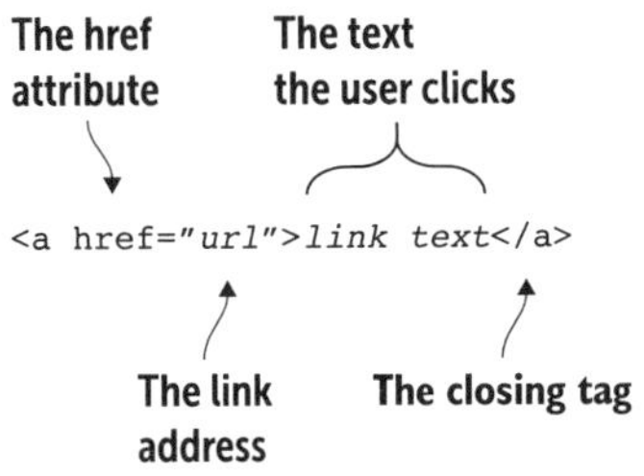

The href attribute — **The text the user clicks**

```
<a href="url">link text</a>
```

The link address — **The closing tag**

▶ Figure 2.3 The syntax to use for the <a> tag

- *Local*—A link to another page on your website. To keep things simple, I'm going to assume that all your website's page files reside in the same directory. (For the slightly more complex case of having page files in multiple directories, see Chapter 16.) In that case, the <a> tag's href attribute value is the name of the page file you're linking to. Here's an example:

```
<a href="wordplay.html">
```

- *Remote*—A link to a page on another website. In that case, the <a> tag's href attribute value is the full URL of the page on the other site. Here's an example:

```
<a href="http://wordspy.com/index.php">
```

Next, you replace link text with the descriptive link text that you want the user to click, and then finish everything with the </a> closing tag. By default, most web browsers display the link in blue underlined text, as shown in the following example.

PLAY

You're given a document with a title, main sections (Section 1, Section 2, and so on), subsections (Section 1.1, Section 1.2, and so on), and sub-subsections (Section 1.1a, Section 1.1b, and so on). Work up a heading scheme for this structure. ⇨ **Online: wdpg.io/2-9-3**

BEWARE

Using uppercase versus lowercase letters can be crucial in entering a URL. On most (but not all) websites, if you enter even a single letter of a directory or filename in the wrong case, you likely won't get where you want to go (that is, you'll get a 404 Not Found error).

FAQ

Does the a in the <a> tag stand for anything? The a is short for anchor, *which comes from the fact that you can create special links called* anchors *that send your readers to other parts of the same page instead of sending them to a different page. You learn how this feature works in Chapter 16.*

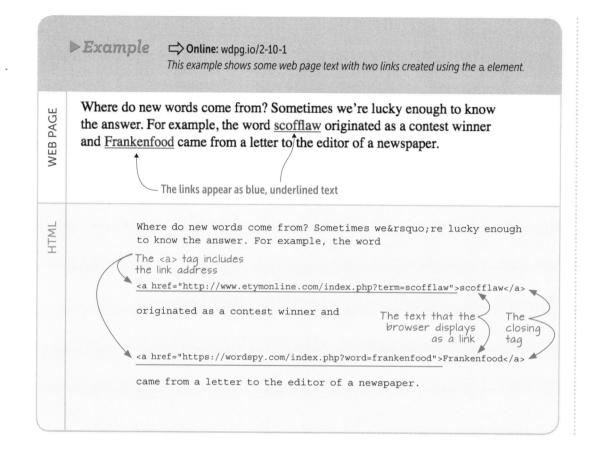

▶ *Example* ⇨ **Online:** wdpg.io/2-10-1

This example shows some web page text with two links created using the a *element.*

WEB PAGE

Where do new words come from? Sometimes we're lucky enough to know the answer. For example, the word <u>scofflaw</u> originated as a contest winner and <u>Frankenfood</u> came from a letter to the editor of a newspaper.

— The links appear as blue, underlined text

HTML

```
Where do new words come from? Sometimes we&rsquo;re lucky enough
to know the answer. For example, the word
```

The <a> tag includes the link address

```
<a href="http://www.etymonline.com/index.php?term=scofflaw">scofflaw</a>

originated as a contest winner and
```

The text that the browser displays as a link

The closing tag

```
<a href="https://wordspy.com/index.php?word=frankenfood">Frankenfood</a>

came from a letter to the editor of a newspaper.
```

Summary

- In the basic HTML page structure, the header is defined by the <head> and </head> tags, and it includes the page title (between the <title> and </title> tags) and the page CSS (between the <style> and </style> tags).

- In the basic page structure, you type your HTML tags and text between the <body> and </body> tags.

- Use <strong> for important text and <b> for keywords.

- Use <em> to emphasize text and <i> to format alternative text.

- You can create a strong visual hierarchy in your page by taking advantage of the heading tags: <h1> through <h6>.

- You set up a link by surrounding text with the <a> and </a> tags. In the <a> tag, use the href attribute to specify the name of a local file or the URL of a remote file.

Chapter 3

Adding Structure to Your Page

> *Organizing is what you do before you do something, so that when you do it, it is not all mixed up.* —A. A. Milne

This chapter covers

- Dividing page text into paragraphs and sections
- Adding numbered lists
- Building bulleted lists

You learned in Chapter 2 that you can create an effective web page by typing some text and then using headings and elements such as `strong` and `em` to make the text more readable and easier to understand. Headings in particular are crucial page devices, not only because they help the reader see where one part of the page ends and another begins, but also because they give the reader a general sense of the page hierarchy. All this falls under the general rubric of page structure, and that's the focus of this chapter.

Thinking about the structure of your web page is important, because a wall of unstructured text is difficult to scan and read, as well as difficult to style. When you add structure (such as the headings from Chapter 2 and the paragraphs, sections, containers, and lists that you learn about in this chapter), each of those substructures is seen by the browser as a separate entity to which you can apply many style properties. As a rule, the more structured your page, the greater the control you have over how it looks. Fortunately, as you see in this chapter, HTML comes with several useful and straightforward tools for adding structure to a page.

HTML Elements for Structuring Page Text

If you work with a word processor, you know that almost all documents have a structure: a title, possibly a subtitle, one or more topic headings, and one or more paragraphs within each topic. This makes the document easy to browse and comfortable to read because the structure guides readers and enables them to focus on the text. You can get those same advantages in your web pages by taking advantage of the various structural elements offered by HTML. I'll begin with one of the most common structures: the paragraph.

Lesson 3.1: **Working with Paragraphs**
Covers: The p element

PLAY

Using the Web Design Playground, modify the first five lines in this example so that the text snippets Line 1, Line 2, Line 3, *and* Line 4 *each appear in a separate paragraph.*
⇨ Online: wdpg.io/3-1-2

⇨ **Online:** wdpg.io/3-1-0

I mentioned in Chapter 2 that web browsers ignore whitespace, including carriage returns created by pressing Enter or Return, which is normally how you'd separate text into paragraphs in a text editor or word processor. The most common way to create a paragraph in HTML is to place a <p> (for paragraph) tag at the beginning of the text and a closing </p> tag at the end of the text.

The following example shows you both the wrong and right ways to create paragraphs.

▶ *Example*   ⇨ **Online:** wdpg.io/3-1-1

In this example, you can see that the web browser ignores the whitespace created by the carriage returns but happily renders text into paragraphs when you use the p element.

WEB PAGE

Line 1 Line 2 Line 3 Line 4 ◀— The web browser ignores the carriage returns.

Paragraph 1
Paragraph 2
Paragraph 3
Paragraph 4

The browser uses the <p> tags to render the text into separate paragraphs.

HTML

```
Line 1
Line 2
Line 3

Line 4
```
Wrong: Separate lines created by pressing only Enter/Return

```
<p>Paragraph 1</p>
<p>Paragraph 2</p>
<p>Paragraph 3</p>
<p>Paragraph 4</p>
```
Right: Paragraphs created by using the p element

Lesson 3.2: *Inserting Line Breaks*
Covers: The br element

USE IT

Use a line break for poems, lyrics, addresses, contact information, or programming statements, or to show a sample of HTML or CSS code.

PLAY

Render the poem "Break, Break, Break," by Alfred Lord Tennyson, correctly by adding line breaks to each line that isn't the end of a stanza.
⇨ Online: wdpg.io/3-2-2

⇨ **Online:** wdpg.io/3-2-0

When you separate page text into paragraphs, the web browser renders this text by (among other things) creating a bit of space between paragraphs. This space is normally what you want because that vertical gap gives the reader a visual clue as to where one paragraph ends and the next one begins, as well as a chance to take a quick breather between sections of text. This space isn't *always* what you want, however. If your page text is a poem, for example, you almost certainly don't want paragraphs between lines. The same is true if your text is programming code or song lyrics.

When you want to start a new line but don't want to have any space between the two lines, you need the br (short for *line break*) element. As you can see in the following example, the web browser renders the br element by inserting a carriage return and beginning the next line immediately below the previous one.

▶*Example* ⇨ **Online:** wdpg.io/3-2-1

In this example, you can see that the web browser renders the br element by inserting a carriage return and beginning the next line immediately below the previous one.

WEB PAGE

Contact Info

Manning Publications Co.
PO Box 761
Shelter Island, NY 11964
support@manning.com
203-626-1510

HTML

```
<h3>Contact Info</h3>
Manning Publications Co.<br>
PO Box 761<br>
Shelter Island, NY  11964<br>
support@manning.com<br>
203-626-1510
```

The <br> tag tells the browser to start the following text on a new line.

Lesson 3.3: *Dividing Web Page Text*
Covers: The `div` element

⇨ **Online:** wdpg.io/3-3-0

In Chapter 11, I show you the HTML5 sectioning elements, including `<section>` and `<article>`. These elements enable you to structure your page semantically by designating containers as sections and articles within those sections, as well as headers, footers, navigation, and more. Not all text falls neatly into any of the HTML5 semantic categories, however. For text that requires a container but for which none of the semantic elements (including the `p` element) is appropriate, HTML offers the `div` (short for *division*) element. The `<div>` tag and its corresponding `</div>` end tag create a simple container for text. The web browser applies no inherent formatting to the text, including not rendering any space between consecutive `div` elements, as you see in the following example.

PLAY

The `br` element is often a poor choice for structuring page text because it doesn't provide a container for the text, so you can't style the text. On the Web Design Playground, replace the `br` elements with `div` elements.
⇨ Online: wdpg.io/3-3-2

▶ *Example*   ⇨ **Online:** wdpg.io/3-3-1

This example uses the `div` element to divide a web page into two text blocks.

WEB PAGE

The `<div>` blocks

Shortening

The **shortening** process is based mostly on a kind of linguistic laziness called **clipping** that causes us to lop off great chunks of words. For example, we end up with *fridge* from *refrigerator* and *flu* from *influenza*. Often we clip everything after the first syllable: *dis* (from *disrespect*) and *gym* (from *gymnasium*).

A related process is the creation of **acronyms,** which form a pronounceable word using the first letters of each word in a phrase. For example, *UNICEF* from United Nations International Children's Emergency Fund, and *NATO* from North Atlantic Treaty Organization.

HTML

```
<h2>Shortening</h2>
<div>
The <b>shortening</b> process is based mostly on a kind of
linguistic laziness called <b>clipping</b> that causes us to lop
off great chunks of words. For example, we end up with <i>fridge</
i> from <i>refrigerator</i> and <em>flu</em> from <i>influenza</
i>. Often we clip everything after the first syllable: <i>dis</i>
(from <i>disrespect</i>) and <i>gym</i> (from <i>gymnasium</i>).
</div>
<div>
A related process is the creation of <b>acronyms</b>, which
form a pronounceable word using the first letters of each word
in a phrase. For example, <i>UNICEF</i> from United Nations
International Children&rsquo;s Emergency Fund, and <i>NATO</i>
from North Atlantic Treaty Organization.
</div>
```

The `<div>` and `</div>` tags divide your web page text into blocks.

REMEMBER

Elements such as div *and* p *are known as block-level elements because they create a boxlike container that begins on a new line and within which the content (such as text) flows. Elements such as* span *are known as inline elements because each one creates a container that exists within some larger element and flows with the rest of the content in that larger element.*

Lesson 3.4: **Creating Inline Containers**
Covers: The span element

⇨ **Online:** wdpg.io/3-4-0

Elements such as div and p are important because they provide containers in which you add and style text. Sometimes, however, you want to style just a subset of the text within such a container. You may want to apply a font effect or color to a few words or to a sentence, for example. In that case, you can create an *inline container* by surrounding the text with the <span> tag and its </span> end tag. The following example creates several inline containers, and a CSS property is defined for the span element to apply a yellow background to each container.

▶ *Example* ⇨ **Online:** wdpg.io/3-4-1
This example creates several inline containers, and a CSS property is defined for the span element to apply a yellow background to each container.

WEB PAGE

Throughout this document, screen items that you click and text that you type appear with a yellow background. Here are some examples:

- Click the File menu and then click Save.
- Set the number of copies and then click Print.
- Click Search, type blockquote, and then press Enter.

CSS

```
span {
    background-color: yellow;
}
```

This style definition tells the browser to apply yellow as the background color to all the span elements.

HTML

```
<p>
Throughout this document, screen items that you click and text
that you type appear with a <span>yellow background</span>. Here
are some examples:
</p>

<ul>
    <li>Click the <span>File</span> menu and then click
<span>Save</span>.</li>
        <li>Set the number of copies and then click <span>Print</span>.</
li>
    <li>Click <span>Search</span>, type <span>blockquote</span>,
and then press <span>Enter</span>.</li>
</ul>
```

The <span> and </span> tags
create inline containers.

Lesson 3.5: **Adding a Visual Break between Blocks**
Covers: The hr element

⇨ **Online:** wdpg.io/3-5-0

As I mention earlier, the p element automatically adds whitespace between paragraphs, and for other block-level elements such as div, you can use CSS to create your own vertical spacing between blocks. Sometimes, however, you want a more direct or more emphatic visual indicator of a break between blocks. In such a case, you can insert the hr (short for *horizontal rule*) element. As you can see in the following example, the web browser displays a horizontal line across the page. If you don't want the line to extend the width of its container, you can use the width CSS property and set it to the width (measured in, say, pixels or a percentage) you prefer.

PLAY

To get some practice with the span *element, try the exercises on the Web Design Playground.*
⇨ Online: wdpg.io/3-4-2

▶ *Example* ⇨ **Online:** wdpg.io/3-5-1

This example shows that when you add the hr element, the web browser displays a horizontal line across the page.

WEB PAGE

Word Origins: Introduction

In a cynical world where attention spans are 140-characters long and where much of the populace is obsessed with the low-brow goings-on of Kim or Miley or Kylie, one amazing fact rises above the muck: it's rare to meet someone who isn't in some way interested in words and language. From slang-slinging youngsters to crossword-solving oldsters, from inveterate punsters to intrepid neologists, some aspect of language appeals to everyone.

The <hr> tag creates a line.

Is there one slice of the language pie that everyone likes? Probably not. People are just too complex to like any one thing universally. However, in my own admittedly limited experience (I haven't met every person in the world), I have yet to come across a person who doesn't appreciate a good story about the origins of a word or phrase.

HTML

```
<h2>Word Origins: Introduction</h2>
<div>In a cynical world where attention spans are 140-characters
long and where much of the populace is obsessed with the low-
brow goings-on of Kim or Miley or Kylie, one amazing fact rises
above the muck: it's rare to meet someone who isn't in some way
interested in words and language. From slang-slinging youngsters to
crossword-solving oldsters, from inveterate punsters to intrepid
neologists, some aspect of language appeals to everyone.</div>
<hr>
<div>Is there one slice of the language pie that everyone likes?
Probably not. People are just too complex to like any one thing
universally. However, in my own admittedly limited experience (I
haven't met every person in the world), I have yet to come across
a person who doesn't appreciate a good story about the origins of
a word or phrase.</div>
```

The <hr> tag inserts a horizontal line between two text blocks.

I should note here that many web-design gurus recommend that instead of using the hr element to get a horizontal line between two blocks, you should add a bottom border to the top block or a top border to the bottom block. See Chapter 7 for more info on styling borders.

Organizing Text Into Lists

It's tough to surf the web these days and not come across a list or three in your travels—a top-ten list, a best-of list, a point-form summary of an event, or any of a thousand other variations on the list theme. A list is often the perfect way to display certain types of information, such as a series of steps or an unordered collection of items.

HTML offers these two list types:

- A *numbered list* (sometimes called an *ordered list*) presents its items in numeric order, with each item's number on the left and the item text indented to the right.

- A *bulleted list* (sometimes called an *unordered list*) presents its items in the order you specify, with each item having a bullet (usually, a small dot) on the left and the item text indented to the right.

Lesson 3.6: *Adding a Numbered List*
Covers: The ol element

⇨ **Online:** wdpg.io/3-6-0

If the things you want to display have an inherent numeric order, such as you might find in the steps of a procedure or the elements in a series, a numbered list is the way to go. The good news is that you don't have to enter the numbers yourself, because the browser takes care of them for you automatically. The first item in the list is given the number 1, the second is given 2, and so on. If you insert or delete items, the browser adjusts all the list numbers as needed to keep everything in numeric order.

You start to construct a numbered list by creating a container that consists of the <ol> tag (short for *ordered list*) and its closing </ol> tag. Between those tags, you add one or more <li> (short for *list item*) tags followed by the item text and the closing </li> tag:

```
<li>Item text</li>
```

The browser displays the item with a number on the left (the value of which is determined by the item's position in the list), followed by item text, which is indented from the number, and the entire item is indented from the left margin of whatever element contains it.

The following example shows a basic numbered list and the HTML tags and text used to create it.

REMEMBER

Although this type of list is used far less than numbered and bulleted lists, you should also be aware of description list, which is a list of terms and descriptions. The entire list uses the <dl> and </dl> tags as a container; you specify each term within the <dt> and </dt> tags and each description within the <dd> and </dd> tags.

USE IT

Use a numbered list for any collection that must appear in sequential, numeric order. Examples are the steps the reader must follow in a how-to procedure, the tasks involved in a recipe, the sections in a document (particularly a contract or other legal document), or the items in a ranking such as a top-ten list.

▶ *Example*   ⇨ **Online:** wdpg.io/3-6-1
This example shows how to use a numbered list to set up a top-ten list.

WEB PAGE

Top 10 Modern Words of Unknown Origin

1. *jazz* (1909)
2. *jive* (1928)
3. *bozo* (1920)
4. *dork* (1964)
5. *pizzazz* (1937)
6. *humongous* (1970)
7. *gismo* (1943)
8. *zit* (1966)
9. *reggae* (1968)
10. *mosh* (1987)

HTML

```
<h3>Top 10 Modern Words of Unknown Origin</h3>
<ol>
    <li><em>jazz</em> (1909)</li>
    <li><em>jive</em> (1928)</li>
    <li><em>bozo</em> (1920)</li>
    <li><em>dork</em> (1964)</li>
    <li><em>pizzazz</em> (1937)</li>
    <li><em>humongous</em> (1970)</li>
    <li><em>gismo</em> (1943)</li>
    <li><em>zit</em> (1966)</li>
    <li><em>reggae</em> (1968)</li>
    <li><em>mosh</em> (1987)</li>
</ol>
```

Within the container, enter each item's text between the <li> and </li> tags.

Use the <ol> and </ol> tags as the container for the numbered list.

PLAY

To get some practice with the ol *and* li *elements, try the exercises on the Web Design Playground.*
⇨ Online: wdpg.io/3-6-2

By default, the numbers used in the list are standard decimal values (1, 2, 3, and so on). You can change the number type by specifying the list-style-type CSS property. Table 3.1 lists the most common numbered-list values for this property.

▶ Table 3.1 Common Numbered-List Values for the list-style-type CSS Property

Value	Description	Example Numbers
decimal	Decimal numbers	1, 2, 3, 4, …
decimal-leading-zero	Decimals numbers with a leading 0	01, 02, 03, 04, …
lower-alpha	Lowercase letters	a, b, c, d, …
upper-alpha	Uppercase letters	A, B, C, D, …
lower-roman	Lowercase Roman numerals	i, ii, iii, iv, …
upper-roman	Uppercase Roman numbers	I, II, III, IV, …
lower-greek	Lowercase Greek letters	α, β, γ, δ, …
upper-greek	Uppercase Greek letters	Α, Β, Γ, Δ, …

LEARN

Quite a few values for list-style-type *are associated with various other languages, such as Chinese, Hebrew, and Japanese. See the following page for the complete list:* https://developer.mozilla.org/en-US/docs/Web/CSS/list-style-type.

Lesson 3.7: **Adding a Bulleted List**
Covers: The ul element

⇨ **Online:** wdpg.io/3-7-0

If the items you want to display have no inherent numeric order, such as you might find in a to-do list or a set of characteristics, a bulleted list is the way to go. Each item appears in its own paragraph, preceded by a bullet (usually, a black dot). You don't have to enter the bullets manually because the browser adds them automatically.

You start building a bulleted list by creating a container that consists of the `<ul>` (short for *unordered list*) tag and its closing `</ul>` tag. Between these tags, as with a numbered list, you add one or more `<li>` tags, followed by the item text and the closing `</li>` tag:

```
<li>Item text</li>
```

The browser displays the item with a bullet on the left, followed by item text, which is indented from the bullet, and the entire item is indented from the left margin of the element that contains it.

The following example shows a basic bulleted list and its underlying HTML tags and text.

USE IT

Use a bulleted list for any collection of items that are related in some way but don't have to appear in numeric order. Examples include a to-do list or grocery list, a set of traits or properties associated with an object, or a collection of prerequisites for a course.

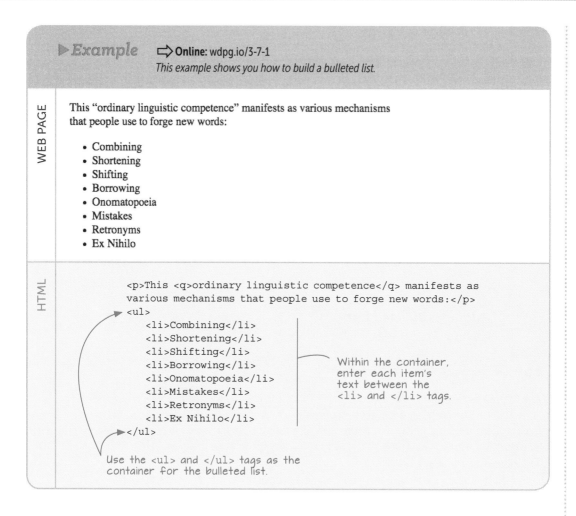

▶ *Example*   ⇨ **Online:** wdpg.io/3-7-1
This example shows you how to build a bulleted list.

WEB PAGE

This "ordinary linguistic competence" manifests as various mechanisms that people use to forge new words:

- Combining
- Shortening
- Shifting
- Borrowing
- Onomatopoeia
- Mistakes
- Retronyms
- Ex Nihilo

HTML

```
<p>This <q>ordinary linguistic competence</q> manifests as
various mechanisms that people use to forge new words:</p>
<ul>
    <li>Combining</li>
    <li>Shortening</li>
    <li>Shifting</li>
    <li>Borrowing</li>
    <li>Onomatopoeia</li>
    <li>Mistakes</li>
    <li>Retronyms</li>
    <li>Ex Nihilo</li>
</ul>
```

Within the container, enter each item's text between the <li> and </li> tags.

Use the <ul> and </ul> tags as the container for the bulleted list.

PLAY

To get some practice with the ul *and* li *elements, try the exercises on the Web Design Playground.*
⇨ Online: wdpg.io/3-7-2

By default, the bullets used in the list are filled circles (•). You can change the number type by specifying the `list-style-type` CSS property. Table 3.2 lists the available bulleted-list values for this property.

▶ Table 3.2 The Bulleted-List Values for the list-style-type CSS Property

Value	Description	Example Bullet
disc	Filled circle	●
circle	Unfilled circle	○
square	Filled square	■

Summary

- To structure your page text into paragraphs, use the `p element`.

- To separate one line from the next, insert the `br` element to add a line break.

- Use the `div` element to divide the page into text blocks.

- You can create an inline container for text by surrounding the text with the `<span>` and `</span>` tags.

- Use the `hr` element to separate text blocks with a horizontal rule.

- Use the `<ol>` tag to create a numbered list and the `<ul>` tag to create a bulleted list. In both cases, you use the `<li>` tag to designate each item in the list.

Chapter 4

Formatting Your Web Page

Digital design is like painting, except the paint never dries. —Neville Brody

This chapter covers

- Styling the text font, size, and style
- Aligning and indenting paragraphs
- Adding text and background colors

You now know how to display important and emphasized text, create links and headings, and display items in bulleted or numbered lists, but although these important techniques give your web page a bit of visual interest, they won't win you any design awards. To get people to sit up and take notice of your page, you need to concentrate on the CSS side of things for a bit, and that's what you'll do in this chapter. First, you'll learn a few ways to style your web page text, including specifying the typeface you want to use and setting the size of the text. You'll also learn how to apply bold to any text (not only important terms or keywords), as well as how to add italic to any text (not only emphasized words or alternative terms). From words and phrases, you jump to paragraphs, learning how to align text horizontally and indent paragraph text. The chapter closes on a colorful note as you learn how to apply CSS colors to text and to the page background.

As you'll see, these basic CSS techniques are straightforward to learn and implement, but don't let their inherent simplicity fool you. These are powerful tools that you'll use over and over to make your pages look great and to give them your personal touch. Those design awards are right around the corner.

Styling Text

Each browser uses default styles to render text such as headings and paragraphs. Although some differences exist among browsers, for the most part these styles are rendered similarly in Google Chrome, Mozilla Firefox, Apple Safari, and so on. These styles are perfectly good design choices, but if you use these default styles, you run the risk of having your web page end up with a default look. That's the last thing you want as a web page designer, so one of your most important tasks is to override those defaults and specify your own text formatting.

Web typography is a huge, fascinating topic that you'll learn in depth in Chapter 14. For now, I'll keep things simple by focusing on four of the most important text-formatting features: typeface, type size, bolding, and italics.

Styling the Typeface

I like to describe fonts as the architecture of characters. When you examine a building, certain features and patterns help you identify the building's architectural style. A flying buttress, for example, usually is a telltale sign of a Gothic structure. Fonts, too, are distinguished by a unique set of characteristics, and those characteristics are embodied in the typeface.

A *typeface* is a distinctive design that's common to any related set of letters, numbers, and symbols. What's the difference between a typeface and a font? For all practical purposes, the two terms are interchangeable. For all impractical purposes, however, a *font* is a particular implementation of a typeface, meaning the typeface as rendered with a specific size, weight, and style. Helvetica is a typeface; Helvetica 16-point bold is a font.

The typeface design gives each character a shape and thickness that's unique to the typeface and difficult to classify. Five main categories serve to distinguish most typefaces you'll come across in your web-design career:

Serif—A *serif* (rhymes with *sheriff*) typeface contains fine cross strokes (called *feet*) at the extremities of each character. These subtle appendages give the typeface a traditional, classy look, but they can get lost when displayed on a screen at small sizes.	Playground
Sans serif—A *sans-serif* typeface doesn't contain cross strokes on the extremities of characters. These typefaces usually have a clean, modern look that's well suited to screen text, particularly at small sizes.	Playground
Monospace—A *monospace* typeface (also called a *fixed-width* typeface) uses the same amount of space for each character, so skinny letters such as *i* and *l* take up as much space as wider letters such as *m* and *w*.	Playground
Cursive—The *cursive* typefaces are designed to resemble handwritten pen or brush writing.	Playground
Fantasy—*Fantasy* typefaces usually are fanciful designs that have some extreme elements (such as being extra-thick).	**Playground**

In CSS, you tell the web browser which typeface you want to apply to an element by using the `font-family` property. You have several ways to set the `font-family` value, but I begin by looking at the method that requires the least amount of work.

USE IT

On a screen, serif usually works best for headings and other text set at large sizes; sans serif makes good body text; monospace works well for code listings; cursive is best for short bits of text that require elegance or playfulness; and fantasy should be used only when a special effect is required.

Lesson 4.1: *Specifying a Generic Font*
Covers: The `font-family` property and generic fonts

⇨ **Online:** wdpg.io/4-1-0

The simplest way to use `font-family` is to specify a *generic font*, which is a standard font implemented by all modern web browsers. There are five generic font families, and their names correspond to the five typeface categories discussed in the preceding section: `serif`, `sans serif`, `monospace`, `cursive`, and `fantasy`. The following example puts the `font-family` property through its paces.

▶ *Example*   ⇨ **Online:** wdpg.io/4-1-1
This example shows you how to use the font-family *property to apply the* sans-serif *generic font to the* h3 *element and the* serif *generic font to the* p *element.*

WEB PAGE

The Web Design Playground ◄——— The h3 element

Why work towards web design proficiency when you can play your way there? ◄——— The p element

CSS

```
h3 {
    font-family: sans-serif;
}
p {
    font-family: serif;
}
```

The h3 element gets the sans-serif generic font.

The p element gets the serif generic font.

HTML

```
<h3>The Web Design Playground</h3>

<p>Why work towards web design proficiency when you can play your
way there?</p>
```

Generic fonts are useful because they're supported by all web browsers, but with only five font families, they lack variety. If you'd like a bit more choice for your web page text, you need to access a broader collection of fonts.

Lesson 4.2: *Specifying a System Font*
Covers: The font-family property and system fonts

⇨ **Online:** wdpg.io/4-2-0

REMEMBER

Using quotation marks and capitalizing the first letter of each word in a system font name are optional, but they're good habits to get into because they make your code more readable.

Besides the built-in generic fonts, each web browser can access the fonts that a site visitor has installed on her computer. Most computers have the serif typeface Times New Roman installed, for example, so your web page could use that typeface instead of the generic serif font. These installed typefaces are known as *system fonts*.

When you specify a system font, here are two things to keep in mind:

- If the font name includes one or more spaces, numbers, or punctuation characters other than a hyphen (-), surround the name with quotation marks:

```
font-family: "Times New Roman";
```

- Capitalize the first letter (or, for multiword names, capitalize the first letter of each word):

```
font-family: Georgia;
```

Note that it's perfectly legal to specify more than one font name as long as you separate the names with commas. In that case, the browser checks the fonts in the order in which they appear and uses the first one that's installed on the user's computer. This arrangement is useful because you can't be sure which system fonts each user has installed. In particular, it's good practice to include a similar generic font family after the system font. If you specify a serif system font such as Times New Roman or Georgia (or both), for example, include the `serif` generic font as the last item in the `font-family` value:

```
font-family: "Times New Roman", Georgia, serif;
```

The following example applies the Verdana system font to the `div` element, which (as you might recall from Chapter 2) is the element you use to divide the web page content into separate sections.

LEARN
To get the installation percentages for many popular system fonts, see https://www.cssfontstack.com.

REMEMBER
Some system fonts are installed on at least 90 percent of both Macs and Windows PCs. For sans-serif, these fonts are Arial, Arial Black, Tahoma, Trebuchet MS, and Verdana. For serif, these fonts are Georgia and Times New Roman. For monospace, this font is Courier New.

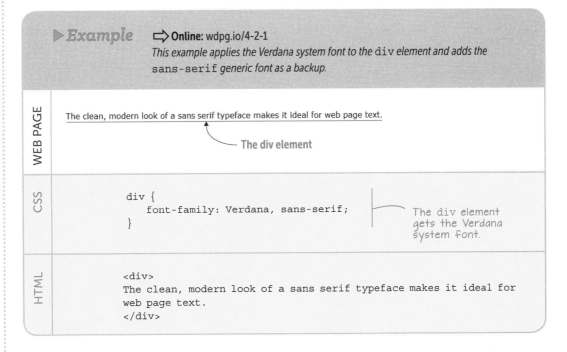

▶ *Example*   ⇨ **Online:** wdpg.io/4-2-1
This example applies the Verdana system font to the `div` *element and adds the* `sans-serif` *generic font as a backup.*

WEB PAGE

The clean, modern look of a sans serif typeface makes it ideal for web page text.

The div element

CSS

```
div {
    font-family: Verdana, sans-serif;
}
```

The div element gets the Verdana system font.

HTML

```
<div>
The clean, modern look of a sans serif typeface makes it ideal for
web page text.
</div>
```

Lesson 4.3: **Setting the Type Size**
Covers: The `font-size` property

⇨ **Online:** wdpg.io/4-3-0

REMEMBER

You can specify font sizes in units other than pixels. I take you through all the available CSS units in Chapter 7.

In the same way that the web browser defines a default typeface for each element, it defines default type sizes, particularly for the heading elements `h1` (largest) through `h6` (smallest). Again, these defaults are usually reasonable, but I'm going to urge you to forget about the defaults and set up your own type sizes. Why? One of the secrets of good web design is assuming control of every aspect of the design, which is the only way to be sure that the web page looks the way you or your client wants it to look. One of your main jobs as a web page designer is to set your own type sizes not only for headings, but also for all your page elements, including body text, captions, sidebars, and navigation.

You specify the type size of an element by setting the `font-size` property equal to a value in pixels, which you indicate with the unit px. The example that follows tells the web browser to render all text that appears within a `div` element at a text size of 24 pixels. By comparison, the example also shows some text within a p element displayed in the default size, which in all modern browsers is 16 pixels.

▶ *Example* ⇨ **Online:** wdpg.io/4-3-1
This example formats the `div` element with a text size of 24 pixels.

WEB PAGE

From Milan to Markup ← — The h1 element

The strange-but-true story of one woman's epic journey from fashion designer to web geek. ← — The div element

Hyperia Marcupala always loved design, but one day she discovered she'd rather work with pixels than pleats. ← — The p element

CSS

```
div {
    font-size: 24px;
}
```
The div element is given a font size of 24px.

```
HTML
        <h1>From Milan to Markup</h1>

        <div>
        The strange-but-true story of one woman's epic journey from
        fashion designer to web geek.
        </div>

        <p>
        Hyperia Marcupala always loved design, but one day she discovered
        she'd rather work with pixels than pleats.
        </p>
```

Working with Text Styles

When you have your typeface picked out and your page elements set up with different type sizes, you're well on your way to making typographically pleasing web pages. But to make your pages stand out from the herd, you need to know two more CSS properties related to styling text. The next couple of sections take you through these styles.

Lesson 4.4: **Making Text Bold**
Covers: The font-weight property

⇨ **Online:** wdpg.io/4-4-0

In Chapter 2, you learned that you can display text as bold by using the <strong> tag or the <b> tag. You use these tags when the affected text has semantic significance: The strong element is for important text, whereas the b element is for keywords. But what if you have text that doesn't fit into either of these semantic categories, but you want it to appear bold anyway for the sake of appearance? In that case, you can turn to the CSS property font-weight. Table 4.1 lists the weights and keywords you can assign to this property.

USE IT

Nonsemantic uses for bold text include a title used at the beginning of each item in a bulleted list, the lead words or the lead sentence in a paragraph, and contact information.

BEWARE

Not all the values in Table 4.1 work in all systems. If whatever typeface you're using doesn't support one or more of the weights, specifying that weight won't have any effect.

FAQ

When would I ever use the normal (or 400) value? When you're working with an element that defaults to bold styling, such as a heading. To prevent such an element from appearing with bold text, assign its font-weight *property a value of* normal *(or* 400*).*

▶ Table 4.1 Possible Values for the `font-weight` Property

Weight	Keyword	Description
100		Thin text
200		Extra light text
300		Light text
400	normal	Regular text
500		Medium text
600		Semibold text
700	bold	Bold text
800		Extra-bold text
900		Black text

The following example gives you a taste of what bold text looks like by applying the weights 100, 400, and 700 to several span elements. (Recall from Chapter 2 that you use span to create an inline container that applies to a word or three.)

▶ *Example* ⇨ **Online:** wdpg.io/4-4-1

This example demonstrates the weights 100, 400, and 700 of the Calibri typeface by applying each weight to a separate span element.

WEB PAGE

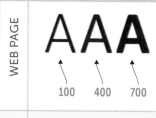

100   400   700

CSS

```css
span {
    font-family: Calibri, sans-serif;
    font-size: 5em;
}
```

HTML

```html
<span style="font-weight: 100">A</span>
<span style="font-weight: 400">A</span>
<span style="font-weight: 700">A</span>
```

The span elements apply the various weights to the letter A.

Lesson 4.5: **Making Text Italic**
Covers: The font-style property

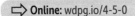

⟹ **Online:** wdpg.io/4-5-0

As you learned in Chapter 2, you can display text in italics semantically by using the `<em>` tag when you want to emphasize text or the `<i>` tag when you want to format alternative text. If you have text that isn't semantic, but you want it to appear italic anyway, use the CSS property `font-style`, and set it to the value `italic`. Here's an example:

USE IT

Nonsemantic uses for italic text include pull quotes, the lead words or the lead sentence in a paragraph, and article metadata (such as the author name and date).

▶ *Example*   ⟹ **Online:** wdpg.io/4-5-1

This example applies the italic font style to the span *element. There are two instances: the* `<span>` *that's nested within the h1 element and the* span *that's nested at the beginning of the* div *element.*

WEB PAGE

Italic Text: *A History*

The first use of italics came in 1500 when Aldus Manutius of the Aldine Press wanted a typeface that resembled the handwritten humanist script that was then in common use. He asked his typecutter Francesco Griffo to make the typeface, which Manutius first used in the frontispiece of a book of the letters of Catherine of Siena. He produced the first book set entirely in italics the next year.

CSS

```css
body {
    font-family: Georgia, serif;
}
span {
    font-style: italic;
}
div {
    font-size: 1.25em;
}
```

The span element is formatted as italic.

HTML

```html
<h1>Italic Text: <span>A History</span></h1>

<div>
<span>The first use of italics came in 1500</span> when Aldus
Manutius of the Aldine Press wanted a typeface that resembled
the handwritten humanist script that was then in common use. He
asked his typecutter Francesco Griffo to make the typeface, which
Manutius first used in the frontispiece of a book of the letters
of Catherine of Siena. He produced the first book set entirely in
italics the next year.
</div>
```

The first span instance

The second span instance

Styling Paragraphs

When (or perhaps I should say *if*) people think of typography, they tend to look at individual letters or letter combinations. That's important, for sure, but it's only the "trees" view of typography. If you want your web pages to look their best, you also need to take in the "forest" view, which encompasses the larger text blocks on the page, including titles, subtitles, headings, and especially paragraphs. As you see in the next couple of sections, paying attention to important styling touches such as alignment and indents can go a long way toward changing your pages from drab to fab.

Lesson 4.6: *Aligning Paragraphs Horizontally*
Covers: The text-align property

⇨ **Online:** wdpg.io/4-6-0

To control how a paragraph or block of text is aligned horizontally—that is, with respect to the left and right page margins—use the CSS text-align property, which takes any of the keywords shown in Table 4.2.

▶ Table 4.2 Possible Values for the **text-align** Property

Keyword	Description
left	Aligns the left edge of the text block with the left margin; the right edge of the text block is not aligned (and so is said to be *ragged*); this is the default in languages that read left to right.
right	Aligns the right edge of the text block with the right margin; the left edge of the text block is not aligned (ragged); this is the default in languages that read right to left.
center	Centers each line of the text block between the left and right margin; both the left and right edges of the text block are ragged.
justify	Aligns the left edge of the text block with the left margin and the right edge of the text block with the right margin.

❝ *The four modes of alignment (centered, justified, flush left, and flush right) form the basic grammar of typographic composition.* —Ellen Lupton

The following example tries each of the four text-align values.

▶ *Example*　⇨ **Online:** wdpg.io/4-6-1
This example shows the four alignment styles at work: centered for the title and subtitle, and left, right, and fully justified text blocks.

WEB PAGE

Centered ————→ # Aligning Web Page Text

————→ ## Notes From the Field

Left-aligned ——{ We read text (in English, anyway) from left to right. This means that when we get to the end of each line, to continue we must jump down one line and then scan to the beginning of that line. That leap-and-scan is most easily made when we "know" where the next line begins. That's why left-justified text is the easiest alignment to read.

Compare the left-justified text block above with this right-justified paragraph. In this case, when you reach the end of each line, jumping down to the next isn't a problem, but because the left side of the text block is set ragged, the beginning of each line isn't in a predictable place, which makes right-justified text a tad more difficult to read. }—— Right-aligned

Many books are set with justified paragraphs because it looks more elegant without the right-ragged edges. However, pro book designers use sophisticated layout software to manage things like hyphenation (particularly if the text includes a long word such as *honorificabilitudinitatibus*). These aren't available for the web, so it's often best not to justify.

———————— Justified ————————

CSS

```
h1, h2 {
    text-align: center;
}
```
— Centers the h1 and h2 elements

HTML

```
<h1>Aligning Web Page Text</h1>
<h2>Notes From the Field</h2>
<div style="text-align: left;">
```
— Left-aligns the first paragraph
```
We read text (in English, anyway) from left to right. This means
that when we get to the end of each line, to continue we must
jump down one line and then scan to the beginning of that line.
That leap-and-scan is most easily made when we "know" where the
next line begins. That's why left-justified text is the easiest
alignment to read. </div>
<div style="text-align: right;">
```
— Right-aligns the second paragraph
```
Compare the left-justified text block above with this right-
justified paragraph. In this case, when you reach the end of each
line, jumping down to the next isn't a problem, but because the
left side of the text block is set ragged, the beginning of each
line isn't in a predictable place, which makes right-justified
text a tad more difficult to read. </div>
<div style="text-align: justify;">
```
— Justifies the third paragraph
```
Many books are set with justified paragraphs because it looks
more elegant without the right-ragged edges. However, pro book
designers use sophisticated layout software to manage things like
hyphenation (particularly if the text includes a long word such as
<i>honorificabilitudinitatibus</i>). These aren't available for
the web, so it's often best not to justify. </div>
```

Lesson 4.7: *Indenting Paragraph Text*

Covers: The text-indent property

LEARN

Some browsers support the `text-align-last` *property, which sets the alignment of the last line in a text block when the* `text-align` *property is set to* `justify`*. Possible values include* `left`, `right`, `center`, *and* `justify`*. See* http://caniuse.com/#feat=css-text-align-last *to follow the support for this property.*

Online: wdpg.io/4-7-0

You can indent paragraph text by using the CSS `text-indent` property, which takes either of the values shown in Table 4.3. Note that the indent applies only to the beginning of the first line of the text block.

▶ Table 4.3 Values You Can Apply to the **`text-indent`** Property

Value	Description
`length`	A numeric value entered with a unit, such as `px`.
`percentage`	A percentage value. The computed indent is the width of the text block multiplied by the percentage.

As with most things typographical, much debate exists about whether text blocks should be indented. Some typographers eschew indents because they believe that nonindented text is more aesthetically pleasing; others embrace indents because they believe that indented text is more readable. Whichever side you end up on, you should keep the following points in mind:

- Never indent the first paragraph of the page or the first paragraph after a heading. The purpose of an indent is to separate the paragraph from the one above it, but that doesn't apply to the first paragraph.
- If you indent your paragraphs, you don't need to add space between paragraphs.
- If you don't indent your paragraphs, you should add some margin or padding between the paragraphs for readability. See Chapter 6 to find out how to set the margins and padding.

REMEMBER

A commonly used value for a paragraph indent is `16px`*.*

BEWARE

If you want to create an outdent for a text block, make sure that the block has a left margin that's wide enough to accommodate the outdented text. See Chapter 7 to learn how to set the left margin for a text block.

> *Using paragraph spacing and indents together squanders space and gives the text block a flabby, indefinite shape.* —Ellen Lupton

▷ **Example**   ⇨ **Online:** wdpg.io/4-7-1

This example displays the three possible indent styles: flush (the first paragraph); a positive indent (second paragraph); and a negative indent (third paragraph), which is usually called an outdent *or a* hanging indent.

WEB PAGE

Flush ——→ The first word of the first line is the critical word of that particular body of text. Let it start flush, at least. —William Addison Dwiggins

Indented ——→ Typographers generally take pleasure in the unpredictable length of the paragraph while accepting the simple and reassuring consistency of the paragraph indent. —Robert Bringhurst

Outdented ——→ OUTDENTS work well when dramatic effect is desired. They sometimes have a second emphasis factor, such as a style or case change, that contrasts with the body text. —Kristin Cullen

HTML

The text-indent property isn't set, so the first line is flush with the rest of the paragraph.

```
<div>
The first word of the first line is the critical word of that
particular body of text. Let it start flush, at least. —William
Addison Dwiggins
</div>
<div style="text-indent: 16px;">
Typographers generally take pleasure in the unpredictable length
of the paragraph while accepting the simple and reassuring
consistency of the paragraph indent. —Robert Bringhurst
</div>
<div style="text-indent: -64px;">
<span style="font-variant: small-caps;">Outdents</span> work
well when dramatic effect is desired. They sometimes have a second
emphasis factor, such as a style or case change, that
contrasts with the body text. —Kristin Cullen
</div>
```

Indents the first line of the paragraph

Outdents the first line of the paragraph

Working with Colors

By default, most web browsers display the page by using black text on a white background. That combination is certainly readable but not interesting. Our marvelous eyes are capable of distinguishing millions of colors, so a palette of only black and white seems wrong somehow. Fortunately, CSS enables you to put your designer eyes to good use by offering several methods for accessing any of the 16 or so million colors that are available in the digital realm. Alas, most of those methods are a bit complicated, so I'm going to put them off until later (see Chapter 13).

For now, you get access to colors using the keywords that CSS defines. Table 4.4 lists the keywords for a few common colors.

▶ Table 4.4 The CSS Keywords for Nine Common Colors

Keyword	Color
red	
lime	
blue	
yellow	
magenta	
cyan	
black	
gray	
white	

There are more than 140 defined keywords in all, so you shouldn't have any trouble finding the right shade (or shades) for your next web project. I've put the complete list of color keywords on the Web Design Playground at wdpg.io/colorkeywords. Figure 4.1 shows a partial list.

Color	Keyword	RGB Value							
				lightpink	#ffb6c1		pink	#ffc0cb	
	crimson	#dc143c		lavenderblush	#fff0f5		palevioletred	#db7093	
	hotpink	#ff69b4		deeppink	#ff1493		mediumvioletred	#c71585	
	orchid	#da70d6		thistle	#d8bfd8		plum	#dda0dd	
	violet	#ee82ee		magenta	#ff00ff		fuchsia	#ff00ff	
	darkmagenta	#8b008b		purple	#800080		rebeccapurple	#663399	
	mediumorchid	#ba55d3		darkviolet	#9400d3		darkorchid	#9932cc	
	indigo	#4b0082		blueviolet	#8a2be2		mediumpurple	#9370db	
	mediumslateblue	#7b68ee		slateblue	#6a5acd		darkslateblue	#483d8b	
	lavender	#e6e6fa		ghostwhite	#f8f8ff		blue	#0000ff	
	mediumblue	#0000cd		midnightblue	#191970		darkblue	#00008b	
	navy	#000080		royalblue	#4169e1		cornflowerblue	#6495ed	
	lightsteelblue	#b0c4de		lightslategray	#778899		slategray	#708090	
	dodgerblue	#1e90ff		aliceblue	#f0f8ff		steelblue	#4682b4	
	lightskyblue	#87cefa		skyblue	#87ceeb		deepskyblue	#00bfff	
	lightblue	#add8e6		powderblue	#b0e0e6		cadetblue	#5f9ea0	
	azure	#f0ffff		lightcyan	#e0ffff		paleturquoise	#afeeee	

▶ Figure 4.1 To see a complete list of the CSS color keywords on the Web Design Playground, surf to wdpg.io/colorkeywords.

Lesson 4.8: *Applying Color to Text*
Covers: The color property

⇨ **Online:** wdpg.io/4-8-0

Several CSS properties have a color component, including borders, backgrounds, and shadows. You learn about all those properties and more in this book (including backgrounds in the next section), but so far you know about text, so I'll start there. Here's the general CSS syntax for applying color to a text element:

```
selector {
    color: keyword;
}
```

The text item to which you want the color applied

The color property and its value

The selector can be an HTML element, such as an h1 heading or p element, or it can be any of the CSS selectors that you see in Chapter 7. The real work is done by the color property and its associated value, which can be any of the CSS color keywords (or any of the other color values supported by CSS, which you learn about in Chapter 17).

The following example shows the color definition for purple h1 text.

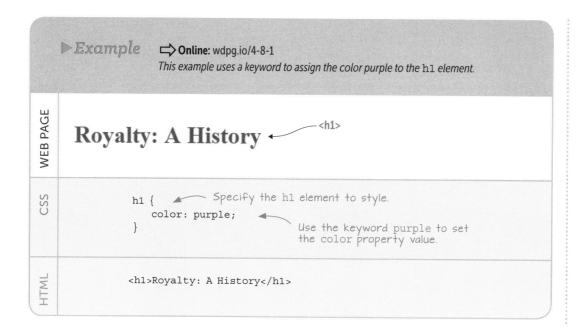

> *Example*   ⇨ **Online:** wdpg.io/4-8-1
> *This example uses a keyword to assign the color purple to the h1 element.*

Royalty: A History ← `<h1>`

```
h1 {           ← Specify the h1 element to style.
    color: purple;  ←
}                    Use the keyword purple to set
                     the color property value.
```

```
<h1>Royalty: A History</h1>
```

Lesson 4.9: **Applying Color to a Background**
Covers: The `background-color` property

PLAY

Style the a element to display the link text as yellow. Then add a second rule that displays the link text red and underlined when you hover the mouse over the link.
⇨ Online: wdpg.io/4-8-4

⇨ **Online:** wdpg.io/4-9-0

So far, I've looked only at setting the color of the foreground—the web page text—but you can use CSS to apply a color to a background. This color could be the background of the entire page (that is, the body element), a heading, a paragraph, a link, or part of a page such as a `<div>` or `<span>` tag.

Here's the general CSS syntax for applying a background color to a web page item:

```
           The item to which you want the
           background color applied
selector {
    background-color: keyword;  ←
}                    The background-color
                     property and its value
```

The selector can be an HTML element or any of the CSS selectors that you learn about in Chapter 7. The key is the `background-color` property and its associated value, which can be any of the color keywords you learned about earlier.

The following example shows a web page with a Table of Contents sidebar that has a black background and white text. The example also gives you a partial look at the HTML and CSS used to set it up.

▶ *Example*   ⇨ **Online:** wdpg.io/4-9-1
This example shows a web page with a Table of Contents sidebar that has a black background and white text.

WEB PAGE

<div>

Using Colors Effectively

"There are only 3 colors, 10 digits, and 7 notes; its what we do with them that's important." —Jim Rohn

"Some colors reconcile themselves to one another, others just clash." —Edvard Munch

"All colors are the friends of their neighbors and the lovers of their opposites." —Marc Chagall

Color Psychology

When selecting colors, think about the psychological impact that your scheme will have on your users. Studies have shown that "cool" colors such as blue and gray evoke a sense of dependability and trust. Use these colors for a more business-like appearance. For pages that require a little more excitement, "warm" colors such as red, yellow, and orange can evoke a festive, fun atmosphere. For a safe, comfortable ambiance, try using brown and yellow. For an environmental touch, use green and brown.

Color Schemes

Table of Contents

Color Psychology
Color Schemes
Color Caveats
A Few Examples
Best Practices
CSS and Color

CSS

```css
div {
    background-color: black;
    color: white;
    float: right;
    font-size: 16px;
    font-weight: bold;
    margin-left: 0.5em;
    padding: 0 10px 5px 10px;
    text-align: left;
}
```

The background-color property sets the <div> background to black.

These properties apply various styles to the <div>.

The color property sets <div> text to white.

HTML

```html
<div>
    <h3>Table of Contents</h3>
    Color Psychology<br>
    Color Schemes<br>
    Color Caveats<br>
    A Few Examples<br>
    Best Practices<br>
    CSS and Color
</div>
```

The <div> tag and its associated HTML and text

PLAY

How would you modify the CSS in this example to display the Table of Contents sidebar with light gray text on a purple background?
⇨ Online: wdpg.io/4-9-2

PLAY

Write a CSS rule that styles links with blue text and a yellow background.
⇨ Online: wdpg.io/4-9-4

Summary

- You can use the `font-family` property to assign a typeface to a page element. This typeface can be one of the five generic fonts—`serif`, `sans-serif`, `monospace`, `cursive`, or `fantasy`— or a system font that's already installed on the user's computer.

- Use the `font-size` property to control the size of your text elements.

- Use the `font-weight` property to apply bolding nonsemantically.

- Use the `font-style` property to apply italics nonsemantically.

- Use `text-align` to set the horizontal alignment, such as centering headings and left-aligning text.

- Use `text-indent` to indent or outdent the first line of a text block.

- To color an element's text, use the `color` property.

- To color an element's background, use the `background-color` property.

Chapter 5

PROJECT: Creating a Personal Home Page

> *Creation is a better means of self-expression than possession; it is through creating, not possessing, that life is revealed.* —Vida Dutton Scudder

This chapter covers

- Planning and sketching your personal home page
- Choosing typefaces for your page
- Adding the header and navigation links
- Adding the body text

With four chapters under your belt, it's time to put your newfound HTML and CSS knowledge to work by building something substantial. Specifically, this chapter takes you through the process of putting together a simple personal home page. *Simple* is the operative word here because you don't yet know enough HTML tags and CSS properties to construct anything complex. Fortunately, you know more than enough to create a great-looking home page for yourself. You know about headings and paragraphs; you know how to create sections by using the `<div>` and `<span>` tags; you know how to create bulleted and numbered lists; you know how to create links; you know how to add typographic touches such as bold and italics; and you know how to apply colors to the background and to the text. As you see in this chapter, all that is more than enough to create a home page to be proud of.

What You'll Be Building

This project is a basic "Look, Ma, I'm on the web!" home page that enables you to take the tools and techniques you learned in this book's first four chapters and apply them in the virtual world of the web. The result is a simple but beautiful page that enables you to stake out a bit of online turf. To what end? That depends on you, but most personal home pages serve as an introduction to anyone who comes surfing by: who you are, what you like (and even what you dislike), what you've done in the past, what you're doing now, and what you'd like to do in the future. As I go along, I'll show you an example based on my information, but naturally, you'll want to replace my text with your own. Your web page is your house, and you can fill it with whatever you want.

Sketching the Layout

All your web projects should begin with a pen or pencil and a cocktail napkin or other handy writing surface. Creating a web page is first and foremost a *design* process, so before you start slinging code, you need to have a decent idea of what you're building. Sure, you can construct a mental image of the page, but it's better to begin with the more tactile approach afforded by pen and paper.

As you can see in Figure 5.1, this sketch doesn't have to be detailed. Lay out the main sections of the page with a phrase or sentence that describes the content of each section.

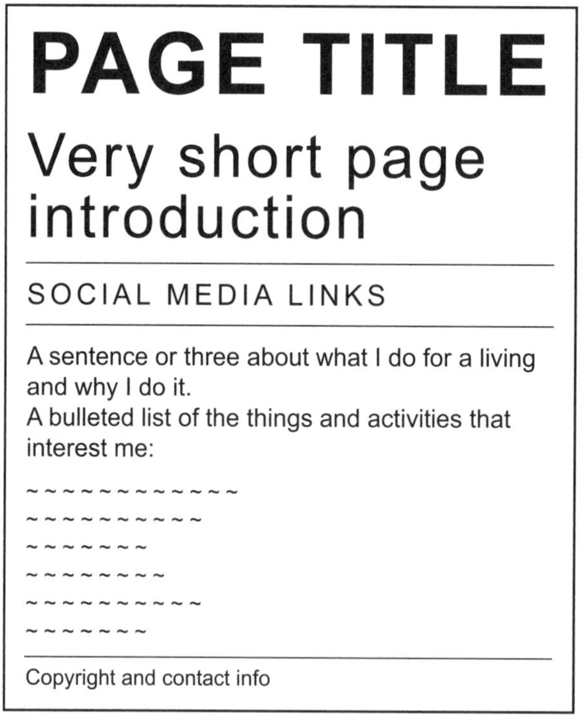

▶ Figure 5.1
Before starting to code your HTML and CSS, use a pen or pencil to work up a quick sketch of the page layout and content.

PAGE TITLE
Very short page introduction

SOCIAL MEDIA LINKS

A sentence or three about what I do for a living and why I do it.
A bulleted list of the things and activities that interest me:

~ ~ ~ ~ ~ ~ ~ ~ ~ ~ ~ ~
~ ~ ~ ~ ~ ~ ~ ~ ~ ~
~ ~ ~ ~ ~ ~
~ ~ ~ ~ ~ ~ ~
~ ~ ~ ~ ~ ~ ~ ~ ~
~ ~ ~ ~ ~ ~

Copyright and contact info

Figure 5.1 shows the layout of a page with the following six sections:

- The title of the page
- A short introduction to the page
- Links to social media sites such as Facebook and Twitter
- Text about what I do for a living
- Text and a bulleted list of things that interest me
- The page footer with a copyright notice and contact info

Your next page-planning task is deciding which typefaces you want to use for your page.

Choosing Typefaces

Because I haven't discussed images yet in this book, this first version of your personal home page is dominated by text, particularly what's known as *body text*—the large blocks of nonheading text that comprise the bulk of your page. Because a good chunk of your audience will be reading your page on devices such as laptops, tablets, and smartphones, it's important to take a bit of time up front to choose typefaces that will be legible and readable on these smaller screens.

You could build your page with a single typeface, but mixing two typefaces—one for headings and the other for body text—adds dynamism and contrast to the page. My preferred use is a sans-serif typeface for headings and a serif typeface for body text, but feel free to reverse them or to use two serifs or sans serifs. The only criterion to look for is two typefaces that work in harmony.

For this project, I'm going to use two perennial web favorites: the sans-serif typeface Verdana for the headings and the serif typeface Georgia for the body text. In my CSS, I'll use the following rules to specify these families:

```
font-family: Georgia, serif;
font-family: Verdana, sans-serif;
```

With the page layout in place and your typefaces chosen, the next step is to pick out a color scheme.

Choosing a Color Scheme

In this simple page, colors won't play a huge role, but you'll want to inject some color to avoid the monotony of all black text on a white background. You can add a background color or even a gradient by using the Web Design Playground's Gradient Construction Kit (see wdpg.io/kits/gradient). I prefer a simple white background for this project, so my own colors focus on the text. Using the Web Design Playground's RGB Color Scheme Calculator (see wdpg.io/colorcalc), I chose a color scheme based on the color value #ffc200, as shown in Figure 5.2. You, of course, should choose a color scheme that suits your style.

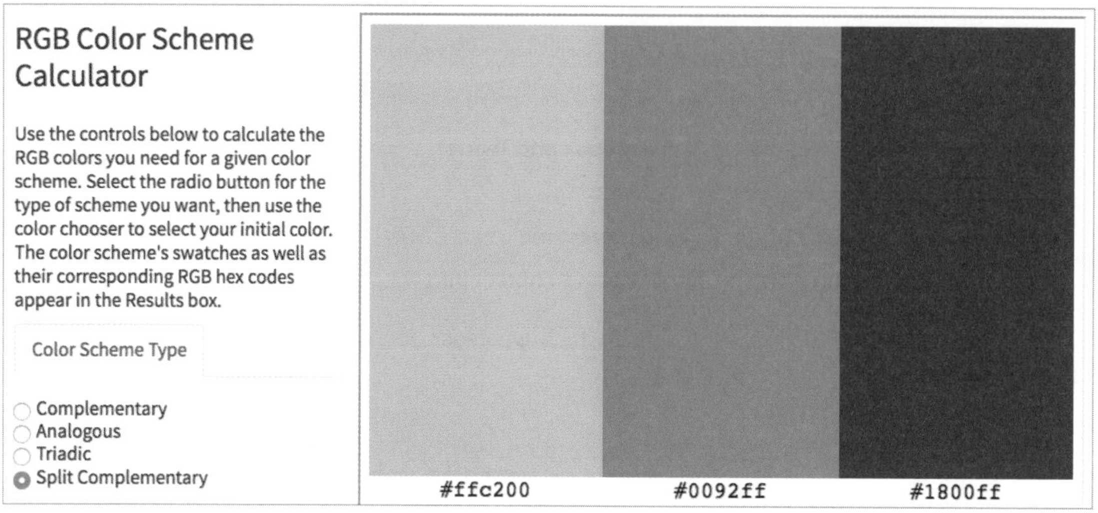

RGB Color Scheme Calculator

Use the controls below to calculate the RGB colors you need for a given color scheme. Select the radio button for the type of scheme you want, then use the color chooser to select your initial color. The color scheme's swatches as well as their corresponding RGB hex codes appear in the Results box.

Color Scheme Type

○ Complementary
○ Analogous
○ Triadic
● Split Complementary

#ffc200 #0092ff #1800ff

▶ Figure 5.2 A split complementary color scheme based on the hex color value `#ffc200`

With the page layout in place and your colors chosen, it's time to translate this rough sketch into precise HTML and CSS code.

Building the Page

To build your personal home page, you'll start with the skeleton code that I introduced you to in Chapter 2. From there, you'll go section by section, adding text, HTML tags, and CSS properties.

The Initial Structure

To start, take the basic page structure from Chapter 2 and add the tags and some placeholder text for each of the page's six sections. Here's a summary of those tags:

- The page title is an h1 heading element.
- The page introduction is an h2 heading element.
- The social media links are within an h3 heading element.
- The first text block is a div element.
- The second text block is another div element, which is followed by a ul element for the bulleted list.
- The page footer is another div element.

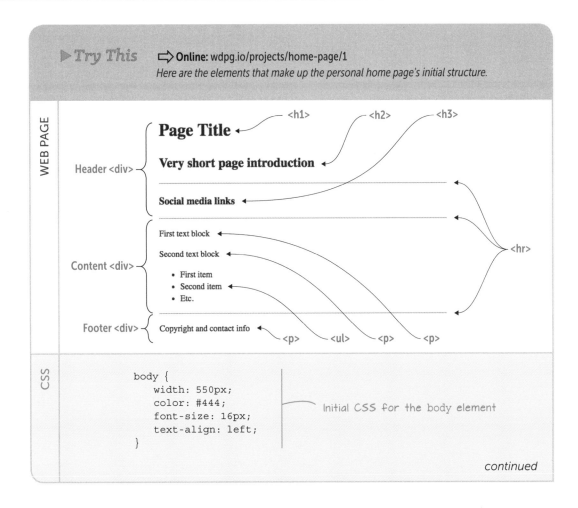

▶ *Try This*   ⇨ **Online:** wdpg.io/projects/home-page/1
Here are the elements that make up the personal home page's initial structure.

WEB PAGE

Header <div>
Content <div>
Footer <div>

Page Title ◄ — <h1>   <h2>   <h3>

Very short page introduction ◄

Social media links ◄

First text block ◄
Second text block ◄
• First item
• Second item ◄
• Etc.

Copyright and contact info ◄

<hr>

<p>   <ul>   <p>   <p>

CSS

```css
body {
    width: 550px;
    color: #444;
    font-size: 16px;
    text-align: left;
}
```

Initial CSS for the body element

continued

HTML

```
<!--START OF HEADER-->
<div>
    <h1>Page Title</h1>
    <h2>Very short page introduction</h2>
    <hr>
    <h3>Social media links</h3>
    <hr>
</div>
<!--END OF HEADER-->
<!--START OF CONTENT-->
<div>
    <p>
        First text block
    </p>
    <p>
        Second text block
    </p>
    <ul>
        <li>First item</li>
        <li>Second item</li>
        <li>Etc.</li>
    </ul>
</div>
<!--END OF CONTENT-->
<!--START OF FOOTER-->
<div>
    <hr>
    <p>
        Copyright and contact info
    </p>
</div>
<!--END OF FOOTER-->
```

Comments denote the beginning and end of each section.

The header section

The content section (two paragraphs and a bulleted list)

The footer section

PLAY

I've left-aligned everything in the page to get a nice clean line down the left side of the page. There's no reason why you couldn't mess with the alignment, however. Try centering the three page header elements (title, introduction, and social media links). ⇨ **Online:** *wdpg.io/projects/home-page/2*

Notice that the initial structure also includes a few CSS properties applied to the body element. These global properties set the width of the page and the default values for the text color, font size, and alignment. The most surprising might be the `width` value of `550px`. Why restrict the width at all, and why use such a relatively small value? One key element in good web typography is line length. If your lines are too long, they become hard to scan, and if they're too short, the text becomes choppy. In both cases, the resulting text is difficult to read. For screen text, the optimum line length is between 65 and 75 characters, so you need to set the width so that all or most of the lines in your body text fit within that range.

Here are a few other things to note about the HTML tags used in the initial structure:

- The page is divided into three sections: a header, the content, and a footer.
- Each section is embedded within a `<div></div>` block. This block organizes the structure and enables you to apply a style (such as a font family) to everything within a particular section.
- Each section of the page is surrounded by special tags called *comments* that mark the beginning (e.g., `<!—START OF HEADER-->`) and the end (e.g., `<!—END OF HEADER-->`) of the section. I use all-uppercase characters to help the comments stand out from the regular code, but that practice is optional. See Chapter 16 to learn more about using comments in your code.

The Page Title

Not surprisingly, you want your page title to be more prominent than the rest of the page text. Setting the text within an h1 element is a good start, but you'll likely need to style the text even more to get the effect you want. Here are some ideas:

- *Apply a different color.* If you make the color unique, the title will stand out from the rest of the text.
- *Apply a larger font size.* Because your page title may be something as simple as your name, a larger size makes it pop.

In the following example, I used my name as the title, but feel free to use whatever text you prefer. I applied the sans-serif system font Verdana to the header section's `div` element (which means that this font is also applied to the rest of the headings). I've also styled the page title (the h1 element) with one of the colors from my color scheme (#1800ff) and a 52px font size.

FAQ

Why didn't you use *#000* or *black* as the default text color? *With a white page background, pure black text can be difficult to read because of the extreme contrast between the two colors. Backing off the text color to #444 or #333 makes it easier to read.*

PLAY

To help you get a feel for the ideal line lengths for onscreen reading, I've set up an exercise on the Web Design Playground. Given a paragraph of text, adjust the body element's width *property to bring the line lengths into the ideal 65- to 75-character range. Try changing the* font-size *property to see what effect that change has on line length.* ⇨ Online: wdpg .io/projects/home-page/3

REMEMBER

Don't be shy about adding comments to your code. Comments help you keep track of the page structure, and they're often indispensable when someone else needs to read your code or when you haven't looked at your page code for a few months.

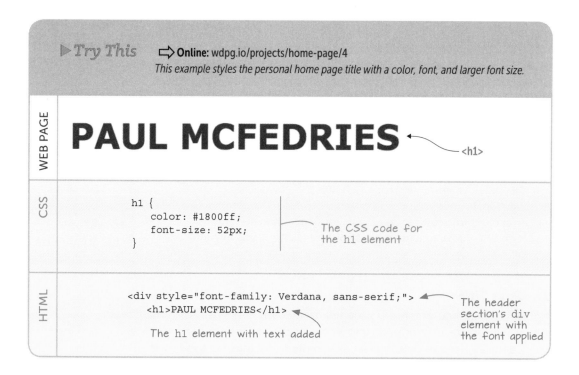

▶ *Try This*   ⇨ **Online:** wdpg.io/projects/home-page/4
This example styles the personal home page title with a color, font, and larger font size.

WEB PAGE

PAUL MCFEDRIES ← `<h1>`

CSS

```
h1 {
    color: #1800ff;
    font-size: 52px;
}
```

The CSS code for the h1 element

HTML

```
<div style="font-family: Verdana, sans-serif;">
    <h1>PAUL MCFEDRIES</h1>
```

The header section's div element with the font applied

The h1 element with text added

PLAY

If your page title is long, it will likely wrap to a second line. That's fine, but you'll want to reduce the line height to bring the two lines closer together. For the h1 *element, try setting the* line-height *property to a value below 1 (such as* 0.8 *or* 0.9*).* ⇨ Online: wdpg. io/projects/home-page/5

The Page Introduction

The page introduction acts as a kind of subtitle. It should be a brief snippet of text that introduces you to the reader. Because the text is a subtitle, the font size should be smaller than the title text but larger than the body text. Again, setting the text within an h2 element should do the job, but you'll want to set the size yourself, depending on what you used for the title.

In the following example, I styled my page introduction with gray text (#666) and a 22px font size. I also used an inline <span> tag to style a key phrase—*technical writer*—with another color from my color scheme (#ffc200). Note as well that this h2 element inherits the font that I applied to the header's <div> tag in the preceding section.

▶ *Try This*   ⇨ **Online:** wdpg.io/projects/home-page/6

This example styles the personal home page introduction with a color and a larger font size. Within the text, a `<span>` tag applies a different color to the key phrase technical writer.

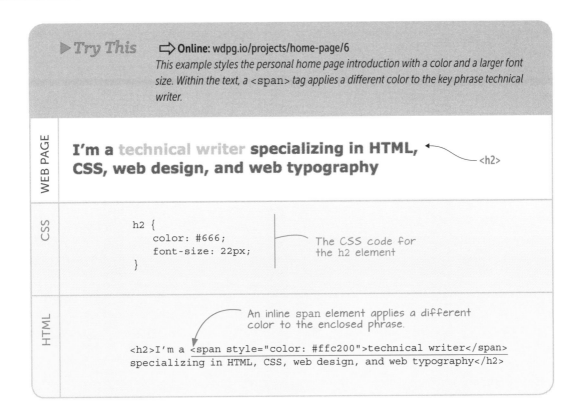

WEB PAGE

I'm a technical writer specializing in HTML, CSS, web design, and web typography ← `<h2>`

CSS

```
h2 {
    color: #666;
    font-size: 22px;
}
```
The CSS code for the h2 element

HTML

An inline span element applies a different color to the enclosed phrase.

```
<h2>I'm a <span style="color: #ffc200">technical writer</span>
specializing in HTML, CSS, web design, and web typography</h2>
```

The Social Media Links

The final element of the page header is the collection of links to your social media sites, such as Facebook, Twitter, and Pinterest. This collection is a key element of the page, so you should make it stand out from regular body text by using a larger font size or a unique color (or both).

For my own page, as shown in the following example, I styled the social media text with a sans-serif font and a 16px font size, and I typed the names in uppercase letters. For the links, I applied the third color from my color scheme (#0092ff) and removed the underline. Hovering over each link changes the text to the #ffc200 color and underlined. Note, too, the use of a vertical-bar symbol (|) to separate items.

PLAY

The page introduction should be short—ideally, no more than two lines. At the same time, it should be balanced visually on the screen, with each line extending as close to the right edge of the text block as possible. I've set up an exercise on the Web Design Playground to help give you some practice doing this.
⇨ *Online: wdpg.io/ projects/home-page/7*

▶ *Try This* ⇨ **Online:** wdpg.io/projects/home-page/8

This example styles the personal home page's social media text with a font, font size, uppercase letters, and link colors and underlines that change when each link is hovered over.

WEB PAGE

FACEBOOK | TWITTER | PINTEREST | CODEPEN | LINKEDIN ← `<h3>`

CSS

```
h3 {
    font-size: 16px;
}
a {
    color: #0092ff;
    text-decoration: none;
}
a:hover {
    color: #ffc200;
    text-decoration: underline;
}
```

The CSS code for the h3 element

The CSS code for the regular link text

The CSS code for the link text when the reader hovers over it using the mouse pointer

HTML

```
<h3> <a href="http://www.facebook.com/PaulMcFedries">FACEBOOK</
a> | <a href="https://twitter.com/paulmcf">TWITTER</a> | <a
href="https://www.pinterest.com/mcfedries/">PINTEREST</a> | <a
href="http://codepen.io/paulmcf/">CODEPEN</a> | <a href="https://
www.linkedin.com/in/paulmcfedries">LINKEDIN</a></h3>
```

FAQ

What happened to the `<hr>` tags? *In the initial page structure, I used horizontal rules above and below the social media links to separate them from the other page text. With the styles I've applied to the links, however, they already appear fully separate from the rest of the text, so the horizontal rules became redundant.*

The Body Text

The bulk of the personal home page is taken up by text that describes who you are, what you do for a living, what you do for fun, and so on. This text is the page's *body text*, and its content is entirely up to you.

You've already set the default text color, font size, and text alignment for the body element, and those values are inherited by the `div` element that contains the content section of the page. All that remains is to apply the body text typeface, which in my example is the serif font Georgia. To ensure that this typeface gets applied to the entire content section, I add the font to the `div` element's `font-family` property.

WEB PAGE

▶ *Try This* ⇨ **Online:** wdpg.io/projects/home-page/10

This example styles the personal home page text with the Georgia typeface. It also changes the bulleted list's bullets to circles.

I've been a professional technical writer for more than 25 years. I have over 90 books to my credit, which have sold more than four million copies worldwide. I've been building websites since 1996, so I have intimate knowledge of HTML, CSS, and web design. My passion is to write books and articles to pass along that knowledge and to create tools that help people build awesome web pages. ⎫ `<p>`

That's my work side, so what about my personal side? That is, what do I do in my spare time? I'm glad you asked! Here's a partial (and alphabetical) list of things and activities that interest me: ⎫ `<p>`

- ○ Chariot racing
- ○ Dog polishing
- ○ Duck herding ← `<ul>`
- ○ Extreme ironing
- ○ Navel fluff sculpture
- ○ Staycationing

CSS

```css
ul {
    list-style-type: circle;
}
```
The list-style-type property is set to circle to change the bullet.

HTML

A `<p></p>` block is used for each paragraph.

The content section's div element with the Georgia font stack applied

```html
<div style="font-family: Georgia, serif;">
    <p>
    I've been a professional technical writer for more than 25 years.
    I have over 90 books to my credit, which have sold more than four
    million copies worldwide. I've been building websites since 1996, so
    have intimate knowledge of HTML, CSS, and web design. My passion
    is to write books and articles to pass along that knowledge and to
    create tools that help people build awesome web pages.
    </p>
    <p>
    That's my work side, so what about my personal side? That is, what
    do I do in my spare time? I'm glad you asked! Here's a partial (and
    alphabetical) list of things and activities that interest me:
    </p>
    <ul>
        <li>Chariot racing</li>
        <li>Dog polishing</li>
        <li>Duck herding</li>
        <li>Extreme ironing</li>
        <li>Navel fluff sculpture</li>
        <li>Staycationing</li>
    </ul>
</div>
```

In this example, note two things:

- I embedded each of the two paragraphs inside a `<p></p>` block to honor the semantic role of the text.

- To give the bulleted list a bit of pizzazz, I set the `ul` element's `list-style-type` property to `circle` to change the default bullets.

The Page Footer

The final element of the personal home page is the page footer. As you can see in the following example, I used the footer to display a copyright notice and my contact information (which in this case consists of my email address). Feel free to use the footer to add any other information you see fit, such as a "thank you for reading" message, a slogan or favorite epigram, or extra contact details.

▶ *Try This*   ⇨ **Online:** wdpg.io/projects/home-page/12

This example separates the footer text from the body text by adding a horizontal rule and by styling the footer text with a lighter gray color, a smaller font size, and italics.

WEB PAGE

© *2019 Paul McFedries*
Contact: mail at my-last-name dot com

CSS

```
hr {
    color: #666;
}
```

The hr element is given a lighter color.

HTML

```
<div style="font-family:Georgia, serif; color: #666; font-size: 14px; font-style: italic;">
    <hr>
    &copy; 2019 Paul McFedries<br>
    Contact: mail at my-last-name dot com
</div>
```

The div element is styled with a font, lighter color, smaller font size, and italics.

The email address is obfuscated.

From Here

The final version of the personal home page (mine is shown in Figure 5.3) is pretty much what you'd expect: a simple, straightforward page that establishes your first home on the web. (If you're itching to get your code out there for all to see, check out Appendix A to get the details.)

PAUL MCFEDRIES

I'm a technical writer **specializing in HTML, CSS, web design, and web typography**

FACEBOOK | TWITTER | PINTEREST | CODEPEN | LINKEDIN

I've been a professional technical writer for more than 25 years. I have over 90 books to my credit, which have sold more than four million copies worldwide. I've been building websites since 1996, so I have intimate knowledge of HTML, CSS, and web design. My passion is to write books and articles to pass along that knowledge and to create tools that help people build awesome web pages.

That's my work side, so what about my personal side? That is, what do I do in my spare time? I'm glad you asked! Here's a partial (and alphabetical) list of things and activities that interest me:

- o Chariot racing
- o Dog polishing
- o Duck herding
- o Extreme ironing
- o Navel fluff sculpture
- o Staycationing

© 2019 Paul McFedries
Contact: mail at my-last-name dot com

▶ Figure 5.3 A personal home page, ready for the web.

Even though you're only getting started with HTML and CSS, you still have plenty of ways to add personal touches to your humble home page. You can always add more text, of course, including a numbered list (such as a top-ten list of your favorite books or bands). You can also play with the colors, try different typefaces, mess with typographical details such as the font size and alignment, and add some links.

If you find yourself slightly disappointed with your page, that's to be expected. After all, at this early stage in your web-design education, you have only limited control of the elements on the page, and you're missing key design ingredients such as images, margins, and page layout. Not to worry—you'll be learning all that and more in Part 2.

PLAY

Although dark gray (#333 or #444) text is most often used with a white background, other text colors can achieve subtle effects. A dark brown text color exudes warmth, for example. On the Web Design Playground, I've set up an example. ⇨ Online wdpg.io/projects/home-page/11

FAQ

Why does your email address look so weird? If you're going to include your email address in your contact info, never display the address in plain text; you run the risk of the address being harvested by spammers. Instead, obfuscate the address in a way that foils the spammers' bots but is still easy for a human to figure out.

BEWARE

When adding a copyright notice, you may be tempted to include both the word Copyright and the copyright symbol (©), but this format is redundant. Use one or the other, but not both.

Summary

- Sketch out the page you want to build.

- Choose the typefaces for the headings and body text.

- Choose a color scheme.

- Build the initial page structure: the barebones HTML tags and the global CSS properties applied to the body element.

- Fill in and style each section one by one: the title, the introduction, the social media links, the body text, and the footer.

Part 2

Working with Images and Styles

HTML tags are vital parts of every web designer's toolbox. You simply must familiarize yourself with all the basic HTML tags—from `<a>` to `<var>`—to build a decent page. But even if you memorized all the 100 or so tags in the HTML5 specification, any page you make that consisted only of tags and text would look . . . well, boring. Alas, it would also look utterly generic because the default renderings for things like text, headings, and lists are more or less the same in all modern browsers.

I know you're not reading this book because you want to be boring and generic! So here in Part 2, you expand your web design horizons with tools and techniques that go well beyond the basics. You learn about images, video, and audio in Chapter 6, and you gain advanced-but-practical style-sheet know-how in Chapter 7. In Chapter 8, you learn how to position web page elements like a pro, and Chapter 9 introduces you to the all-important CSS box model, which lets you size elements and add borders and margins around elements.

Finally, in Chapter 10, you summon all your newfound HTML and CSS knowledge and use it to build a slick landing page for a product.

Chapter 6

Adding Images and Other Media

> ❝ *It's like what they say about the perfect picture book. The art and the text stand alone, but together, they create something even better.* —Deborah Wiles

 This chapter covers

- Embedding an image on a web page
- Working with background images
- Optimizing images for the web
- Adding videos, music, and other media

When you come across a page that's nothing but text, how does it make you feel? It probably makes you feel disappointed or perhaps even sad. And unless the text is absorbing and the typography exceptionally good, it also probably makes you want to click the Back button and look for some place where your sore eyes can catch a break. You don't want people feeling disappointed, sad, or eager to leave your site, so throw them a visual bone or two by sprucing up your pages with images and perhaps even a video once in a while. In this chapter, I show you how it's done.

Lesson 6.1: **Adding an Image to the Page**
Covers: The `img` element

⇨ **Online:** wdpg.io/6-1-0

So far in this book, you've seen that the innards of a web page are text with a few HTML tags and CSS rules sprinkled strategically here and there. So you may be wondering how images fit into this text-only landscape. The short answer is that they don't! Unlike with a word processing document or a presentation, you don't insert images directly into a web page. Instead, you upload the image as a separate file to your website and then insert into your page text a special HTML tag that tells the browser where to locate the image. Then the browser retrieves the file from the server and displays the image on the page in the location you specified.

The special tag that gets the browser to add an image to a web page is the `img` element, which uses the partial syntax shown in Figure 6.1.

▶ **Figure 6.1**
You insert an image into a web page by using the `<img>` tag.

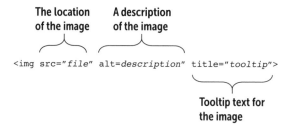

You have three attributes to consider here:

- `src`—This attribute (short for *source*) specifies where the image file is located. If the file is on a remote server, use the full URL of the file; if the file is in the same directory as the HTML file, use the name of the file; otherwise, use the image's path and filename. If you've created in your site's main folder a subfolder named `images`, and your image file is `logo.png`, your `src` value would be `/images/logo.png`.

- `alt`—This attribute (short for *alternative*) is a word or short phrase that describes the image and that could be used in place of the image in case the image file can't be displayed. A company logo, for example, might use the alternative text *logo*, preceded by the company name. Alt text is also used by screen readers and Braille apps to give the user some idea of what the image is.

- `title`—You can use this optional attribute to specify tooltip text that appears when the user hovers the mouse pointer over the image, as shown in the example that follows.

The following example shows an `img` element in action.

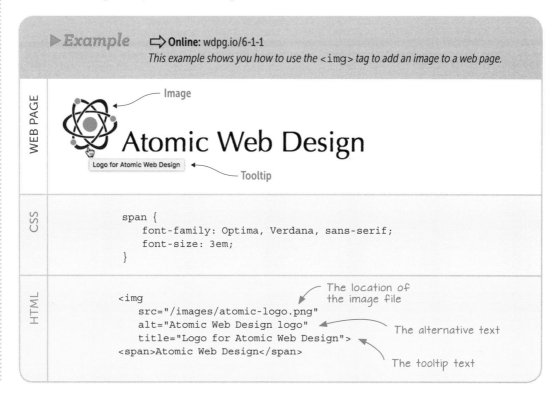

> ▶ *Example*   ⇨ **Online:** wdpg.io/6-1-1
> *This example shows you how to use the `<img>` tag to add an image to a web page.*

WEB PAGE

Image

Atomic Web Design

Logo for Atomic Web Design ← Tooltip

CSS

```css
span {
    font-family: Optima, Verdana, sans-serif;
    font-size: 3em;
}
```

HTML

```html
<img
    src="/images/atomic-logo.png"
    alt="Atomic Web Design logo"
    title="Logo for Atomic Web Design">
<span>Atomic Web Design</span>
```

The location of the image file

The alternative text

The tooltip text

> 66 *Your website needs a proper balance between textual and visual content. Awesome images or videos without text will give your visitor little to no useful data, but you might find it hard to engage users with large slabs of plain text.* —Helen Stark

Understanding Image File Formats

In the preceding example, you may have noticed that the image file was named `atomic-logo.png`, meaning that it uses the PNG image file format. That format is common on the web, but it's not the only one you can use. In fact, the web has standardized on four formats that account for almost all web imagery, and I summarize them in Table 6.1.

Adding Images and Other Media

▶ Table 6.1 Image File Formats

Name	Extension	Description	Uses
GIF	.gif	The original web graphics format (the name is short for Graphics Interchange Format and it's pronounced giff or jiff). GIFs are limited to 256 colors, can have transparent backgrounds, and can be combined into short animations.	Use GIFs if you want to combine multiple images into a single animated image.
JPEG	.jpg .jpeg	This format (which gets its name from Joint Photographic Experts Group and is pronounced jay-peg) supports complex images that have many millions of colors. The main advantage of JPEG files is that they're compressed, so even digitized photographs and other high-quality images can be a reasonably small size for faster downloading. Note, however, that JPEG compression is *lossy*, which means that it makes the image smaller by discarding redundant pixels. The higher the compression, the more pixels are discarded and the less sharp the image appears.	If you have a photo or similarly complex image, JPEG is almost always the best choice because it gives the smallest file size. How small is small enough for the web? You learn about that topic in "Optimizing Images" later in this chapter.
PNG	.png	This format (short for Portable Network Graphics and pronounced p-n-g or ping) supports millions of colors. It's a compressed format, but unlike JPEGs, PNGs use *lossless* compression. Images retain sharpness, but the file sizes can get quite big. PNG also supports transparency.	If you have an illustration or icon that uses solid colors, or a photo that contains large areas of near-solid color, PNG is best because it gives you a reasonably small file size while retaining excellent image quality. You can also use PNG if you need transparency effects.
SVG	.svg	This format (short for Scalable Vector Graphics) uses vectors rather than pixels to generate an image. These vectors are encoded as a set of instructions in XML format, meaning that the image can be altered in a text editor and can be manipulated to produce animations.	If you have a logo or icon and have a graphics program that can save files as SVG (such as Adobe Illustrator or Inkscape), this format is a good choice because it produces small files that can be scaled to any size without distortion.

LEARN

If you want to join the animated-GIF fun, lots of sites on the web can help. The easiest route is to use an online tool such as GIFCreator (http://gifcreator.me) or GIFMaker.me (http://gifmaker.me).

Getting Graphics

The text part of a web page is, at least from a production standpoint, a piece of cake for most folks. Graphics, on the other hand, are another kettle of digital fish entirely. Creating a snazzy logo or eye-catching illustration requires a modicum of artistic talent, which is a bit harder to come by than basic typing skills.

•

If you have such talent, however, you're laughing: Create the image in your favorite graphics program and save it in JPEG or PNG format. The nonartists in the crowd have to obtain their graphics goodies from other sources. Besides uploading your own photos or scanning your own images, you can find no shortage of other images floating around. Here are some ideas:

- Many programs (including Microsoft Office and most paint and illustration programs) come with clip-art libraries. Clip art is professional-quality artwork that you can incorporate into your own designs. In almost all cases, you're free to use the clip art in your own designs without worrying about copyright.

- Take advantage of the many graphics archives online. Sites all over the web store hundreds and even thousands, of images: stock photos, illustrations, icons, and more. Many of these images are free, but check each site's terms of use.

- Grab an image from a web page. When your browser displays a web page with an image, the corresponding graphics file is stored temporarily on your computer's hard disk. In most browsers, you can right-click the image to save that file permanently. As I elaborate in the note off to the side, however, there are copyright concerns, because you shouldn't use images that you don't own without permission and/or credit.

BEWARE

Don't forget that many images are the property of the people or companies that created them in the first place. Unless you're absolutely sure that a picture is in the public domain (for example, it comes with a Creative Commons license that lets you reuse the image), you need to get permission from the owner before using it. Either way, be sure to give credit to the image owner on your site.

Inserting an HTML5 Figure

Although many of your images are purely decorative or designed to catch a site visitor's eye, you may also use plenty of graphics that tie in with your page text. When you reference an image directly in the text, that image is known as a *figure*. In HTML5, a figure is a semantic page element that you designate with the `figure` element. If the figure has a caption, that caption too is a semantic element that you designate with the `figcaption` element. Here's the basic structure to use:

```
<figure>
    <img src="file" alt="description" title="tooltip">
    <figcaption>Caption text</figcaption>
</figure>
```

Following is an example.

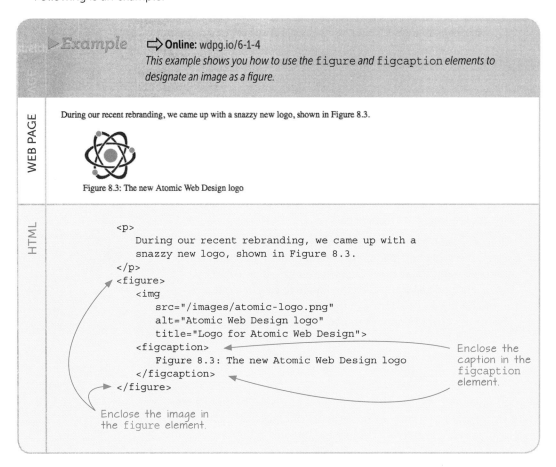

Setting Up an Image as a Link

You already know that you can set up a word or phrase as a link, but you can do the same with images. You arrange things in the same way, surrounding the `<img>` tag with the `<a>` and `</a>` tags, like so:

```
<a href="url"><img src="file"></a>
```

Here's an example.

▶ *Example*   ⇨ **Online:** wdpg.io/6-1-6
This example shows you how to use the a *element and the* img *element to turn an image into a link.*

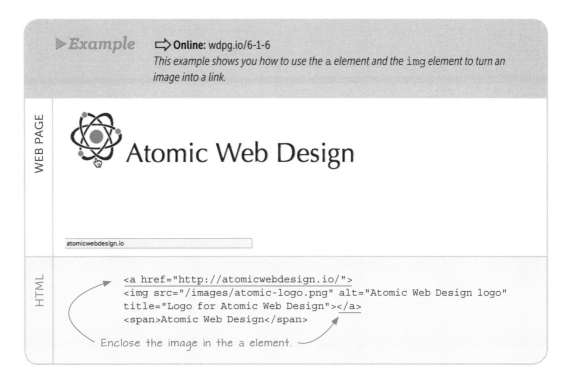

WEB PAGE

HTML

```
<a href="http://atomicwebdesign.io/">
<img src="/images/atomic-logo.png" alt="Atomic Web Design logo"
title="Logo for Atomic Web Design"></a>
<span>Atomic Web Design</span>
```

Enclose the image in the a element.

Using an Image as a Custom Bullet

As you learned in Chapter 2, CSS offers the list-style-type property that enables you to specify another type of bullet character to use with an unordered list. You can kick that property up a notch by using the list-style-image property to specify an image to use as a custom bullet:

```
ul {
    list-style-image: url(file);
}
```

As with the <img> tag, the file value specifies the location of the image file. Note, however, that you don't have to surround the value with quotation marks. Following is an example.

BEWARE

I've shown the code for turning an image into a link on one line for a purpose. If you place these tags on separate lines—particularly the closing </a> tag—you end up with weird artifacts in the text (essentially, underlined carriage returns).

▶ *Example* ⇨ **Online:** wdpg.io/6-1-7

This example shows you how to use the `list-style-image` *property to specify an image as a custom bullet.*

WEB PAGE	**Prepare Images for the Web:** ✓ Remove unnecessary images ✓ Choose the correct image format ✓ Size the images appropriately ✓ Compress JPEGs as needed ✓ Optimize PNGs
| **CSS** | ```css
ul {
    list-style-image: url(/images/checkmark.png);
}
```<br><br>Set the `list-style-image` property to the image file location. |
| **HTML** | ```html
<h3>
    Prepare Images for the Web:
</h3>
<ul>
    <li>Remove unnecessary images</li>
    <li>Choose the correct image format</li>
    <li>Size the images appropriately</li>
    <li>Compress JPEGs as needed</li>
    <li>Optimize PNGs</li>
</ul>
``` |

Aligning Images and Text

The `<img>` tag is an inline element, so you can insert it into, say, a paragraph or similar block element, and it will flow along with the rest of the content. By default, the bottom edge of the image aligns with the baseline of the current line, but you can control that vertical alignment by using the `vertical-align` property:

```css
element {
    vertical-align: baseline | bottom | middle | top;
}
```

- `baseline`—The bottom of the image is aligned with the baseline of the current line (the default).

- `bottom`—The bottom of the image is aligned with the bottom of the current line (that is, the bottommost extent of descending letters such as y and g).
- `middle`—The middle of the image is aligned with the baseline of the current line, plus one half of the x-height of the current font.
- `top`—The top of the image is aligned with the top of the current line.

The following example shows the `vertical-align` property at work.

MASTER

If you need even finer control of the vertical placement of an image, you can specify a length value, in pixels (px), for the `vertical-align` *property. To move the image up, specify a negative value.*

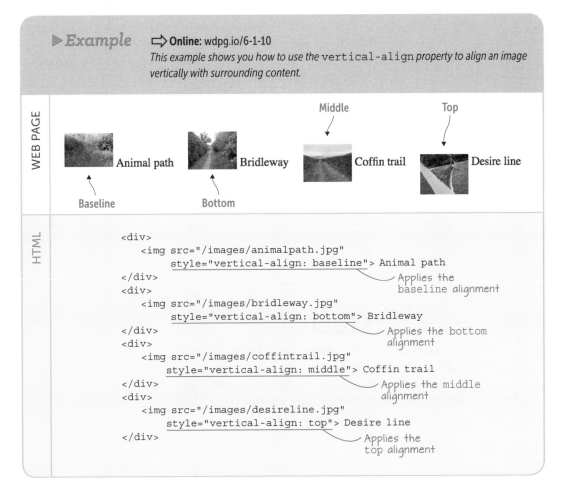

▶ *Example*   ⇨ **Online:** wdpg.io/6-1-10
This example shows you how to use the `vertical-align` *property to align an image vertically with surrounding content.*

WEB PAGE

Middle   Top

Animal path   Bridleway   Coffin trail   Desire line

Baseline   Bottom

HTML

```
<div>
    <img src="/images/animalpath.jpg"
        style="vertical-align: baseline"> Animal path
</div>                                    Applies the
<div>                                     baseline alignment
    <img src="/images/bridleway.jpg"
        style="vertical-align: bottom"> Bridleway
</div>                                  Applies the bottom
<div>                                   alignment
    <img src="/images/coffintrail.jpg"
        style="vertical-align: middle"> Coffin trail
</div>                                   Applies the middle
<div>                                    alignment
    <img src="/images/desireline.jpg"
        style="vertical-align: top"> Desire line
</div>                                Applies the
                                     top alignment
```

⇨ **Online:** wdpg.io/6-2-0

Lesson 6.2: *Working with Background Images*

Covers: `background-image` and related properties

To add some visual interest to an element, you can use the `background-image` property to specify an image file to use as the background:

```
element {
    background-image: url(file);
}
```

The *file* value specifies where the image file is located. If the file is on a remote server, use the full URL of the file; if the file is in the same directory as the HTML file, use the name of the file; otherwise, use the image's path and filename.

The following example shows this property in action.

▶*Example*   ⇨ **Online:** wdpg.io/6-2-1

This example shows you how to use the `background-image` *property to apply an image as the background of an element.*

WEB PAGE

Original image   Tiled background images

Tiling

When you add a background image, the browser doesn't just add the image once and move on to the next task. Instead, it takes the image and repeats it until it fills the entire parent block element, a process known as *tiling*.

CSS

```
div {
    background-image: url(/images/bg.png);
    width: 500px;
    height: 200px;
}
```

The div element gets a background image.

```
HTML

            <img src="/images/bg.png">          The image is displayed on
            <div>                               its own for comparison.
                <h1>Tiling</h1>
                <p>When you add a background image, the browser doesn't just
            add the image once and move on to the next task. Instead, it takes
            the image and repeats it until it fills the entire parent block
            element, a process known as <i>tiling</i>.
                </p>
            </div>
```

When working with background images, you should assume that the image may not load properly for some reason. Therefore, it's always a good idea to specify the `background-color` property with a value that matches the main color of the image. Here's an example:

```
div {
    background-color: #fec72f;
    background-image: url(/images/bg.png);
}
```

Controlling the Background Repeat

You saw in the preceding example that the browser's default behavior for a background image that's smaller than the element is to repeat the image horizontally and vertically until the element is filled. This behavior is called *tiling* the background, and it's usually the behavior you want. However, you can control whether the background repeats horizontally, vertically, or doesn't repeat by using the `background-repeat` property:

```
element {
    background-image: url(file);
    background-repeat: repeat | repeat-x | repeat-y | no-repeat;
}
```

- `repeat`—Tiles the image horizontally and vertically (the default)
- `repeat-x`—Tiles the image only horizontally, as shown in Figure 6.2
- `repeat-y`—Tiles the image only vertically, as shown in Figure 6.3
- `no-repeat`—Displays the image once

BEWARE

A background image can add a nice bit of eye candy to a page, but it leaves a bitter taste if it interferes with the legibility of your page text. Always ensure that you've got lots of contrast between the text and the background.

PLAY

You can try out all the `background-repeat` *values interactively in the Web Design Playground.* ⇨ Online: wdpg.io/6-2-2

REMEMBER

The `repeat` *value is the default, so declaring* `background-repeat: repeat` *is optional.*

▶ Figure 6.2
With background-repeat: repeat-x, the background image repeats horizontally.

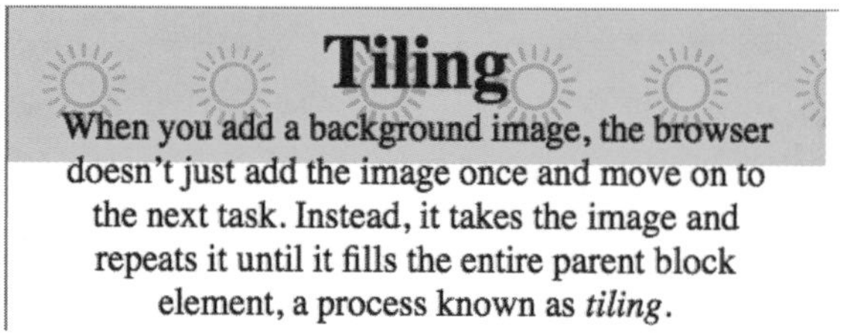

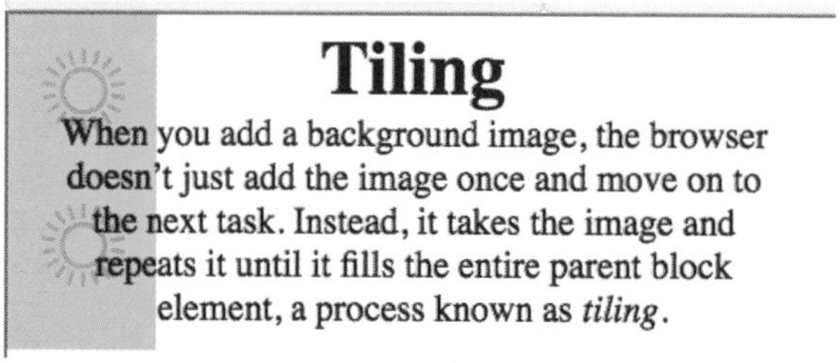

> **Tiling**
> When you add a background image, the browser doesn't just add the image once and move on to the next task. Instead, it takes the image and repeats it until it fills the entire parent block element, a process known as *tiling*.

▶ Figure 6.3
With background-repeat: repeat-y, the background image repeats vertically.

> **Tiling**
> When you add a background image, the browser doesn't just add the image once and move on to the next task. Instead, it takes the image and repeats it until it fills the entire parent block element, a process known as *tiling*.

PLAY

You can try out all the background-position *keywords interactively in the Web Design Playground.*

⇨ Online: wdpg.io/6-2-3

REMEMBER

The left top *value is the default, so declaring* background-position: left top *is optional. Note, too, that this value is equivalent to* background-position: 0px 0px *or* background-position: 0% 0%.

Setting the Background Position

By default, the background image tiling starts in the top-left corner of the parent element. You can change that setting by applying the background-position property:

```
element {
    background-image: url(file);
    background-position: horizontal vertical;
}
```

- horizontal—Specifies the starting horizontal position of the background image tiling. You can use the keywords left, center, or right; a percentage; or a pixel value.

- vertical—Specifies the starting vertical position of the background image tiling. You can use the keywords top, center, or bottom; a percentage; or a pixel value.

Figure 6.4 is a composite that shows the nine possible positions when you use the three horizontal keywords (left, center, and right) and three vertical keywords (top, center, and bottom). Note that in each case, I set the background-repeat property to no-repeat.

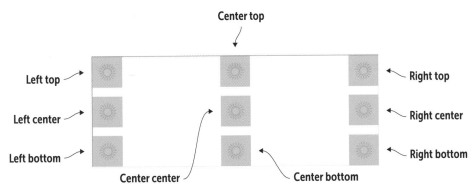

▶ Figure 6.4 The nine possible keyword-based positions for the `background-position` property

Adding a Hero Image

One of the most popular web design trends of the past few years is the *hero image*: an eye-catching photo or illustration that takes up the entire width (and usually the entire height) of the browser window when you first land on a page. Using a hero image is a great way to grab a visitor's attention right off the bat.

To set up a hero image, you need to do the following:

1   Begin the page with a block element (such as a `div`) that's styled to take up the entire browser window:

```
width: 100vw;
height: 100vh;
```

2   For that same block element, add a background image and set its position to `background-position: center center`.

3   Add the declaration `background-size:  cover`, which tells the browser to size the image so that it covers the entire background of the block element.

Following is an example.

PLAY

Another way to use an image as a custom bullet is to set the image as the background for the `li` element, which enables you to use `background-position` to control the alignment of the bullet and the item text.
⇨ Online: wdpg.io/6-2-4

REMEMBER

The `vw` and `vh` units represent one one-hundredth of the browser window's width and height, respectively. For more on these units, see Chapter 7.

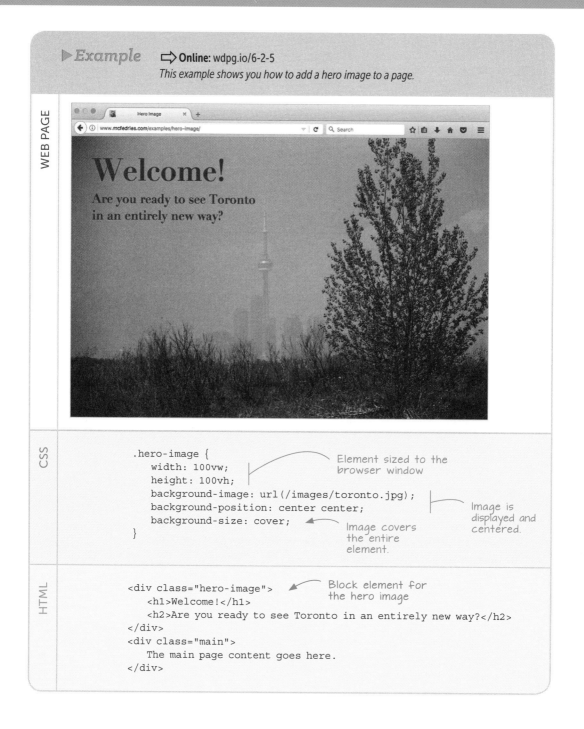

WEB PAGE

▶ *Example*   ⇨ **Online:** wdpg.io/6-2-5

This example shows you how to add a hero image to a page.

Welcome!

Are you ready to see Toronto in an entirely new way?

CSS

```
.hero-image {
    width: 100vw;
    height: 100vh;
    background-image: url(/images/toronto.jpg);
    background-position: center center;
    background-size: cover;
}
```

Element sized to the browser window

Image is displayed and centered.

Image covers the entire element.

HTML

```
<div class="hero-image">
    <h1>Welcome!</h1>
    <h2>Are you ready to see Toronto in an entirely new way?</h2>
</div>
<div class="main">
    The main page content goes here.
</div>
```

Block element for the hero image

The Background Shorthand Property

CSS has five main background-related components: color, image, repeat, attachment, and position. These components are represented, respectively, by the CSS properties background-color, background-image, background-repeat, background-attachment, and background-position. Handily, you can apply any or all of these properties with a single statement by using the background shorthand property, which takes the syntax shown in Figure 6.5.

PLAY

You can make the background stay in place while you scroll the rest of the page by adding the declaration background-attachment: fixed. ⇨ Online: wdpg.io/6-2-6

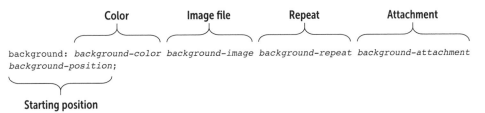

```
background: background-color background-image background-repeat background-attachment
background-position;
```

Starting position

▶ Figure 6.5   You can apply up to five background properties at the same time by using the background property.

This syntax is a straightforward repetition of everything you've learned so far, and you're free to enter the properties in any order you prefer.

Optimizing Images

There's a common saying in web-design circles: "Color is free on the web." This saying means that you can add colors to text, backgrounds, borders, and other elements without paying a performance price. This is decidedly *not* the case with images, which, thanks to their potential to be huge (particularly those hero images I talked about earlier), can come with high performance costs indeed. To help ensure that your pages aren't bandwidth hogs that take ages to load, here are a few tips to bear in mind for optimizing the images you use:

- *Don't use unnecessary images.* Before adding an image to a page, ask yourself whether the image is needed to convey your message. If so, go for it. If not, leave it behind. Your users will thank you.

- *Watch your image sizes.* Web browsers can resize images as needed, but they shouldn't have to. If you want a 100x100 logo in the top-left corner, don't upload a 2,048x2,048 version of that image and force the browser to resize (by, say, specifying the smaller width and height in your CSS). That bigger file will take a long time to download, which is a waste of bandwidth.

- *Choose your file format wisely.* As a general rule, you should use the image file format that produces the smallest file size while still retaining a satisfactory level of image quality for the job at hand. A hero image should look good, but a tiny thumbnail doesn't have to be high-resolution.

PLAY

One of the most surprising aspects of background images is that you can use multiple backgrounds on the same element. You can repeat the same background image in two or more places or use two or more background images (or both!). ⇨ Online: wdpg.io/6-2-7

BEWARE

If you plan to overlay text on your hero image, make sure that the image includes an area that's not too busy so that your text will be readable. Also, make sure that you have sufficient contrast between the colors of your image and your text.

LEARN

If you need to use 24-bit PNGs, software tools are available that can help reduce the size of those files. If you use a Mac, try ImageAlpha (https://pngmini.com); if you run Windows, check out PNGoo (https://pngquant.org).

- *Take advantage of JPEG compression.* If you're saving your image in the JPEG format, your imaging software allows you to choose a compression level for the file. You'll need to experiment a bit to get the right level, but for most uses, a compression level in the range of 60 to 75 percent is a good place to start. More compression usually leads to poor image quality, and less compression usually results in large file sizes.

- *Optimize PNG images.* When you're working with a PNG image, decide whether you can get away with 8-bit color, which is a mere 256 colors. For a simple logo or icon, 8-bit color may be more than enough, and you'll end up with quite a small file. For more complex images, you'll probably need the full 24-bit palette.

Adding Video and Audio to the Page

You know that people love their cat videos and podcasts, so you want a piece of the action by adding video or audio content to your own web pages. Great idea! I'll begin with the good news: HTML5 comes with the `<video>` and `<audio>` tags, which offer a somewhat straightforward way to embed media content in a page. Notice that I said *somewhat*. Why the hedge? Ah, that's where the bad news rears its complexifying head. Right now, web media is a crazy quilt of standards, compression algorithms, and file formats. It's borderline absurd, but if you want to serve your visitors sights or sounds, you need to wade into the deep end.

I'll begin by defining two aspects of web media formats:

- *Container*—The file format, called a *container* because it acts like the media equivalent of a zip file—that is, it's an archive that contains multiple items, particularly the media codecs (discussed next) and the media metadata.

- *Codec*—The algorithm used to encode and compress the video or audio in a digital format and to decode and decompress the media for playback. (The word *codec* is a blend of *code/decode* and *compress/decompress*.)

So a web media file that you'd embed in a page comes in a specific media format that uses a particular container, and within that container are all the codecs that the format supports. Sounds simple enough, right? The absurdity comes into play when you understand that there's no such thing as a standard or universal media format.

Web Video Formats

For video, in fact, you have three main formats to worry about:

- *WebM*—This format uses the WebM container, inside which is either the VP8 or VP9 video codec, as well as the Vorbis or Opus audio codec. This format is open source and royalty free. File extension: `.webm`.

- *Ogg*—This format uses the Ogg container, inside which is the Theora video codec, as well as the Vorbis or Opus audio codec. This format is open source and royalty free. File extension: `.ogg` or `.ogv`.

- *MPEG-4*—This format uses the MPEG-4 container, inside which is the H.264 video codec, as well as the AAC audio codec. This format is patented but free for end users. File extension: `.mp4`.

Which one should you use? Most of the time, you can get away with using the MPEG-4 format, which is supported by all major browsers. That support is a bit problematic, however. First, Firefox doesn't support MPEG-4 natively; instead, it relies on the operating system's built-in support for MPEG-4. Second, Google has hinted that it may not support MPEG-4 in future releases of Chrome. It's a good idea to serve your visitors both an MPEG-4 version and a WebM version (which is newer and better supported than Ogg).

Web Audio Formats

For audio, there are even more formats:

- *MP3*—This format is both the container and the audio codec. This format is patented but free for end users. File extension: `.mp3`.

- *WAV*—This format is both the container and the audio codec. File extension: `.wav`.

- *WebM*—This format uses the WebM container, inside which is Vorbis or Opus audio codec. This format is open source and royalty free. File extension: `.webm`.

- *Ogg*—This format uses the Ogg container, inside which is the Vorbis or Opus audio codec. This format is open source and royalty free. File extension: `.ogg`. or `.oga`.

- *MPEG-4*—This format uses the MPEG-4 container, inside which is the AAC audio codec. This format is patented but free for end users. File extension: `.m4a`.

Things are a bit saner in the audio world, where every browser now supports the MP3 format, so you can get away with using the one file type.

LEARN

*Many tools are available to convert videos to formats supported by HTML5. Two online tools that are worth checking out are Zamzar (*https://www.zamzar.com*) and Online-Convert (*https://www.online-convert.com/*).*

LEARN

*The two online tools I mentioned earlier also support the HTML5 web audio formats. You may also want to have a look at media.io (*https://media.io*).*

Lesson 6.3: **Embedding Video in a Web Page**
Covers: The video element

⇨ **Online:** wdpg.io/6-3-0

HTML5's video element offers a no-nonsense way of embedding video content in your web page. Well, *no-nonsense* may be wishful thinking. You can use two syntaxes, depending on the number of video file formats you want to serve.

First, here's the syntax to use if you're offering a single video format:

```
<video src="file"
       poster="file"
       width="value"
       height="value"
       controls
       autoplay
       loop>
</video>
```

- src—Specifies the location of the video file, so it's much the same as the src attribute for the <img> tag

- poster—Specifies the location of an image, such as a title frame or still frame from the video, to display before video playback begins

- width and height—Specify the dimensions of the video playback window

- controls—When included, tells the browser to display the playback controls in the video window

- autoplay—When included, tells the browser to automatically start playing the video as soon as it has downloaded enough of the video file

- loop—When included, tells the browser to begin playback from the beginning each time the video ends

Following is an example.

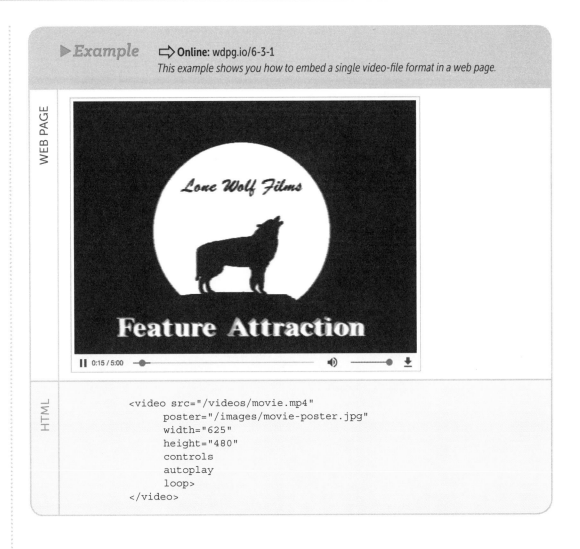

▶ *Example*   ⇨ **Online: wdpg.io/6-3-1**
This example shows you how to embed a single video-file format in a web page.

WEB PAGE

Feature Attraction

HTML

```
<video src="/videos/movie.mp4"
       poster="/images/movie-poster.jpg"
       width="625"
       height="480"
       controls
       autoplay
       loop>
</video>
```

To offer two or more video formats, you need to remove the `src` attribute from the `<video>` tag and replace it with multiple `source` elements, one for each format you want to offer:

```
<video poster="file"
       width="value"
       height="value"
       controls
       autoplay
       loop>
    <source src="file"
            type='type; codecs="codecs"'>
</video>
```

- `src`—As before, the `src` attribute for each `<source>` tag specifies the name and/or location of the video file.

- `type`—This string (surrounded by single quotation marks) specifies the video format type (as shown earlier in this chapter in the "Web Video Formats" section), a comma-separated and double-quotation-mark-surrounded list of the format's video and audio codecs:

- *MPEG-4*—Use the following:

```
type='video/mp4; codecs="avc1.4D401E, mp4a.40.2"'
```

- *WebM*—Use one of the following:

```
type='video/webm; codecs="vp8, vorbis"'
type='video/webm; codecs="vp9, vorbis"'
type='video/webm; codecs="vp9, opus"'
```

- *Ogg*—Use one of the following:

```
type='video/ogg; codecs="theora, vorbis"'
type='video/ogg; codecs="theora, opus"'
```

Here's an example.

▶ *Example*   ⇨ **Online:** wdpg.io/6-3-2

This example shows you how to embed multiple video-file formats in a web page.

WEB PAGE

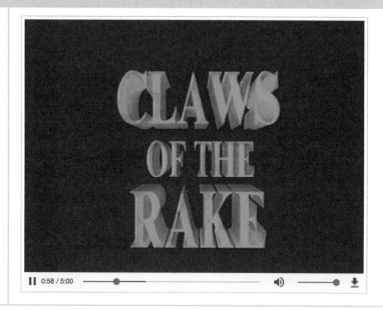

```
HTML    <video poster="/images/movie-poster.jpg"
               width="625"
               height="480"
               controls
               autoplay
               loop>
           <source src="/videos/movie.mp4"
                   type='video/mp4; codecs="avc1.4D401E, mp4a.40.2"'>
           <source src="/videos/movie.webm"
                   type='video/webm; codecs="vp8, vorbis"'>
           <source src="/videos/movie.ogv"
                   type='video/ogg; codecs="theora, vorbis"'>
        </video>
```

Lesson 6.4: *Embedding Audio in a Web Page*

Covers: The audio element

⇨ **Online:** wdpg.io/6-4-0

You'll be delighted to hear that embedding audio in a web page is nearly identical to embedding video, because the <audio> and <video> tags have many of the same attributes.

First, here's the syntax to use if you're offering a single audio format:

```
<audio src="file"
       controls
       autoplay
       loop>
</video>
```

- src—Specifies the location of the audio file
- controls—When included, tells the browser to display the playback controls in the audio window
- autoplay—When included, tells the browser to automatically start playing the audio as soon as it has downloaded enough of the audio file
- loop—When included, tells the browser to begin playback from the beginning each time the audio ends

Following is an example.

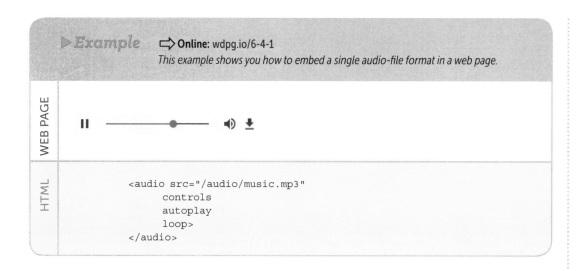

Online: wdpg.io/6-4-1

▶*Example*

This example shows you how to embed a single audio-file format in a web page.

WEB PAGE

HTML

```
<audio src="/audio/music.mp3"
       controls
       autoplay
       loop>
</audio>
```

To offer two or more audio formats, remove the src attribute from the <audio> tag and replace it with multiple <source> tags, one for each format you want to offer:

```
<audio controls
       autoplay
       loop>
   <source src="file"
           type="type">
</audio>
```

- src—As before, the src attribute for each <source> tag specifies the name and/or location of the audio file

- type—Specifies the audio format type (as shown earlier in the section "Web Audio Formats")

Here's an example.

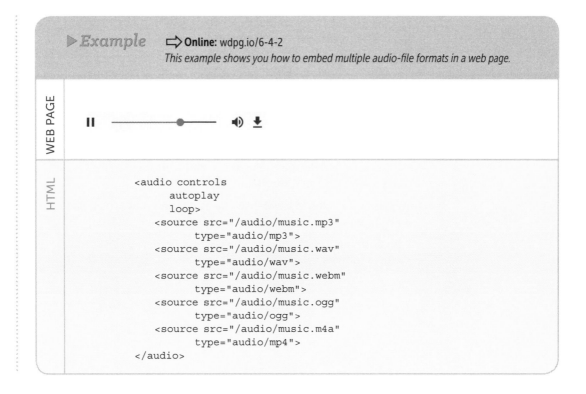

▶ *Example*   ⇨ **Online:** wdpg.io/6-4-2

This example shows you how to embed multiple audio-file formats in a web page.

WEB PAGE

HTML

```
<audio controls
    autoplay
    loop>
  <source src="/audio/music.mp3"
        type="audio/mp3">
  <source src="/audio/music.wav"
        type="audio/wav">
  <source src="/audio/music.webm"
        type="audio/webm">
  <source src="/audio/music.ogg"
        type="audio/ogg">
  <source src="/audio/music.m4a"
        type="audio/mp4">
</audio>
```

Summary

- There are four main image-format types—GIF, JPEG, PNG, and SVG—although most of your pages will use JPEG for photos and complex images, and PNG for illustrations, logos, and icons that use mostly solid colors and/or transparency.

- To add an image to the page, use the `<img>` tag:

  `<img src="file" alt="description" title="tooltip">`

- To infuse your images with HTML5 semantic flavor, surround the `img` element with the `figure` element and, optionally, add a `figcaption` element.

- To make an image do double duty as a link, surround the `img` element with the `a` element.

- You can set up an image as an element background by adding the following property to the element's CSS:

```
background-image: url(file);
```

- You can control the background image's display by adding one or more of the following properties: `background-repeat`, `background-position`, and `background-attachment`.

- You can set all three of these properties, as well as the `background-color` and `background-image` properties, by using the `background` shorthand property.

- You embed a video in a web page by using the `<video>` tag, and you embed sound in a web page by using the `<audio>` tag.

- With both the `<video>` tag and the `<audio>` tag, you can specify multiple formats by adding a separate `<source>` tag for each.

Learning More About Styles

This chapter covers

- Learning the three methods for adding styles to a web page
- Adding power and flexibility with classes
- Understanding the units of measurement you can use in your CSS

How do you craft pages that rise above the humdrum? How do you design pages that go beyond the same old, same old? One word: *styles*. If you've seen a web page that you think is well designed, know that the page uses styles to achieve that look. If there's a web designer whose work you admire, know that the designer mastered styles that make her work stand out. You saw several useful styles in Part 1 of the book, but those styles are only a taste of what's out there. To help you get started down the road to becoming truly style-savvy, this chapter takes your style knowledge to the next level.

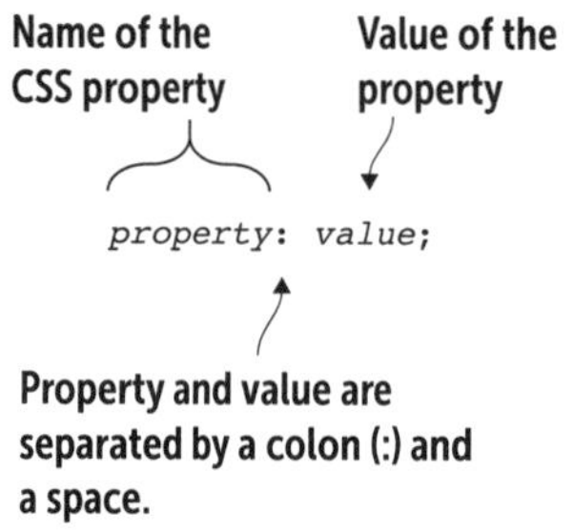

▶ Figure 7.1

The syntax of a property-value pair

Adding Styles to a Page

I mentioned in Chapter 1 that a web page is a text file filled with words, numbers, and a few strategically placed HTML tags that provide structure for the text. You'll be happy to hear that CSS is also a text-based business, so you don't need anything grander than a simple text editor (or this book's handy Web Design Playground) to get started with styles.

That said, although *what* styles consist of is simple enough, *how* you add styles to a web page is a bit more complex. First, recall from Chapter 1 that a single style declaration consists of a property-value pair that uses the syntax shown in Figure 7.1.

Name of the CSS property

Value of the property

property: value;

Property and value are separated by a colon (:) and a space.

The `property` name is almost always written in lowercase letters (although it doesn't have to be). If the `value` includes one or more spaces, numbers, or punctuation characters other than a hyphen (-), surround the value with quotation marks.

The added complexity of CSS comes from the fact that you have not one, not two, but *three* ways to tell the web browser what style declarations you want to use:

- Inline styles
- Internal styles
- External styles

The next three lessons introduce you to these methods.

Lesson 7.1: **Inserting Inline Styles**
Covers: The `<style>` attribute

⇨ **Online:** wdpg.io/7-1-0

Probably the most straightforward way to add styles to your web page is to insert them directly into the element you want to modify. This technique is called an *inline style*, and you insert a style by including the `style` attribute within the HTML element you want to change. Figure 7.2 shows the general syntax to use.

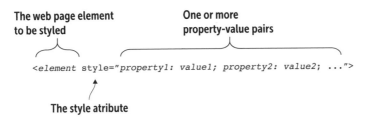

The web page element to be styled

One or more property-value pairs

```
<element style="property1: value1; property2: value2; ...">
```

The style atribute

▶Figure 7.2   The syntax to use for inline styles

Here are a few points to keep in mind when you use inline styles:

- If you want to include two or more property-value pairs in a single inline style, be sure to separate each pair with a semicolon (;).

- If a value needs to be quoted, use single quotation marks (').

- An inline style affects only the element in which you place the `style` attribute.

Following are a couple of examples of inline styles.

BEWARE

Because the `style` *attribute's value is itself surrounded by double quotation marks, be careful if one of your property-value pairs requires quotation marks of its own. In that case, surround the value with single quotation marks (for example,* `style="font-family: 'PT Sans';").`

▶*Example*   ⇨**Online:** wdpg.io/7-1-1
This example shows an inline style applied to a `<p>` *tag, as well as an inline style with multiple property-value pairs applied to a* `<ul>` *tag.*

WEB PAGE

The *snowclone* is a kind of *phrasal template* since it comes with one or more empty "slots" that get filled with words to create a new phrase. Some examples:

⎫ The <p> text

- I'm not an X, but I play one on TV
- In X, no one can hear you Y
- X and Y and Z, oh my!

⎬ The <ul> text

continued

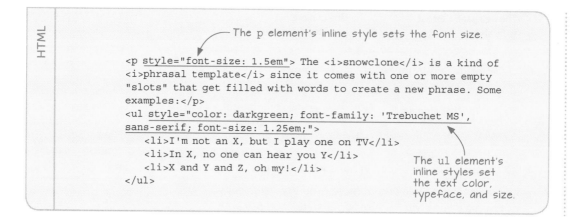

The p element's inline style sets the font size.

```html
<p style="font-size: 1.5em"> The <i>snowclone</i> is a kind of
<i>phrasal template</i> since it comes with one or more empty
"slots" that get filled with words to create a new phrase. Some
examples:</p>
<ul style="color: darkgreen; font-family: 'Trebuchet MS',
sans-serif; font-size: 1.25em;">
    <li>I'm not an X, but I play one on TV</li>
    <li>In X, no one can hear you Y</li>
    <li>X and Y and Z, oh my!</li>
</ul>
```

The ul element's inline styles set the text color, typeface, and size.

PLAY

Can you spot the style *attribute error in the following* <a> *tag?* <a href="https:// www.w3.org/TR/ css-style-attr/" style="color: indianred; font-weight: bold, text-decoration: none;"> ⇨ **Online:** wdpg.io/7-1-3

Although inline styles are the easiest way to add CSS code to your page, they're not the most convenient method for anything other than the simplest of pages because they require you to add the style attribute directly to every element you want styled. If your page consists of, say, a dozen h2 elements, and you want to apply the same style to them all, you must add a dozen style attributes. Even worse, if you later decide to change how your h2 elements appear, you have to change every instance of the style value. That's a lot of work, so most web designers eschew inline styles or use them only for specific instances.

What do these designers do instead? Ah, that's where internal styles come in.

Lesson 7.2: **Adding an Internal Style Sheet**
Covers: The style element

⇨ **Online:** wdpg.io/7-2-0

The second method for getting styles into a web page involves adding a <style></style> tag pair in the page's head section (that is, between the page's <head> and </head> tags) and then defining the styles within those tags. This method is called an *internal style sheet* (or sometimes an *embedded style sheet*), and it uses the following general syntax:

The web page elements
to be styled

```
<style>
    selectorA {
        propertyA1: valueA1;
        propertyA2: valueA2;
        ...
    }
    selectorB {
        propertyB1: valueB1;
        propertyB2: valueB2;
        ...
    }
    ...
</style>
```

Declarations are
surrounded by opening
and closing braces.

One or more
declarations

A style rule

From this syntax, you can see that an internal style sheet consists of one or more *style rules*, each of which defines one or more property-value pairs to be applied to the specified web page elements. Each rule has the following characteristics:

- A *selector* that specifies the web page elements to which you want the style applied. This selector is often a tag name, but it can also specify any other type of CSS selector (such as the class selector, described in Lesson 7.4).

- An opening left brace: {.

- One or more property-value pairs, separated by semicolons.

- A closing right brace: }.

In CSS lingo, a property-value pair is called a *declaration*, and the collection of declarations applied to a selector—that is, the braces and the property-value pairs between them—is called a *declaration block*. The combination of a selector and its declaration block is called a *style rule*.

The following example uses an internal style sheet to format the dt element.

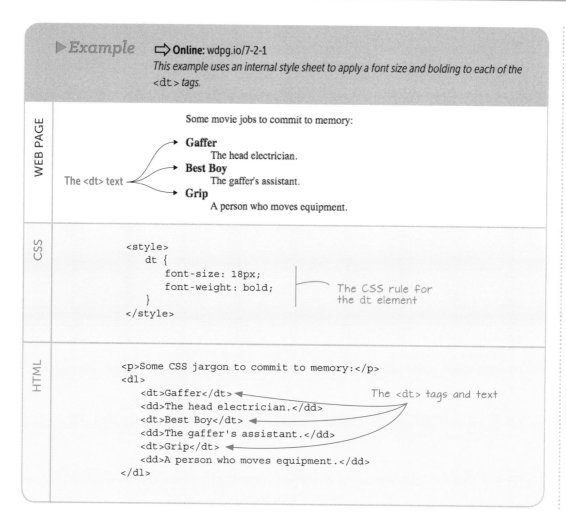

▶ *Example*   ⇨ **Online:** wdpg.io/7-2-1

This example uses an internal style sheet to apply a font size and bolding to each of the
<dt> tags.

WEB PAGE

Some movie jobs to commit to memory:

Gaffer
> The head electrician.

Best Boy
> The gaffer's assistant.

Grip
> A person who moves equipment.

The <dt> text

CSS

```
<style>
    dt {
        font-size: 18px;
        font-weight: bold;
    }
</style>
```

The CSS rule for
the dt element

HTML

```
<p>Some CSS jargon to commit to memory:</p>
<dl>
    <dt>Gaffer</dt>
    <dd>The head electrician.</dd>
    <dt>Best Boy</dt>
    <dd>The gaffer's assistant.</dd>
    <dt>Grip</dt>
    <dd>A person who moves equipment.</dd>
</dl>
```

The <dt> tags and text

MASTER

Declaration blocks can get quite long, with some containing a dozen or more property-value pairs. One way to make reading and working with these big blocks easier is to add the declarations in alphabetical order by property name.

Here, you see one of the great advantages of using internal styles. If your page has a dozen dt elements, this one style applies to them all, which gives the page a consistent look. Even better, if you decided that a size of 20px would look better for your dt text, you'd have to change the value only once in the style declaration; that change would get reflected automatically in all your dt elements.

Internal styles work beautifully if your site consists of a single web page. Such sites aren't rare, but it's far more likely that your or your client's site will consist of several pages, perhaps even several dozen. If you want your pages to have a consistent look—and you should, because consistency across pages is one of the hallmarks of good web design—using internal style sheets means copying the same `<style>` tag to each and every page. Also, if you change even one aspect of any style rule, you must make the same change to the same rule in every page.

The bigger your site is, the less appealing all that maintenance sounds and the more likely you'll be to switch to external style sheets.

Lesson 7.3: **Referencing an External Style Sheet**
Covers: The `link` element

Online: wdpg.io/7-3-0

The third and final method for adding styles to a page involves creating a second text file that you use to define your style rules. This method is called an *external style sheet*, and by tradition, its filename uses the `.css` extension (as in `styles.css`). Within that file, you use the same syntax that you saw earlier for an internal style sheet, but you do without the `style` element:

REMEMBER

Traditionally, you save an external style sheet text file with the `.css` *extension (*`styles.css`*).*

```
The web page elements
to be styled

selectorA {                     Declarations are
    propertyA1: valueA1;        surrounded by opening
    propertyA2: valueA2;        and closing braces.
    ...                  One or more
}                         declarations
selectorB {
    propertyB1: valueB1;
    propertyB2: valueB2;
    ...                     A style rule
}
    ...
```

To let the web browser know that you have an external style sheet, you add a `<link>` tag to your web page's head section. Figure 7.3 shows the syntax.

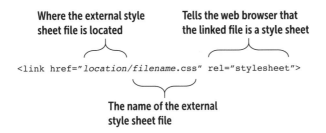

Where the external style sheet file is located

Tells the web browser that the linked file is a style sheet

`<link href="location/filename.css" rel="stylesheet">`

The name of the external style sheet file

▶ Figure 7.3
The `<link>` tag syntax for attaching an external style sheet to a web page

In this syntax, the `location` value is perhaps the trickiest. There are four possibilities:

- *Referencing a CSS file in the same directory.* Leave out the location and reference only the filename, like so:

```
<link href="styles.css" rel="stylesheet">
```

- *Referencing a CSS file in a subdirectory of the web page directory.* The location is the name of the subdirectory. If the subdirectory is named `css`, for example, you'd use the following:

```
<link href="css/styles.css" rel="stylesheet">
```

- *Referencing a CSS file in a subdirectory of the website's main subdirectory.* The location is the root directory (/) followed by the name of the subdirectory. If the subdirectory is named `css`, for example, you'd use the following:

```
<link href="/css/styles.css" rel="stylesheet">
```

- *Referencing a CSS file on a remote server.* The location is the full URL of the CSS file. Here's an example:

```
<link href="https://fonts.googleapis.com/css?family=Lato"
rel="stylesheet">
```

Using an external style sheet brings three major advantages to your web pages:

- *It makes applying a consistent look across multiple pages much easier.* If you attach the same external style sheet to several pages, and that CSS styles, say, your h1 elements, those tags will look exactly the same on all the pages.

- *It makes updating and maintaining your pages much easier.* If you make a change to the CSS in an external style sheet, that change is automatically propagated to every web page that links to the CSS file.

- *It enhances the separation between structure and presentation.* By using an external style sheet, you separate your project into two distinct layers: a *structural layer* of files that contain only HTML tags and a *presentation layer* of files that contain only CSS rules. Nice.

REMEMBER

As with the `<style>` tag, you may see some CSS external file `<link>` tags that include the `type="text/css"` attribute. That attribute was required with HTML 4.01, but you don't need it with HTML5.

This isn't to say that you should use only external style sheets rather than inline styles or internal style sheets. You have plenty of good reasons to use the `style` element, and you'll find that some web-page design problems are most easily solved by using a `style` attribute in an HTML tag. There's no need for taking a dogmatic approach to CSS; do what works.

Lesson 7.4: *Using Class Selectors*
Covers: The `.class` selector

⇨ **Online:** wdpg.io/7-4-0

Earlier, you learned that when you're defining a style rule, the first thing you specify is the web page object you want styled, followed by the declaration block:

```
selector {
    property1: value1;
    property2: value2;
    ...
}
```

The specified object is called a *selector*, and so far in this book, you've seen it used only with tag names, such as `h1` and `div`. This selector is known as the *type selector* because it targets a specific type of HTML element.

Type selectors are handy, and you'll use them frequently in your web-design career, but it doesn't take long before you come across a conundrum: What are you supposed to do when you have multiple instances of the same element that need different styling? A web page can easily have a few dozen `<div>` tags, so what's a coder to do if some of those `div`s require, say, right-aligned, italic, light gray text set at 20px and others require centered, bold, dark gray text set at 24px? You could insert all these styles as inline styles, sure, but that task quickly gets unwieldy when you're working with more than a half dozen elements.

You work around this and similar problems by taking advantage of the many other types of CSS selectors available. CSS derives most of its tremendous flexibility and power through these selectors. I don't think I'm exaggerating in the least when I say that if you want to become a CSS wizard—or (which is sort of the same thing) if you want to make yourself irresistibly hirable as a web designer—mastering selectors is the royal road to that goal. To get started down that road, check out perhaps the most powerful CSS selector: the class selector.

One of the most common web design scenarios is having multiple page objects that require the same styling. Whenever you have a set of elements that require the same styling, you can group those elements under a single HTML-and-CSS umbrella. In HTML, that umbrella takes the form of the `class` attribute, and the syntax appears in Figure 7.3.

REMEMBER

Although exceptions occur, for purposes of this book, your class names must begin with a letter; the rest of the name can include any combination of letters, numbers, hyphens (-), and underscores (_). See **wdpg.io/7-4-3/**.

▶ Figure 7.4
Use the class attribute to
assign a class name to an
HTML element.

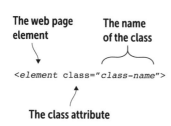

The web page element

The name of the class

```
<element class="class-name">
```

The class attribute

BEWARE

Class names are case-sensitive, meaning that the browser treats, say, myClassName *and* myclassname *as two separate classes.*

The following code assigns the class name custom-bullet-text to a <span> tag:

```
<span class="custom-bullet-text">
```

The key point here—and the source of the power inherent in using classes—is that you can assign the same class to multiple elements. When that's done, you can use an internal or external style sheet to define the styles for that class by using the class name, preceded by a dot (.) as the selector in your CSS:

```
.class-name {
    property1: value1;
    property2: value2;
    ...
}
```

The following example shows you how to use a class selector.

▶ *Example* ⇨ **Online:** wdpg.io/7-4-1
This example assigns a class name to each <span> tag and then uses a CSS class selector to apply a rule to those span elements.

WEB PAGE

Cube, Dice, or Mince? What's the Diff?

- Chop: To cut into small pieces.
- Cube: To cut into cube-shaped pieces.
- Dice: To cut into small, cube-shaped pieces.
- Mince: To cut into very small pieces.
- Shred: To cut or tear into long, thin irregular strips.

class="custom-bullet-text"

The styles aren't applied to the bullets.

CSS

```
.custom-bullet-text {
    color: brown;
    font-size: 18px;
    line-height: 1.5;
}
```

Rule for the custom-bullet-text class

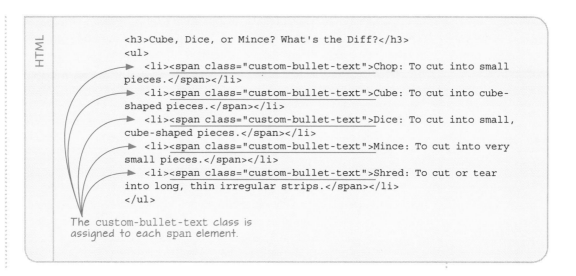

HTML

```
<h3>Cube, Dice, or Mince? What's the Diff?</h3>
<ul>
    <li><span class="custom-bullet-text">Chop: To cut into small
pieces.</span></li>
    <li><span class="custom-bullet-text">Cube: To cut into cube-
shaped pieces.</span></li>
    <li><span class="custom-bullet-text">Dice: To cut into small,
cube-shaped pieces.</span></li>
    <li><span class="custom-bullet-text">Mince: To cut into very
small pieces.</span></li>
    <li><span class="custom-bullet-text">Shred: To cut or tear
into long, thin irregular strips.</span></li>
</ul>
```

The custom-bullet-text class is
assigned to each span element.

Units of Measurement in CSS

Many web page styles require measurement values, including font sizes, border widths, and margin sizes. So far in this book, I've used pixels (px) to specify measurements, but you can use several other units, which I've laid out in Table 7.1.

▶ Table 7.1 Units of Measurement for CSS Properties

Unit	Name	Description
px	pixel	An absolute measurement equal to 1/96 of an inch
pt	point	An absolute measurement equal to 1/72 of an inch
em	em	A relative measurement equal to the element's default, inherited, or defined font size
rem	root em	A relative measurement equal to the font size of the root element of the web page
vw	viewport width	A relative measurement equal to 1/100 of the current width of the browser window
vh	viewport height	A relative measurement equal to 1/100 of the current height of the browser window

MASTER

Why not apply the CSS to the li element in this example? Such a rule would also style the bullet. By wrapping each list item in a <span>, you can style only the text.

Table 7.1 lists two types of units: absolute and relative. *Absolute* measures have a fixed size—a pixel is a pixel, for example—so you can be sure that an element sized with an absolute measure always appears consistently. As a designer, you may think this fact is a good thing, but it isn't always—especially on the web, where users sometimes change the default size of text in their browser settings. As a designer, your job should be to honor that change, not override it. Absolute values are frowned upon because they overrule type size changes set by the user, which is a design no-no. Also, as you'll see in Chapter 14, absolute values make your page design too rigid, so it doesn't show up well on both large and small screens.

Therefore, modern web-design best practices eschew absolute units in favor of relative units, usually rems or percentages. Relative measures don't have a fixed size. Instead, they're based on whatever size is supplied to the element. This size could be inherited from the parent element, or it could be the default specified by the user. If the browser's default type size is 16px, and you set your <p> type to 1.5rem, your paragraph text will be rendered at 24px. If the user bumped up the default text size to 20px, your paragraphs will render at 30px, thus preserving the relative size of the text. Also, relative measures scale well on devices of different sizes, so a design that looks good on a desktop screen can be made to look as good on a smartphone screen. (Again, Chapter 14 is the place to get the details.)

Summary

- Inline styles are added directly to a tag using the style attribute.
- You create an internal style sheet by adding your definitions to the <style> tag.
- An external style sheet exists as a separate .css file and is referenced through a <link> tag.
- A *class selector* applies CSS rules to any element that uses the specified class name.
- For CSS properties that require measurement values, use one of the following units: px, pt, em, rem, vw, or vh.

Chapter 8

Floating and Positioning Elements

> *The float property is a valuable and powerful asset to any web designer/developer working with HTML and CSS.* —Noah Stokes

This chapter covers

- Learning how elements flow down the page
- Interrupting the normal flow by floating elements
- Using floats to create drop caps and pull quotes
- Interrupting the normal flow by positioning elements

Left to its own devices, the web browser imposes an inflexible structure on your web pages, and your site is in danger of becoming boring (at least from a design perspective). To avoid that fate, you need to take control of your page elements and free them from the web browser's fixed ideas about how things should be laid out. You do that by wielding two of the most powerful CSS tools in the web designer's arsenal: floating and positioning. With these tools, you can break out of the browser's default element flow and build interesting, creative pages that people will be itching to visit. This chapter tells you everything you need to know.

Understanding the Default Page Flow

When you add elements to a web page, the browser lays out those elements in the order in which they appear in the HTML file according to the following rules:

- Block-level elements are stacked vertically, with the first element on top, the second element below it, and so on.

- Each inline element is rendered from left to right (in English and other left-to-right languages) within its parent block element.

Figure 8.1 shows a schematic diagram of a few block-level elements, stacked as the browser would render them. Figure 8.2 shows the corresponding web page with inline elements added.

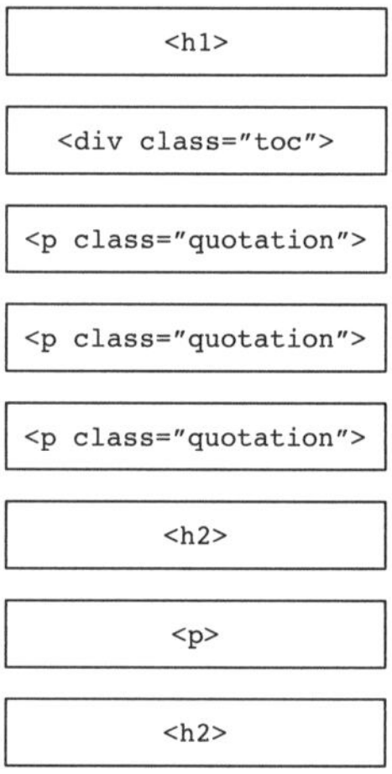

`<h1>`
`<div class="toc">`
`<p class="quotation">`
`<p class="quotation">`
`<p class="quotation">`
`<h2>`
`<p>`
`<h2>`

▶ Figure 8.1
The browser stacks block-level elements one on top of another.

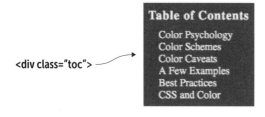

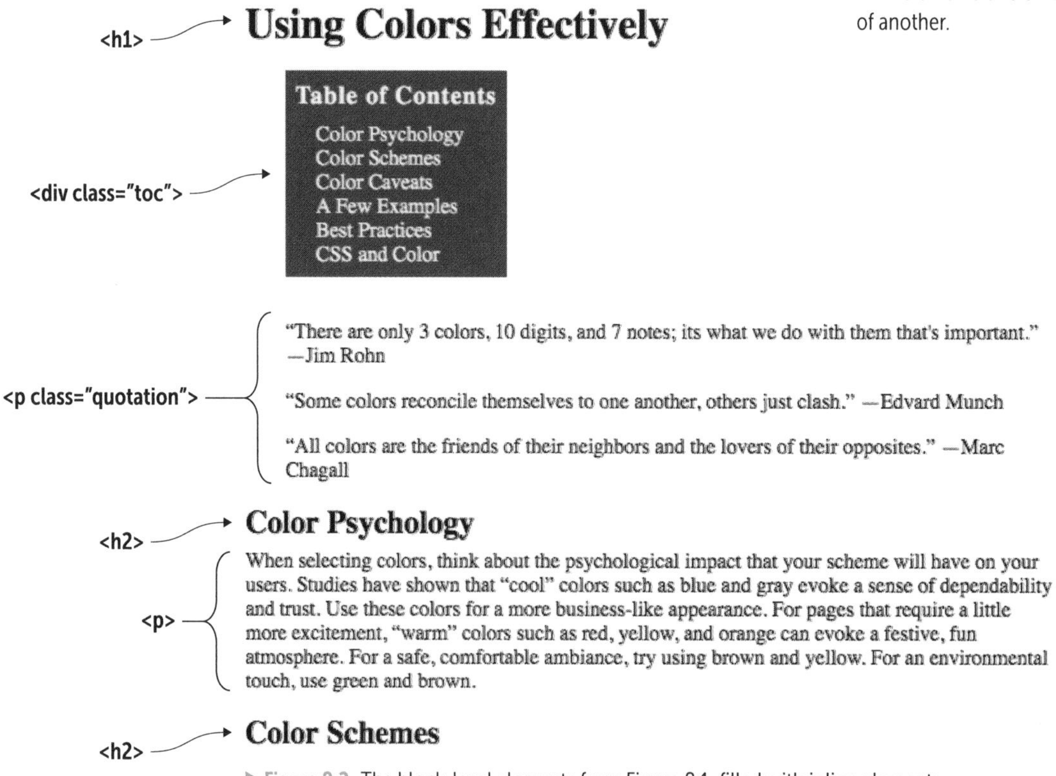

`<h1>` ⟶ # Using Colors Effectively

`<div class="toc">` ⟶
Table of Contents
Color Psychology
Color Schemes
Color Caveats
A Few Examples
Best Practices
CSS and Color

`<p class="quotation">` ⟶
"There are only 3 colors, 10 digits, and 7 notes; its what we do with them that's important."
—Jim Rohn

"Some colors reconcile themselves to one another, others just clash." —Edvard Munch

"All colors are the friends of their neighbors and the lovers of their opposites." —Marc Chagall

`<h2>` ⟶ ## Color Psychology

`<p>` ⟶
When selecting colors, think about the psychological impact that your scheme will have on your users. Studies have shown that "cool" colors such as blue and gray evoke a sense of dependability and trust. Use these colors for a more business-like appearance. For pages that require a little more excitement, "warm" colors such as red, yellow, and orange can evoke a festive, fun atmosphere. For a safe, comfortable ambiance, try using brown and yellow. For an environmental touch, use green and brown.

`<h2>` ⟶ ## Color Schemes

▶ Figure 8.2 The block-level elements from Figure 8.1, filled with inline elements

Lesson 8.1: **Floating Elements**
Covers: The `float` property

⇨ **Online:** wdpg.io/8-1-0

You can interrupt the top-to-bottom flow of elements by *floating* one or more elements to the left or right. *Floating* means that the browser takes the element out of the usual flow and places it as far as possible to the left or to the right (depending on the value you provide) and as high as possible (depending on other content) in its parent element. Then the rest of the page content flows around the floated element.

You float an element by setting its `float` property:

```
element {
    float: left|right|none;
}
```

In Figure 8.2, for example, the page would look nicer and make better use of space if the table of contents could be pushed to the right with the quotations flowing around it. That's readily done with the `float` property, as shown in the following example.

MASTER

Because the nearby nonfloated page elements wrap around the floated element, you should ensure that adequate whitespace exists between them by adding a margin around the floated element.

REMEMBER

Unlike with a nonfloated element, the top and bottom margins of a floated element do not collapse. See Chapter 9 to learn more about collapsing margins.

▶ *Example*   ⇨ **Online:** wdpg.io/8-1-1
This example uses the `float` *property to float the table of contents to the right.*

WEB PAGE

Using Colors Effectively

"There are only 3 colors, 10 digits, and 7 notes; its what we do with them that's important." —Jim Rohn

"Some colors reconcile themselves to one another, others just clash." —Edvard Munch

"All colors are the friends of their neighbors and the lovers of their opposites." —Marc Chagall

Table of Contents
Color Psychology
Color Schemes
Color Caveats
A Few Examples
Best Practices
CSS and Color
Color Resources

Color Psychology

When selecting colors, think about the psychological impact that your scheme will have on your users. Studies have shown that "cool" colors such as blue and gray evoke a sense of dependability and trust. Use these colors for a more business-like appearance. For pages that require a little more excitement, "warm" colors such as red, yellow, and orange can evoke a festive, fun atmosphere. For a safe, comfortable ambiance, try using brown and yellow. For an environmental touch, use green and brown.

Color Schemes

continued

```css
.toc {
    float: right;
    margin-left: 2em;
    margin-bottom: 2em;
    etc.
}
```

The float property applied to the toc class

```html
<h1>Using Colors Effectively</h1>
<div class="toc">
    <h3>Table of Contents</h3>
    <div>Color Psychology</div>
    <div>Color Schemes</div>
    <div>Color Caveats</div>
    <div>A Few Examples</div>
    <div>Best Practices</div>
    <div>CSS and Color</div>
    <div>Color Resources</div>
</div>
<p class="quotation">
"There are only 3 colors, 10 digits, and 7 notes; its what we do
with them that's important." —Jim Rohn
</p>
etc.
```

This <div> tag uses the toc class.

BEWARE

If you float an inline element, be sure to give it a width so that the browser knows how much space to give the element.

FAQ

Can I float only block-level elements? *No, you can also apply the* float *property to an inline element, such as a* span. *When you do, however, the browser takes the element out of the normal flow, turns it into a block-level element, and then floats it.*

Clearing Floated Elements

In the preceding example, notice that not only do the three quotations wrap around the floated table of contents; so do the first h2 element ("Color Psychology") and part of the paragraph that follows it. That behavior normally is what you want. But what if, for aesthetic or other reasons, you prefer that the h2 element and its text do *not* wrap around the table of contents?

You can do that by telling the browser that you want the h2 element to *clear* the floated element. *Clearing* a floated element means that the browser renders the element after the end of the floated element. You clear an element by setting its clear property:

```css
element {
    clear: left|right|both|none;
}
```

You use left to clear element of any elements that have been floated left, right to clear element of any elements that have been floated right, or both to clear element of both left- and right-floated elements. To clear the h2 element in the example, I'd use the following code:

```css
h2 {
    clear: right;
}
```

Figure 8.3 shows the page with the h2 (Color Psychology) now clearing the floated table of contents.

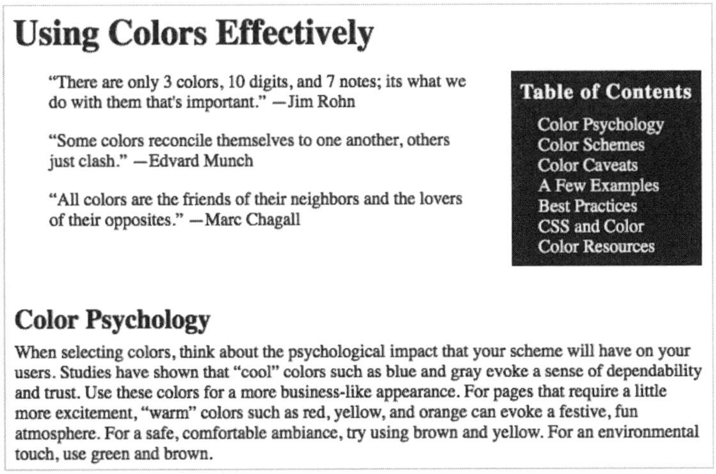

Using Colors Effectively

"There are only 3 colors, 10 digits, and 7 notes; its what we do with them that's important." —Jim Rohn

"Some colors reconcile themselves to one another, others just clash." —Edvard Munch

"All colors are the friends of their neighbors and the lovers of their opposites." —Marc Chagall

Table of Contents

Color Psychology
Color Schemes
Color Caveats
A Few Examples
Best Practices
CSS and Color
Color Resources

Color Psychology

When selecting colors, think about the psychological impact that your scheme will have on your users. Studies have shown that "cool" colors such as blue and gray evoke a sense of dependability and trust. Use these colors for a more business-like appearance. For pages that require a little more excitement, "warm" colors such as red, yellow, and orange can evoke a festive, fun atmosphere. For a safe, comfortable ambiance, try using brown and yellow. For an environmental touch, use green and brown.

▶ **Figure 8.3**
The Color Psychology **h2** element now clears the floated table of contents.

Preventing Container Collapse

Floated elements have a few gotchas that you need to watch for. The biggest one is that under certain circumstances, a floated element will overflow or drop right out of its parent container. To see what I mean, take a look at the following code (see Figure 8.4), which has two <p> tags in a <div> container that has been styled with a light blue background and a red border:

CSS:

```
div {
    border: 1px solid red;
    background-color: lightcyan;
}
```

HTML:

```
<div>
    <p>
        If you float two consecutive elements, the second floated
element will always appear either beside the first floated element
or below it.
    </p>
    <p>
        For example, if you float the elements left, the second
will appear to the right of the first. If there isn't enough room
to the right, it will appear below the first element.
    </p>
</div>
```

PLAY

You can float multiple elements. ⇨ **Online:** wdpg.io/8-1-3

▶ Figure 8.4

Two `<p>` elements inside a `<div>` container

> If you float two consecutive elements, the second floated element will always appear either beside the first floated element or below it.
>
> For example, if you float the elements left, the second will appear to the right of the first. If there isn't enough room to the right, it will appear below the first element.

Figure 8.5 shows the result when I style the `<p>` tags with a width and float them to the left:

CSS:

```
.col {
    float: left;
    width: 300px;
}
```

HTML:

```
<p class="col">
```

▶ Figure 8.5

When I float the `<p>` elements, the `<div>` container collapses on itself.

The <div> has collapsed.

If you float two consecutive elements, the second floated element will always appear either beside the first floated element or below it.

For example, if you float the elements left, the second will appear to the right of the first. If there isn't enough room to the right, it will appear below the first element.

MASTER

Some web developers prefer to use a more semantic name for the class, such as group.

REMEMBER

This solution is sometimes called a clearfix hack.

Bizarrely, the `<div>` container nearly disappears! That red line across the top is all that's left of it. What happened? When I floated the `<p>` elements, the browser took them out of the normal flow of the page. The `<div>` container saw that it no longer contained anything, so it collapsed on itself. This always occurs when a parent element contains only floated child elements.

To fix this problem, you can tell the parent element to clear its own child elements, thus preventing it from collapsing. Figure 8.6 shows a class that does this.

After the parent...

```
.self-clear::after {
    content: "";
    display: block;
    clear: both;
}
```

...insert an empty string...

...make it a block...

...and clear both left and right.

▶Figure 8.6
A class that enables a parent element to clear its own child elements

This class tells the browser to insert an empty string, rendered as a block-level element, and have it clear both left- and right-floated elements. The following example shows the fix in action and the full code.

▶ *Example*   ⇨ **Online:** wdpg.io/8-1-5
This example fixes the collapsing parent problem by telling the parent to self-clear its own floated child elements.

WEB PAGE	If you float two consecutive elements, the second floated element will always appear either beside the first floated element or below it.	For example, if you float the elements left, the second will appear to the right of the first. If there isn't enough room to the right, it will appear below the first element.

CSS

```
div {
    border: 1px solid red;
    background-color: lightcyan;
    width: 675px;
}
.col {
    float: left;
    width: 300px;
}
.self-clear::after {
    content: "";
    display: block;
    clear: both;
}
```

This rule styles the div element.

This class adds a width and floats the element.

This class prevents the parent from collapsing.

continued

HTML

```
<div class="self-clear">
<p class="col">
If you float two consecutive elements, the second floated element
will always appear either beside the first floated element or
below it.
</p>
<p class="col">
For example, if you float the elements left, the second will
appear to the right of the first. If there isn't enough room to the
right, it will appear below the first element.
</p>
</div>
```

Floating a Drop Cap

Floats have many uses, but one of my favorites is creating a *drop cap*, which is a paragraph's large first letter that sits below the baseline and "drops" a few lines into the paragraph. The trick is to select the opening letter by using the `::first-letter` pseudo-element and float that letter to the left of the paragraph. Then you mess around with font size, line height, and padding to get the effect you want, as shown in the following example.

▶ *Example*   ⇨ **Online:** wdpg.io/8-1-6
This example uses `float` *and the* `::first-letter` *pseudo-element to create a drop cap.*

WEB PAGE

Drop cap

Starting an article doesn't have to be boring! Get your text off to a great beginning by rocking the opening paragraph with a giant first letter. You can use either a *raised cap* (also called a *stick-up cap* or simply an *initial*) that sits on the baseline, or you can use a *drop cap* that sits below the baseline and nestles into the text.

CSS

```
.first-paragraph::first-letter {          1. Select the first letter.
    float: left;
    padding-top: .1em;                  2. Float it to the left.
    padding-right: .1em;
    color: darkred;
    font-size: 5em;                     3. Style to taste.
    line-height: .6em;
}
```

HTML

```
<p class="first-paragraph">
Starting an article doesn't have to be boring! Get your text off
to a great beginning by rocking the opening paragraph with a giant
first letter. You can use either a <i>raised cap</i> (also called
a <i>stick-up cap</i> or simply an <i>initial</i>) that sits on
the baseline, or you can use a <i>drop cap</i> that sits below the
baseline and nestles into the text.
</p>
```

Floating a Pull Quote

Another great use for floats is to add a pull quote to an article. A *pull quote* is a short but important or evocative excerpt from the article that's set off from the regular text. A well-selected and well-designed pull quote can draw in a site visitor who might not otherwise read the article.

You create a pull quote by surrounding the excerpted text in an element such as a span and then floating that element, usually to the right. Now style the element as needed to ensure that it stands apart from the regular text: top and/or bottom margins, a different font size, style, or color, and so on. Following is an example.

MASTER

If you prefer a raised cap to a drop cap, you can modify the example code to accommodate this preference. You need to remove the float *declaration and the* padding-top *and* padding-right *declarations.*

▶ *Example*   ⇨ **Online:** wdpg.io/8-1-7

This example uses `float` *to create a pull quote.*

WEB PAGE

A *pull quote* is a short excerpt or an important phrase or quotation that has been copied ("pulled") from a piece of text and displayed as a separate element between or, more often, to one side of the regular text.
It's important that the pull quote be styled in a way that not only makes it stand apart from the regular text (with, for example, a different font size, style, or color), but also makes it stand out for the reader. After all, it's the job of the pull quote to entice the would-be reader and create a desire to read the article.

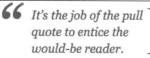 *It's the job of the pull quote to entice the would-be reader.* — Pull quote

CSS

```
.pullquote {
    float: right;                    ← This code floats the element.
    width: 50%;
    margin: 1.25em 0 1em .25em;
    padding-top: .5em;
    border-top: 1px solid black;
    border-bottom: 1px solid black;  This code styles the
    font-size: 1.05em;               pull quote.
    font-style: italic;
    color: #666;
}
.pullquote::before {
    content: "\0201c";
    float: left;
    padding: .1em .2em .4em 0;        Creates an optional
    font-size: 5em;                   large quotation mark.
    line-height: .45em;
}
```

HTML

```
<p>
A <i>pull quote</i> is a short excerpt or an important phrase or
quotation that has been copied ("pulled") from a piece of text and
displayed as a separate element between or, more often, to one
side of the regular text.
<span class="pullquote">
It's the job of the pull quote to entice the would-be reader.
</span>
It's important that the pull quote be styled in a way that not only
makes it stand apart from the regular text (with, for example, a
different font size, style, or color), but also makes it stand out
for the reader. After all, it's the job of the pull quote to entice
the would-be reader and create a desire to read the article.
</p>
```

The pull quote element

Despite head-scratching behaviors such as parent collapse, floating elements are useful for breaking them out of the default flow to achieve interesting layouts and effects. Floats get the browser to do most of the work, but if you want even more control of the look of your pages, you need to get more involved by specifying the positions of your elements.

Lesson 8.2: *Positioning Elements*
Covers: The position property

⇨ **Online:** wdpg.io/8-2-0

I mentioned earlier in this chapter that the default layout the browser uses for page elements renders the elements in the order in which they appear in the HTML file, stacking block-level elements and allowing inline elements to fill their parent blocks left to right. This system rarely produces a compelling layout, so another technique you can use (besides floating elements) to break out of the default flow is positioning one or more elements yourself, using the CSS position property combined with one or more of the CSS offset properties:

```
element {
    position: static|relative|absolute|fixed;
    top: measurement|percentage|auto;
    right: measurement|percentage|auto;
    bottom: measurement|percentage|auto;
    left: measurement|percentage|auto;
    z-index: integer|auto;
}
```

For the first four offset properties—top, right, bottom, and left—you can use any of the CSS measurement units you learned about in Chapter 7, including px, em, rem, vw, and vh. You can also use a percentage or auto (the default). The z-index property sets the element's position in the *stacking context*, which defines how elements are layered "on top" of and "under" one another when they overlap. An element with a higher z-index value appears layered over one with a lower value.

For the position property, here's a quick summary of the four possibilities:

- static—Ignores the offset properties (this is the default positioning used by the browser)
- relative—Positions the element offset from its default position while keeping the element's default position within the page flow
- absolute—Positions the element at a specific place within the nearest ancestor that has a nonstatic position while removing the element from the page flow
- fixed—Positions the element at a specific place within the browser viewport while removing the element from the page flow

The next few sections give you a closer look at relative, absolute, and fixed positioning.

Relative Positioning

When you position an element relatively, the element's default position remains in the normal page flow, but the element is shifted by whatever value or values you specify as the offset:

- If you supply a top value, the element is shifted down.
- If you supply a right value, the element is shifted from the right.
- If you supply a bottom value, the element is shifted up.
- If you supply a left value, the element is shifted from the left.

Having the element's default page-flow position maintained by the browser can lead to some unusual rendering, as shown in the following example.

REMEMBER

These shifts assume that you supply positive values to each property. Negative values are allowed (and are used often in web-design circles) and result in shifts in the opposite direction. A negative top value shifts the element up, for example.

WEB PAGE

Relative positioning shifts an element out of its default position while preserving the element's original space in the page flow. This can cause page weirdness. For example, if you set the top property, the element ⟶　　　　　　. This leaves a gap where the element would have been, which can look odd. 　shifts down

Gap where the span
element would have been

The shifted
span element

CSS

```
span {
    position: relative;
    top: 3em;
    border: 2px solid blue;
}
```

Applies relative positioning
and a top offset to the
span element

HTML

```
<div>
Relative positioning shifts an element out of its default position
while preserving the element's original space in the page flow.
This can cause page weirdness. For example, if you set the top
property, the element <span>shifts down</span>. This leaves a gap
where the element would have been, which can look odd.
</div>
```

The span element

You probably won't use relative positioning much for laying out page elements directly, but as you see in the next section, it comes in handy when you want to prepare elements to use absolute positioning.

PLAY

*Use relative positioning
to add watermark
text to a paragraph.*
⇨ Online: wdpg.io/8-2-2

XA 849 9116

Absolute Positioning

When you position an element absolutely, the browser does two things: It takes the element out of the default page flow, and it positions the element with respect to its nearest nonstatic (that is, positioned) ancestor. Figuring out this ancestor is crucial if you want to get absolute positioning right:

- Move up the hierarchy to the element's parent, grandparent, and so on. The first element you come to that has had its `position` property set to something other than `static` is the ancestor you seek.

- If no such ancestor is found, the browser uses the viewport, meaning that the element's absolute position is set with respect to the browser's content area.

With the ancestor found, the browser sets the element's absolute position with respect to that ancestor as follows:

- If you supply a `top` value, the element is moved down from the ancestor's top edge.

- If you supply a `right` value, the element is moved left from the ancestor's right edge.

- If you supply a `bottom` value, the element is moved up from the ancestor's bottom edge.

- If you supply a `left` value, the element is moved right from the ancestor's left edge.

REMEMBER

As with relative positioning, negative values are allowed and position the element in the opposite direction. A negative `left` *value moves the element left with respect to the ancestor's left edge, for example.*

WEB PAGE

▶ *Example*   ⇨ **Online:** wdpg.io/8-2-3
This example sets both a span *element and a* strong *element to absolute positioning.*

Browser window   <div>

<span>

Lesson 7.6

Absolute Positioning

Intro

<strong>

Absolute positioning moves an element from its default position, but doesn't preserve the its original space in the page flow. The element's new position is set with respect to the nearest ancestor in the hierarchy that has a non-static position, or the browser window if no such ancestor exists.

CSS

```css
h1, div {
    position: relative;
    z-index: 2;
}
span {
    position: absolute;
    top: 0;
    left: 0;
    z-index: 1;
    padding: 0.25em 6em 3em 0.25em;
    background-color: yellow;
    color: blue;
}
strong {
    position: absolute;
    top: 0;
    left: 0;
    z-index: -1;
    padding: 0.25em 5em 2.5em 0;
    background-color: orange;
    color: purple;
}
```

The div element is nonstatic.

The span and strong elements are positioned absolutely.

continued

```
HTML    <h1>
        Absolute Positioning
        </h1>
        <div>
        Absolute positioning moves an element from its default position,
        but doesn't preserve the its original space in the page flow. The
        element's new position is set with respect to the nearest ancestor
        in the hierarchy that has a non-static position, or the browser
        window if no such ancestor exists. <strong>Intro</strong>
        </div>
        <span>Lesson 8.6</span>
```

The span element

The strong element

SEE IT

To see an animation of how the browser positions the elements in this example, open the example in the Web Design Playground and click the See It button.

⇨ Online: wdpg.io/8-2-3

MASTER

This example also demonstrates the z-index property. The h1 and div elements have been given a z-index value of 2. The span element is given a z-index of 1; therefore, it appears "behind" the h1. The strong element is given a z-index of -1; therefore, it appears "behind" the div.

In this example, two elements are positioned absolutely:

- span—This element has no nonstatically positioned ancestor, so it's positioned with respect to the browser window. When you set both top and left to 0, the span element moves to the top-left corner of the window.

- strong—This element is nested inside a div element that's positioned relatively. Therefore, the strong element's absolute position is with respect to the div. In this case, when you set both top and left to 0, the strong element moves to the top-left corner of the div.

Fixed Positioning

The final position property value that I'll consider is fixed. This value works just like absolute, except for two things:

- The browser always computes the position with respect to the browser window.

- The element doesn't move after it has been positioned by the browser, even when you scroll the rest of the page content.

As you might imagine, this value would be useful for adding a navigation bar that's fixed to the top of the screen or a footer that's fixed to the bottom. You see an example of the latter in Chapter 15.

Summary

- In the default page flow, block-level elements are stacked vertically, and inline elements are rendered from left to right within their parent blocks.

- To pull an element out of the default page flow, set its `float` property to `left` or `right`.

- To position an element, set its `position` property to `relative`, `absolute`, or `fixed`; then specify the new position with `top`, `right`, `bottom`, and `left`.

- Set an element's position within the stacking context by using the `z-index` property, which layers higher-value elements over smaller-value elements.

FAQ

Why did you use -1 for the strong element's z-index? *The* `strong` *element is a descendant of the* `div` *element, and in CSS, the only way to make a descendant appear lower in the stacking context than its ancestor is to give the descendant a negative* `z-index` *value.*

PLAY

You can use absolute positioning to add tooltips (pop-up descriptions) to your links. ⇨ Online: wdpg.io/8-2-4

Chapter 9

Styling Sizes, Borders, and Margins

> *Understanding the CSS box model is crucial for getting your designs to behave as you want them to.* —Craig Campbell

This chapter covers

- Understanding the CSS box model
- Setting the width and height of an element
- Adding padding around an element's content
- Applying a border to an element
- Surrounding an element with a margin

When you learn about design, one of the first concepts that comes up is the principle of proximity: Related items should appear near one another, and unrelated items should be separated. This practice gives the design clear visual organization, which makes it easier for the reader to understand and navigate the design. The principle of proximity applies to your web page designs as well, but there's a problem. If you stick with the browser's default styling, your web page elements have no proximity structure; no elements are grouped or separated, so there's no organization. Fortunately, CSS offers a robust set of properties that enable you to apply the principle of proximity by sizing, spacing, and separating elements on the page. You learn about web page layout in earnest in Part 3, but this chapter introduces you to some vital foundations.

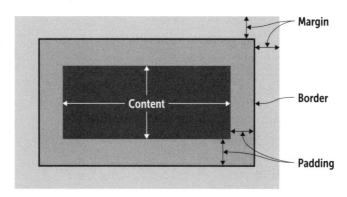
The Anatomy of an Element Box

The key to getting your web page content to bend to your will is to understand that every element you add to a page—every `<div>`, every `<p>`, every `<span>`, even every `<strong>` and every `<em>`—is surrounded by an invisible box. Why is that such a big deal? Because you can use CSS to control many aspects of that box, including its height, width, spacing, borders, and position on the page. To get there, you need to become acquainted with the various parts of the box.

Figure 9.1 gives you an abstract look at the basic box parts, and Figure 9.2 shows how these same parts affect some actual page content.

▶ Figure 9.1 ·
The main parts of an element box

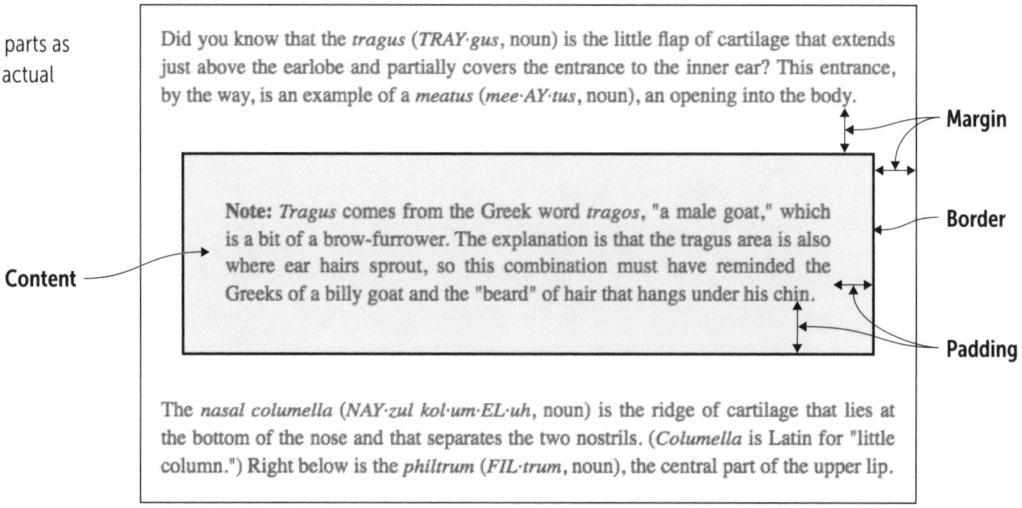

Content

Margin

Border

Padding

▶ Figure 9.2
The element box parts as they appear with actual page content

Did you know that the *tragus* (*TRAY·gus*, noun) is the little flap of cartilage that extends just above the earlobe and partially covers the entrance to the inner ear? This entrance, by the way, is an example of a *meatus* (*mee·AY·tus*, noun), an opening into the body.

Note: *Tragus* comes from the Greek word *tragos*, "a male goat," which is a bit of a brow-furrower. The explanation is that the tragus area is also where ear hairs sprout, so this combination must have reminded the Greeks of a billy goat and the "beard" of hair that hangs under his chin.

Content

Margin

Border

Padding

The *nasal columella* (*NAY·zul kol·um·EL·uh*, noun) is the ridge of cartilage that lies at the bottom of the nose and that separates the two nostrils. (*Columella* is Latin for "little column.") Right below is the *philtrum* (*FIL·trum*, noun), the central part of the upper lip.

> *At the risk of over-repeating myself: every element in web design is a rectangular box. This was my ah-ha moment that helped me really start to understand CSS-based web design and accomplish the layouts I wanted to accomplish.* —Chris Coyier

There are four parts to each element box:

- *Content*—This area is the inner rectangle of the box, consisting of the content—such as some text or an image—that's contained within the box.
- *Padding*—This area between the content and the border represents extra whitespace added outside the top, right, bottom, and left edges of the content area.
- *Border*—This part runs along the outer edges of the padding area and surrounds the content and padding with lines.
- *Margin*—This area is the outer rectangle of the box, representing extra whitespace added outside of the top, right, bottom, and left borders.

The combination of the content area, padding, border, and margin is known in CSS circles as the *box model*. Surprisingly, this box model applies not only to the usual block-level suspects (such as <div>, <h1>, and <p>), but also to all inline elements (such as <span>, <em>, and <a>). Why is the box model so important? There are two main reasons: appearance and positioning.

Appearance is crucial because the box model enables you to control the *whitespace*—the padding and margins—that surround the content. As any designer will tell you, making good use of whitespace is a key part of any successful layout.

Positioning is vital because CSS also gives you quite a bit of control of where the element boxes appear on the page. Rather than the default—and *boring*—layout of one element stacked on the next all the way down the page, CSS offers box model-related properties that let you shift each box to the position that gives you the layout you prefer.

Keeping all this in mind the best you can, it's time to turn your attention to the useful and powerful CSS properties that enable you to manipulate any element box. First up: changing the box dimensions.

Lesson 9.1: **Setting the Width and Height**

Covers: The `width` and `height` properties

⇨ **Online:** wdpg.io/9-1-0

Web browsers perform a great many automatic calculations when they load a page. Two of those automatic values are the width and the height of each element box on the page, which are set according to the following guidelines:

- The width of each element box is set to the width of the element's container, which by default is the width of the browser window.

- The height of each element box is set to a value that's tall enough to contain all the element's content.

One of the main tenets of good web design is that you should override these and similar browser defaults so that you have maximal control of the look and layout of your page. To do that with the dimensions of any block-level element box, use the CSS `width` and `height` properties. These properties take any of the CSS measurement units you learned about in Chapter 7, including `px`, `em`, `rem`, `vw`, and `vh`. You can also set `width` or `height` to a percentage or to `auto` (the default, which allows the browser to set the dimensions automatically).

At this point, you may be asking yourself an important question. When you set the width or height, which of the element box's four rectangular areas—content, padding, border, or margin—are you sizing? Intuitively, you might guess the border, because that area contains the content and padding, or what feels like the "inside" of the element box. Surprisingly, that's not the case. By default, the `width` and `height` properties apply only to the *content* area. That's most unfortunate, because when you size an element, to get its true size as rendered on the page you must add the values of its padding and border. If that sounds like an unnecessarily complicated way to go about things, you're right. Instead, you can set the `box-sizing` property to `border-box` for the element:

```
element {
    box-sizing: border-box;
}
```

This code tells the web browser to apply the `width` and `height` values all the way out to (and including) the border of the element box. Note that the margin is *not* included in the width and height.

REMEMBER

I should clarify here that these calculations apply only to block-level elements such as `<div>` and `<p>`. Inline elements such as `<span>` and `<a>` flow with the text, so `width` *and* `height` *are ignored.*

MASTER

If you want to work with an inline element's `width`, `height`, *and other block-related properties but keep the element inline, add* `display: inline-block` *to the element's CSS. To make the element a true block-level element, add* `display: block`, *instead.*

BEWARE

You should rarely, if ever, set an element's `height` *property. Setting the height is useful for images, but with text, there are too many variables to know for sure whether everything will fit into the height you specify. Let the content create the element's height naturally.*

The width property is useful for setting the text line length for optimum reading. For ideal screen reading, your body text blocks should contain between 50 and 80 characters per line (including spaces and punctuation). In most cases, a line length of around 65 characters is optimum, but it's okay to set a longer line if you're using a larger font size or a shorter line if you're using a smaller font size. You set the line length by adjusting the text block's width property. Consider the text shown in Figure 9.3.

> On March 19, 1988, a man named Robert Muller Jr. was a passenger in a car driving along US Route 441 in Florida. At some point in the journey, the car was cut off (or, at least, it appeared that way), enraging the car's occupants. Unfortunately, Mr. Muller had access to a gun, which he subsequently used to shoot out the back window of the other car, wounding 20-year-old Cassandra Stewart in the neck. Police described the shooting as an incident of "road rage," and a name for an all-too-common form of motorist madness was born.

▶ Figure 9.3 In the default width on a large screen, the line lengths of this text are too long for comfortable reading.

With line lengths of well over 150 characters, this text is hard to scan. You can fix that problem by adjusting the width of the text's containing element, as shown in the following example.

MASTER

Rather than apply box-sizing *to individual elements, assign it once by using the universal element (**)*, and it will be applied to every element. Also, if you ever want to return to the default sizing behavior for an element, use the declaration* box-sizing: content-box.

PLAY

If you set the height of an element, you may find that its content overflows its element box. To control this behavior, you can use the overflow *property.*
➡ Online: wdpg.io/9-1-4

▶ *Example* ➡ **Online:** wdpg.io/9-1-1
This example reduces the width of the containing div *element to make the line lengths easier to read.*

WEB PAGE

On March 19, 1988, a man named Robert Muller Jr. was a passenger in a car driving along US Route 441 in Florida. At some point in the journey, the car was cut off (or, at least, it appeared that way), enraging the car's occupants. Unfortunately, Mr. Muller had access to a gun, which he subsequently used to shoot out the back window of the other car, wounding 20-year-old Cassandra Stewart in the neck. Police described the shooting as an incident of "road rage," and a name for an all-too-common form of motorist madness was born.

630px

continued

<table>
<tr>
<td>CSS</td>
<td>

```
div {
    box-sizing: border-box;
    width: 630px;
}
```

border-box is applied.

The width is set for the ideal line length.

</td>
</tr>
<tr>
<td>HTML</td>
<td>

```
<div>
On March 19, 1988, a man named Robert Muller Jr. was a passenger
in a car driving along US Route 441 in Florida. At some point in
the journey, the car was cut off (or, at least, it appeared that
way), enraging the car's occupants. Unfortunately, Mr. Muller had
access to a gun, which he subsequently used to shoot out the back
window of the other car, wounding 20-year-old Cassandra Stewart
in the neck. Police described the shooting as an incident of "road
rage," and a name for an all-too-common form of motorist madness
was born.
</div>
```

</td>
</tr>
</table>

Lesson 9.2: **Adding Padding**

Covers: The `padding-*` properties

PLAY

You can specify a maximum width for an element by using the max-width *property; similarly, you can set the minimum width by using the* min-width *property.* ⇨ *Online: wdpg.io/9-1-3*

⇨ **Online:** wdpg.io/9-2-0

In the element box, the padding is the whitespace added above, below, to the left, and to the right of the content. If you add a border to your element, as described in Lesson 9.3, the padding is the space between your content and the border. The padding gives the element a bit of room to breathe within its box, ensuring that the content isn't crowded by its own border or by nearby elements.

You set the padding by applying a value to each of the four sides:

```
element {
    padding-top: top-value;
    padding-right: right-value;
    padding-bottom: bottom-value;
    padding-left: left-value;
}
```

Each value can take any of the standard CSS measurement units, including px, em, rem, vw, and vh, or you can set the value to a percentage. Here's an example:

```
.pullquote {
    padding-top: 1em;
    padding-right: 1.5em;
    padding-bottom: .75em;
    padding-left: 1.25em;
}
```

You can also use a `padding` shorthand property to set all the padding values with a single declaration. You can use four syntaxes with this property, as shown in Figure 9.4.

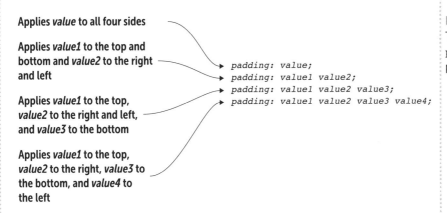

Applies *value* to all four sides

Applies *value1* to the top and bottom and *value2* to the right and left

Applies *value1* to the top, *value2* to the right and left, and *value3* to the bottom

Applies *value1* to the top, *value2* to the right, *value3* to the bottom, and *value4* to the left

```
padding: value;
padding: value1 value2;
padding: value1 value2 value3;
padding: value1 value2 value3 value4;
```

▶ Figure 9.4
The syntaxes of the padding shorthand property

You can duplicate the rule in the preceding example by using the shorthand syntax as follows:

```
.pullquote {
    padding: 1em 1.5em .75em 1.25em;
}
```

To see how you can use padding to make your web page more readable, consider the simple navigation bar shown in Figure 9.5.

HOME RESEARCH PAPERS BLOG CONTACT INFO

▶ Figure 9.5
A navigation bar without any horizontal padding

The big problem is that it's impossible to tell by looking how many navigation items there are. You could have as many as six (Home, Research, Papers, Blog, Contact, and Info) or as few as three (Home, Research Papers Blog, and Contact Info). To fix this problem, you can use padding to add some horizontal breathing room between the items, as shown in the following example.

MASTER

This example transforms an unordered list into a navigation menu by doing two things: setting the ul *element's* list-style-type *property to* none *to hide the bullets, and setting the* li *element's* display *property to* inline-block, *which tells the browser to treat the items as blocks but display them inline.*

❝❝*Horizontal navigation with tight spacing between nav items is a common issue I often encounter on otherwise well-designed sites. Without adequate padding, navigation items begin to run together and become more difficult to quickly scan.* —Jeremiah Shoaf

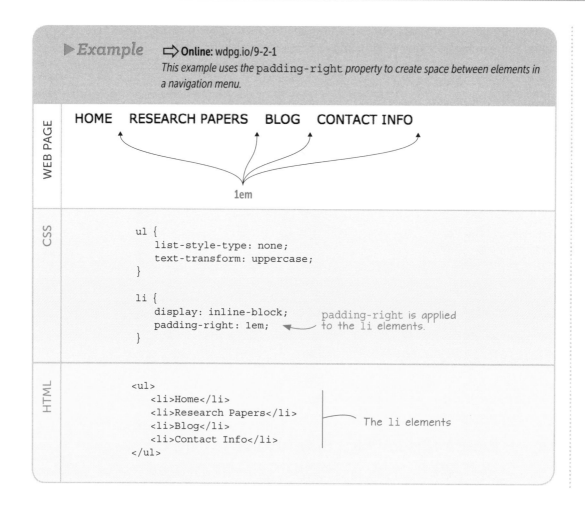

▶ *Example*   ⇨ **Online:** wdpg.io/9-2-1

This example uses the `padding-right` *property to create space between elements in a navigation menu.*

WEB PAGE

HOME   RESEARCH PAPERS   BLOG   CONTACT INFO

1em

CSS

```
ul {
    list-style-type: none;
    text-transform: uppercase;
}

li {
    display: inline-block;
    padding-right: 1em;          padding-right is applied
}                                to the li elements.
```

HTML

```
<ul>
    <li>Home</li>
    <li>Research Papers</li>          The li elements
    <li>Blog</li>
    <li>Contact Info</li>
</ul>
```

Lesson 9.3: **Applying a Border**
            Covers: The `border-*` properties

SEE IT

To see an animation of how the browser adds the padding in the above example, open the example in the Web Design Playground and click the See It button.
⇨ Online: wdpg.io/ 9-2-1

⇨ **Online:** wdpg.io/9-3-0

In the element box, the *border* is the line that defines the outer edge of the padding on four sides: top, right, bottom, and left. In this way, the border comes between the element's padding and its margin. The border is optional, but it's often useful for providing the reader a visual indicator that the enclosed content is separate from any nearby content.

To create a basic border around an element, use the `border` property, as shown in Figure 9.6.

The element to style

The border width

The border color

```
element {
    border: width style color;
}
```

The border style

▶ Figure 9.6 The syntax of the `border` property

USE IT

Add a border to an element to provide a visual indication that the content is self-contained or separate from the surrounding page content.

The *width* value can take any standard CSS measurement unit, including `px`, `em`, `rem`, `vw`, and `vh`. You can also set the value to any of the following keywords: `thin`, `medium`, or `thick`. For the *style* value, you can use any of the following keywords: `dotted`, `dashed`, `solid`, `double`, `groove`, `ridge`, `inset`, or `outset`. For the *color* parameter, you can use any of the color names that you learned about in Chapter 4.

Here's an example:

```
.pullquote {
    border: 1px solid black;
}
```

This rule defines the `pullquote` class with a one-pixel wide, solid, black border.

The following example takes the navigation list from Lesson 9.2 and adds a border around it.

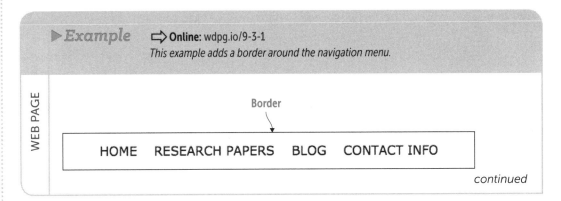

▶ *Example* ⇨ **Online: wdpg.io/9-3-1**
This example adds a border around the navigation menu.

WEB PAGE

Border

HOME   RESEARCH PAPERS   BLOG   CONTACT INFO

continued

```css
ul {
    border: 1px solid black;
    padding-top: .75em;
    padding-bottom: .75em;
    list-style-type: none;
    text-align: center;
    text-transform: uppercase;
}

li {
    display: inline-block;
    padding-right: 1em;
}

li:first-child {
    padding-left: 1em;
}
```

CSS

The border

Padding added to the top and bottom

The items are centered.

Extra padding on the left

```html
<ul>
    <li>Home</li>
    <li>Research Papers</li>
    <li>Blog</li>
    <li>Contact Info</li>
</ul>
```

HTML

PLAY

The CSS box model can be confusing at first because it's hard to visualize the box that surrounds each element. To help, use the outline *property, which adds a line around the outside edge of the box border. The* outline *property uses the same syntax as the* border *property.*

➡ Online: wdpg.io/9-3-3

❝❝ *Use a border when you need to separate content into logical sections if your design requires content to be separate, and without it the design would appear cluttered.* —Andrew Stoker

One odd detail may have you furrowing your brow: The `li:first-child` element gets a `padding-left` value of 1em. What's going on? Recall from Lesson 9.2's example that you needed to add 1em of padding between the menu items to separate them. You did that by using the `padding-right` property, but doing so also meant adding 1em of padding to the right of the Contact Info item. To compensate for that extra padding on the right, you need to add an equal amount on the left so the menu centers properly. The `li:first-child` rule adds the required padding to the first `li` element.

Lesson 9.4: *Controlling the Margins*
Covers: The `margin-*` properties

⇨ **Online:** wdpg.io/9-4-0

In the element box, the *margin* is the whitespace added above, below, to the left, and to the right of the border. The margin lets you control the space between elements. Positive margin values, for example, keep the page elements from bumping into one another or overlapping, and also keep the elements from brushing up against the edges of the browser viewport. On the other hand, if your design requires elements to overlap, you can achieve this effect by using negative margin values.

You apply the margin by setting a value to one or more of an element's four sides:

```
element {
    margin-top: top-value;
    margin-right: right-value;
    margin-bottom: bottom-value;
    margin-left: left-value;
}
```

Each margin value can use any of the standard CSS measurement units, such as px, em, rem, vw, and vh. You can also use a percentage or the auto keyword (to have the browser set the margin automatically to fit the available space). Here's an example:

```
.pullquote {
    margin-top: 1.5em;
    margin-right: 2.5em;
    margin-bottom: 2em;
    margin-left: 3em;
}
```

As with `padding`, a `margin` shorthand property lets you apply the margins by using a single declaration. Figure 9.7 shows the four syntaxes you can use with this property.

Applies *value* to all four sides

Applies *value1* to the top and bottom and *value2* to the right and left

Applies *value1* to the top, *value2* to the right and left, and *value3* to the bottom

Applies *value1* to the top, *value2* to the right, *value3* to the bottom, and *value4* to the left

```
margin: value;
margin: value1 value2;
margin: value1 value2 value3;
margin: value1 value2 value3 value4;
```

MASTER

Positive margin values serve to push the element away from surrounding elements (or the edges of the browser viewport). Sometimes, however, you'll want to bring elements closer, and you can do that by setting a negative margin value.
⇨ **Online:** wdpg.io/9-4-5

USE IT

Margins are especially useful for establishing the spacing between your page's text blocks, particularly its paragraphs. A good general rule for spacing each paragraph is to set the bottom margin to 1em.

▶ Figure 9.7
The syntax possibilities of the margin shorthand property

You can rewrite the rule in the preceding example by using the shorthand syntax like so:

```
.pullquote {
    margin: 1.5em 2.5em 2em 3em;
}
```

It's important to remember that the web browser sets a default margin for all the elements by using its internal style sheet. That sounds handy, but one of the key principles of web design is to gain maximum control of the look of the page by styling everything yourself. A big step in that direction is adding the following code to the top of your style sheet:

> ❝ We think of our CSS as modifying the default look of a document—but with a "reset" style sheet, we can make that default look more consistent across browsers, and thus spend less time fighting with browser defaults. —Eric Meyer

```
html, body, abbr, article, aside, audio, blockquote, button,
canvas, code, div, dl, dt, embed, fieldset, figcaption,
figure, footer, form, h1, h2, h3, h4, h5, h6, header, iframe,
img, input, label, legend, li, nav, object, ol, option, p,
pre, q, section, select, table, tbody, td, tfoot, th, thead,
tr, ul, video {
    margin: 0;
    padding: 0;
}
```

This code gets rid of the browser's default margins and padding on all these elements, enabling you to adjust these settings yourself as needed on your page. If your page is small, you can use the following simplified version:

```
* {
    margin: 0;
    padding: 0;
}
```

Note, however, that you *do* need to set your margins. To see why, Figure 9.8 shows the simple navigation bar when the margins have been reset to 0.

▶ Figure 9.8
The navigation bar without any margins

As you can see, the navigation bar is rendered tight to the top, right, and left edges of the browser window, with little room between the bottom of the navigation bar and the text. To fix this problem, you can set the navigation bar's margins to add some welcome whitespace around it, as shown in the following example.

PLAY

You can also use a margin trick to center a child element vertically within its parent.
⇨ Online: wdpg.io/9-4-4.

▶ *Example* ⇨ **Online:** wdpg.io/9-4-1
This example uses the `margin` *properties to create space around the navigation menu.*

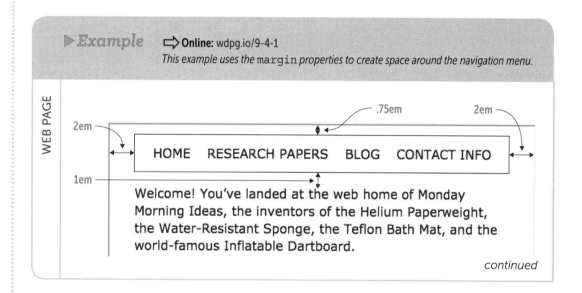

continued

```
CSS

ul {
    border: 1px solid black;
    margin-top: .75em;
    margin-right: 2em;           Margin properties applied
    margin-bottom: 1em;          to the ul element
    margin-left: 2em;
    padding-top: .75em;
    padding-bottom: .75em;
    list-style-type: none;
    text-align: center;
    text-transform: uppercase;
}
div {
    margin-right: 2em;           Margin properties applied
    margin-left: 2em;            to the div element
}
```

```
HTML

<ul>
    <li>Home</li>
    <li>Research Papers</li>
    <li>Blog</li>
    <li>Contact Info</li>
</ul>
<div>
Welcome! You've landed at the web home of Monday Morning Ideas,
the inventors of the Helium Paperweight, the Water-Resistant
Sponge, the Teflon Bath Mat, and the world-famous Inflatable
Dartboard.
</div>
```

PLAY

If you've set an element's width, you can quickly center the element horizontally by using the declaration margin: top/bottom auto, *where top/bottom is the value for both the top and bottom margins.*

⇨ Online: wdpg.io/9-4-3.

Watch Out for Collapsing Margins!

In the preceding example, I added margin-bottom: 1em to the ul element to separate it from the div text. Suppose that I decide that I want 2em of space between these elements, so I adjust the div rule as follows. Figure 9.9 shows the result:

```
div {
    margin-top: 1em;        A top margin
    margin-right: 2em;      added to the
    margin-left: 2em;       div element
}
```

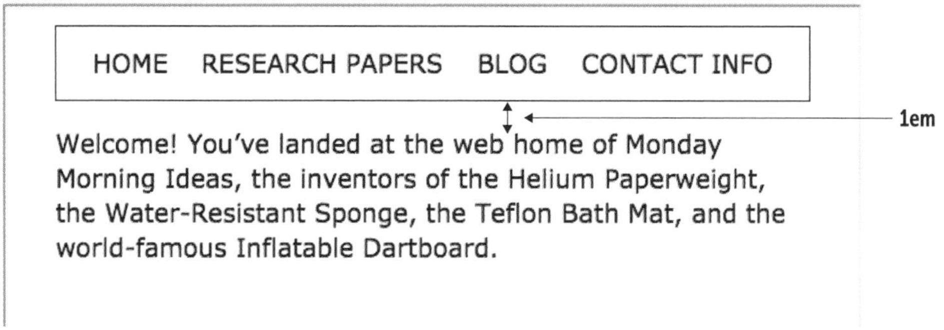

HOME   RESEARCH PAPERS   BLOG   CONTACT INFO

— 1em

Welcome! You've landed at the web home of Monday Morning Ideas, the inventors of the Helium Paperweight, the Water-Resistant Sponge, the Teflon Bath Mat, and the world-famous Inflatable Dartboard.

▶ Figure 9.9 The div text with a 1em top margin added

No, your eyes aren't deceiving you: The space between the navigation bar and the div text is exactly the same as it was before! What's going on here is a tricky CSS phenomenon known as *collapsing margins*. When one element's bottom margin meets another element's top margin, the web browser doesn't add the two values, as you might expect. Instead, it determines which of the two margin values is larger, and it uses that value as the vertical margin between the two elements. It throws out the smaller margin value, thus collapsing the two margins into a single value.

If you ever find that the top or bottom margins of one or more page elements are behaving strangely—that is, are bigger or smaller than you think they should be—there's an excellent chance that collapsing margins are the culprit.

Summary

- The four main parts of a CSS element box are the content, the padding around the content, the border around the padding, and the margin around the border.
- You specify an element's dimensions by setting its width and height properties.
- You add padding around an element's content by using the four padding properties: padding-top, padding-right, padding-bottom, and padding-left. Alternatively, use a padding shortcut property, such as padding: *top right bottom left*.
- The simplified border syntax is border: *width style color*.
- You add a margin around an element by using the four margin properties: margin-top, margin-right, margin-bottom, and margin-left. Alternatively, use a margin shortcut property, such as margin: *top right bottom left*.

MASTER

If you do want extra vertical space between two elements, you can increase the larger of the two margin values (setting margin-bottom: 2em *on the* ul *element, for example). Alternatively, change the collapsing margin to padding (such as by replacing the* margin-top *property with* padding-top: 1em *on the* div *element).*

REMEMBER

The left and right margins never collapse. Also, margin collapse doesn't occur for elements that are floated or positioned absolutely (see Chapter 8).

Chapter 10

PROJECT: Creating a Landing Page

The one key feature of the online marketing landscape is the landing page—that (hopefully welcoming) doorway to your online storefront, which you present to your Web site visitors. —Martin Harwood

This chapter covers

- Planning and sketching your landing page
- Choosing fonts and colors for the page
- Understanding and implementing banded content
- Adding the images and text

Okay, you're nine chapters into this adventure, and you've come a long way. Here in Part 2 alone, you've mastered using images and media; making style sheets; using classes; floating elements; using absolute and relative positioning; and manipulating sizes, borders, and margins. That's a lot, and (most important) it's enough know-how to start building some amazing pages. As proof, in this project you'll be putting all those HTML and CSS skills to good use to create a professional-looking landing page for a marketing campaign for a product or service. If that project sounds out of your depth, not to worry: You know more than enough to ace this assignment, and I'll be building my own (rather silly, as you'll see) landing page right alongside you. If you get stuck, I (or, at least, my code) will be right there with you to help or give you a nudge in the right direction. Let's get started!

What You'll Be Building

In its most general sense, a *landing page* is the page visitors first see when they navigate to (land on) your website. That's often your home page, but it could also be any page that the person comes across via a Google search or a link that someone else posts to social media.

But a more specific sense of the term is relevant to this project. In this sense, a *landing page* is the first page that people see when they click a link in an ad, blog post, or social media update that's part of a marketing or awareness campaign for a specific product or service. The landing page's job is to explain the product or service and to induce the user to perform some action, such as buy the item, subscribe to the service, or sign up for a newsletter.

This project takes the HTML and CSS skills you learned in the preceding nine chapters and shows you how to use them to build a basic landing page for a product or service. It includes images, descriptive text, and "call-to-action" buttons that ask the reader to perform some action (such as buy or subscribe). The general structure of the pages uses a popular modern layout called *banded content*, in which the text and images appear in horizontal strips that run the full width of the browser window. As you go along, I'll build an example landing page based on a fictitious book that I'm "selling," but of course you'll want to build your own page with your own text and images.

Sketching the Layout

Because you've likely seen a landing page or two in your day, you may have a reasonable idea of what you want your landing page to look like. If so, great! You're way ahead of most people at this stage of the project. But believe me, a design that exists only in your head is hard to translate into HTML and CSS code. To make the transition from design to code much easier, you need to get that design out of your head and into concrete form. You can use a graphics program such as Adobe Photoshop or Illustrator for this purpose, but I prefer to sketch the basic components of the page with pencil and paper.

As Figure 10.1 shows, your sketch doesn't have to be a work of art or even all that detailed. Draw the main sections of the page and include some text that describes the content of each section.

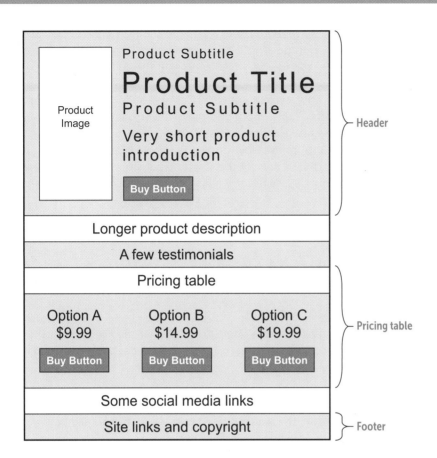

▶ Figure 10.1
Before you begin coding,
get a pencil and some
paper and create a quick
sketch of the page layout
and content.

Your next page-planning task is deciding which typefaces you want to use for your landing page.

Choosing Typefaces

As a rule, landing pages shouldn't burden the user with tons of text. You want to highlight the key features of your product or service, give the users reasons why they should want it, and then give them the opportunity to get it. So if you're building a page without lots of body text, your typeface needs to be clean and legible, and it shouldn't call attention to itself (and thus take attention away from the product).

REMEMBER

When you specify multiple typefaces in the `font-family` *property, the web browser checks to see whether they're installed on each user's computer in the order in which they appear and uses the first typeface it finds.*

In such cases, a sans-serif typeface is often the best choice, because the lack of serifs gives these fonts a clean appearance. Sans serifs also have a more modern feel than serifs, which gives you the added advantage of making your product look new and fresh.

One of my favorite system fonts is Optima, a gorgeous sans-serif designed by Hermann Zapf (whom you may know from the famous Zapf Dingbats typeface available on most PCs). Alas, although Optima is installed on all Mac computers, it's available on few Windows PCs. So as a backup font for Windows, I'll also specify the Calibri typeface, which has similar characteristics. In my CSS, I'll use the following rule to apply these families to all the page text:

```
body {
    font-family: Optima, Calibri, sans-serif;
}
```

With your page layout sketched and your typeface chosen, the next step is picking out a color scheme.

Choosing a Color Scheme

Because the landing page uses a single typeface, you need to turn to other page elements to add some dynamism and contrast. A good place to do that is the color scheme:

LEARN

If you're not comfortable choosing colors, a great online tool called Palettable (https://www.palettable.io) can help. Enter your initial color, and Palettable suggests a compatible color. Click Like to keep it or Dislike to try another.

- *Accent color*—This color is used as the background for page elements such as the call-to-action buttons and text that you want to make sure the reader doesn't miss. As such, it should be a bold, unmistakable hue that stands out.

- *Secondary color*—This color is mostly used as the background for some of the content bands. It should be similar to the accent color: bold enough to tell the reader that the content is important but not so bold that it clashes with or overshadows the accent color.

- *Tertiary color*—This color is used as the background for content that's less important.

Figure 10.2 shows the colors I chose for my landing page. You, of course, should choose a color scheme that suits your style.

With the page layout in place and your fonts and colors chosen, it's time to bring everything together by slinging some HTML and CSS code.

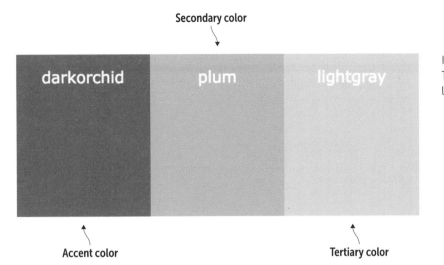

Secondary color

darkorchid plum lightgray

Accent color

Tertiary color

▶ Figure 10.2
The color scheme for my landing page

Building the Page

To construct your landing page, start with the skeleton code that I introduced in Chapter 1. From there, go section by section, adding text, HTML tags, and CSS properties.

The Initial Structure

To get started, take the basic page structure from Chapter 1 and add the tags, a placeholder image, and some placeholder text for each of the page's main sections.

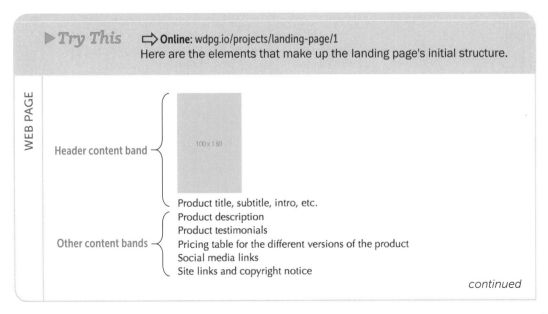

▶ *Try This*   ⇨ **Online:** wdpg.io/projects/landing-page/1
Here are the elements that make up the landing page's initial structure.

WEB PAGE

Header content band

100 x 150

Product title, subtitle, intro, etc.

Other content bands

Product description
Product testimonials
Pricing table for the different versions of the product
Social media links
Site links and copyright notice

continued

```
HTML

        <div class="header">
           <div class="header-image">
              <img src="http://placehold.it/100x150" alt="">
           </div>
           <div class="header-info">
              Product title, subtitle, intro, etc.
           </div>
        </div>
        <div class="description">
           Product description
        </div>
        <div class="testimonials">
           Product testimonials
        </div>
        <div class="product-versions">
           Pricing table for the different versions of the product
        </div>
        <div class="social">
           Social media links
        </div>
        <div class="footer">
           Site links and copyright notice
        </div>
```

Header content band

Description content band

Testimonials content band

Pricing table content band

Social media content band

Footer content band

Here are a few things to note about the HTML tags used in the initial structure:

- The page is divided into six sections: header, description, testimonials, pricing table, social media, and footer.

- Each section is embedded within a `<div></div>` block.

- Each `div` element is assigned a class, which enables you to apply CSS properties to everything within that section.

The Header

The header is probably the most important section of the landing page, because it's the first section that visitors see when they arrive. You want the header not only to have an impact, but also to start the job of selling your product. The project's header accomplishes these goals by including the following features:

- *Hero background image*—This image should be visually striking or should tell a story that's relevant to your product. Either way, be sure that the image doesn't interfere with the readability of the header text.

- *Product image*—This image should be a simple illustration or photo that enables the would-be buyer to see what the product looks like.

- *Product info*—At a minimum, this info should include the product name or title, a short (two or three sentences) introduction, and the price. I've also chosen to include a surtitle (which could be something like Available Now! or Special Offer!) and a subtitle.

- *Call-to-action button*—The user clicks this button to perform the action you want, such as buying, subscribing to, or downloading the product.

Because the header is so crucial to the success of a landing page, take it slow and build the header one feature at a time, beginning with the hero background.

The Hero Background Image

You may recall from Chapter 6 that a hero image is an eye-catching photo or illustration that takes up the entire width, and often the entire height, of the browser window when you first land on a page. The following example shows the header for my fictitious product with a hero background image applied.

▶ *Try This*   ⇨ **Online:** wdpg.io/projects/landing-page/2
This example shows a landing page header's hero background.

WEB PAGE

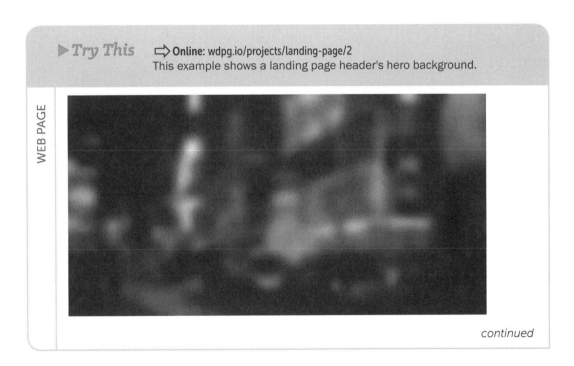

continued

CSS

```css
.header {
    background: url(/images/landing-page-header-bg.jpg);
    background-attachment: fixed;
    background-position: right center;
    background-size: cover;
    padding-bottom: 1em;
    width: 100vw;
    height: 100vh;
}
```

Prevent the hero image from scrolling with the content.

HTML

```html
<div class="header">
</div>
```

REMEMBER

I added the height: 100vh *definition to give the header some height, because it has no content. Later, after I add the header content, I'll take out that definition.*

This photo (which you'll barely recognize as a blurred image of a nighttime city scene) uses the standard code for a hero image that you learned in Chapter 6. I added the property background-attachment: fixed to prevent the image from scrolling with the rest of the page, which is a nice effect.

The Product Image

Next, add the photo or illustration that shows the user the product. This image should be a decent size, big enough to give the reader a good idea of what the product looks like but not so big that it overwhelms your hero background. Following is an example.

▶ *Try This* ⇨ **Online:** wdpg.io/projects/landing-page/3
This example adds the product image to the landing-page header.

WEB PAGE

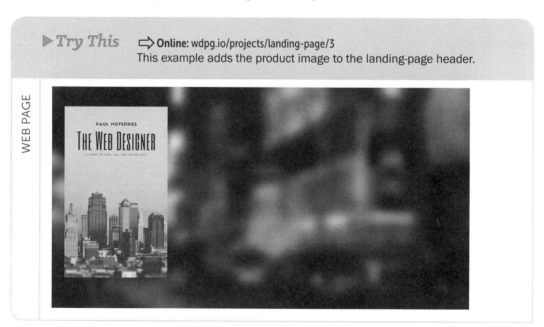

```
CSS     .header-image {
            float: left;
            width: 33%;
            margin-top: 3em;              The CSS code
            padding-right: 3em;           for the image
            text-align: right;
        }
```

```
HTML    <div class="header">
         <div class="header-image">
           <img src="/images/landing-page-book-cover.png"      The image
        alt="Front cover">                                     is added as
         </div>                                                a standard
        </div>                                                 HTML img
                                                               element.
```

The image is floated to the left and given some margins and padding to provide some separation from the rest of the content.

The Product Info

Now it's time to add the product info to the header. Again, this info needs to include at least the product title and a brief introduction, but feel free to add elements such as a surtitle and subtitle, as shown in the following example.

▶ *Try This*   ⇨ **Online:** wdpg.io/projects/landing-page/4
This example adds the product info to the landing-page header.

continued

CSS

```css
.header-info {
    float: right;
    width: 67%;
    margin-top: 4em;
    color: white;
}
```

The CSS code for the product info div

HTML

The info is added within a div element.

```html
<div class="header">
  <div class="header-image">
    <img src="/images/landing-page-book-cover.png" alt="Front
cover">
  </div>
  <div class="header-info">
    <div class="surtitle">Coming Soonish!</div>
    <h1 class="title">The Web Designer</h1>
    <h3 class="subtitle">
        A story of HTML, CSS, and the big city</h3>
    <p class="intro">
        She knew HTML. She knew CSS. But did she know love?
Read this destined-to-be-remaindered novel that <em>The New
York Times Book Review</em> described as &ldquo;reasonably
grammatical&rdquo; and the <em>Times Literary Supplement</em>
called &ldquo;bathroom-worthy.&rdquo;  Pre-order your paperback
copy now for just $14.99.
    </p>
  </div>
</div>
```

The `div` element that holds all the product info is floated to the right and given some margins. The various bits of product info—the surtitle, title, subtitle, and intro—appear in their own block-level elements. To save space, I haven't shown the CSS properties applied to these block-level elements, but they include styles such as margins and font sizes. (See the online version of the example for the complete code.)

The Call-to-Action Button

The final piece of the header puzzle is the call-to-action button that the reader can click to order, subscribe, download, or do whatever your preferred action is for the landing page. This button should be easy to find, so make it visible and bold, as shown in the following example.

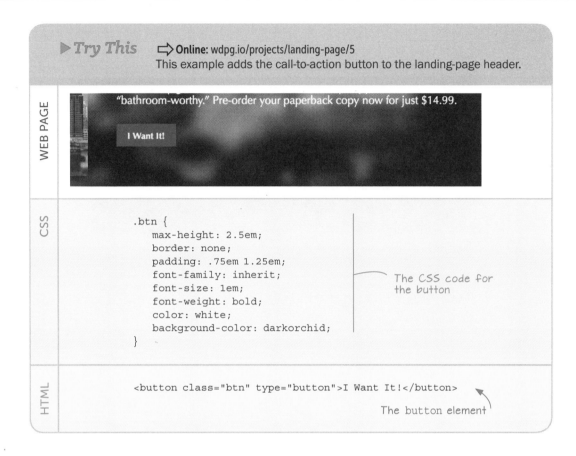

▶ **Try This**   ⇨ **Online:** wdpg.io/projects/landing-page/5
This example adds the call-to-action button to the landing-page header.

WEB PAGE

"bathroom-worthy." Pre-order your paperback copy now for just $14.99.

I Want It!

CSS

```css
.btn {
    max-height: 2.5em;
    border: none;
    padding: .75em 1.25em;
    font-family: inherit;
    font-size: 1em;
    font-weight: bold;
    color: white;
    background-color: darkorchid;
}
```

The CSS code for the button

HTML

```html
<button class="btn" type="button">I Want It!</button>
```

The button element

I use the `<button>` tag to create the button, and then I apply various styles to make the button stand out, including my accent color (`darkorchid`) as the background and bold white text as the foreground.

The Product Description

The next element of the landing page is a brief description of the product, which is your first chance to try to sell the user on your product or service. How you go about that depends on the product and on your comfort level when it comes to playing the huckster, but here are a few ideas:

- A simple paragraph that explains the product
- A bulleted list of the product's main features
- A paragraph or list that tells the user why the product is right for her
- A paragraph or list that briefly outlines a series of problems and explains how the product solves them

For my landing page, I went with a short recap of the book's plot, as shown in the following example.

▶ **Try This**   ⇨ **Online:** wdpg.io/projects/landing-page/6
This example shows the product description added to the landing page.

WEB PAGE

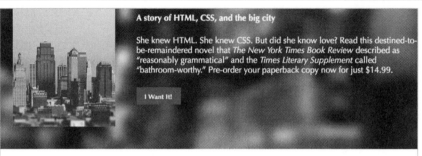

A story of HTML, CSS, and the big city

She knew HTML. She knew CSS. But did she know love? Read this destined-to-be-remaindered novel that *The New York Times Book Review* described as "reasonably grammatical" and the *Times Literary Supplement* called "bathroom-worthy." Pre-order your paperback copy now for just $14.99.

I Want It!

At High Falutin High, the arts high school in her home town, Daisy Fontana fell in love. Not with a boy, or even with a girl, for that matter, but with something altogether more interesting: web design. Instead of a BFF, she had CSS. Instead of singing and dancing with the other kids, she spent her time coding alone. But when she graduated and moved to the city to find a job, she knew everything about HTML, but nothing about life. Will the town eat her alive, or will she survive and rise to the top of the cutthroat world of coding websites? Daisy Fontana is a nerd heroine for our times, and *The Web Designer* tells her gripping tale.

CSS

```css
.description {
    width: 100%;
    padding: 1em 0;
    font-size: 1.25em;
    background-color: white;
}
```

The CSS code for the description class

HTML

```html
<div class="description">
At High Falutin High, the arts high school in her home town, Daisy
Fontana fell in love. Not with a boy, or even with a girl, for
that matter, but with something altogether more interesting: web
design. Instead of a BFF, she had CSS. Instead of singing and...
</div>
```

Setting Up the Content Bands

At this point in the construction of your landing page, you've run into a problem. In the preceding example, the text in the description extends across the entire width of the browser window, which makes the line lengths too long for comfortable reading. The solution is to structure the landing page by using horizontal bands of content that have two characteristics:

- A background color or image that extends across the entire browser window.
- Foreground content that's given a maximum width to retain readability. This content usually appears in the center of the browser window.

Depending on the width of the browser window and the maximum width you assign to the content block, however, that block takes up only part of the window width. The problem, then, is how to get the background to extend across the entire width of the window while restricting the content to some subset of that width.

The answer is to structure each content band with two `div` elements:

- An outer `div` element that spans the width of the browser window and is styled with the background color or image you want to use with the band

- A nested `div` element that contains the content, is given a maximum width, and is centered horizontally within the browser window

In the following example, I've applied the nested `div` (using a class named `container`) to both the header and the product description.

▶ *Try This* ⇨ **Online:** wdpg.io/projects/landing-page/7
This example shows the nested `div` element that will hold the content within each content band.

WEB PAGE

She knew HTML. She knew CSS. But did she know love? Read this destined-to-be-remaindered novel that *The New York Times Book Review* described as "reasonably grammatical" and the *Times Literary Supplement* called "bathroom-worthy." Pre-order your paperback copy now for just $14.99.

I Want It!

At High Falutin High, the arts high school in her home town, Daisy Fontana fell in love. Not with a boy, or even with a girl, for that matter, but with something altogether more interesting: web design. Instead of a BFF, she had CSS. Instead of singing and dancing with the other kids, she spent her time coding alone. But when she graduated and moved to the city to find a job, she knew everything about HTML, but nothing about life. Will the town eat her alive, or will she survive and rise to the top of the cutthroat world of coding websites? Daisy Fontana is a nerd heroine for our times, and *The Web Designer* tells her gripping tale.

continued

CSS

```css
.container {
    max-width: 800px;
    margin: 0 auto;
    clear: both;
}
```

The CSS code for the content container

```css
.container::after {
    content: "";
    display: block;
    clear: both;
}
```

This CSS enables the container to clear its own floats.

HTML

```html
<div class="header">
    <div class="container">
    ...
    </div>
</div>
...
<div class="description">
    <div class="container">
    ...
    </div>
</div>
```

The nested div elements that hold the band content

The container class does three things:

- It uses max-width to set a maximum width of 800 pixels for the content.

- It uses the margin: 0 auto shorthand to center the element horizontally. This declaration sets the top and bottom margins to 0 and the left and right margins to auto. The latter tells the web browser to set the margins automatically based on the element width. Because both left and right are set together, the browser parcels out the same margin size to each, thus centering the element.

- It uses clear: both to place the element after any floated elements that come before it in the document flow.

The container::after pseudo-element uses the clearfix trick that you learned about in Chapter 8, enabling the element to clear any floated elements that it contains and preventing the container from collapsing.

The Product Testimonials

It's always a good idea to add some third-party positivity to your landing page, such as glowing reviews from the media, favorable user ratings from another site, or positive feedback you've received directly from product testers or users. The following example shows my landing page with a few reviews added, as well as a related illustration.

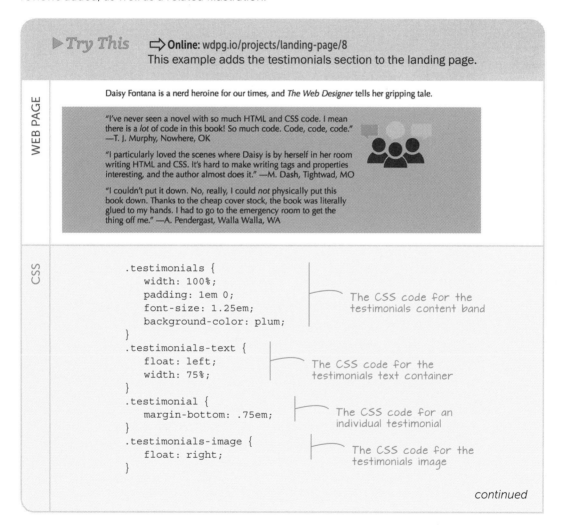

▶ *Try This*   ⇨ **Online:** wdpg.io/projects/landing-page/8
This example adds the testimonials section to the landing page.

WEB PAGE

Daisy Fontana is a nerd heroine for our times, and *The Web Designer* tells her gripping tale.

"I've never seen a novel with so much HTML and CSS code. I mean there is a *lot* of code in this book! So much code. Code, code, code."
—T. J. Murphy, Nowhere, OK

"I particularly loved the scenes where Daisy is by herself in her room writing HTML and CSS. It's hard to make writing tags and properties interesting, and the author almost does it." —M. Dash, Tightwad, MO

"I couldn't put it down. No, really, I could *not* physically put this book down. Thanks to the cheap cover stock, the book was literally glued to my hands. I had to go to the emergency room to get the thing off me." —A. Pendergast, Walla Walla, WA

CSS

```css
.testimonials {
    width: 100%;
    padding: 1em 0;
    font-size: 1.25em;
    background-color: plum;
}
.testimonials-text {
    float: left;
    width: 75%;
}
.testimonial {
    margin-bottom: .75em;
}
.testimonials-image {
    float: right;
}
```

The CSS code for the testimonials content band

The CSS code for the testimonials text container

The CSS code for an individual testimonial

The CSS code for the testimonials image

continued

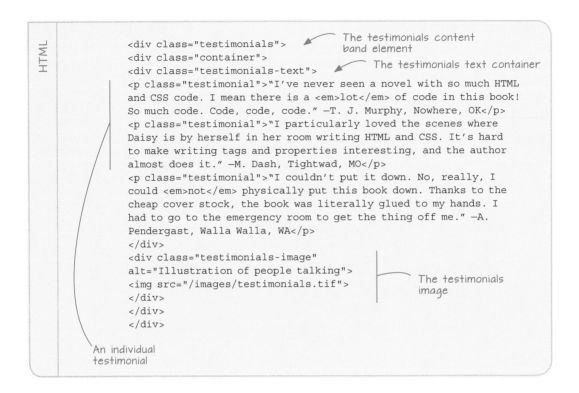

In this example, the content band is a `div` element with a class named `testimonials`, which is styled with a `plum` background color. Within the content container are a `testimonials-text` element that's floated left and a `testimonial-image` element that's floated right.

The Pricing Table

In your ideal world, someone visiting your landing page will be so enamored of your product or service that he'll click the call-to-action button that you've placed in the page header. Failing that, you need to give the person a second chance to purchase or subscribe. One of the best ways to do that is to create a *pricing table*, which outlines the versions of your product that are available and the pricing for each version. If your product doesn't have versions (or even if it does), you can create packages that include other items, such as a companion e-book, a newsletter subscription, a discount coupon for future purchases, and so on.

USE IT

On most landing pages, the preferred option is the one that returns the seller the highest net profit. You can use other criteria to determine which option you want to feature, such as most popular, most cost-effective, and best overall value.

The pricing table should have at least two versions or packages but generally not more than four. One of those versions should be your preferred version—the one you ideally want each person to choose. That version may be the one that nets you the most money, offers the best value to the user, or has some other advantage over the others. This preferred version should stick out from the others in some way. You could add a Best Value! heading over it, for example, or use one of the bold accent colors in your color scheme.

On my own landing page, I precede the pricing table with a content band that acts as a kind of title but is in fact an exhortation to the user to choose a package, as you can see in the following example.

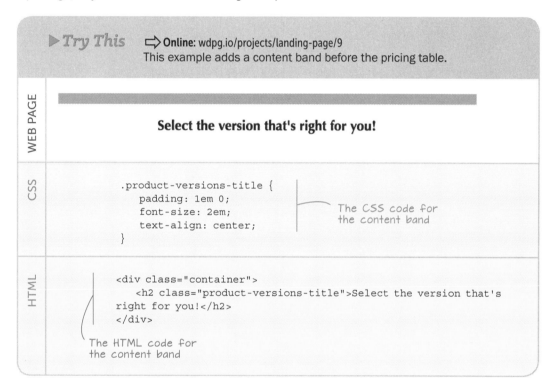

▶ *Try This* ⇨ **Online:** wdpg.io/projects/landing-page/9
This example adds a content band before the pricing table.

WEB PAGE

Select the version that's right for you!

CSS

```
.product-versions-title {
    padding: 1em 0;
    font-size: 2em;
    text-align: center;
}
```

The CSS code for the content band

HTML

```
<div class="container">
    <h2 class="product-versions-title">Select the version that's
right for you!</h2>
</div>
```

The HTML code for the content band

For the pricing table itself, the standard format is to place each version or package in a vertical column that tells the reader everything she needs to know: the title, price (if any), and features. Then you add a call-to-action button at the bottom of the column. The following example shows one column from the pricing table on my fictitious landing page.

▶ *Try This*   ⇨ **Online:** wdpg.io/projects/landing-page/10
This example adds the first column of the pricing table.

WEB PAGE

thing on me. —A. Pendergast, Walla Walla, WA

Select the version that's right for you!

eBook Version
$9.99
300-page PDF
Free ebook
Free newsletter subscription
10% off your next purchase
Order Now!

CSS

```css
.product-versions {
    padding: 1em 0;
    background-color: plum;}
.product-version {
    float: left;
    width: 33.33%;
    border: 1px solid gray;
    text-align: center;
    background-color: white;}
.version-title {
    padding: .75em 0;
    font-size: 1.5em;}
.version-price {
    padding: .75em 0;
    font-size: 2em;
    background-color: lightgray;}
.version-item {
    border-bottom: 1px solid gray;
    width: 100%;
    padding: .75em 0;
    font-size: 1.25em;}
.version-item:last-child {
    border-bottom: 0;}
.btn-plain {
    font-weight: normal;
    color: black;
    background-color: lightgray;}
```

HTML

The product version container

The content band

The content container

```
<div class="product-versions">
  <div class="container">
    <div class="product-version">
      <h3 class="version-title">eBook Version</h3>
      <h4 class="version-price">$9.99</h4>
      <div class="version-item">
        300-page PDF
      </div>
      <div class="version-item">
        Free ebook
      </div>
      <div class="version-item">
        Free newsletter subscription
      </div>
      <div class="version-item">
        10% off your next purchase
      </div>
      <div class="version-item">
        <button class="btn btn-plain" type="button">Order
Now!</button>
      </div>
    </div>
  </div>
</div>
```

The version title

The version price

The version items

Seven classes are used here, and this is what they do:

- product-versions—This outer div creates the content band. It's given a plum background.

- container—This class is the content div.

- product-version—This div creates the column for a single version or package. It's floated left and, because there are three columns, is given a 33.33 percent width.

- version-title—This div holds the title of the version or package.

- version-price—This div holds the price of the version or package. For most of the versions, the price is given a plain gray background.

REMEMBER

When you specify two classes on an element—as I do in the following example in the second h4 element—the web browser applies the properties of both classes to the element.

- `version-item`—This class holds the rest of the items in the version or package, with one `div` for each feature plus another at the bottom for the call-to-action button.

- `btn-plain`—This class is used for call-to-action buttons that you don't want to highlight. The text is given a normal weight; the text color reverts to black; and the background is set to light gray.

To complete the pricing table, you add the versions or packages, using the same styles as before, but styling your optimum version in a way that highlights it for the reader, as shown in the next example.

▶ *Try This*   ⇨ **Online:** wdpg.io/projects/landing-page/11
This example completes the pricing table, including one column that highlights a version for the reader.

WEB PAGE

eBook Version	Print Version	eBook+Print Bundle
$9.99	**$14.99**	**$19.99**
300-page PDF	300-page paperback	PDF *and* paperback versions
Free ebook	Free ebook	Free ebook
Free newsletter subscription	Free newsletter subscription	Free newsletter subscription
10% off your next purchase	10% off your next purchase	15% off your next purchase
Order Now!	Order Now!	**Order Now!**

CSS

```
.version-price-featured {
    color: white;
    background-color: darkorchid;
}
```

The CSS code for highlighting an item price

```
HTML          <div class="product-version">
                  <h3 class="version-title">Print Version</h3>
                  <h4 class="version-price">$14.99</h4>
                  <div class="version-item">
                      300-page paperback
                  </div>
                  <div class="version-item">
                      Free ebook
                  </div>
                  <div class="version-item">
                      Free newsletter subscription
                  </div>
                  <div class="version-item">
                      10% off your next purchase
                  </div>
                  <div class="version-item">
                      <button class="btn btn-plain" type="button">Order Now!</
              button>
                  </div>
              </div>
              <div class="product-version">
                  <h3 class="version-title">eBook+Print Bundle</h3>
                  <h4 class="version-price version-price-featured">$19.99</h4>
                  <div class="version-item">
                      PDF <em>and</em> paperback versions
                  </div>
                  <div class="version-item">
                      Free ebook
                  </div>
                  <div class="version-item">
                      Free newsletter subscription
                  </div>
                  <div class="version-item">
                      15% off your next purchase
                  </div>
                  <div class="version-item">
                      <button class="btn" type="button">Order Now!</button>
                  </div>
              </div>
```

The HTML code for the highlighted price

MASTER

If your CSS specifies two classes on an element, and those classes have one or more properties in common, the properties in the second class (that is, the class that appears later in the CSS file) take precedence.

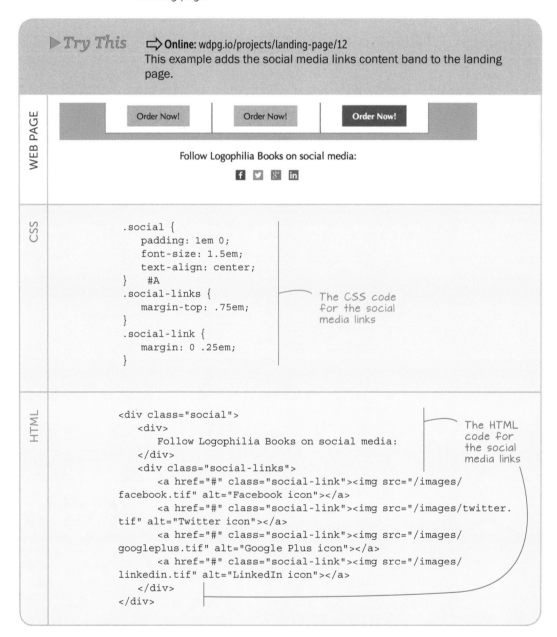
The Social Media Links

The next content band on the landing page is a collection of social media links, which appear centered on the page, with each social network's icon used as the link. The following example shows the links I set up for my landing page.

▶ *Try This* ⇨ **Online:** wdpg.io/projects/landing-page/12
This example adds the social media links content band to the landing page.

WEB PAGE

| Order Now! | Order Now! | **Order Now!** |

Follow Logophilia Books on social media:

CSS

```
.social {
    padding: 1em 0;
    font-size: 1.5em;
    text-align: center;
}    #A
.social-links {
    margin-top: .75em;
}
.social-link {
    margin: 0 .25em;
}
```

The CSS code for the social media links

HTML

```
<div class="social">
    <div>
        Follow Logophilia Books on social media:
    </div>
    <div class="social-links">
        <a href="#" class="social-link"><img src="/images/
facebook.tif" alt="Facebook icon"></a>
        <a href="#" class="social-link"><img src="/images/twitter.
tif" alt="Twitter icon"></a>
        <a href="#" class="social-link"><img src="/images/
googleplus.tif" alt="Google Plus icon"></a>
        <a href="#" class="social-link"><img src="/images/
linkedin.tif" alt="LinkedIn icon"></a>
    </div>
</div>
```

The HTML code for the social media links

Three classes are used here:

- `social`—This outer `div` creates the content band. It's given a `white` background, and the `text-align` property is set to `center`.
- `social-links`—This `div` creates the container for all the links.
- `social-link`—This class is used to style the individual links.

Note that you don't need a `container` element in this content band because the text and links are centered on the page.

The Page Footer

The final element of the landing page is the footer. As you can see in the following example, I used the footer to display a copyright notice and my contact information (which consists of my email address). Feel free to use the footer to add any other information you see fit, such as a "thank you for reading" message, a slogan or favorite epigram, or extra contact details.

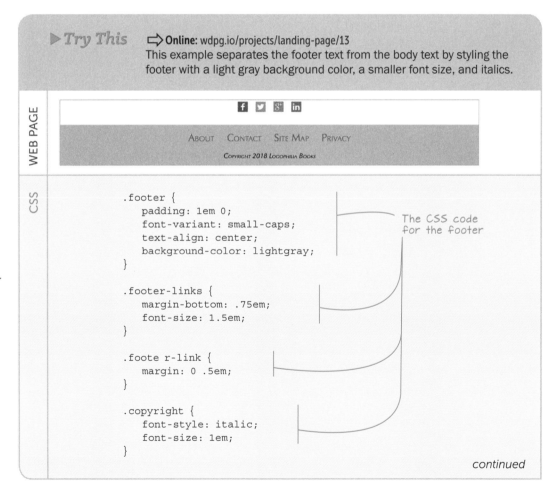

▶ **Try This** ⇨ **Online:** wdpg.io/projects/landing-page/13
This example separates the footer text from the body text by styling the footer with a light gray background color, a smaller font size, and italics.

WEB PAGE

CSS

```
.footer {
    padding: 1em 0;
    font-variant: small-caps;
    text-align: center;
    background-color: lightgray;
}

.footer-links {
    margin-bottom: .75em;
    font-size: 1.5em;
}

.foote r-link {
    margin: 0 .5em;
}

.copyright {
    font-style: italic;
    font-size: 1em;
}
```

The CSS code for the footer

continued

HTML

```html
<div class="footer">
    <div class="footer-links">
        <a href="#" class="footer-link">About</a>
        <a href="#" class="footer-link">Contact</a>
        <a href="#" class="footer-link">Site Map</a>
        <a href="#" class="footer-link">Privacy</a>
    </div>
    <div class="copyright">
        Copyright 2018 Logophilia Books
    </div>
</div>
```

The HTML code for the footer

Four classes are used here:

- footer—This outer div creates the content band. It's given a lightgray background, and the text-align property is set to center.

- footer-links—This div creates the container for all the footer links. Note that each link URL points to #, which is a placeholder that, when clicked, takes the user to the top of the page. In a production landing page, you'd replace each # with the URL of an file on your site.

- footer-link—This class styles the individual footer links.

- copyright—This class styles the copyright notice.

Again, you don't need a container element in this band because the content is already centered on the page.

From Here

Considering that you're only halfway through the book, I have to say that the final version of the landing page (mine is shown in Figure 10.3) is a fine-looking web page. It's easy to read, easy to understand, and isn't boring. (If you're as pleased with your landing page as I think you ought to be and are looking forward to getting your code online, check out Appendix A to get the details.)

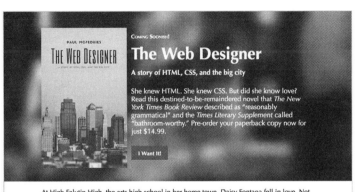

▶ Figure 10.3
The landing home page for my book

If there's a problem with the landing page, it's that we had to use lots of padding and margin fiddling (among other CSS hacks) to get things to line up somewhat neatly. That fussing happened because we're not using a true page layout. With our elements floated here and there we're almost in layout land, but not quite. But that's no problem because page layouts are the topic of Part 3, so you'll soon learn all you need to know to create rock-solid layouts for your landing pages and all your other pages.

Summary

- Sketch out the page you want to build.
- Choose the typeface for the text.
- Choose a color scheme.
- Build the initial page structure: the barebones HTML tags and the global CSS properties.
- Fill in and style each section one by one: header, description, testimonials, pricing table, social media links, and footer.

Part 3

Laying Out a Web Page

A big part of designing web pages is the ability to lay out the page elements in a way that's not only pleasing to the eye, but also easy to understand and navigate. That sounds like a tall order, I'm sure, but the chapters here in Part 3 will help you do that. You start with a look at some page layout basics in Chapter 11, including learning the important HTML5 semantic page elements such as `<header>` and `<article>`. From there, Chapter 12 takes you on a tour of one of the hottest and most powerful modern page layout technologies: flexbox.

Modern web design is all about responsive web design that enables pages to look good and work well on any size screen, and that's the subject of Chapters 13 and 14. Finally, you put all this newfound page layout know-how to work in Chapter 15 as you build a sophisticated photo-gallery page.

Learning Page Layout Basics

 This chapter covers

- Understanding web page layout types, technologies, and strategies
- Getting to know the HTML5 semantic page layout elements
- Examining modern, real-world page layouts

The first half of this book served to lay down a solid foundation for creating web pages. When you got past the basics of HTML and CSS, you learned about text tags, fonts, colors, CSS classes, the box model, floating and positioning elements, and images and other media. So congratulations are in order: You've graduated from being able merely to *build* web pages to being able to *design* them.

Alas, you'll have little time to bask in your newfound glory, because this chapter dives right into the next stage of web design. Here, you take a step back from the "trees" of HTML tags and CSS properties to examine the "forest" of page layout. This refers to the overall structure and organization of a web page, and if that sounds trivial or unimportant, consider this: Every single person who visits your page will, consciously or not, be asking a bunch of questions. What is the page about? Am I interested? Does this page have the information I'm looking for? If so, where can I find it?

All those questions are—or, at least, *should* be—answerable by glancing at your layout. If your structure is wonky or your organization is haphazard, I guarantee you that most people will move on after a few seconds. Avoiding that fate means taking a bit of time to plan and code a layout that shows your content in its best, visitor-friendliest light.

The Holy-Grail Layout

To help you learn the various web page layout techniques, I'm going to use a version of the so-called *holy-grail* layout that consists of the following parts:

- A header at the top of the page

- A navigation bar below the header

- Two full-height columns consisting of the main page content in the left column and a sidebar of related content in the right (or sometimes the left) column

- A footer at the bottom of the page

USE IT

The holy-grail layout is useful for blog posts, articles, essays, how-tos, and similar content-focused pages.

There are a number of variations on this theme, depending on how strictly you want to define the layout. You may want three columns between the navigation bar and the footer instead of two, for example. Another common variation is to have the footer appear at the bottom of the browser window if the content doesn't extend that far.

Figure 11.1 shows a schematic of the layout you're going to build.

▶ Figure 11.1
A version of the holy-grail
web page layout

To build this layout, you need to understand the available page layout methods.

Understanding Web Page Layout Methods

As I mentioned in Chapter 7, by default the web browser lays out HTML content with the blocks stacked in the order in which they appear in the source document. Within each block, the text runs left to right (for languages that read that way). For the simplest web pages (such as the personal home page you built in Chapter 5), that default layout is fine, but at this point in your web-design career, you're already way beyond that. At this level, you need to know how to break out of that default layout to gain some control of how web content appears on the page.

Fortunately, you have no shortage of ways to do that, but you need to know about three main methods:

- *Floats*—As you learned in Chapter 8, you can use the `float` property to break an element out of the normal page flow and send it to the left or right inside its parent container. By doing this with multiple items, you can organize content into columns and other sophisticated page layouts. See "Creating Page Layouts with Floats" later in this chapter.

- *Inline blocks*—The `display: inline-block` declaration takes a block-level element out of the default vertical page flow and adds it to the horizontal (usually, left-to-right) flow of the other inline elements. This creates many interesting page layout opportunities, and you learn about some of them in "Creating Page Layouts with Inline Blocks" later in this chapter.

- *Flexbox*—This powerful but underused CSS module enables you to organize page content in containers that can wrap, grow, and shrink in flexible ways. See Chapter 12 to learn how it works.

Which one should you use? I recommend that you *not* use floats or inline blocks. I do recommend that you learn how floats and inline blocks work for layout—which is why I talk about them in this chapter—because you need to understand the techniques used on so many legacy sites, and you may find these techniques handy for small page components. That leaves flexbox, which you learn about in Chapter 12 and put to good use in Chapter 15's project.

> *Flexbox is certainly something you should take seriously. It paves the way for the modern style of laying out content, and it's not going away anytime soon. It has emerged as a new standard. So, with outstretched arms, embrace it!* —Ohans Emmanuel

Learning the HTML5 Semantic Page Elements

The last piece of the page layout puzzle you need to know before getting started is the collection of HTML5 elements that enable you to create semantic layouts. Why is this important? Because every page you upload to the web will be read and parsed in some way by automated processes, such as search-engine crawlers and screen readers for the disabled. If your page is nothing but a collection of anonymous `<div>` and `<span>` tags, that software will be less likely to analyze the page to find the most important content.

To help you solve that problem, HTML5 offers a collection of semantic elements that you can use to specify the type of content contained in each area of your page. There are quite a few of these elements, but the following seven are the most important:

```
<header>
<nav>
<main>
<article>
<section>
<aside>
<footer>
```

The next few sections explain each of these elements.

Proper semantics . . . increase accessibility, as assistive technologies such as screen readers can better interpret the meaning of our content. —Anna Monus

<header>

You use the `header` element to define a page area that contains introductory content. This content is most often the site title (which should be marked up with a heading element, such as `h1`), but it can also include things such as a site logo. Here's an example:

```
<body>
    <header>
        <img src="logo.tif" alt="Semantics Depot logo">
        <h1>Semantics Depot</h1>
    </header>
    etc.
</body>
```

<nav>

You use the `nav` element to define a page area that contains navigation content, such as links to other sections of the site or a search box. This element can appear anywhere on the page but typically appears right after the page's main `header` element:

```
<body>
    <header>
        <img src="logo.tif" alt="Semantics Depot logo">
        <h1>Semantics Depot</h1>
    </header>
    <nav>
        <a href="#">Home</a>
        <a href="#">Blog</a>
        <a href="#">Contact</a>
        <a href="#">About Us</a>
    </nav>
    etc.
</body>
```

<main>

The main element is used as a container for the content that's unique to the current page. Whereas the `header`, `nav`, `aside`, and `footer` elements are often common to all or most of the pages in the site, the `main` element is meant to mark up the content that's unique. The `main` element typically appears after the `header` and `nav` elements:

```
<body>
    <header>
        ...
```

```
    </header>
    <nav>
        …
    </nav>
    <main>
        Unique content goes here
    </main>
    etc.
</body>
```

<article>

The `article` element is used to mark up a complete, self-contained composition. The model here is the newspaper or magazine article, but this element can also apply to a blog entry, a forum post, or an essay. Most pages have a single `article` element nested within the `main` element:

```
<body>
    <header>
        …
    </header>
    <nav>
        …
    </nav>
    <main>
        <article>
            Article content goes here
        </article>
    </main>
    etc.
</body>
```

It's perfectly acceptable, however, to have multiple `article` elements within a single `main` element. Note, too, that it's okay to nest a `header` element inside an `article` element if doing so is semantically appropriate:

```
<article>
    <header>
        <h2>Isn't It Semantic?</h2>
        <p>By Paul McFedries</p>
    </header>
    Article content goes here
</article>
```

<section>

You use the `section` element to surround any part of a page that you'd want to see in an outline of the page. That is, if some part of the page consists of a heading element (`h1` through `h6`) followed by some text, you'd surround the heading and its text with `<section>` tags. This typically happens within an `article` element, like so:

```
<article>
    <section>
        <h3>Introduction</h3>
        Introduction text
    </section>
    <section>
```

```
        <h3>Argument</h3>
        Argument text
    </section>
    <section>
        <h3>Summary</h3>
        Summary text
    </section>
</article>
```

<aside>

You use the `aside` element to mark up a page area that isn't directly related to the page's unique content. A typical example is a sidebar that contains the latest site news, a Twitter feed, and so on. The `aside` element can appear anywhere within the `main` element (and, indeed, can appear multiple times on the page), but it's a best practice to have the `aside` appear after the page's `article` element, as shown here:

```
<body>
    <header>
        ...
    </header>
    <nav>
        ...
    </nav>
    <main>
        <article>
            ...
        </article>
        <aside>
            ...
        </aside>
    </main>
    etc.
</body>
```

<footer>

You use the `footer` element to define a page area that contains closing content, such as a copyright notice, address, and contact information.

Here's the semantic layout of a typical HTML5 page:

```
<body>
    <header>
        ...
    </header>
    <nav>
        ...
    </nav>
    <main>
        <article>
            <section>
                ...
            </section>
            <section>
                ...
            </section>
            <aside>
```

```
                        ...
                </aside>
            </article>
        </main>
        <footer>
                ...
        </footer>
    </body>
```

The Holy-Grail Layout, Revisited

Earlier, you learned about the holy-grail layout, which I can reintroduce within the context of the HTML5 semantic page elements. Figure 11.2 shows the same schematic that you saw in Figure 11.1, but with HTML5 semantic layout tags identifying each part.

▶ Figure 11.2
The holy-grail web page layout with HTML5 semantic tags

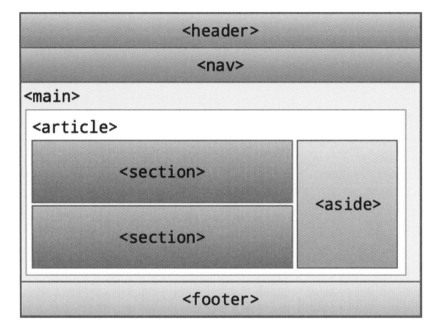

Here's the bare-bones HTML code for the layout:

```
<header>
    <img src="logo.tif" alt="Our logo">
    <h1>Site Title</h1>
</header>
<nav>
    <ul>
        <li>Item 1</li>
        etc.
    </ul>
</nav>
<main>
    <article>
        <section>
            <h2>Article Title</h2>
```

```
            <p>Article paragraph</p>
            etc.
        </section>
        <aside>
            <p>Sidebar paragraph</p>
            etc.
        </aside>
    </article>
</main>
<footer>
    <p>Footer paragraph</p>
    etc.
</footer>
```

Creating Page Layouts with Floats

I'm simplifying somewhat, but building a page layout with floating elements consists of repeating the following three steps:

1 Let the elements flow in the default manner.

2 When you need two or more elements to appear beside each other, float them (usually to the left).

3 When you want to resume the default page flow, clear the floats.

If you look at the source code for any page that has side-by-side content or content arranged in columns, most of the time that site used floated elements to achieve the effect. That said, floats are losing favor with web designers who yearn for a more straightforward and solid approach to layout. That approach will one day be flexbox combined with a new technology called CSS Grid, but until that day comes, you should be familiar with float-based layouts because they're still used so often.

LEARN

To get up to speed with CSS Grid basics, see the tutorial "Getting Started with CSS Grid" on the Web Design Playground.
⇨ Online: **wdpg.io/grid**

Lesson 11.1: **Creating the Holy Grail Layout with Floats**
Covers: Layout with the `float` property

⇨ **Online:** wdpg.io/11-1-0

The holy grail includes three instances of side-by-side content:

- In the header, you usually want a site title beside the site logo.

- In the navigation bar, you usually want the navigation items to appear in a row.

- The sidebar must appear to the right of the main content.

All these instances require the use of the `float` property to get the elements out of the default page flow and rendered beside each other.

Begin with the header, as shown in the following example.

▶ *Example*   ⇨ **Online:** wdpg.io/11-1-1
This example shows you how to use `float` *to get the header logo and title side by side.*

WEB PAGE

| YOUR LOGO HERE | **Site Title** |

CSS

```
header {
    border: 1px solid black;
    padding: .25em 0;
}
header img {                    Float the img element to the left.
    float: left;
    padding-left: 1em;
}
h1 {                            Float the h1 element to the left.
    float: left;
    padding-left: .5em;
}
.self-clear::after {
    content: "";
    display: block;             Clearfix to prevent the
    clear: both;                header from collapsing.
}
```

HTML

```
<header class="self-clear">
    <img src="/images/your-logo-here.tif" alt="Our logo">
    <h1>Site Title</h1>
</header>
```

REMEMBER

I'm using type selectors (such as header img*) here to make the code as simple as possible. In practice, it's usually better to assign classes to each element and then select the classes in your CSS.*

As you can see, both the `img` element and the `h1` element are assigned `float: left`, which places them beside each other on the left edge of the header element. Because these elements are out of the default page flow, you'll usually have to adjust the padding or margins to get them placed where you want them, as I've done in the example.

Now float the navigation bar's items, as shown in the following example.

▶*Example* ⇨ **Online:** wdpg.io/11-1-2

This example shows you how to use `float` *to get the navigation bar items side by side.*

WEB PAGE

| Home | Item | Item | Item |

CSS

```
nav {
    border: 1px solid black;
    padding: .5em;
}
nav ul {
    list-style-type: none;
}
nav li {                    ← Float the li elements to the left.
    float: left;
    padding-right: 1.5em;
}
```

HTML

```
<nav class="self-clear">
    <ul>
        <li>Home</li>
        <li>Item</li>
        <li>Item</li>
        <li>Item</li>
    </ul>
</nav>
```

In this case, the `li` elements are assigned `float: left`, which places them beside each other on the left edge of the `nav` element. Again, I've used padding to adjust the placement of the elements.

Next, float the `main` element's `<article>` and `<aside>` tags to create the two-column content layout. The following example shows how it's done.

▶ **Example**   ⇨ **Online:** wdpg.io/11-1-3
This example shows you how to use `float` *to get the* `article` *and* `aside` *elements side by side in a two-column layout.*

WEB PAGE

Article Title

Article paragraph 1

Article paragraph 2

Sidebar Title

Sidebar paragraph

CSS

```css
article {                    ┌─ Float the article element to the left.
    float: left;
    width: 75%;          ┌─ Set the width of the article element.
    border: 1px solid black;
}
aside {                      ┌─ Float the aside element to the left.
    float: left;
    width: 25%;          ┌─ Set the width of the aside element.
    border: 1px solid black;
}
```

HTML

```html
<main>
    <article>
        <h2>Article Title</h2>
        <p>Article paragraph 1</p>
        <p>Article paragraph 2</p>
    </article>
    <aside>
        <h3>Sidebar Title</h3>
        <p>Sidebar paragraph</p>
    </aside>
</main>
```

In this case, both the `article` element and the `aside` element are assigned `float: left`, which places them beside each other on the left side of the `main` element. (You could float the `aside` element to the right to get the same layout.) You also need to assign a `width` value to each element to set the size of your columns.

The width of your columns depends on what you'll be using them for. In general, if one of the columns is a sidebar, it shouldn't take up much more than 25 percent of the available width. Note, too, that if you've applied `box-sizing: border-box`, your column percentages can add up to 100 to fill the width of the main element.

Note, too, that the bottom borders of the two columns don't line up because, in the absence of a CSS `height` declaration, the browser assigns a height to an element based on the height of its contents. This problem is common with floated columns, but I'll show you a workaround after the next example.

Finally, you're ready to add the `footer` element, as shown in the example that follows.

PLAY

How would you modify this layout to display three content columns: a sidebar to the left and to the right of the `article` element? ⇨ Online: wdpg.io/11-1-7

▶ *Example*   ⇨ **Online:** wdpg.io/11-1-4

This example shows adding the `footer` to the bottom of the page by clearing the floated columns. Colors have been added to all the elements, but most aren't shown in the code.

WEB PAGE

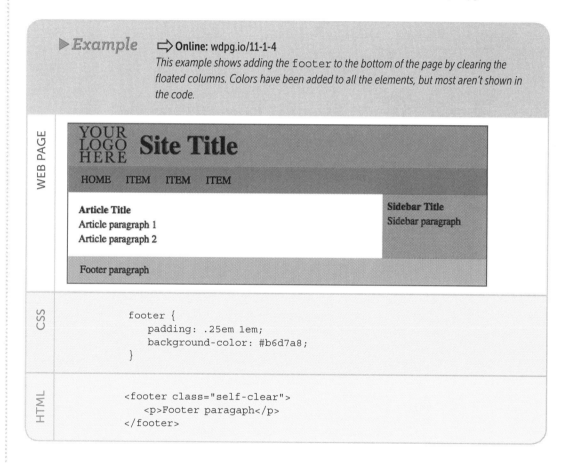

CSS

```css
footer {
    padding: .25em 1em;
    background-color: #b6d7a8;
}
```

HTML

```html
<footer class="self-clear">
    <p>Footer paragaph</p>
</footer>
```

Note, too, that in this example the `article` and `aside` columns are the same height. How did I do that? I faked it by using a technique called *faux columns*. Here's how it works:

1 Put a wrapper element around both the `article` and the `aside` elements.

   In this example, the `main` element can serve as the wrapper.

PLAY

How would you modify this layout to display the sidebar on the left instead of the right? ⇨ Online: wdpg.io/11-1-6

2 Assign the same background color to the wrapper and the `aside` element.

In the example, I assigned the color #b6d7a8 to both.

3 Assign a different background color to the `article` element.

In the example, I assigned white to the article background.

Because the wrapper and the `aside` use the same background color, the sidebar appears to reach all the way down to the footer. Here's a skeleton version of the code:

```
<main class="self-clear">
    <article>
    </article>
    <aside>
    </aside>
</main>
<footer class="self-clear">
</footer>
<style>
    main, aside {
        background-color: #b4a7d6;
    }
    article {
        background-color: white;
    }
    .self-clear {
        content: "";
        display: block;
        clear: both;
    }
</style>
```

Using floats to lay out web page content is an old, common CSS trick. As you saw in this section, however, it has some problems. You must remember to clear your floats when needed, for example; margins tend to collapse; and you often have to resort to kludgy tricks such as faux columns to make things look good. You can solve some of these problems by using inline blocks, which I turn to in the next section.

Creating Page Layouts with Inline Blocks

Building a page layout with inline block elements is similar to using floats:

1 Let the page elements flow in the default manner.

2 When you need two or more elements to appear beside each other, display them as inline blocks.

Notice that one of the main advantages of using inline blocks is that you don't have to explicitly clear elements.

Lesson 11.2:   **_Creating the Holy-Grail Layout with Inline Blocks_**
Covers: Layout with the `inline-block` property

⇨ **Online:** wdpg.io/11-2-0

As before, the holy grail includes three instances in which you need content side by side: the header, the navigation bar, and the content columns. All these instances require the use of the `display: inline-block` declaration to get the elements out of the default page flow and rendered beside each other. By default, inline blocks are displayed left to right (or according to the default inline orientation), so they're similar to declaring `float: left`.

I begin at the beginning with the header, as shown in the following example.

REMEMBER

I'm using type selectors (such as `header img`) *here to make the code as simple as possible. In practice, it's usually better to assign classes to each element and then select the classes in your CSS.*

▶ *Example*   ⇨ **Online:** wdpg.io/11-2-1

This example shows you how to use inline blocks to get the header logo and title side by side.

WEB PAGE

YOUR
LOGO
HERE **Site Title**

CSS

```css
header {
    border: 1px solid black;
    padding: .5em 0 .1em 1em;
}
h1 {
    display: inline-block;      ← Display the h1 element
    padding-left: .5em;           as an inline block.
    font-size: 2.5em;
}
```

HTML

```html
<header>
    <img src="/images/your-logo-here.tif" alt="Our logo">
    <h1>Site Title</h1>
</header>
```

The `img` element is an inline block by default, and I've declared the h1 element with `display: inline-block`, which places these two elements beside each other from left to right.

Now convert the navigation bar's items to inline blocks, as shown in the following example.

▶ *Example*   ⇨ **Online:** wdpg.io/11-2-2

This example shows you how to use inline blocks to get the navigation-bar items side by side.

WEB PAGE

> **Home   Item   Item   Item**

CSS

```
nav {
    padding: .5em;
    border: 1px solid black;
}
nav ul {
    list-style-type: none;
    padding-left: .5em;
}
nav li {
    display: inline-block;        Display the li elements
    padding-right: 1.5em;         as inline blocks.
}
```

HTML

```
<nav>
    <ul>
        <li>Home</li>
        <li>Item</li>
        <li>Item</li>
        <li>Item</li>
    </ul>
</nav>
```

In this case, the `li` elements are declared `display: inline-block`, which places them beside each other on the left edge of the nav element.

Next, convert the `main` element's `<article>` and `<aside>` tags to inline blocks, which gives you the two-column content layout. The following example shows how it's done.

▶ Example   ⇨ **Online:** wdpg.io/11-2-3
This example shows you how to use inline blocks to get the article *and* aside
elements side by side in a two-column layout.

WEB PAGE

Article Title

Article paragraph 1

Article paragraph 2

Sidebar Title

Sidebar paragraph

CSS

```
article {
    display: inline-block;          Display the article
    width: 75%;                     element as an inline block.
    border: 1px solid black;
}
aside {                             Display the aside element
    display: inline-block;          as an inline block.
    vertical-align: top;
    width: 25%;                     Align the aside element
    border: 1px solid black;        text with the top.
}
```

HTML

```
<main>
    <article>
        <h2>Article Title</h2>
        <p>Article paragraph 1</p>
        <p>Article paragraph 2</p>
    </article><aside>                No whitespace between
        <h3>Sidebar Title</h3>       the column elements
        <p>Sidebar paragraph</p>
    </aside>
</main>
```

In this case, both the article element and the aside element are
assigned display: inline-block, which places them beside each other
on the left side of the main element. You also need to assign a width value
to each element to set the size of your columns.

Notice, too, that in the HTML code, I crammed the </article> end tag
and the <aside> start tag together so that there's no whitespace between
them. This is crucial when working with inline blocks because otherwise,
the browser will add a bit of space when it renders the elements, which can
mess up your width calculations.

You've no doubt noticed that as with floats, the bottom borders of the two columns don't line up. You'll use the same workaround to fix that problem. Finally, add the `footer` element, as shown in the example that follows.

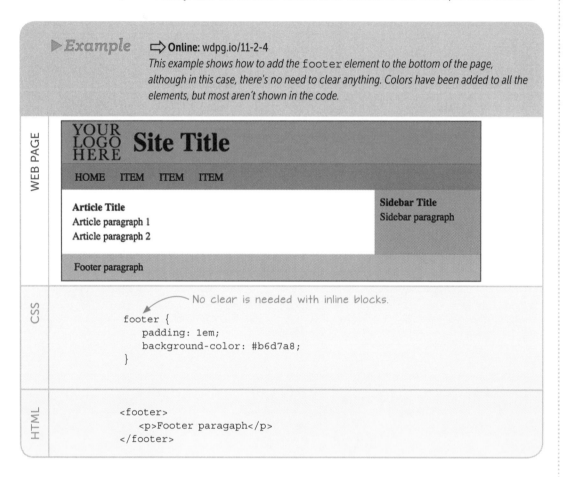

▶*Example* ⇨ **Online:** wdpg.io/11-2-4

This example shows how to add the `footer` element to the bottom of the page, although in this case, there's no need to clear anything. Colors have been added to all the elements, but most aren't shown in the code.

WEB PAGE

YOUR
LOGO
HERE **Site Title**

HOME   ITEM   ITEM   ITEM

Article Title
Article paragraph 1
Article paragraph 2

Sidebar Title
Sidebar paragraph

Footer paragraph

CSS

No clear is needed with inline blocks.

```css
footer {
    padding: 1em;
    background-color: #b6d7a8;
}
```

HTML

```html
<footer>
    <p>Footer paragaph</p>
</footer>
```

PLAY

How would you modify this layout to display the sidebar on the left instead of the right? ⇨ Online: wdpg.io/11-2-6

As I did with the floated layout, I made the `article` and `aside` columns appear to be the same height by using faux columns. (Note that these faux columns work properly only as long as the `article` element is taller than the `aside` element.)

Using inline blocks to lay out web page content isn't common despite the ease with which you can create fairly sophisticated layouts. Inline blocks have their drawbacks, of course. You have to watch your vertical alignment; you often have to ensure that there's no whitespace between the blocks; and you can't send elements to the right side of the parent as you can with `float: right`. To solve these problems and gain extra power over your layouts, you need to shun these old technologies in favor of the newest layout kid on the block: flexbox. You learn everything you need to know in Chapter 12.

Summary

- You can make your pages more semantic by using the HTML5 page layout tags: `<header>`, `<nav>`, `<main>`, `<article>`, `<section>`, `<aside>`, and `<footer>`.

- To use a float-based layout, let the elements flow in the default manner; then, when you need two or more elements to appear beside each other, float them (usually to the left). Remember that when you want to resume the default page flow, clear the floats.

- To use an inline block-based layout, let the page elements flow in the default manner; then, when you need two or more elements to appear beside each other, display them as inline blocks.

PLAY

How would you modify this layout to display three content columns: a sidebar to the left and to the right of the `article` *element?* ⇨ Online: wdpg.io/11-2-7

Chapter 12

Creating Page Layouts with Flexbox

Flexbox is the first CSS layout technique that works for the modern web. —Paddi MacDonnell

This chapter covers

- Understanding how flexbox works
- Learning the techniques for working with flexbox containers and items
- Putting flexbox to good use with real-world ideas
- Building the holy grail layout with flexbox

In Chapter 11, you saw that floats and inline blocks can get the job done, but not without running into problems, quirks, and workarounds such as clearing floats, creating faux columns, and avoiding whitespace. Even with all that, these layout strategies can't accomplish one of the features of the holy-grail layout: displaying the footer at the bottom of the screen if the page content doesn't fill the screen height.

This chapter's layout strategy prevents all these quirks, solves the footer problem, and has the fresh-faced appeal of a modern technology. I'm talking about flexbox, and before you can start using it for layout, you need to understand what it is and how it works. The next few sections explain everything you need to know.

Understanding Flexbox

Flexbox is the welcome shorthand for this method's cumbersome official moniker: Flexible Box Layout Module. The underlying principle behind flexbox is to provide a way around the rigid, cumbersome way that the browser handles blocks of content. The default is to stack them. Consider the following collection of `div` elements:

```
<div class="container">
    <div class="item itemA">A</div>
    <div class="item itemB">B</div>
    <div class="item itemC">C</div>
    <div class="item itemD">D</div>
    <div class="item itemE">E</div>
    <div class="item itemF">F</div>
</div>
```

Not shown here are the classes I've applied to give each item element a unique background color, and Figure 12.1 shows the results. As you can see, the `div` elements are stacked and extend the width of the browser window.

▶ Figure 12.1
The default browser layout of the `div` elements

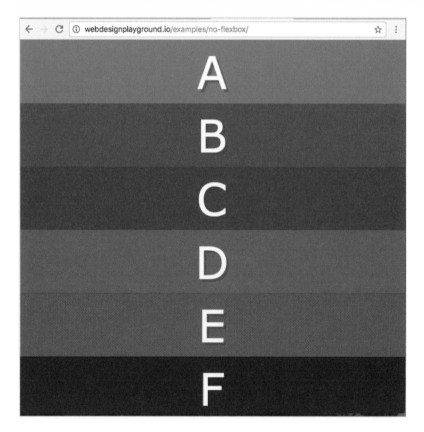

Even if you break out of this default flow with floats or inline blocks, the uncomfortable sense remains that the browser is still in charge and is fitting your blocks where *it* thinks they should go. Yes, you can tame the browser somewhat by styling your floats and inline blocks just so, but there's a brittleness to these tweaks. Try to imagine what happens to the float and inline-block holy-grail layouts if the sidebar text is longer than the article text. (Hint: It's not pretty.)

Flexbox rides to the rescue by offering simple but extremely powerful methods for laying out, distributing, aligning, sizing, and even ordering the child elements in a parent container. The *flex* part of the name comes from one of this technology's main tenets: The child items in a container should be able to change dimensions (width *and* height) by growing to fill in empty space if there's too much of it or by shrinking to allow for a reduction in space. This happens whether the amount of content changes or the size of the screen changes (such as by maximizing a window or by changing a device's screen orientation).

So flexbox is perfect, then? No, it's not. It has two main drawbacks:

- Its inherit flexibility means that it sometimes behaves in ways that appear nonsensical. It can be maddening at first, but when you've used it a few times, you begin to see why flexbox behaves the way it does.

- It's not suitable for large-scale layouts. Flexbox works wonderfully for components of a page—such as a header or sidebar—and is fine for small-scale layouts (such as the holy-grail practice layout). But big, complex projects are almost always too much for flexbox to handle. (If you have the time, wait for CSS Grid Layout to have sufficient browser support.)

When you work with flexbox, you work with two kinds of page objects: containers and items. A *flex container* is any type of parent block element— div, p, any of the HTML semantic page elements you learned in Chapter 11, even the body element—that surrounds one or more elements. These child elements are called *flex items*.

Okay, that's enough theory. It's time to start learning how flexbox works.

Working with Flexbox Containers

Before you can do anything with flexbox, you need to decide which block-level element will be the flex container. When you've done that, you convert that element to a container with a single CSS declaration: display: flex. The following rule turns the header element into a flex container:

```
header {
    display: flex;
}
```

LEARN

To learn CSS Grid basics now, see my tutorial "Getting Started with CSS Grid" on the Web Design Playground.
⇨ Online: wdpg.io/grid

The container's child elements automatically become flex items; no extra rules or declarations or code are required. From there, you can start customizing your flex container and its items to suit the task at hand.

I find that the best way to learn about and use flexbox is to ask yourself a series of questions—one set for containers and another for items. Here are the container questions:

- In which direction do you want the container's items to run?
- How do you want the items arranged along the main axis?
- How do you want the items arranged along the cross axis?
- Do you want the items to wrap?
- How do you want multiple lines arranged along the cross axis?

(Don't worry if you're not sure what I mean by *main axis* and *cross axis*. All will be revealed in the next section.) The next few sections ask and show you the possible answers to each of these questions.

In which direction do you want the container to run?

The first thing that's flexible about flexbox is that it doesn't dictate one and only one direction for the container's items. Although the browser's default layout rigidly enforces a vertical direction, and although floats and inline blocks work only horizontally, flexbox is happy to go either way. With flexbox, *you* decide.

Perhaps the most important flexbox concept to grasp right from the get-go is the notion that flexbox containers always have two axes:

- *Main*—The axis that runs in the same direction as the container's items
- *Cross*—The axis that runs perpendicular to the main axis (the cross axis is also called the *secondary axis*)

You determine the main-axis direction when you set the `flex-direction` property on a container:

```
container {
    display: flex;
    flex-direction: row|row-reverse|column|column-reverse;
}
```

- `row`—Sets the main axis to horizontal, with items running from left to right (the default)
- `row-reverse`—Sets the main axis to horizontal, with items running from right to left
- `column`—Sets the main axis to vertical, with items running from top to bottom
- `column-reverse`—Sets the main axis to vertical, with items running from bottom to top

Using the `div` elements shown in Figure 12.1 earlier in this chapter, here's how you'd turn the parent `div` into a flex container by using the right-to-left (`row`) direction:

```
.container {
    display: flex;
    flex-direction: row;
}
```

Figure 12.2 shows the results, and Figure 12.3 shows what happens when you use `flex-direction: row-reverse`.

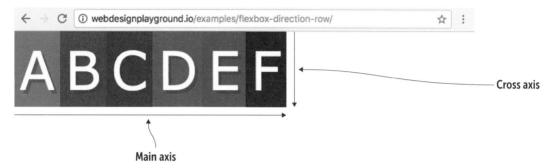

▶ Figure 12.2 The `div` elements with a flex container and the `row` direction applied

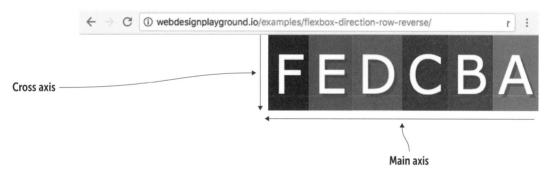

▶ Figure 12.3 The `div` elements with a flex container and the `row-reverse` direction applied

Figure 12.2 shows the same result as using `float: left` or `display: inline-block`, and Figure 12.3 shows the same result as using `float: right` (and isn't possible with inline blocks). With flexbox, however, you get the result by adding a couple of declarations to the container rather than styling each child element, as you do with floats and inline blocks. Right off the bat, you can see that flexbox is easier and more efficient.

PLAY

How would you use flexbox to display a numbered list in reverse order? ⇨ **Online: wdpg .io/12-1-4**

How do you want the items arranged along the main axis?

When you've used flex-direction to set the main axis for the container, your next decision is how you want the items to be arranged along that axis. Use the justify-content property on a container:

```
container {
    display: flex;
    justify-content: flex-start|flex-end|center|space-between|space-around;
}
```

- flex-start—Places the items at the beginning of the container (the default)

- flex-end—Places the items at the end of the container

- center—Places the items in the middle of the container

- space-between—Places the items with the first item at the beginning of the container, the last item at the end, and the rest of the items evenly distributed in between

- space-around—Distributes the items evenly within the container by supplying each item the same amount of space on either side

Figure 12.4 shows the effect that each value has on the arrangement of the items within the container when the main axis is horizontal. (Note that I've added an outline around each container so you can visualize its boundaries.)

How do you want the items arranged along the cross axis?

With the items arranged along the main axis, your next task is choosing an arrangement along the cross axis. You set this by using the container's align-items property:

```
container {
    display: flex;
    align-items: stretch|flex-start|flex-end|center|baseline;
}
```

- stretch—Expands each item along the cross axis to fill the container (the default)

- flex-start—Aligns the items with the beginning of the cross axis

- flex-end—Aligns the items at the end of the cross axis

- center—Aligns the items in the middle of the cross axis

- baseline—Aligns the items along their baseline of the flex container

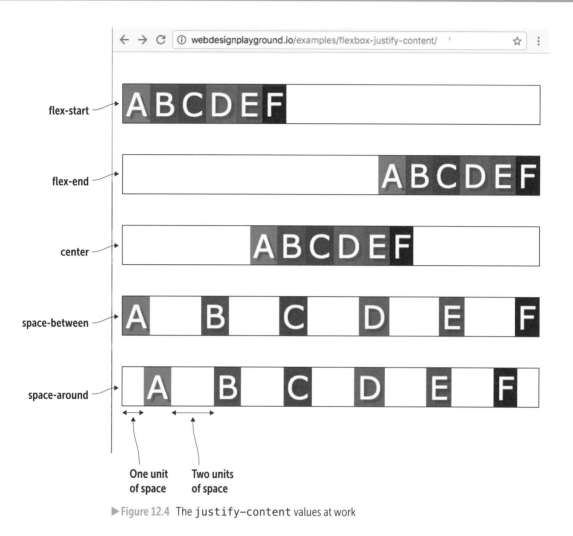

▶ Figure 12.4 The justify-content values at work

Figure 12.5 shows the effect that each value has on the arrangement of the items within the container when the cross axis is vertical. (I've added an outline around each container so you can visualize its boundaries.)

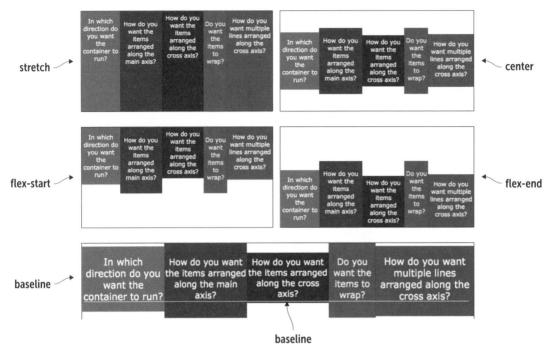

▶ Figure 12.5 The `align-items` values in action

FAQ

Are these alignment options confusing, or is it just me? *Almost everyone getting started with flexbox finds alignment to be the most confusing part. It may help to think of the main axis as the* justification axis, *because you use the* justify-content *property to arrange items on that axis. Similarly, think of the cross axis as the* alignment axis, *because you arrange items on it using the* align-items *property.*

Do you want the items to wrap?

By default, flexbox treats a container as a single row (if you've declared `flex-direction` as `row` or `row-reverse`) or as a single column (if you've declared `flex-direction` as `column` or `column-reverse`). If the container's items are too big to fit into the row or column, flexbox shrinks the items along the main axis to make them fit. Alternatively, you can force the browser to wrap the container's items to multiple rows or columns rather than shrinking them. You do this by using the container's `flex-wrap` property:

```
container {
    display: flex;
    flex-wrap: nowrap|wrap|wrap-reverse;
}
```

- `nowrap`—Doesn't wrap the container's items (the default)
- `wrap`—Wraps the items to as many rows or columns as needed
- `wrap-reverse`—Wraps the items at the end of the cross axis

Figure 12.6 shows the effect that each value has on the arrangement of the items within the container when the main axis is horizontal. (I've added an orange outline around each container so you can visualize its boundaries.)

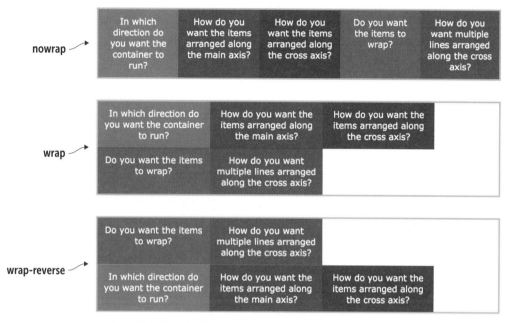

▶ Figure 12.6 How the flex-wrap values work

How do you want multiple lines arranged along the cross axis?

Your final container-related decision is how you want multiple lines—that is, multiple rows or columns—arranged along the cross axis. This is similar to arranging individual flex items along the main axis, except that here, you're dealing with entire lines of items. You control this arrangement by using the container's align-content property:

```
container {
    display: flex;
    align-content: stretch|center|flex-start|flex-end|space-
between|space-around;
}
```

- stretch—Expands the wrapped lines along the cross axis to fill the container height (the default)
- center—Places the lines in the middle of the cross axis
- flex-start—Places the lines at the beginning of the cross axis

PLAY

You can try out the different align-items *values interactively on the Playground.*
⇨ Online: wdpg.io/12-1-6

REMEMBER

The nowrap *value is the default, so declaring* flex-wrap: nowrap *is optional.*

PLAY

You can wrap your head around the three flex-wrap *values by trying them out interactively on the Playground.*
⇨ Online: wdpg.io/12-1-8

REMEMBER
The stretch *value is the default, so declaring* align-content: stretch *is optional.*

PLAY
You can try out all the align-content *values interactively on the Playground.* ⇨Online: wdpg.io/12-1/10

- flex-end—Places the lines at the end of the cross axis
- space-between—Places the first line at the beginning of the cross axis, the last line at the end, and the rest of the lines evenly distributed in between
- space-around—Distributes the lines evenly within the container by supplying each line with a set amount of space on either side

Figure 12.7 shows the effect that each value has on the arrangement of the lines within the container when the main axis is horizontal. (I've added an orange outline around each container so you can visualize its boundaries.)

▶Figure 12.7 Using the align-content values

Lesson 12.1: ***Dead-Centering an Element with Flexbox***
Covers: flex *and other flex container properties*

BEWARE
As with justify-content, *the* space-around *value gives one unit of space before the first line and after the last line but two units of space between all the other lines.*

⇨ **Online:** wdpg.io/12-1-1

By far the most common question related to web page layouts is a deceptively simple one: How do I center an element horizontally and vertically? That is, how can you use CSS to place an element in the dead center of the browser window? Over the years, many clever tricks have been created to achieve this goal, with most of them using advanced and complex CSS rules. Fortunately, you don't have to worry about any of that because flexbox lets you dead-center any element with four lines of CSS, as shown in the following example.

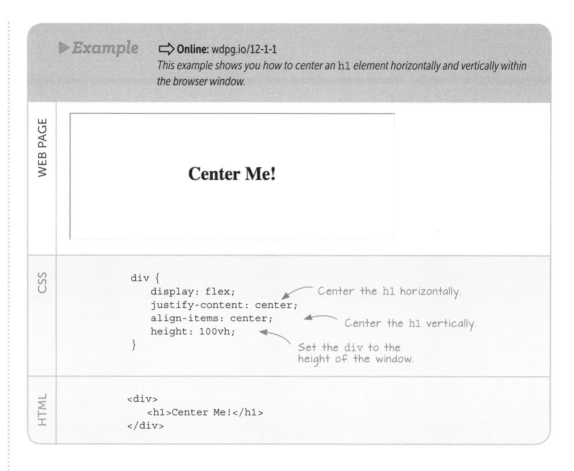

▶ *Example*   ⇨ **Online:** wdpg.io/12-1-1
This example shows you how to center an h1 *element horizontally and vertically within the browser window.*

WEB PAGE

Center Me!

CSS

```css
div {
    display: flex;              Center the h1 horizontally.
    justify-content: center;
    align-items: center;        Center the h1 vertically.
    height: 100vh;
}                               Set the div to the
                                height of the window.
```

HTML

```html
<div>
    <h1>Center Me!</h1>
</div>
```

This example works by turning the div element into a flex container, which automatically converts the h1 element to a flex item. By setting both justify-content and align-items to center, and by giving the div the full height of the browser window (it's the width of the browser window by default), you center the h1 in the window.

Working with Flexbox Items

Now that you know everything that's worth knowing about flexbox containers, turn your attention to the flexbox items inside those containers. As before, learning about and using flex items is best approached by asking yourself a series of questions:

- Do you want the item to grow if there's extra room?
- Do you want the item to shrink if there's not enough room?
- Do you want to suggest an initial size for an item?
- Do you want to change an item's order?
- Do you want to override an item's alignment?

The next few sections discuss these questions and provide you some answers.

Do you want the item to grow if there's extra room?

If you look back at Figure 12.4, notice that in the flex-start example, the flex items are bunched up at the beginning of the container, leaving a chunk of empty space to the right. This effect may be what you want, or you may prefer to have the items fill that empty space. You can do that by applying the flex-grow property to the item you want to expand:

```
item {
    flex-grow: value;
}
```

By default, all flex items are given a flex-grow value of 0. To grow items to fill a container's empty space, you assign positive numbers to those items as follows (see Figure 12.8):

- If you assign any positive number to one flex item in a container, the amount of empty space in the container is added to that item.

- If you assign the same positive number to multiple flex items in a container, the amount of empty space in the container is divided evenly among those items.

- If you assign different positive numbers to multiple flex items in a container, the amount of empty space in the container is divided proportionally among those items, based on the values you provide. If you assign the values 1, 2, and 1 to three items, those items get 25 percent, 50 percent, and 25 percent of the empty space, respectively.

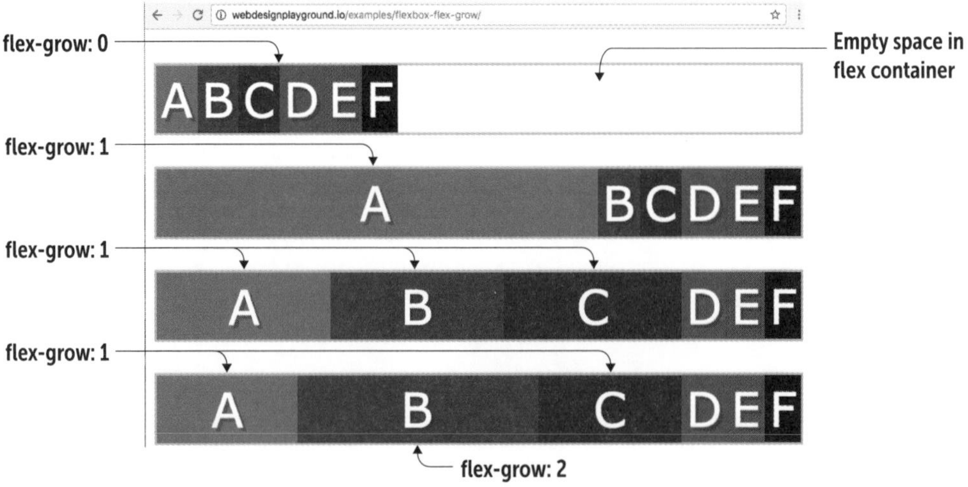

MASTER

To calculate what proportion of the empty space is assigned to each item, add all the flex-grow values for a given container and then divide the individual flex-grow values by that total. Values of 1, 2, and 1 add up to 4, for example, so the percentages are 25 (¼), 50 (²⁄₄), and 25 (¼), respectively.

flex-grow: 0

flex-grow: 1

flex-grow: 1

flex-grow: 1

Empty space in flex container

flex-grow: 2

▶Figure 12.8 The effect of different flex-grow values

Do you want the item to shrink if there's not enough room?

The opposite problem of expanding flex items to fill a container's empty space is shrinking flex items when the container doesn't have enough space. This shrinking is activated by default, so if the browser detects that the flex items are too large to fit the container, it automatically reduces the flex items to fit.

How much each item shrinks depends on its size in relation to the other items and the size of the container. Suppose that you're working with a horizontal main axis (that is, `flex-direction` is set to `row`) and that the container is 1200px wide, but each of its five items is 400px wide. That's 2000px total, so the browser must reduce the items by 800px to fit the container. In this case, because all the items are the same width, the browser reduces the width of each by 160px.

If the items have different widths, the calculations get more complicated, so I won't go into them here. Suffice it to say that the amount each item's width gets reduced depends on its initial width. The greater the initial width is, the more the item shrinks.

Rather than let the browser determine how much each item gets reduced, you can specify that a particular item be reduced more than or less than the other items. You do that by applying the `flex-shrink` property to the item:

```
item {
    flex-shrink: value;
}
```

By default, all flex items are given a `flex-shrink` value of 1, which means that they're all treated equally when it comes time to calculate the shrink factor. To control the shrink factor yourself, assign positive values to those items as follows (see Figure 12.9):

- If you set `flex-shrink` to a number greater than 1, the browser shrinks the item more than the other items by a factor that's somewhat proportional to the value you provide. (Again, the math is quite complicated.)

- If you set `flex-shrink` to a number greater than 0 but less than 1, the browser shrinks the item less than the other items.

- If you set `flex-shrink` to 0, the browser doesn't shrink the item.

PLAY

You can play with various `flex-grow` *values interactively on the Playground.*
⇨ Online: wdpg.io/12-2-2

LEARN

Mike Reithmuller has a lucid explanation of the math involved in calculating item shrinkage here: https://madebymike.com.au/writing/understanding-flexbox.

BEWARE

The browser won't shrink an item to a size less than the minimum required to display its content. If you keep increasing an item's `flex-shrink` *value, and the item refuses to get smaller, the item is probably at its minimum possible size.*

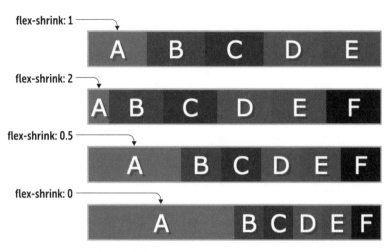

flex-shrink: 1

flex-shrink: 2

flex-shrink: 0.5

flex-shrink: 0

▶ Figure 12.9 The effect of different `flex-shrink` values. Each item is 300px, and the container is 600px.

Do you want to suggest an initial size for an item?

You've seen that flex items can grow or shrink depending on how they fit in the container and that you have some control of this process via the `flex-grow` and `flex-shrink` properties. But when I say that flex items can grow or shrink, what are they growing and shrinking *from*? That depends:

- If the item has a declared `width` value (if `flex-direction` is set to `row`) or a declared `height` value (if `flex-direction` is set to `column`), the item grows or shrinks from this initial size.

- If the item doesn't have a declared width or height, the item's dimensions are set automatically by the browser to the minimum values required to fit the item's content. The item can grow from this initial value, but it can't shrink to a smaller value.

The latter case—that is, not having a declared width (for `flex-direction: row`) or height (for `flex-direction: column`)—causes two problems. First, it prevents an item from shrinking smaller than its content. Second, the initial size (that is, the minimum required to display the content) may be smaller than you require. You can solve both problems by declaring a *flex basis*, which is a suggested size for the item. You do that by applying the `flex-basis` property:

```
item {
    flex-basis: value|auto|content;
}
```

- `value`—Sets a specific measure for the width (with `flex-direction: row`) or height (with `flex-direction: column`). You can use any of the CSS measurement units you learned about in Chapter 7, including `px`, `em`, `rem`, `vw`, and `vh`. You can also set *value* to a percentage.

- `auto`—Lets the browser set the initial value based on the item's `width` or `height` property (the default). In the absence of a declared width or height, `auto` is the same as `content`, discussed next.

- `content`—Sets the initial width or height based on the content of the item.

Using the flex shorthand property

You should know that flexbox offers a shorthand property for `flex-grow`, `flex-shrink`, and `flex-basis`. This property is named `flex`, and it uses any of the following syntaxes:

```
item {
    flex: flex-grow flex-shrink flex-basis;
    flex: flex-grow flex-shrink;
    flex: flex-grow flex-basis;
    flex: flex-grow;
    flex: flex-basis;
}
```

Here's an example declaration that uses the default values for each property:

```
flex: 0 1 auto;
```

This example sets `flex-grow` to 1 and `flex-shrink` to 0:

```
flex: 1 0;
```

This final example styles an item with a fixed size of 10em:

```
flex: 0 0 10em;
```

Do you want to change an item's order?

One of the most surprising—and surprisingly handy—tricks offered by flexbox is the ability to change the order of the items in a container. When would you use this feature? Here are two common scenarios:

- One of the important tenets of accessibility is to place a page's main content as near the top of the page as possible. If you have ads or other nonessential content in, say, a left sidebar, that content necessarily appears first in the source document. With flexbox, however, you can put the sidebar's code after the main content and then change its position so that it still appears on the left side of the page.

- A similarly important tenet of mobile web design is to place the main content on the initial screen seen by mobile users. If you don't want to restructure the content for desktop users, you can add a CSS media query that uses flexbox to change the content order, depending on the device being used.

Creating Page Layouts with Flexbox

MASTER

Negative order *values are allowed, so an easy way to move an item to the front of its container is to set its* order *value to -1.*

PLAY

You can mess around with some order *values interactively on the Playground.* ⇨ Online: wdpg.io/12-2-6

You change the order of a flex item by using the order property:

```
item {
    order: value;
}
```

By default, all the items in a flex container are given an order value of 0. You can manipulate the item order as follows:

- The higher an item's order value, the later it appears in the container.
- The item with the highest order value appears last in the container.
- The item with the lowest order value appears first in the container.

Figure 12.10 puts a few order values through their paces.

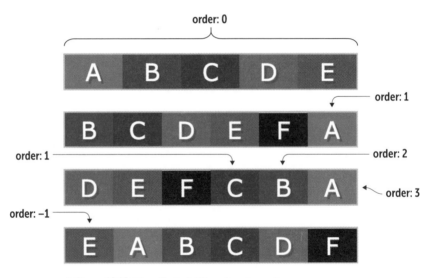

▶ Figure 12.10 The effect of different order values

Do you want to override an item's alignment?

You saw earlier that you can use the align-items property to arrange items along a container's cross axis. Rather than align all the items the same way, you may prefer to override this global alignment and assign a different alignment to an item. You can do that by setting the item's align-self property:

```
item {
    align-self: stretch|flex-start|flex-end|center|baseline;
}
```

The possible values act in the same manner as I outlined earlier (see "How do you want the items arranged along the cross axis?"). You can also assign the value `auto` to revert the item to the current `align-items` value. Figure 12.11 shows a container with `align-items` set to `flex-start` but with the last item having `align-self` set to `flex-end`.

align-items: flex-start

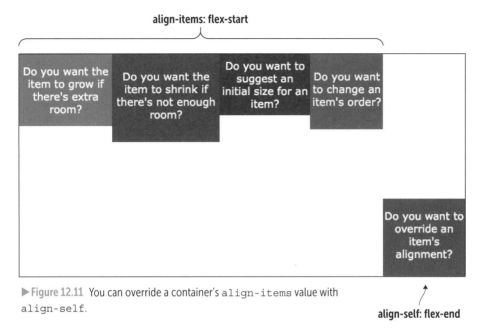

▶ Figure 12.11 You can override a container's `align-items` value with `align-self`.

align-self: flex-end

Flexbox Browser Support

The good news about flexbox browser support is that it works in all current browsers. In fact, it works even in the vast majority of recent browsers, so for the most part, you don't have to worry about using browser prefixes.

If you have to support old browsers, however, some prefixing is required to get flexbox to work. These prefixes can get complex because the flexbox syntax changed between versions, so supporting older browsers means supporting these older syntaxes. Rather than run through all these prefixes, I'm going to pass the buck to a fantastic tool called Autoprefixer (http://autoprefixer.github.io), shown in Figure 12.12. You paste your nonprefixed code into the left pane, and fully prefixed code appears automagically in the right pane. It also comes with a Filter box that you can use to specify how far back you want to go with browser support:

- Type `last x versions` to support that most recent *x* versions of all browsers (such as `last 4 versions`).
- Type `> y%` to support only web browsers that have at least *y%* market share (such as `> .5%`).

▶Figure 12.12
Use the online version of Autoprefixer to add browser vendor prefixes to your flexbox code.

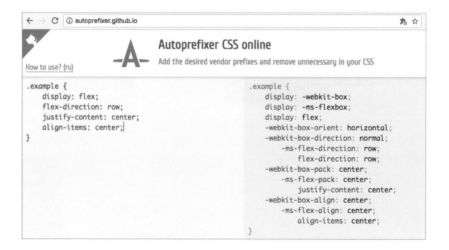

Lesson 12.2: *Creating a Thumbnail List*
Covers: The `flex-grow` and `flex-shrink` properties

⇨ **Online:** wdpg.io/12-2-0

A common web page component is a simple thumbnail list that has a thumbnail image on the left and a description or other information on the right. These elements are used for photo galleries, user directories, book lists, project summaries, and much more. Getting the image and the text to behave is tricky with garden-variety CSS, but it's a breeze with flexbox, as shown in the following example.

▷ *Example*   ⇨ **Online:** wdpg.io/12-2-1
This example shows you how to use flexbox to create a thumbnail list of items.

WEB PAGE

 animal path
A footpath or track made by the constant and long-term walking of animals.

 bridleway
A footpath that is also suitable for a horse and rider.

 coffin trail
A footpath used for transporting a coffin to a cemetary for burial.

 desire line
An informal path that pedestrians prefer to take to get from one location to another rather than using a sidewalk or other official route.

CSS

```css
.dictionary-container {
    list-style-type: none;
}
.dictionary-item {
    display: flex;                  ← Each li becomes a flex
}                                      container.
.dictionary-image {
    flex-shrink: 0;                 ← Prevent the thumbnail
}                                      from shrinking.
.dictionary-entry {
    flex-grow: 1;                   ← Allow the text to use the
}                                      rest of the container.
```

HTML

```html
<ul class="dictionary-container">
    <li class="dictionary-item">
        <div class="dictionary-image">
            <img src="/images/animalpath.jpg" alt="Photo of an
animal path">
        </div>
        <div class="dictionary-entry">
            <h4>animal path</h4>
            <p>A footpath or track made by the constant and long-
term walking of animals.</p>
        </div>
    </li>
    etc.
</ul>
```

Lesson 12.3: ***Creating the Holy-Grail Layout with Flexbox***
Covers: Layout with `flex` and other flexbox properties

⇨ **Online:** wdpg.io/12-3-0

Okay, now you can turn your attention to building the holy-grail layout with flexbox. As before, the holy grail includes three instances in which you need content side by side: the header, the navigation bar, and the content columns. In all three instances, you'll place the elements in a flexbox container with a horizontal main axis.

First, however, note that you want these elements stacked, which means that they need a flex container that uses a vertical main axis. The `<body>` tag does the job nicely, so set `body` as a flex container with a vertical main axis and the content starting at the top:

```
body {
    display: flex;
    flex-direction: column;
    justify-content: flex-start;
    max-width: 50em;
    min-height: 100vh;
}
```

Note, too, that I specified a maximum width for the container and a minimum height. You'll see why I used 100vh when I talk about adding a footer a bit later.

Now do the header, as shown in the following example.

▶ *Example*   ⇨ **Online:** wdpg.io/12-3-1
This example shows you how to use flexbox to get the header logo and title side by side.

WEB PAGE

 **Site Title**

CSS

```
header {
    display: flex;
    justify-content: flex-start;
    align-items: center;
    border: 1px solid black;
    padding: 1em;
}
header img {
    flex-shrink: 0;
}
h1 {
    flex-grow: 1;
    padding-left: .5em;
    font-size: 2.5em;
}
```

Display the header element as a flex container.

Prevent the logo from shrinking.

Let the h1 element use the rest of the header space.

HTML

```
<header>
    <img src="/images/your-logo-here.tif" alt="Our logo">
    <h1>Site Title</h1>
</header>
```

In this code, I converted the header element to a flex container with the items arranged at the start of the main (horizontal) axis and centered on the cross (vertical) axis.

Now convert the navigation bar to a horizontal flex container, as shown in the following example.

▶ *Example* ⇨ **Online:** wdpg.io/12-3-2
This example shows you how to use flexbox to get the navigation-bar items side by side.

WEB PAGE

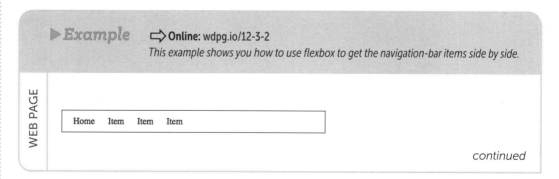

continued

CSS

```css
nav {
    padding: .5em;
    border: 1px solid black;
}
nav ul {
    display: flex;
    justify-content: flex-start;
    list-style-type: none;
    padding-left: .5em;
}
nav li {
    padding-right: 1.5em;
}
```

Display the ul element as a flex container.

HTML

```html
<nav>
    <ul>
        <li>Home</li>
        <li>Item</li>
        <li>Item</li>
        <li>Item</li>
    </ul>
</nav>
```

In this case, the `ul` element is converted to a flex container, meaning that the `li` elements become flex items arranged horizontally from the start of the container.

Next, convert the `main` element's `<article>` and `<aside>` tags to flex items, which gives you the two-column content layout. The following example shows how it's done.

▶ *Example* ⇨ **Online:** wdpg.io/12-3-3

This example shows you how to use flexbox to get the article *and* aside *elements side by side in a two-column layout.*

WEB PAGE

Article Title

Article paragraph 1

Article paragraph 2

Sidebar Title

Sidebar paragraph

CSS

```
main {
    display: flex;          ← Display main as
    flex-grow: 1;           ← a flex container.
}                             Let it grow vertically.
article {
    flex-grow: 3;
    border: 1px solid black;   Let article use
}                              three units of space
aside {
    flex-grow: 1;
    border: 1px solid black;  ← Let aside use one
}                               unit of space.
```

HTML

```
<main>
    <article>
        <h2>Article Title</h2>
        <p>Article paragraph 1</p>
        <p>Article paragraph 2</p>
    </article>
    <aside>
        <h3>Sidebar Title</h3>
        <p>Sidebar paragraph</p>
    </aside>
</main>
```

A couple of interesting things are going on here. First, note that the main element does double duty: It acts as the flex container for the article and aside elements, *and* it's a flex item in the body element's flex container. Setting flex-grow to 1 for the main element tells the browser to give main all the empty vertical space in the body container. Again, why you're doing this will become apparent when you get to the footer.

For the article and aside flex items, I assigned flex-grow values of 3 and 1, respectively, meaning that article gets 75 percent of the available horizontal space and aside gets the remaining 25 percent.

Finally, add the footer element in the same way that you did with the float and inline block layouts in Chapter 11. Figure 12.13 shows the result.

MASTER

Note, too, that the article *and* aside *items are the same height—a pleasant bonus that comes courtesy of the* body *container's default* stretch *value for* align-items. *You get a true full-height sidebar and don't have to resort to a faux column.*

▶ Figure 12.13 The complete holy-grail layout using flexbox

PLAY

How would you modify this layout to display the sidebar on the left instead of the right?
⇨ Online: wdpg.io/12-3-5

PLAY

How would you modify this layout to display three content columns: a sidebar to the left and to the right of the article *element?* ⇨ Online: wdpg.io/12-3-6

Can you see what's different? That's right: The footer element appears at the bottom of the browser window, which is where it should be in a true holy-grail layout. You got that nice touch by doing three things:

- Turning the body element into a flex container with a vertical main axis

- Declaring min-height: 100vh on the body element, which forces the body element to always be at least the same height as the browser window

- Setting flex-grow: 1 on the main element to force it to use any available empty vertical space in the body container

Summary

- In which direction do you want the container to run? Use `flex-direction`.
- How do you want the items arranged along the main axis? Use `justify-content`.
- How do you want the items arranged along the cross axis? Use the `align-items` property.
- Do you want the items to wrap? Use `flex-wrap`.
- How do you want multiple lines arranged along the cross axis? Add the `align-content` property.
- Do you want the item to grow if there's extra room? Use `flex-grow`.
- Do you want the item to shrink if there's not enough room? Use `flex-shrink`.
- Do you want to suggest an initial size for an item? You can use the `flex-basis` property.
- Do you want to change an item's order? You can use the `order` property.
- Do you want to override an item's alignment? Use `align-self`.

Chapter 13

Designing Responsive Web Pages

 Rather than tailoring disconnected designs to each of an ever-increasing number of web devices, we can treat them as facets of the same experience. We can design for an optimal viewing experience, but embed standards-based technologies into our designs to make them not only more flexible, but more adaptive to the media that renders them. In short, we need to practice responsive web design. —Ethan Marcotte

This chapter covers

- Learning why you should avoid fixed-width layouts
- Creating page layouts that are liquid and flexible
- Using media queries to build pages that adapt to changing screen sizes
- Creating layouts designed first for mobile screens

I'll begin by defining what I mean when I describe a web page as responsive: A *responsive* page is one that automatically adapts its layout, typography, images, and other content to fit whatever size screen a site visitor is using to access the page. In other words, the page content should be usable, readable, and navigable regardless of the dimensions of the screen it's being displayed on.

Responsive web design—or RWD, as it's colloquially known in the web-design community—wouldn't be a big deal if only the occasional site user were surfing with a smartphone or tablet. However, sometime back in 2014 the worldwide percentage of web users on mobile devices *surpassed* that of users with desktop browsers.

> *Web design is responsive design. Responsive web design is web design, done right.* —Andy Clarke

There are many reasons why it's good practice to make all your pages responsive, and you'll learn about many of them as you progress through this chapter. But arguably the most important reason is also the most basic: *When reading a web page, nobody should have to scroll horizontally.*

Although it's true that a few pages are designed to be navigated by scrolling from left to right, the vast majority of pages are oriented vertically, so you read or scan them from top to bottom. One of the most annoying and maddening web page experiences occurs when a page doesn't fit the width of your screen, so seeing all the content requires scrolling to the right, back to the left, then to the right again, and so on. It's maddening and a sure way to drive people to another site—any site—within seconds.

Lesson 13.1: *Why Fixed-Width Layouts Are the Enemy*
Covers: Fixed-width page layouts

> **⇨ Online:** wdpg.io/13-1-1

Why don't web pages fit whatever screen they're being displayed on? In most cases, the culprit is the use of large, fixed-width elements. These elements stay the same size no matter how wide a screen they're shown on, so if their width is greater than that of the screen, the dreaded horizontal scrollbar appears. To see what I mean, consider the following example.

▶ *Example*   ➡ **Online:** wdpg.io/13-1-1
This example shows you the bare-bones version of a typical fixed-width layout.

CSS

```css
body {
    width: 960px;
}
header {
    padding: 16px;
}
article {
    float: left;
    width: 640px;
    padding: 16px;
}
aside {
    float: left;
    width: 320px;
    padding: 12px;
}
footer {
    padding: 16px;
}
```

The body element uses a fixed width of 960px.

The article element uses a fixed width of 640px.

The aside element uses a fixed width of 320px.

HTML

```html
<header>
    <h1>Responsive Web Design</h1>
</header>
<main>
    <article>
        <h2>A Brief History</h2>
        <p>Early in the new millennium, etc.</p>
    </article>
    <aside>
        <h3>Links</h3>
        etc.
    </aside>
</main>
<footer>
    <p>&copy; Logophilia Limited</p>
</footer>
```

This example is a basic two-column floated layout where the body and the page's two columns—the article and aside elements—all used widths with fixed values in pixels. If the browser viewport is at least 960 pixels wide, this web page displays well, as shown in Figure 13.1. But what happens when the page is accessed by a smaller screen? As you can see in Figure 13.2, a tablet in portrait mode isn't wide enough, so some content gets cut off, and the horizontal scrollbar appears. Even worse is the page on a smartphone screen, as shown in Figure 13.3, where even less of the content is visible, which means even more horizontal scrolling for the poor reader.

▶ Figure 13.1
The web page fits a desktop screen.

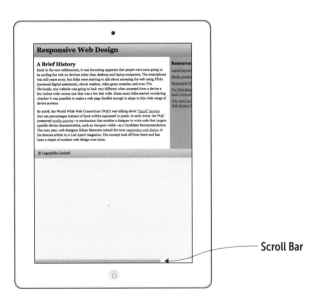

Scroll Bar

▶ Figure 13.2   The web page is a bit too wide for a tablet screen.

Scroll Bar

▶ Figure 13.3   The web page is far too wide for a smartphone screen.

> *Developing fixed-size web pages is a fundamentally flawed practice. Not only does it result in web pages that remain at a constant size regardless of the user's browser size, but it fails to take advantage of the medium's flexibility.* —Jim Kalbach

Creating a Responsive Layout

Now that you know fixed-width layouts are bad, you can take steps to make sure that your layouts display nicely on any size screen. You have several ways to achieve this responsive ideal, and the next few sections take you through these methods. But first, you need to take care of some prerequisites.

First, you need to make sure that all your block-level elements are being sized out to the border and not to the content, which is the default sizing. As I explained in Chapter 9, the easiest way to do this is to include the following rule at the top of your CSS:

```
* {
    box-sizing: border-box;
}
```

Second, you need to configure the browser viewport's default width and scale by adding the following tag somewhere within your page's <head> section:

```
<meta name="viewport" content="width=device-width, initial-
scale=1.0">
```

By setting `width=device-width`, you're telling the browser to set the width of the page to be the same as the width of whatever device the page is being displayed on. By setting `initial-scale=1.0`, you're telling the browser to display the page initially without zooming in or out.

With those tweaks added, you're ready to get responsive.

Lesson 13.2: **Creating a Liquid Layout**
 Covers: Using percentages for liquid layouts

⇨ **Online:** wdpg.io/13-2-0

As you saw earlier, the real problem with a fixed-width layout is setting the `width` property to an absolute value, such as `960px`. You can remedy that problem by converting your absolute `width` values to relative widths that use percentages instead of pixels. This solution is often called a *liquid layout*.

 Converting a fixed-width layout to a liquid layout is most often a three-stage process. The first stage is deciding a maximum width for your layout.

REMEMBER

A layout that uses relative measurement units, such as percentages, is known as a liquid layout.

The goal of a liquid layout is to allow the content to scale down when faced with smaller screen sizes and to scale up when a larger screen comes along. Most of the time, however, you don't want the content to get too wide, because that can result in text lines that are too long for comfortable reading. Examine your content and then decide on the maximum width that still allows for good reading and navigation. With that number in mind, apply the `max-width` property to the outermost container (such as the body element). The following example declares the body element with a maximum width of 960 pixels:

```
body {
    max-width: 960px;
}
```

REMEMBER

When using percentages for widths, remember that CSS doesn't base that percentage on the viewport width. Instead, it calculates that percentage based on the width of the element's parent.

The second stage is determining the percentage widths to use for the rest of the elements. By default, any block-level element takes up 100 percent of its parent's width, so you need to calculate percentages only for elements that you want to use less than the full parent width. If an `article` element is 1,000 pixels wide, and a child `div` is declared with `width: 75%`, that `div` is 750 pixels wide. If the screen is resized so that the `article` element is 800 pixels wide, the child `div` automatically scales down to 600 pixels wide.

To convert your fixed-width elements to percentages, you apply the following formula to each:

```
element percentage = (element fixed width / parent fixed width) * 100
```

The example shown in Lesson 13.1 earlier in this chapter has two fixed-width components:

- An `article` element set to 640 pixels wide. Because the parent (the `body` element) is 960 pixels wide, the `article` element's percentage width value is (640 / 960) * 100 = 66.67%.

- An `aside` element set to 320 pixels wide. Again, the parent (the `body` element) is 960 pixels wide, so the `aside` element's percentage width value is (320 / 960) * 100 = 33.33%.

The third stage in converting a fixed-width layout to a liquid layout is applying the same formula to any other horizontal items that are part of the layout, such as margins and padding. If an element is declared with `padding: 12px`, and its parent is 960 pixels wide, the liquid margin width becomes (12 / 960) * 100 = 1.25%.

The following updates the earlier example with a liquid layout.

▶ *Example*   ⇨ **Online:** wdpg.io/13-2-1
This code shows the conversion of the fixed-width layout to a liquid layout.

CSS

```css
body {
    max-width: 960px;
}
article {
    float: left;
    width: 66.67%;
    padding: 1.67%;
}
aside {
    float: left;
    width: 33.33%;
    padding: 1.25%;
}
```

The body element now has a
maximum width of 960px.

The article element now
has a width of 66.67%.

The aside element now
has a width of 33.33%.

The padding properties are now percentages.

HTML

```html
<header>
    <h1>Responsive Web Design</h1>
</header>
<main>
    <article>
        <h2>A Brief History</h2>
        <p>Early in the new millennium, etc.</p>
    </article>
    <aside>
        <h3>Links</h3>
        etc.
    </aside>
</main>
<footer>
    <p>&copy; Logophilia Limited</p>
</footer>
```

With the liquid layout in place, you can see in Figure 13.4 that a tablet in portrait mode displays the web page content completely. Looking good! Figure 13.5 shows that a smartphone screen also displays the content without requiring the reader to scroll horizontally. Nice. But you can also clearly see that the resulting columns are alarmingly narrow, which makes reading difficult. To fix that problem, you need to learn another responsive design technique. But first, an aside on viewport units.

PLAY

You can get some practice converting a fixed-width layout to a liquid layout on the Playground. ⇨ Online: wdpg.io/13-2-2

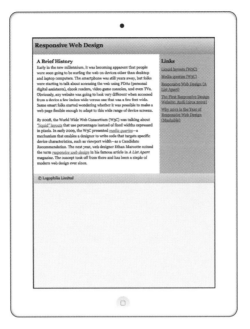

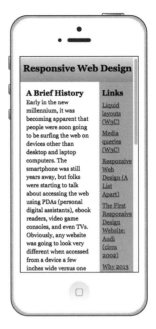

▶Figure 13.4 With a liquid layout, the web page fits a tablet screen perfectly.

▶Figure 13.5 The liquid layout also fits a smartphone screen but at the cost of too-narrow columns.

Liquid Layouts with Viewport Units

When dealing with percentage units, it's important to remember that assigning a percentage width to an element means that you're styling that element to be a percentage of its *parent's* width. If a parent element is 800 pixels wide, and you declare `width: 75%` on a child element, that child is 600 pixels wide. It doesn't matter whether the browser's screen width is 2,000 pixels; that child takes up only 600 pixels across the screen.

What if you want that child element to be 75 percent of the screen instead of its parent? In that case, you need to switch from percentages to viewport units, which act as percentage-like units that apply to the entire browser viewport. The four units you can use are

- `vw`—The viewport width unit, where `100vw` equals 100 percent of the current viewport width. If the viewport is 1,600 pixels wide, `1vw` is equivalent to `16px`.

- `vh`—The viewport height unit, where `100vh` equals 100 percent of the current viewport height. If the viewport is 2,000 pixels high, `1vh` is equivalent to `20px`.

- vmin—The viewport minimum unit, where `100vmin` equals 100 percent of the smaller of the two viewport dimensions. If the viewport is 800 pixels wide and 600 pixels high, `1vmin` is equivalent to `6px` (because in this case, the viewport height is the smaller of the two dimensions).

- vmax—The viewport maximum unit, where `100vmax` equals 100 percent of the larger of the two viewport dimensions. If the viewport is 1,200 pixels wide and 1,024 pixels high, `1vmax` is equivalent to `12px` (because the viewport width is the larger of the two dimensions).

Suppose that you want to display an image so that it automatically takes up the entire height of the viewport. You can do that by applying the following rule to the image:

```
.image-full {
    height: 100vh;
    width: auto;
}
```

I added the `width: auto` declaration to tell the browser to calculate the width automatically based on the height, which maintains the image's original aspect ratio.

PLAY

You can try out this full-height image technique on the Playground.
⇨ Online: **wdpg.io/13-2-4**

Lesson 13.3: **Creating a Flexible Layout**
Covers: Using flexbox to wrap elements

⇨ **Online: wdpg.io/13-3-0**

When the screen gets too narrow to display side-by-side content effectively, it's time for your layout to change. Specifically, you need your layout to stop using side-by-side columns and switch to a more vertical layout that gives each element the full width of the screen.

You'll see in the next section that CSS offers a technique that enables you to directly access the width of the current device. That tool is a powerful one, but for many layouts it's overkill, because you have ways to get elements to wrap automatically and create a so-called *flexible layout*.

One possibility is to convert your floats to inline blocks. When you set the widths to percentages and add a `min-width` declaration to ensure that your blocks are always greater than or equal to some minimum size, your blocks will wrap when the viewport no longer has enough horizontal room to display the blocks. Unfortunately, if you use the faux-column trick that I told you about in Chapter 11, there are certain widths at which the block gets wrapped but you can still see part of the faux column, which is unsightly. Inline blocks are suitable only if you don't use the faux-column technique.

REMEMBER

A layout in which elements wrap when there isn't enough horizontal room to display them side by side is known as a flexible layout.

PLAY

You can see the inline-block technique in action on the Playground.
⇨ Online: **wdpg.io/13-3-2**

A better solution is flexbox, which offers the `flex-wrap` property to activate wrapping within a container. It also enables you to use `flex-grow` to ensure that your blocks use the proportions you want, and you can establish minimum block widths by adding a `flex-basis` value and setting `flex-shrink` to `0`.

The following updates the earlier example with a flexible layout.

▶**Example**   ⇨**Online:** wdpg.io/13-3-1
This code shows the conversion of the liquid layout to a flexible layout.

CSS

```
body {
    display: flex;
    flex-direction: column;
    align-items: center;
}
```
The body element is a column flex container.

```
.container {
    display: flex;
    flex-direction: column;
    max-width: 960px;
}
```
The container element is a column flex container.

```
main {
    display: flex;
    flex-wrap: wrap;
    flex-grow: 1;
}
```
The main element is a flex container that wraps.

```
article {
    flex-grow: 2;
    flex-shrink: 0;
    flex-basis: 300px;
}
```
The article element can grow, but not shrink, from a basis of 300px.

```
aside {
    flex-grow: 1;
    flex-shrink: 0;
    flex-basis: 150px;
}
```
The aside element can grow, but not shrink, from a basis of 150px.

HTML

```
<div class="container">
    <header>
        <h1>Responsive Web Design</h1>
    </header>
    <main>
        <article>
            <h2>A Brief History</h2>
            <p>Early in the new millennium, etc.</p>
        </article>
        <aside>
            <h3>Links</h3>
            etc.
        </aside>
    </main>
    <footer>
        <p>&copy; Logophilia Limited</p>
    </footer>
</div>
```

Here, I'm using the body element as a column flex container, which enables me to center the div horizontally by using align-items: center. The main element is also set up as a flex container with flex-wrap: wrap declared. The article and aside elements (which are flex items) get flex-grow values of 2 and 1, respectively, which are the flex equivalents of the 66.67 percent and 33.33 percent width values from the liquid layout. In both cases, I also added a flex-basis to each (300px and 150px, respectively) and set flex-shrink to 0, which creates a minimum width value for each element.

❝ The web's greatest strength, I believe, is often seen as a limitation, as a defect. It is the nature of the web to be flexible, and it should be our role as designers and developers to embrace this flexibility and produce pages which, by being flexible, are accessible to all. —John Allsop

Figure 13.6 shows the flexible page layout as it appears on a smartphone screen. If you scroll down, as shown in Figure 13.7, you see that the `aside` element has wrapped under the `article` element.

▶ **Figure 13.6**
The top portion of the flexible page layout as viewed on a smartphone screen

▶ **Figure 13.7**
The bottom portion of the flexible layout shows that the `aside` element has wrapped under the `article` element.

Lesson 13.4: **Creating an Adaptive Layout**
Covers: Using `@media` queries

⇨ **Online:** wdpg.io/13-4-0

In Lesson 13.3, you learned how to use flexbox to get liquid elements to wrap when the device viewport gets too narrow to accommodate the elements' minimum widths. That technique is handy, but it's not always going to be one you can turn to, because there may be times when you can't use flexbox (because you need to support older versions of Internet Explorer, for example).

On a different but related note, take a look back at Figure 13.6. See how the page title (Responsive Web Design) barely fits the width of the smartphone viewport? If that element were even a few pixels bigger or a few letters longer, it would wrap and look quite awful, as shown in Figure 13.8.

▶ Figure 13.8
Increase the size of the page title a bit, and the design breaks.

How are these scenarios related? You can solve the underlying problems by asking questions about the width of the browser viewport:

- Is the viewport width less than 450 pixels? If so, remove the floats from the elements so that they display in the default stacked layout.

- Is the viewport width less than 350 pixels? If so, reduce the type size of the page title to 24px.

- Is the viewport width greater than 1,024 pixels? If so, display the aside element.

You can ask these and many other types of questions by defining *media queries* within your CSS. A *media query* is an expression accompanied by a code block consisting of one or more style rules. The expression interrogates some feature of the screen, such as its width. If that expression is true for the current device, the browser applies the media query's style rules; if the expression is false, the browser ignores the media query's rules. A layout that uses media queries is often called an *adaptive layout* because it adapts itself to the screen on which it's displayed.

Here's the general syntax:

```
@media (expression) {
    selector {
        declarations
    }
    etc.
}
```

The *expression* is most often min-width or max-width, followed by a colon and a value.

If you want to apply styles on a screen no wider than a specified value, use max-width. The following code tells the browser to display the h1 element with a type size of 24px whenever the screen width is less than or equal to 350 pixels:

```
@media (max-width: 350px) {
    h1 {
        font-size: 24px;
    }
}
```

If you want to apply styles on a screen that's at least as wide as a specified value, use min-width. The following code sets display: inline-block on the aside element whenever the screen width is greater than or equal to 1,024 pixels:

```
@media (min-width: 1024px) {
    aside {
        display: inline-block;
    }
}
```

The following code updates the example to use a media query that removes the floats from the article and aside elements whenever the screen width drops to 450 pixels or less.

For good measure, the media query also does the following:

- It applies width: 100% to the article and the aside element.

- It reduces the font size of the h1 element (that is, the page title) to 24px.

- It changes the background color of the main element to white, which effectively turns off the faux-column effect because you don't need it while the aside element isn't floated.

CSS

> ▶ *Example*   ⇨ **Online:** wdpg.io/13-4-1
> *This code uses a media query to remove the floats from the* article *and* aside
> *elements, as well as perform a few other tasks as noted.*

```css
h1 {
    float: left;
    font-size: 32px;
}
main {
    background-color: #b4a7d6;
}
article {
    float: left;
    width: 66.67%;
}
aside {
    float: left;
    width: 33.33%;
}
@media (max-width: 450px) {
    article {
        float: none;
        width: 100%;
    }
    aside {
        float: none;
        width: 100%;
    }
    h1 {
        font-size: 24px;
    }
    main {
        background-color: white;
    }
}
```

The media query applies to screen widths up to 450px.

Floats are removed from the article and aside elements.

The page title is reduced to 24px.

The main element background color is changed to white.

Figure 13.9 shows how the page layout appears on a screen with a width greater than 450 pixels. As shown in Figures 13.10 and 13.11, however, the layout changes on a screen with a width of 450 pixels or less.

▶ **Figure 13.9**
Here's the page layout you see when the screen width is greater than 450 pixels.

PLAY

Given a version of the example layout in which the `aside` *element is hidden by default, write a media query that displays the* `aside` *element when the viewport is at least 1,024 pixels wide.* ⇨ Online: **wdpg.io/13-4-2**

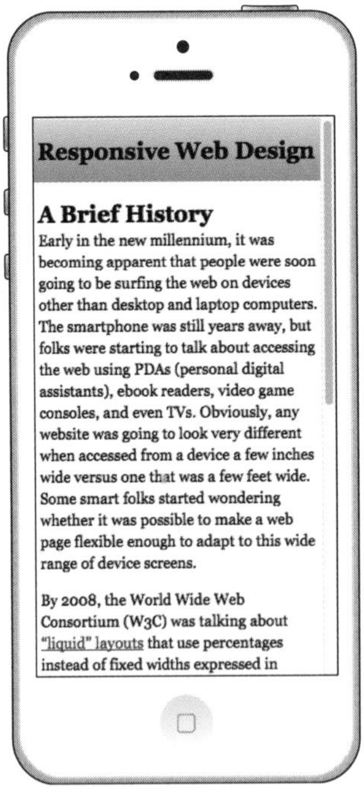

▶ **Figure 13.10** Here's the top portion of the page layout that appears on a screen that is less than 450 pixels wide.

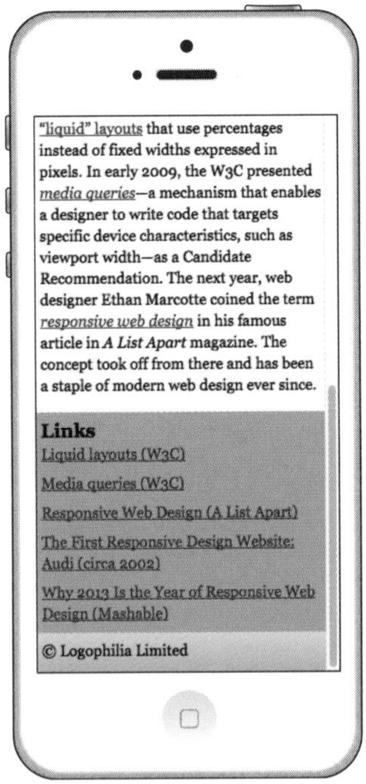

▶ **Figure 13.11** The bottom portion of the screen confirms that the floats have been removed from the `article` and `aside` elements.

A Note about Media Query Breakpoints

You may be tempted to set up your media queries to target specific device widths, such as 320px for an iPhone 5 and earlier, 400px for a Galaxy Note, 768px for an iPad 4 and earlier, and so on. Alas, that way lies madness. There are just too many devices with too many different widths for you to have a hope of targeting them all. Even if you could somehow do that, your code would be out of date by the end of the day, because new devices with new widths are being released constantly. Forget it.

Instead, it's much better to let your content dictate the `min-width` and `max-width` values you use in your media queries. On a desktop screen, for example, you might determine that your text lines are at their most readable when they have about 75 characters per line. If you can get that line length when the container element is 600 pixels wide, it makes sense to set that element's `max-width` property to `600px`. Suppose that you also determine that your lines remain readable down to about 50 characters per line and that you get that line length when the container element is 400 pixels wide.

Experiment with different screen widths to see when that container's width falls below this 400-pixel threshold. This depends on your overall page layout, but suppose that it happens when the screen width falls below 550 pixels because you've got the container floated next to a 150-pixel-wide sidebar. Your page becomes less readable below that width, so the design *breaks* at 550px. That value becomes the *breakpoint* for a media query:

```
@media (max-width: 550px) {
    .container {
        float: none;
        width: 100%;
    }
}
```

In general, you vary the width of the browser window and watch for widths at which the design breaks: text lines getting too short or too long, a type size becoming too big, a block element that ends up in a weird place, and so on. Then use the width as a breakpoint for a media query.

REMEMBER

A layout that begins with a structure designed for mobile devices and adds complexity only when the screen is wide enough is known as a mobile-first layout.

REMEMBER

You don't necessarily have to start with a width as small as 320px. If you have access to your site analytics, they should tell you what devices your visitors use. If you find that all or most of your mobile users are on devices that are at least 400 pixels wide, you should start there.

➡️ **Online:** wdpg.io/13-5-0

In Lesson 13.4, you saw how to use media queries to target mobile screens and adjust layout features such as removing floats. That works fine, but a school of web-design thought says that all CSS should be additive instead of subtractive. That is, your CSS should add or modify properties values, never remove them. Why? In a sense, CSS is like cooking; it's a lot easier to add salt and other seasonings than to remove them. In your web-design kitchen, it's always best to start with the most minimal layout that works and then add things to it.

In almost every conceivable web page scenario, the most minimal layout is the one that's designed to work on the smallest devices, which these days means smartphones. The idea, then, is to build your page to look and work well on the smallest smartphone screen (typically, 320 pixels wide). Only then do you add to and modify the layout for larger screens. This layout is called a *mobile-first layout*, and it's at the heart of responsive web design today.

One of the tenets of mobile-first design is to include in the initial, mobile-focused layout only those page elements that are essential to the user's experience of the page. Many mobile users are surfing over slow connections with limited data plans, so as a conscientious web designer, it's your job to ensure that these users are served nothing frivolous. What counts as "frivolous" or "nonessential" is often a tough call, because what's trivial to one person might be vital to another. You'll need to exercise some judgment here, but that's why they pay you the big bucks.

> ❝ *Mobile devices require software development teams to focus on only the most important data and actions in an application. There simply isn't room in a 320 by 480 pixel screen for extraneous, unnecessary elements. You have to prioritize.* —Luke Wroblewski

As an illustration, suppose that you modify the example page so that it includes a second `aside` element on the left, which you'll use to display a quotation related to responsive web design. This touch is nice but not essential, particularly because in the normal flow of the web page, this element would appear before the `article` element. As shown in the following code, add this new `aside` element with the `display: none` declaration to hide it by default. Then use a media query to display the element on screens that are at least 750 pixels wide.

▶ *Example*   ⇨ **Online:** wdpg.io/13-5-1
This code uses a media query to display the otherwise-hidden `<aside class="quotation">` *element on screens that are at least 750 pixels wide.*

CSS

```css
.quotation {
    display: none;        The quotation class is
}                         hidden by default.

@media (min-width: 750px) {
    .quotation {
        display: block;   On screens at least 750px
    }                     wide, the element is displayed.
}
```

HTML

```html
<header>
    <h1>Responsive Web Design</h1>
</header>
<main>
    <aside class="quotation">
        <h3>Quote</h3>
        etc.                      The new quotation element
    </aside>
    <article>
        <h2>A Brief History</h2>
        <p>Early in the new millennium, etc.</p>
    </article>
    <aside>
        <h3>Links</h3>
        etc.
    </aside>
</main>
<footer>
    <p>&copy; Logophilia Limited</p>
</footer>
```

Figure 13.12 shows that on a smartphone, the layout doesn't include the quotation sidebar, but it does appear on a wider screen like the tablet shown in Figure 13.13.

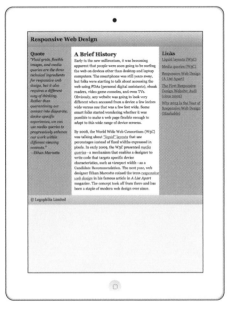

▶Figure 13.12 The quotation sidebar doesn't appear on a narrow smartphone screen.

▶Figure 13.13 The quotation sidebar does appear on a wider screen, such as a tablet.

Which Layout Is the Responsive One?

That's a good question. The answer is that together, they *all* add up to the modern conception of a responsive layout: one that uses relative measurements, a flexible grid, and media queries, all presented with a mobile-first approach. If you incorporate these concepts into your pages, you'll be well along the road to your ultimate destination: a fully responsive web design.

But you're not quite there yet. To complete the journey, you need to know how to make your images and text responsive. You learn how to do that in Chapter 14.

REMEMBER

A layout that uses relative measurement units, a flexible grid, media queries, and a mobile-first approach is known as a responsive layout.

Summary

- Avoid fixed-width layouts in which page elements are sized by using absolute measurements such as pixels.

- Use liquid layouts in which horizontal measures such as widths, paddings, and margins are expressed in percentages.

- If doing so is appropriate for your design, use flexbox or inline blocks to create a flexible layout that allows page elements to wrap as the screen size gets smaller.

- To create an adaptive layout, use media queries to adjust element sizes, change the layout, and hide or display elements depending on the screen size.

- Use a mobile-first approach in which your initial page layout is optimized for a smartphone, and use media queries to add features and change the layout as needed for larger screens.

Making Your Images and Typography Responsive

The most important thing about responsive design is flexibility. Everything must be flexible: layouts, image sizes, text blocks—absolutely everything. Flexibility gives your site the fluidity it needs to fit inside any container. —Nick Babich

 This chapter covers

- Making fluid images that respond to screen size
- Delivering different-size images based on the user's screen size
- Making text adapt to the screen size by specifying responsive font sizes
- Making other page elements adapt to the screen size by specifying responsive measurements

In Chapter 13, you learned not only why you shouldn't use a fixed-width layout, but also why (and how) you should use responsive layouts that are both flexible and adaptive. Having your page layout change in response to different screen widths is a must in these days of wildly different screen sizes, but it's only part of the total responsive package. To make your pages truly adaptable to any device, you need to sprinkle both your page images and page typography with responsive pixie dust. You need to style images to scale up or down depending on the screen width, deliver different images based on the screen size, and use responsive type sizes. You learn these and other powerful responsive techniques in this chapter.

Making Images Responsive

Making an image responsive is one of the biggest challenges that web designers face. The scale of the challenge comes from two problems associated with making images responsive:

- Making a fixed-size image fit into a container with fluid dimensions. An image that's 600 pixels wide will fit nicely inside an element that's 800 pixels wide, but it overflows if that element is scaled down to 400 pixels wide. Solving this problem requires making images fluid so that the size adjusts to the changing screen size.

- Delivering a version of an image that's sized appropriately for the user's screen dimensions. It's one thing to offer up a 2,000 x 1,500-pixel image to desktop users, but sending the same image to smartphone users is a waste of upload time and bandwidth.

The next two lessons show you some basic methods for overcoming these problems.

Lesson 14.1: *Creating Fluid Images*
Covers: Styling the img element for responsiveness

⇨ **Online:** wdpg.io/14-1-0

An image comes with a predetermined width and height, so at first blush, it seems impossible to overcome these fixed dimensions. Fortunately, an <img> tag is another page element. Yes, by default the image is displayed at its full width and height, like a div or any other block element. But in the same way that you can make a block element fluid by using percentages, you can make an image fluid.

You need to be a bit careful when working with images:

- In most cases, you don't want the image to scale larger than its original size since, for most images, this scaling will result in ugly pixilation and jagged edges.

- If you change one dimension of an image, it will almost certainly appear to be skewed because its original aspect ratio—the ratio of the width to the height of the image—will have been altered. Therefore, you have to change both the width and the height proportionally to retain the image's original aspect ratio. Fortunately, you can get the browser to do some of the work for you.

To handle both concerns, you can create a fluid image that responds to changes in screen size by applying the following rule:

```
img {
    max-width: 100%;
    height: auto;
}
```

Setting `max-width: 100%` allows the image to scale smaller or larger as its parent container changes size but also specifies that the image can never scale larger than its original width. Setting `height: auto` tells the browser to maintain the image's original aspect ratio by calculating the height based on the image's current width.

The following code shows an example.

PLAY

In some cases, you don't want the image height to scale larger than its original height, so you need to set `max-height: 100%` *and* `width: auto` *on the image.* ⇨ Online: wdpg.io/14-1-2

▶*Example*   ⇨ **Online:** wdpg.io/14-1-1

This code creates a fluid image that scales smaller or larger as the screen size changes but doesn't scale larger than its original dimensions.

CSS

```
img {
    max-width: 100%;
    height: auto;
}
```

The rule that makes images fluid

HTML

```
<header>
    <h1>Responsive Web Design</h1>
</header>
<main>
    <aside class="quotation">
        <h3>Quote</h3>
        etc.
    </aside>
    <article>
        <h2>A Brief History</h2>
        <p>Early in the new millennium, etc.</p>
    </article>
    <aside>
        <h3>Links</h3>
        etc.
        <img src="/images/rwd.tif" alt="Responsive Web Design
image">
    </aside>
</main>
<footer>
    <p>&copy; Logophilia Limited</p>
</footer>
```

An image added to the aside element

Figures 14.1 and 14.2 show how the image size changes as the width of its parent `aside` element changes.

▶ Figure 14.1 The image as it appears when its `aside` parent element is given the full width of a smartphone screen

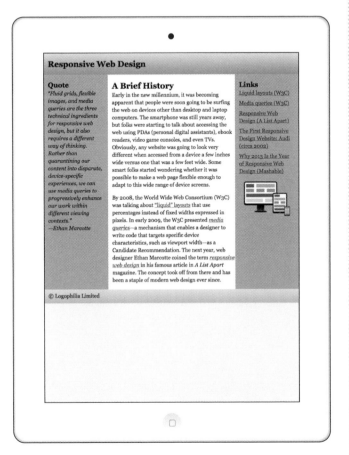

▶ Figure 14.2 When the `aside` element is displayed at a narrower width, the image scales down accordingly.

Lesson 14.2: **Delivering Images Responsively**
Covers: The `sizes` and `srcset` attributes

> ➡ **Online:** wdpg.io/14-2-0

The other side of the responsive-image coin involves delivering to the user a version of the image that has a size that's appropriate for the device screen. You might deliver a small version of the image for smartphone screens, a medium version for tablets, and a large version for desktops. In the past, you needed a script to handle this task, but in HTML5, you can do everything right in your `<img>` tag thanks to two new attributes: `sizes` and `srcset`.

The `sizes` attribute is similar to a media query in that you use an expression to specify a screen feature, such as a minimum or maximum height, and then specify how wide you want the image to be displayed on screens that match that configuration. You can specify multiple expression-width pairs, separated by commas. Here's the general syntax:

```
sizes="(expression1) width1,
       (expression2) width2,
       etc.,
       widthN"
```

Notice that if the last item doesn't specify an expression, the specified width applies to any screen that doesn't match any of the expressions. Suppose that you want images to be displayed with width 90vw on screens that are less than or equal to 500px and 50vw on all other screens. Here's how you'd set that up:

```
sizes="(max-width: 500px) 90vw, 50vw"
```

Next, add to your `<img>` tag the `srcset` attribute, which you set to a comma-separated list of image file locations, each followed by the image width and letter w. Here's the general syntax:

```
srcset="location1 width1w,
        location2 width2w,
        etc.">
```

This code gives the browser a choice of image sizes, and it picks the best one based on the current device's screen dimensions and the preferred widths you specified in the `sizes` attribute. Here's an example:

```
srcset="/images/small.tif 400w,
        /images/medium.tif 800w,
        /images/large.tif 1200w">
```

The following example puts everything together to show you how to deliver images responsively.

BEWARE

When you're testing the `srcset` attribute by changing the browser window size, you may find that the browser doesn't always download a different-size image. Although the browser may detect that a smaller image should be used based on the `srcset` values, it may opt to resize the existing image, because it has already downloaded that image.

REMEMBER

The default image—that is, the image specified with the `src` attribute—is the fallback image that will be displayed in older browsers that don't support the `srcset` attribute. Good mobile-first practice is to make the default image the one you prefer to deliver to mobile users.

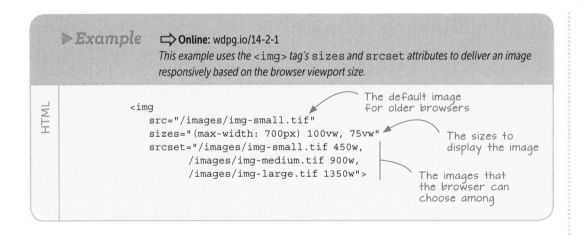

This example uses the `<img>` tag's `sizes` and `srcset` attributes to deliver an image responsively based on the browser viewport size.

HTML

```
<img
    src="/images/img-small.tif"
    sizes="(max-width: 700px) 100vw, 75vw"
    srcset="/images/img-small.tif 450w,
            /images/img-medium.tif 900w,
            /images/img-large.tif 1350w">
```

The default image for older browsers

The sizes to display the image

The images that the browser can choose among

Figures 14.3 through 14.5 show how the image that's delivered to the browser changes as the size of the screen changes.

▶ **Figure 14.3**
A wide browser viewport gets the large image.

▶Figure 14.4 A tablet-size viewport gets the medium image.

▶Figure 14.5 A smartphone-size viewport gets the small image.

Making Typography Responsive

Is your goal to enrage some of the people who visit your website? I thought not, but you may be doing that if you use pixels for your site typography. Web browsers such as Google Chrome and Mozilla Firefox enable users to specify a default font size, which is set to 16px in all modern browsers, but people with aging eyesight or visual impairments often bump this default to 24px, 32px, or even higher. If you use the declaration font-size: 16px for, say, your page's body text, *all* your visitors—and in particular those who increased their default font size—will see your text at that size. Cue the rage.

Fortunately, it's easy to avoid that scenario by switching to relative units for your font-size values. One possibility is the em unit, where 1em corresponds to the browser's default font size—or, crucially, the *user's* specified default font size. If that default is 16px, 1.5em corresponds to 24px, and 3em corresponds to 48px. If the default is 24px, 1.5em would render at 36px, and 3em would render at 72px.

Making Your Images and Typography Responsive

That solution may seem to be perfect, but there's an inheritance fly in this responsive soup. First, let me point out that *inheritance* means that for certain CSS properties, if a parent element is styled with the font-size property, its child and descendant elements are automatically styled the same way. (See Chapter 19 to learn more about this crucial CSS concept.) To see the problem, first consider the following HTML and CSS and then answer one question: If the default font size is 16px, what is the font size, in pixels, of the h1 element?

HTML:

```
<body>
    <header>
        <h1>What's My Font Size?</h1>
    </header>
</body>
```

CSS:

```
body {
    font-size: 1em;
}
header {
    font-size: 1.5em;
}
h1 {
    font-size: 2em;
}
```

Your intuitive guess may be that because the h1 element is declared with font-size: 2em, it must get rendered at 32px. Alas, that's not the case, and to understand why, you need to know that the font-size property is inherited, which leads to the following sequence:

1 The body element's font size (1em) is set to 16px.

2 The header element inherits the font size from the body element, so the header element's font size (1.5em) is set to 24px.

3 The h1 element inherits the font size from the header element, so the h1 element's font size (2em) is set to 48px.

That's not a deal-breaker when it comes to using em units; you need to be aware of this fact and take the inherited font sizes into account.

If you don't feel like doing the math required to work successfully with em units, there's an alternative: the rem unit. rem is short for *root em* and refers to the font size of the page root, which is the html element. Two things to note:

- Because the root's font size is the same as the default font size, and because the rem unit scales in the same way as the em unit, the rem unit is responsive.

- Because the rem unit always inherits its font size only from the html element, there are no inheritance gotchas to worry about. An h1 element declared with font-size: 2rem will always render at twice the default font size.

This isn't to say that you should always use rem over em. There may be situations in which you *want* a child element's font size to be relative to its parent's font size, in which case em units are the best choice.

Lesson 14.3: *Using Responsive Font Sizes*
Covers: Using rem units for font-size

⇨ **Online:** wdpg.io/14-3-0

The following code updates the example page to replace the font-size property's absolute px units with relative rem units.

▶ *Example*　⇨ **Online:** wdpg.io/14-3-1

This code updates the example page to replace the font-size property's absolute px units with relative rem units.

CSS

```css
h1 {
    font-size: 2rem;
}
h2 {
    font-size: 1.5rem;
}
h3 {
    font-size: 1.25rem;
}
@media (min-width: 750px) {
    h1 {
        font-size: 2.5rem;
    }
    h2 {
        font-size: 2rem;
    }
    h3 {
        font-size: 1.5rem;
    }
}
```

The header elements are given mobile-first rem font sizes.

The header elements are also given large-screen rem font sizes.

Lesson 14.4: **Using Responsive Measurements**
Covers: Using `rem` units for measurements

⇨ **Online:** wdpg.io/14-4-0

Unfortunately, the bad design results that come from using absolute units such a `px` aren't restricted to font sizes. To see what I mean, consider the following code, the results of which are shown in Figure 14.6:

```
HTML:
<header>
    <h1>Responsive Web Design</h1>
</header>
CSS:
header {
    height: 64px;
}
h1 {
    font-size: 2rem;
}
```

Responsive Web Design

▶ Figure 14.6 The `h1` text looks good at `2rem`.

Looks good! But what happens when I change the default font in my web browser (Firefox) to 30px? Figure 14.7 shows the sad story.

Responsive Web Design

▶ Figure 14.7 The element doesn't render so well when a larger default font is used.

At the larger default size, the heading is larger than the `header` element in which it's contained, resulting in an overall crowded feel to the text and (much worse) to cutting off the descenders of the *p* and *g*.

Why did this happen? The header element's `height` property uses an absolute value of `64px`. That height won't budge a pixel no matter what font size you use as the default. But consider the following revised code and the result shown in Figure 14.8:

```
HTML:
<header>
    <h1>Responsive Web Design</h1>
</header>
CSS:
header {
    height: 4rem;
}
h1 {
    font-size: 2rem;
}
```

REMEMBER

This example is artificial because in practice, you'd rarely set an explicit height on an element. Instead, it's always better to let the content dictate an element's height naturally.

Responsive Web Design

▶Figure 14.8 With the `header` element's `height` property now using relative `rem` units, the `header` scales along with the text as the default font size changes.

The only change I made was to declare `height: 4rem` on the `header` element. Using the relative unit makes the height responsive, so it increases (or decreases) along with the font size when the default font value is changed.

How you use relative units for measurements depends on many factors, not least of which is the design effect you're trying to achieve. It's possible, however, to suggest a few guidelines:

- For vertical measures such as `padding-top`, `padding-bottom`, `margin-top`, and `margin-bottom`, use `rem` units.

- For horizontal measures such as `width`, `padding-right`, `padding-left`, `margin-right`, and `margin-left`, use percentages.

- For horizontal measures in which you want more control of properties such as `width`, `max-width`, and `min-width`, use `rem` units.

- For vertical measures that you want to scale in relation to the viewport height, use `vh` units.

- For horizontal measures that you want to scale in relation to the viewport width, use `vw` units.

BEWARE

Because a percentage is relative to the parent element, you may find that using percentages for padding or margins leads to unexpected or bizarre results. In such cases, you should switch to rem *units for more control.*

▶ *Example*   ⇨ **Online:** wdpg.io/14-4-1

This code updates the example page to replace all the absolute px measurements with relative rem or percentage units.

CSS

```
.container {
    max-width: 60rem;
}
header {
    padding: 1rem
 1.67%;
}
h1 {
    padding-left: 1.67%;
}
.quotation {
    padding-right: 1.67%;
}
article {
    flex-basis: 20rem;
    padding-top: 1rem;
    padding-left: 1.67%;
}
p {
    margin-bottom: 1rem;
}
aside {
    flex-basis: 10rem;
    padding: 1rem
 1.67%;
}
div {
    padding-bottom: .5rem;
}
footer {
    padding: 1rem
 1.67%;
}
```

rem units used for greater control

rem units used on all vertical measures

Percentages used on all the other horizontal measures

Gallery of Responsive Sites

▶ Hicks Design (https://hicksdesign.co.uk) offers a gallerylike layout that presents a clean, uncluttered look that scales perfectly to any size screen.

Making Your Images and Typography Responsive

▶ The Andersson-Wise site (www.anderssonwise.com) gracefully restructures its layout as it scales from the desktop version to the tablet and smartphone versions.

▶ The Boston Globe front page (www.bostonglobe.com) responsively changes from a three-column layout on the desktop to a two-column layout on a tablet and to a one-column layout on a smartphone.

▶ The Authentic Jobs site (https://authenticjobs.com) displays a simple job list on a smartphone-size screen and progressively adds more detailed information as the screen size increases.

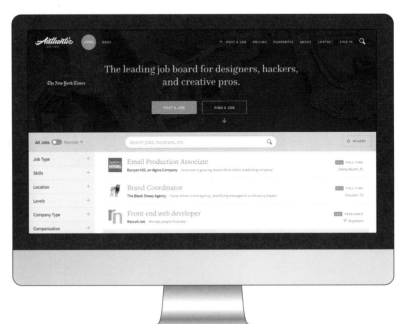

Summary

- Make your images fluid by styling them with the declarations `max-width: 100%` and `height: auto`.

- In your `<img>` tags, add the `sizes` and `srcset` attributes to scale and deliver images that are appropriate for any screen size.

- When styling font sizes, avoid absolute pixel values in favor of `rem` units.

- Also use `rem` units when styling vertical measures such as height, padding, and margins.

Chapter 15

PROJECT: Creating a Photo Gallery

People love photos. If you start publishing photos, they will quickly become the most popular part of your site. —Brian Bailey

 This chapter covers

- Planning and sketching your photo gallery
- Choosing typefaces for your page
- Adding the header and navigation links
- Adding the image thumbnails
- Adding dynamic captions and links to full-size images

Unlike with your first two projects—the personal home page that you built in Chapter 5 and the landing page you built in Chapter 10—you now know enough to create a page that looks like it was designed and coded by a professional. If that seems like a stretch at this point in your web-design journey, this chapter will prove that I'm right. Here, I'll take you through the construction of a full-featured photo gallery, complete with dynamically generated captions, links to full-size versions of each thumbnail, and much more. You'll be leveraging many of the tools and techniques that you've learned so far, including class selectors, the CSS box model, images (of course), and layouts. Let's get to work!

PROJECT: Creating a Photo Gallery

What You'll Be Building

This project is an online gallery for showing off your photos. The page will consist of at least half a dozen *thumbnails*, which are reduced-size versions of your images. The idea is that a site visitor should be able to click one of these thumbnails to display the full-size version of the image. Each thumbnail should also display a short caption that describes the image.

On the surface, this project is a simple one. Truthfully, the resulting page will *look* simple, as well. It will look *nice*, mind you, but it will project to the visitor an air of simplicity. The fact that the site *looks* unsophisticated, however, doesn't mean that it's built that way. As you'll soon learn, this page has some rocking technology under the hood, including a flexbox-based layout, viewport-based sizing, and sophisticated positioning techniques.

Getting Your Photos Ready

You should begin this project by getting at least some of your photos ready to use. You'll want to use JPEGs for everything, because they give you smaller file sizes while maintaining good photo quality. You'll also need two versions of each image: a regular-size version and a thumbnail version. In the page layout I use, all the thumbnails need to be the same size. It doesn't matter what size you use, but in my project, I resized all my thumbnails to a 300-pixel width and a 200-pixel height. The full-size versions can be whatever size you want.

Sketching the Layout

As you've seen in the earlier projects (see Chapters 5 and 10), your web projects should begin with a pencil and paper (or whatever variation on that theme you're most comfortable with). You're learning how to design web pages, and any design worthy of the name always begins with a quick sketch to get an overall feel for the page dimensions and components. *Quick* is the operative word. You don't need to create an artist's rendering of the final page. As shown in Figure 15.1, you need to lay out the main sections of the page and indicate the approximate location, size, and contents of each section.

Figure 15.1 shows the layout of a page with the following four sections:

- A header with a site logo and title
- A navigation area with links to other gallery pages
- The main section of the page containing the image thumbnails
- The page footer with a copyright notice and links to social media sites

With that out of the way, it's time to turn your attention to the typeface or typefaces you want to use for the page.

▶ **Figure 15.1**
Before diving in to the page's HTML and CSS details, use pencil and paper to get a sense of the overall page layout and content.

Choosing Typefaces

This page has little type, so the choice of a typeface shouldn't take up too much of your time. There are three areas where your choice of typeface will come into play:

- *Heading*—Something that looks handwritten would be nice. For my project, I'm going to keep things simple and use the default `cursive` typeface. For something that has good coverage on both Windows PCs and Mac, you could go with Brush Script MT.

- *Navigation and footer*—The text here consists mostly of links, so a nice, clean sans-serif font is a good choice. For my project, I'm going with Calibri (installed on most Windows PCs) and Optima (installed on most Macs).

- *Thumbnail-image captions*—These captions are fairly small, so I recommend a typeface that remains readable even at small sizes. I'll stick with Calibri and Optima for my captions.

In my CSS, I'll use the following declarations to specify these families:

```
font-family: cursive;
font-family: Optima, Calibri, sans-serif;
```

Now turn your attention to a color scheme for the photo gallery.

Choosing the Colors

This page is simple, color wise, so you don't need to build an elaborate color scheme. In fact, in my version of this project, I'm using just three main colors:

- *Header and footer background*—This design looks balanced when the header and the footer have the same color. Because the main background (discussed next) should be relatively plain to show off the thumbnails, the header and footer background gives you a chance to pick something with a bit of pizzazz to liven up the page.

- *Main background*—This area takes up the bulk of the page, and it's used to show both the image thumbnails and the navigation links. A color such as black or dark versions of gray, brown, or blue work best for this purpose.

- *Text*—This color needs to read well in all three sections of the page: header, main, and footer. Assuming these sections are using dark backgrounds, an off-white color such as #eee would work fine, as would something along the lines of a not-too-bright yellow.

Figure 15.2 shows the colors I chose for my project.

▶ Figure 15.2
The color scheme for my project

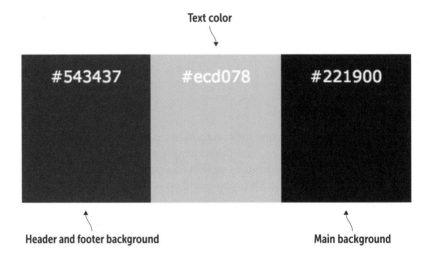

Text color

#543437   #ecd078   #221900

Header and footer background   Main background

With the page layout sketched and your typefaces and colors chosen, it's time to make things more concrete (virtually speaking) by translating everything into HTML and CSS code.

Building the Page

To build your photo gallery, start with the skeleton code that I introduced you to in Chapter 1. From there, go section by section, adding text, HTML tags, and CSS properties.

The Initial Structure

To get things started, take the basic page structure from Chapter 1 and add the gallery layout. I'm going to use the HTML5 semantic elements:

- The page header section uses the `header` element, and it consists of two items: an `img` element for the site logo and an `h1` element for the site title.

- The navigation section uses the `nav` element, and it consists of an unordered list of links to other pages of the gallery.

- The main section uses the `main` element, and it consists of several `img` elements, each of which points to a thumbnail version of a photo.

- The page footer section uses the `footer` element, and it consists of a copyright notice and links to several social media sites.

▶ *Try This* ⇨ **Online:** wdpg.io/projects/photo-gallery/01
Here are the elements that make up the photo gallery's initial HTML structure.

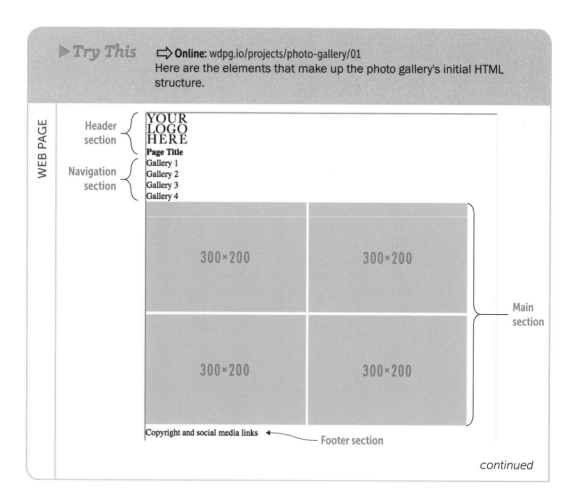

continued

```
<header>
    <img src="/images/your-logo-here.tif" alt="My logo">
    <h1>Page Title</h1>
</header>
    <nav>
    <ul>
        <li>Gallery 1</li>
        <li>Gallery 2</li>
        <li>Gallery 3</li>
        <li>Gallery 4</li>
    </ul>
</nav>
<main>
    <img src="http://placehold.it/300x200" alt="">
    <img src="http://placehold.it/300x200" alt="">
    <img src="http://placehold.it/300x200" alt="">
    <img src="http://placehold.it/300x200" alt="">
</main>
<footer>
    <p>Copyright and social media links</p>
</footer>
```

HTML

The header section

The navigation section

The main section (the image thumbnails)

The footer section

REMEMBER

The initial page layout also includes a CSS reset that sets the margin and padding to 0 and the box sizing to border-box.

The gallery isn't much to look at right now, but you'll soon fix that problem. You start by setting up the page's overall layout.

The Overall Layout

After spending all that time learning how to use flexbox in Chapter 12, you'll be pleased to hear that you'll be putting that effort to good use here, because this project uses flexbox for all its layout.

Get things rolling by setting up the initial flexbox container. The <body> tag will do nicely for that purpose, and you'll use it as a single-column container, which gives you a vertical main axis. You want the items aligned with the start of that axis (that is, the top of the page). You also want everything to be centered horizontally, and you want the footer to appear at the bottom of the screen, even when there isn't enough content to fill the rest of the page. The following example shows you how to set everything up.

> ▶ *Try This*   ⇨ **Online:** wdpg.io/projects/photo-gallery/02
>
> This example shows you how to configure the body element as a flexbox container for the entire page.

```css
body {
    display: flex;
    flex-direction: column;
    justify-content: flex-start;
    align-items: center;
    min-height: 100vh;
    font-family: Optima, Calibri, sans-serif;
    background-color: #221900;
    color: #ecd078;
}
```

Set a minimum height.

Set up the flexbox container.

Apply a font stack and the background and text colors.

The one comment I'll add here concerns the `min-height` property. By declaring this property to be `100vh`, you're telling the browser that the body element is always at least the height of the browser's viewport. Having the body element height greater than or equal to the height of the viewport ensures that the footer section appears at the bottom of the screen, even if there isn't enough content to fill the viewport vertically.

The Header Section

The header section consists of a `header` element that contains two items: an `img` element for the site logo and an `h1` element for the site title. You also want the header to have the following features:

- Because the header background is different from the page background, the header will look best if it extends across the width of the browser window. To do this, declare `width: 100%` on the `header` element.

- The site logo and title should be centered both horizontally and vertically within the header. Configure the `header` element as a flexbox container with a horizontal main axis and both `justify-content` and `align-items` set to `center`.

The following example shows the HTML and CSS that I used to accomplish these goals and to style the rest of the header section.

REMEMBER

*Flexbox now enjoys near-universal browser support, so to keep things simple and uncluttered, the code you see here and on the Playground doesn't include any vendor prefixes. If you need to support old browsers, however, use Autoprefixer (***https:// autoprefixer.github.io***) to generate the prefixes.*

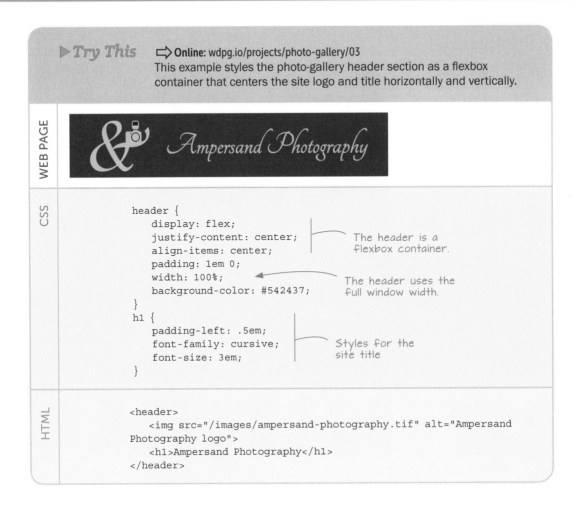

▶ *Try This*   ⇨ **Online:** wdpg.io/projects/photo-gallery/03
This example styles the photo-gallery header section as a flexbox container that centers the site logo and title horizontally and vertically.

WEB PAGE

Ampersand Photography

CSS

```css
header {
    display: flex;
    justify-content: center;
    align-items: center;
    padding: 1em 0;
    width: 100%;
    background-color: #542437;
}
h1 {
    padding-left: .5em;
    font-family: cursive;
    font-size: 3em;
}
```

The header is a flexbox container.

The header uses the full window width.

Styles for the site title

HTML

```html
<header>
    <img src="/images/ampersand-photography.tif" alt="Ampersand Photography logo">
    <h1>Ampersand Photography</h1>
</header>
```

The Navigation Section

The next area of the page is the navigation section, which consists of several links to other gallery pages. This section uses the nav element and contains an unordered list of links. Here's a list of the goals you want to accomplish for this section:

- The links should be centered both horizontally and vertically within the navigation section. Set up the nav element as a flexbox container with a horizontal main axis and both justify-content and align-items set to center.

- The links should appear as a horizontal bulleted list without the bullets. To do this, configure the ul element as a flexbox container and set the list-style-type property to none.

The following example shows the HTML and CSS that I used to accomplish these goals and to style the rest of the navigation section.

▶ *Try This*   ⇨ **Online:** wdpg.io/projects/photo-gallery/04
This example styles the photo gallery's navigation section as a flexbox container that displays the unordered list items horizontally.

WEB PAGE

| GALLERY 1 | GALLERY 2 | GALLERY 3 | GALLERY 4 |

CSS

```css
nav {
    display: flex;
    justify-content: center;
    align-items: center;
    width: 100%;
    background-color: inherit;}
nav ul {
    display: flex;
    list-style-type: none;}
nav li {
    padding: 1em 2.5em;
    text-transform: uppercase;}
```

The nav is a flexbox container.

The ul is a flexbox container, and its bullets are hidden.

Styles for the li elements

HTML

```html
<nav>
    <ul>
        <li><a href="gallery1.html">Gallery 1</a></li>
        <li><a href="gallery2.html">Gallery 2</a></li>
        <li><a href="gallery3.html">Gallery 3</a></li>
        <li><a href="gallery4.html">Gallery 4</a></li>
    </ul>
</nav>
```

You should see two problems with the navigation links right away:

- The link text is the standard blue that browsers use for links. By default, links don't pick up the parent's text color, so you need to tell the browser to use that color for links. In most cases, the easiest way is to declare color: inherit on the a element.

- Nothing indicates which gallery page is currently being displayed. To solve this problem, apply a special style to the navigation text for the current page. I created a class named current-page and used it to style the current li element with the background and text colors switched.

The following example shows the revised navigation links.

MASTER

You could declare the page's text color explicitly, but if you decide to change the text color later, you have to make the change in two places: the body *element and the* a *element. When you use* inherit, *the* a *element automatically picks up any change you make in the* body *element's text color.*

PROJECT: Creating a Photo Gallery

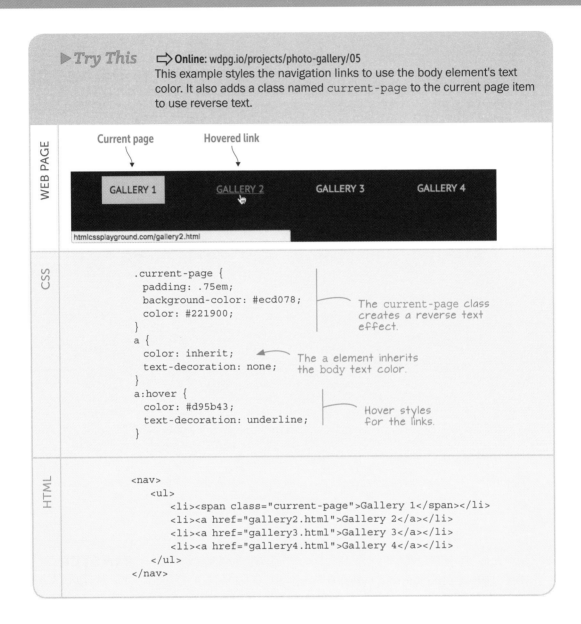

▶ **Try This** ⇨ **Online:** wdpg.io/projects/photo-gallery/05
This example styles the navigation links to use the body element's text color. It also adds a class named `current-page` to the current page item to use reverse text.

WEB PAGE

Current page   Hovered link

GALLERY 1   GALLERY 2   GALLERY 3   GALLERY 4

htmlcssplayground.com/gallery2.html

CSS

```css
.current-page {
  padding: .75em;
  background-color: #ecd078;
  color: #221900;
}
a {
  color: inherit;
  text-decoration: none;
}
a:hover {
  color: #d95b43;
  text-decoration: underline;
}
```

The current-page class creates a reverse text effect.

The a element inherits the body text color.

Hover styles for the links.

HTML

```html
<nav>
    <ul>
        <li><span class="current-page">Gallery 1</span></li>
        <li><a href="gallery2.html">Gallery 2</a></li>
        <li><a href="gallery3.html">Gallery 3</a></li>
        <li><a href="gallery4.html">Gallery 4</a></li>
    </ul>
</nav>
```

The Main Section

The real meat of the photo gallery is, of course, the photos themselves. The basic idea of a gallery is to display a thumbnail of an original photo and enable the visitor to view the original. The simplest way is to set up each thumbnail as a link that points to the original, as I've done in the following example. Note, too, that I set up `main` as a flexbox container that centers the thumbnails horizontally and allows them to wrap.

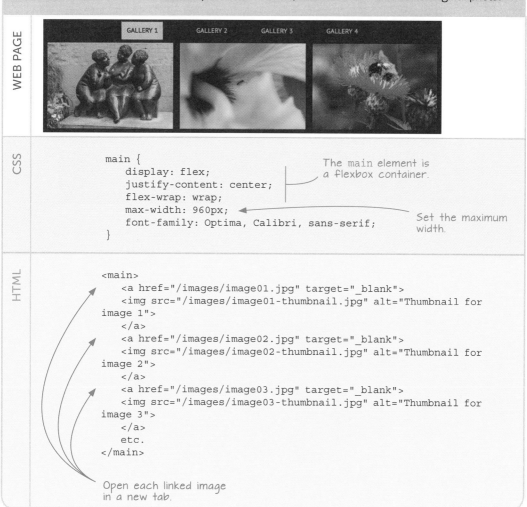

WEB PAGE

GALLERY 1   GALLERY 2   GALLERY 3   GALLERY 4

CSS

```
main {
    display: flex;
    justify-content: center;
    flex-wrap: wrap;
    max-width: 960px;
    font-family: Optima, Calibri, sans-serif;
}
```

The main element is a flexbox container.

Set the maximum width.

HTML

```
<main>
    <a href="/images/image01.jpg" target="_blank">
    <img src="/images/image01-thumbnail.jpg" alt="Thumbnail for
image 1">
    </a>
    <a href="/images/image02.jpg" target="_blank">
    <img src="/images/image02-thumbnail.jpg" alt="Thumbnail for
image 2">
    </a>
    <a href="/images/image03.jpg" target="_blank">
    <img src="/images/image03-thumbnail.jpg" alt="Thumbnail for
image 3">
    </a>
    etc.
</main>
```

Open each linked image in a new tab.

▶ *Try This*   ⇨ **Online:** wdpg.io/projects/photo-gallery/07
This example sets up the `main` element as a flexbox container. The flex items are the photo thumbnails, each of which links to its original photo.

The Footer Section

The final element of the photo gallery page is the footer section, which you'll use to display a copyright notice and links to social media sites. To align these items horizontally and vertically, configure the `footer` element as a flex container.

REMEMBER

In this project's `main` *element, the secondary axis runs vertically, so the declaration* `align-content: flex-start` *tells the browser to keep all the thumbnails aligned with the top of the* `main` *element.*

PROJECT: Creating a Photo Gallery

Note as well that you want the `footer` element to appear at the bottom of the page, even when the `main` element doesn't fill the browser window vertically. You need to set the `main` element's flex-grow property to 1 to force it to fill in the space. That solution creates weird vertical spacing in the thumbnails, however. To fix that problem, add `align-content: flex-start` to the `main` element. The following example shows how.

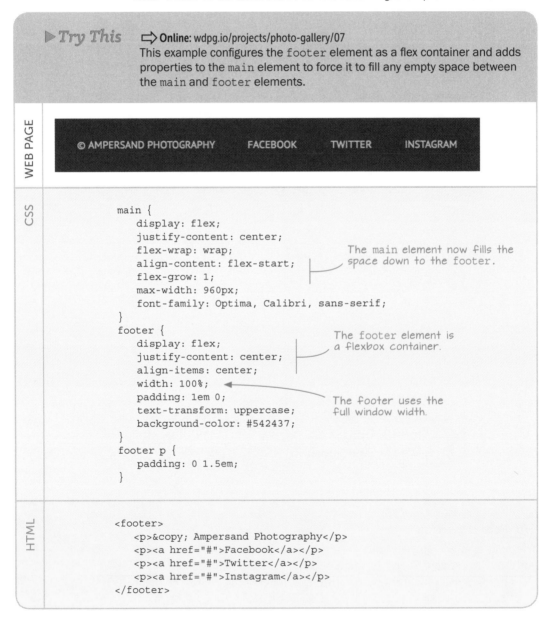

▶ *Try This*   ⇨ **Online:** wdpg.io/projects/photo-gallery/07
This example configures the `footer` element as a flex container and adds properties to the `main` element to force it to fill any empty space between the `main` and `footer` elements.

WEB PAGE

© AMPERSAND PHOTOGRAPHY   FACEBOOK   TWITTER   INSTAGRAM

CSS

```css
main {
    display: flex;
    justify-content: center;
    flex-wrap: wrap;
    align-content: flex-start;
    flex-grow: 1;
    max-width: 960px;
    font-family: Optima, Calibri, sans-serif;
}
footer {
    display: flex;
    justify-content: center;
    align-items: center;
    width: 100%;
    padding: 1em 0;
    text-transform: uppercase;
    background-color: #542437;
}
footer p {
    padding: 0 1.5em;
}
```

The main element now fills the space down to the footer.

The footer element is a flexbox container.

The footer uses the full window width.

HTML

```html
<footer>
    <p>&copy; Ampersand Photography</p>
    <p><a href="#">Facebook</a></p>
    <p><a href="#">Twitter</a></p>
    <p><a href="#">Instagram</a></p>
</footer>
```

Adding a Few Tricks

As it stands, your photo gallery is a decent page that looks good and works well. That may be all you're looking for, and if so, you need read no further. If you've been thinking that the gallery is a bit ho-hum and run-of-the-mill, however, the next few sections show you how to add some dynamic and useful features to the gallery.

Making the Footer Fixed

Earlier, you set things up so that your footer section displays at the bottom of the screen even if there isn't enough content in the main section to fill the browser window. When the `main` element has more content than will fit in the browser window, it pushes the footer down, and the user must scroll to see it. What if you prefer to have your footer always visible?

You can implement the following:

- Set the `footer` element's `position` property to `fixed`.

- Set the `footer` element's `bottom` property to `0`, which tells the browser to fix the footer to the bottom of the viewport.

- Add some padding to the bottom of the `main` element to ensure that the last of its content isn't obscured by the fixed footer. Set the `padding-bottom` value to the same value as the height of the footer element (`3.5em`, in this case).

The following example shows the added code that accomplishes all these tasks.

▶ *Try This*   ⇨ **Online:** wdpg.io/projects/photo-gallery/08
This example fixes the `footer` element to the bottom of the viewport.

WEB PAGE

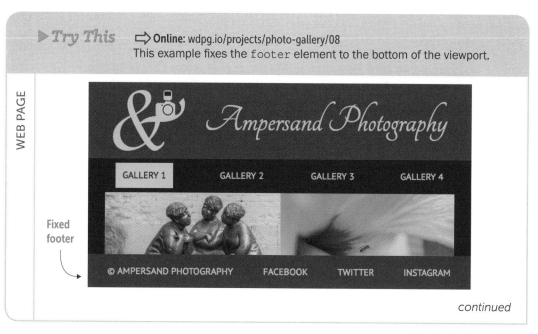

Fixed footer

continued

```
CSS

main {
    display: flex;
    justify-content: center;
    flex-wrap: wrap;
    align-content: flex-start;
    flex-grow: 1;
    max-width: 960px;
    padding-bottom: 3.5em;
}
footer {
    display: flex;
    justify-content: center;
    align-items: center;
    position: fixed;
    bottom: 0;
    width: 100%;
    text-transform: uppercase;
    background-color: #542437;
}
```

Bottom padding on main equals the height of footer.

The footer is fixed.

The footer is positioned at the bottom of the viewport.

PLAY

The full code for the fixed nav element is available on the Playground.
⇨ Online: wdpg.io/ projects/photo-gallery/09

REMEMBER

To make an element sticky in desktop and iOS Safari, you need to use position: -webkit-sticky.

BEWARE

The sticky value is in the early stages of becoming a full member of CSS. As I write this book, it's supported by the most recent versions of Google Chrome, Mozilla Firefox, Apple Safari (desktop and iOS), Microsoft Edge, and Chrome for Android, but not by Internet Explorer.

Making the Nav Bar Sticky

You may not be interested in having a fixed footer, but it's a common layout request to have the navigation bar onscreen full time, no matter how far down the user scrolls. In this case, however, you can't use the same technique that you used for the footer in the preceding section. If you fix the nav bar in place, you also have to fix the header; otherwise, you'd end up with some ugly scrolling. But fixing the header is a waste of screen real estate, so you need a different solution.

One possibility is to switch the positions of the header and nav elements. With the latter now at the top of the screen, you could declare position: fixed and top: 0 on the nav element, and add padding-top: 3.5em to the body element.

That solution is a nice one, but what if (like me) you prefer the nav element to appear below the header? In that case, you can turn to a relatively new CSS position value called sticky. Combined with a specific top or bottom value, sticky tells the browser to scroll the element normally until it hits the specified position and then stick in place.

To set this feature up for your navigation bar, you need to do the following:

- Set the nav element's position property to sticky.

- Set the nav element's top property to 0, which tells the browser to stick the nav bar when it's scrolled to the top of the viewport.

- Set the nav element's z-index property to a positive number (such as 10) to ensure the nav bar always appears on top of the rest of the page elements as they scroll by.

The following example shows the code you need to add to make this happen.

▶ *Try This*   ⇨ **Online:** wdpg.io/projects/photo-gallery/10

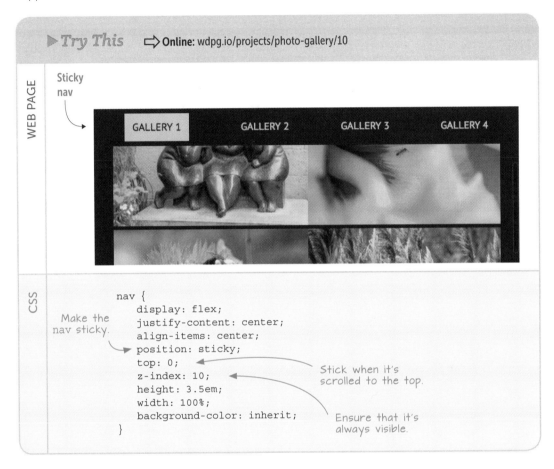

WEB PAGE

Sticky nav

CSS

Make the nav sticky.

Stick when it's scrolled to the top.

Ensure that it's always visible.

```css
nav {
    display: flex;
    justify-content: center;
    align-items: center;
    position: sticky;
    top: 0;
    z-index: 10;
    height: 3.5em;
    width: 100%;
    background-color: inherit;
}
```

Adding Dynamic Captions

One thing your photo gallery lacks is captions for the thumbnails. One straightforward way to add captions is to wrap each thumbnail in a div and configure that div as a flex container with flex-direction set to column. Then you could add the caption as, say, a figcaption element, and it will appear below the thumbnail. The following example demonstrates this technique.

PROJECT: Creating a Photo Gallery

▶ *Try This* ⇨ **Online:** wdpg.io/projects/photo-gallery/11
This example shows one method for adding captions below each thumbnail.

WEB PAGE

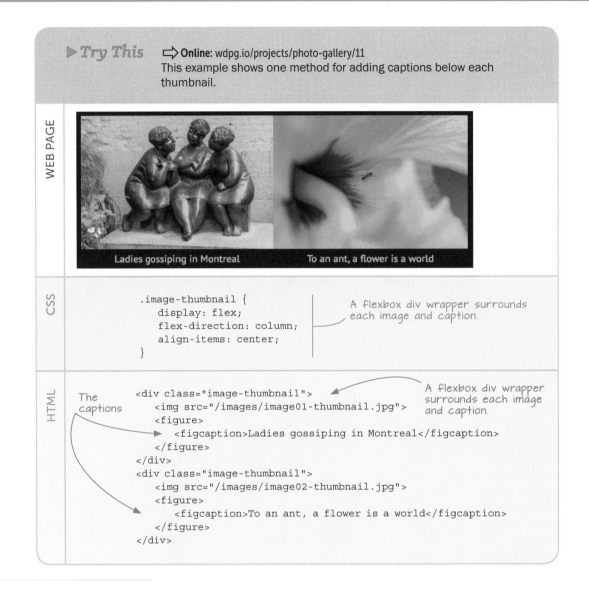

CSS

```css
.image-thumbnail {
    display: flex;
    flex-direction: column;
    align-items: center;
}
```

A flexbox div wrapper surrounds each image and caption.

HTML

The captions

```html
<div class="image-thumbnail">
    <img src="/images/image01-thumbnail.jpg">
    <figure>
        <figcaption>Ladies gossiping in Montreal</figcaption>
    </figure>
</div>
<div class="image-thumbnail">
    <img src="/images/image02-thumbnail.jpg">
    <figure>
        <figcaption>To an ant, a flower is a world</figcaption>
    </figure>
</div>
```

A flexbox div wrapper surrounds each image and caption.

That solution works fine, but I'd like to show you a more advanced technique that comes with a considerable "wow" factor. In this technique, you keep the `figcaption` wrapper but add the `image-caption` class and expand it with `p` elements that you can use for both a caption title and the caption itself:

```html
<div class="image-thumbnail">
    <img src="/images/image01-thumbnail.jpg">
    <figcaption class="image-caption">
        <p class="caption-title">Les Chuchoteuses</p>
        <p class="caption-text">Sculpture of ladies gossiping in
Montreal</p>
    </div>
</div>
```

The caption title and text is enclosed in this figcaption.

Your goal is to hide the caption and display it only when the user hovers the mouse over the thumbnail. In your CSS, you set up the `image-thumbnail` class with relative positioning and a width and height equal to the actual width and height of the thumbnail image:

```
.image-thumbnail {
    position: relative;
    width: 300px;
    height: 200px;        Set these to the same di-
}                         mensions as the thumbnail.
```

Now that `image-thumbnail` is positioned, you're free to use absolute positioning on the `image-caption` class. That's important, because you want to style this class with the same width and height as the thumbnail and then position it in the top-left corner (that is, at `top: 0` and `left: 0`) so that when you display it, it covers the thumbnail. Here's the full CSS for this class:

```
.image-caption {                          Caption is a
    display: flex;                        flex container.
    flex-direction: column;
    justify-content: flex-end;
    position: absolute;
    left: 0;                  Positioned absolutely
    top: 0;                   at top left
    width: 300px;
    height: 200px;          Same dimensions as the thumbnail
    background-color: rgba(32, 32, 32, 0.75);    Dark gray, slightly
    color: #ecd078;                              transparent background
    opacity: 0;         Hidden by default
}
```

Notice that you've set up a flex container with a vertical main axis and the items aligned with `flex-end` so that they appear at the bottom of the container. The background color is set to a dark gray that's slightly transparent, so you'll still be able to see the thumbnail. Finally, the caption has `opacity` set to 0, which means that it's hidden by default.

To show it, add the `hover` pseudo-class to the `image-caption` class and use it to set the `opacity` to 1:

```
.image-caption:hover {
    opacity: 1;
}
```

Figure 15.3 shows an example.

PLAY

The full code for this example is available on the Playground.
⇒ Online: wdpg.io/ projects/photo-gallery/12

▶ Figure 15.3
Hover the mouse over a thumbnail to see the caption.

From Here

The final version of the photo gallery (mine is shown in Figure 15.4) is a great showcase for your photos. (If you want to get your code on the web sooner rather than later, check out Appendix A for the details.)

▶ Figure 15.4
A full-featured photo gallery

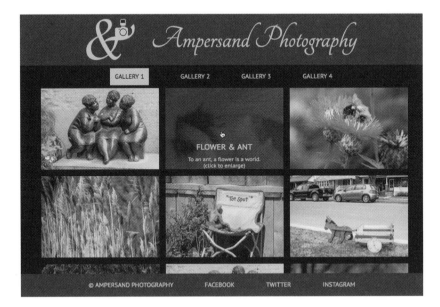

Even though you've built a full-featured photo gallery (especially if you added the extra features from the last section), you still have many ways to add to or modify the gallery. You can always add more images, of course, and if you have a ton of photos to show off, you can add more gallery pages. You can also change the colors, try different typefaces and type sizes, and so on.

Summary

- Prepare thumbnail and full-size versions of the photos you want to display.
- Sketch out the photo gallery you want to build.
- Choose the typefaces for the page title and text.
- Choose colors.
- Build the initial page structure: the barebones HTML tags and the global CSS properties applied to the body element.
- Add the flexbox layout.
- Fill in and style each section one by one: header, navigation, main, and footer.
- Optionally add a few tricks such as a fixed footer, a sticky nav bar, and dynamic captions.

Part 4

Making Your Web Pages Shine

It has been roughly 20 years since most of us started to take notice of the World Wide Web (as we would have long-windedly called it back then). That's not long in the timeline of human history, but it's long enough for us to have mostly forgotten what the web was like back in, say, 1995. If you're old enough to have used the web back then, let me refresh your memory: It was drab. That dreariness was caused by several things, including a universal lack of color, no style sheets, and only a few rudimentary HTML tags. Back then, it didn't even occur to most web surfers that pages could look decent. Ah, now we know better. Now we know that pages can not only look good, but also positively *shine*.

Your own web designs will shine as well when you get through the chapters here in Part 4, where you learn how to use a few sophisticated HTML tags (Chapter 16), how to apply colors and gradients (Chapter 17), gain some advanced web typography skills (Chapter 18), and pick up some professional-level CSS techniques (Chapter 19). Chapter 20 brings everything together by showing you how to build a shiny personal portfolio page.

More HTML Elements for Web Designers

HTML has only a few dozen elements, but we busy developers often forget to use the right tag for the job in hand. It's all too easy to add a `<div>` *or a* `<span>` *when there are more suitable alternatives. —Craig Buckler*

 This chapter covers

- Checking out some underused but important HTML elements
- Linking to files on your site
- Linking to a specific element on a page
- Adding special characters and comments

You may have noticed that after a flurry of HTML-related activity in the early chapters of the book, subsequent chapters had a decidedly CSS flavor. That's not too much of a surprise, because after you know a few basic elements such as `<div>`, `<p>`, and `<span>`, you can hang a lot of CSS baggage on them and create some fine-looking web pages. But there's more to HTML than these basic elements. You saw a few useful page structure elements in Chapter 11, but in this chapter, you'll extend your HTML know-how even further with elements for everything from abbreviations to variables, advanced uses of the `<a>` element, adding nonkeyboard characters to your pages, and even adding comments to make your code more readable. It's a regular HTML extravaganza!

Lesson 16.1: *Other Text-Level Elements You Should Know*
Covers: Text-level elements

⇨ **Online:** wdpg.io/16-1-0

I've mentioned a few times in this book that it's important to construct the HTML portion of your web page code semantically. That is, you should use elements that tell the web browser—not to mention other web designers and developers reading your code—what meaning each element has in the context of the page. This is particularly true when it comes to the overall layout of the page; as you saw in Chapter 11, tags such as `<header>`, `<nav>`, and `<article>` make your code much easier to understand. These elements are block-level elements, but you can also use inline elements and mark them up semantically. HTML5 defines quite a few such text-level elements, and although you may use them only rarely, you should know what they are and what semantic freight they're meant to pull.

<abbr>

This element identifies text as an abbreviation or an acronym. Add the `title` attribute to tell the browser the full version of the abbreviation or the full expansion of the acronym. Most browsers display the `title` value in a tooltip when you hover the mouse pointer over the element. Some browsers (particularly Google Chrome and Mozilla Firefox) add a dotted underline to the text.

▶ *Example*　⇨ **Online:** wdpg.io/16-1-1

WEB PAGE

FOMO

fear of missing out

HTML

```
<abbr title="fear of missing out">FOMO</abbr>
```

<cite>

Use the cite element to mark text that's a reference to a creative work, such as a book, article, essay, poem, blog post, tweet, movie, TV show, play, or work of art. Most browsers display the cited text in italics.

▶*Example*   ⇨ **Online:** wdpg.io/16-1-2

WEB PAGE

"A fine quotation is a diamond on the finger of a man of wit, and a pebble in the hand of a fool".
—*Joseph Roux, Meditations of a Parish Priest*

HTML

```
<q>A fine quotation is a diamond on the finger of a man of wit,
and a pebble in the hand of a fool</q>. —<cite>Joseph Roux,
Meditations of a Parish Priest</cite>
```

<code>

This element identifies text as programming code. Most browsers display the marked-up text in a monospace font.

▶*Example*   ⇨ **Online:** wdpg.io/16-1-3

WEB PAGE

Use the CSS rgb() function.

HTML

```
Use the CSS <code>rgb()</code> function.
```

<dfn>

You use this element to mark the initial or defining instance of a term. Most browsers display the text in italics.

▶ *Example*   ⟹ **Online:** wdpg.io/16-1-4

WEB PAGE

A *header* is an element that appears
at the top of the page.

HTML

```
A <dfn>header</dfn> is an element that appears at the top of the
page.
```

<kbd>

You use the kbd element to indicate text that's entered via the keyboard (such as typed characters or a pressed key, such as Enter or Return) or, more generally, to indicate any type of user input (such as a voice command). Most browsers display the text in a monospace font.

▶ *Example*   ⟹ **Online:** wdpg.io/16-1-5

WEB PAGE

For example, type `Helvetica` and then
press `Enter`.

HTML

```
For example, type <kbd>Helvetica</kbd> and then press
<kbd>Enter</kbd>.
```

<mark>

Use the mark element to highlight page text that has some significance for the reader, similar to the way you'd use a highlighter to mark a passage of text in a book. Most browsers display the text with a yellow background.

▶ *Example* ⇨ **Online:** wdpg.io/16-1-6

WEB PAGE

Futura is a geometric sans-serif typeface
that was designed by Paul Renner in 1927.

HTML

```
Futura is a geometric sans-serif typeface that was <mark>designed
by Paul Renner in 1927</mark>.
```

<pre>

The pre element doesn't have a semantic purpose in HTML5, but it's
used quite often with other semantic elements, such as code. One of the
problems with displaying programming code and similar text is that it's
difficult to show structuring elements such as indents because the web
browser ignores such whitespace. When you mark up the code with the pre
(short for *preformatted text*) element, however, the web browser preserves
all whitespace characters, including multiple spaces and new lines. The
browser also displays the text in a monospace font.

▶ *Example* ⇨ **Online:** wdpg.io/16-1-7

WEB PAGE

```
function helloWorld() {

  //Greet the reader
  alert('Hello World!');
}
```

HTML

```
        <pre><code>
        function helloWorld() {

          //Greet the reader
          alert('Hello World!');
        }</code></pre>
```

<s>

Use the s element to mark text that's inaccurate, outdated, or in some other way incorrect. Why not delete the text instead? Sometimes, you want to leave the inaccurate text in place for comparison purposes, such as to show a correction, updated information, or a revised price. The web browser marks up this text by using a strikethrough effect.

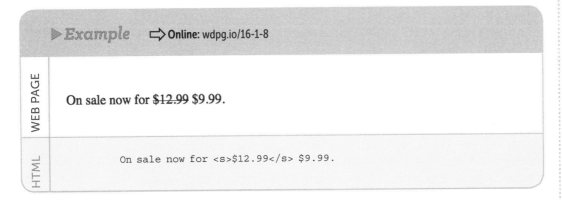

▶ *Example*   ⇨ Online: wdpg.io/16-1-8

WEB PAGE

On sale now for ~~$12.99~~ $9.99.

HTML

```
On sale now for <s>$12.99</s> $9.99.
```

<samp>

The samp element enables you to mark up a passage of text as the sample output from a computer program or similar system. The web browser displays this text by using a monospace font.

▶ *Example*   ⇨ Online: wdpg.io/16-1-9

WEB PAGE

The error message said `Comic Sans?`
`Are you kidding me!?.`

HTML

```
The error message said <samp>Comic Sans!? Are you kidding me!?</
samp>.
```

<small>

You use the small element to mark text as an aside from the regular text, particularly one that has to do with what people often refer to as fine print: copyright or trademark notices, disclaimers or disclosures, legal rights or restrictions, warnings or caveats, or source attribution. The web browser displays this text by using a type size that's slightly smaller than the regular text.

▶ *Example*   ⇨ **Online:** wdpg.io/16-1-10

WEB PAGE

Thank you for reading this essay.
TypeNerdNews is © 2019 Aldus Manutius.
All rights reserved.

HTML

```
Thank you for reading this essay.<br>
<small>TypeNerdNews is &copy; 2019 Aldus Manutius. All rights
reserved.</small>
```

<sub>

The sub element marks text as a subscript, which is handy if your web page requires chemical or mathematical formulas. The web browser displays this text by using a small type size that's set partially below the regular text baseline.

▶ *Example*   ⇨ **Online:** wdpg.io/16-1-11

WEB PAGE

Many illuminated manuscripts are written using iron gall ink, which is iron sulfate ($FeSO_4$) added to gallic acid ($C_7H_6O_5$).

HTML

```
Many illuminated manuscripts are written using iron gall ink,
which is iron sulfate (FeSO<sub>4</sub>) added to gallic acid
(C<sub>7</sub>H<sub>6</sub>O<sub>5</sub>).
```

<sup>

The sup element marks text as a superscript, so it's often used for mathematical formulas, but many web authors also use it to specify footnote markers. The web browser displays this text by using a small type size that's set partially above the regular text baseline.

▶ *Example*   ⇨ **Online:** wdpg.io/16-1-12

WEB PAGE

The W3C standard cautions us not to use subscripts and superscripts "for typographical presentation for presentation's sake."[1]

HTML

```
The W3C standard cautions us not to use subscripts and
superscripts "for typographical presentation for presentation's
sake."<sup>[1]</sup>
```

<time>

You use the `time` element to indicate that a particular bit of text is a date, a time, or a combination of the two:

```
<time datetime="machine-value">human text</time>
```

The idea is to represent the date and/or time in two ways:

- The text between the `<time>` and `</time>` tags is a human-friendly way of showing the date or time, such as 1 p.m. on August 23, 2019.

- The value of the `datetime` attribute is a machine-friendly version of the date and/or time, such as 2019-08-23T16:00:00-05:00. The general syntax to use is shown in Figure 16.1.

▶ Figure 16.1
The syntax to use for the `<time>` tag's `datetime` attribute

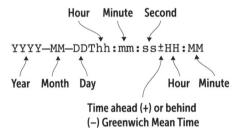

The web browser doesn't format the date/time in a special way. Instead, you use the `time` element to give the browser and other software-based visitors to your page a meaningful, readable date and/or time. It's often useful to include the date and time when a page was created or last edited, for example.

You use the `time` element to indicate that a particular bit of text is a date, a time, or a combination of the two.

▶ *Example*   ⟹ **Online:** wdpg.io/16-1-13

WEB PAGE

This web page was last modified on
August 23rd, 2019 at 9:25AM.

HTML

```
This web page was last modified on <time datetime="2019-08-
23T09:25:00-05:00">August 23rd, 2019 at 9:25AM</time>.
```

<u>

The u element has no semantic use that I can discern. The World Wide Web Consortium (W3C) standard says that it "represents a span of text with an unarticulated, though explicitly rendered, non-textual annotation." I have no idea what that means. The W3C unhelpfully suggests that a possible use may be "labeling the text as being misspelt," but that seems dubious.

The real problem with the u element is that all web browsers render the text as underlined, which means that every person who visits your page will think that the text is a link, and a large subset of those visitors will try to click it (and grow frustrated when nothing happens). You may think that underlining is useful for emphasizing text, but that's what the <em> tag is for. In short, you have no good reason to use the <u> tag and plenty of good reasons *not* to use it. I include it here because you may come across it when looking at the source code of some (no doubt poorly designed) web pages.

▶ *Example*   ⟹ **Online:** wdpg.io/16-1-14

WEB PAGE

It's a really bad idea to use the u element
because its text <u>looks just like a link</u>.

HTML

```
It's a really bad idea to use the <code>u</code> element because
its text <u>looks just like a link</u>.
```

`<var>`

The `var` element enables you to mark up a word or phrase as a placeholder. This placeholder could be a programming variable, a function parameter, or a word or phrase used to represent a general class of things. The web browser displays this text by using italics.

▶ *Example*   ⇨ **Online:** wdpg.io/16-1-15

WEB PAGE

Here's the syntax to use for the `time` element:
`<time datetime="`*`machine-value`*`">`*`human text`*`</time>`.

HTML

```
Here's the syntax to use for the <code>time</code> element:<br>
<code>&lt;time datetime="<var>machine-value</var>"&gt;<var>human
text</var>&lt;/time&gt;.</code>
```

More about Links

When I showed you how to wield the `<a>` tag way back in Chapter 2, you learned that creating a link is a straightforward matter of setting the link address as the value of the `<a>` tag's `href` attribute. That's all true as far as it goes, but there's more to the `<a>` element because your web page links can come in any of the following three varieties:

- Remote links to web pages outside your site
- Local links to other web pages on your site
- In-page links to other sections of the current web page

You learned about remote links in Chapter 2, and you learn about in-page links in the next section. But now, I'm going to talk about local links to your other web pages.

Linking to Local Files

The first thing to note is that for local links, the URL doesn't require either the protocol or the domain name. With an internal link, the browser assumes that the protocol is HTTP (or HTTPS, if you use the secure version of HTTP on your site) and that the domain name is the name of your host server. That's straightforward enough, but before continuing with the link lesson, I want to take a short side trip to help you understand how directories work in the web world.

When you sign up with a company that will host your web pages, that company gives you your own directory on its server. If you're putting together only a few pages, that directory should be more than adequate. If you're constructing a larger site, however, you should give some thought to how you organize your files. Why? Well, think of your own computer. It's unlikely that you have everything crammed into a single directory. Instead, you probably have separate directories for the different programs you use and other directories for your data files.

There's no reason why you can't cook up a similar scheme in your web home. With this type of multidirectory setup, however, how you link to files in other directories can be a bit tricky. As an example, consider a website that has three directories:

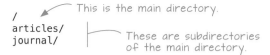

There are three scenarios to watch out for:

- *Referencing a file in the same directory*—This scenario is easiest because you don't have to include any directory information. Suppose that the HTML file you're working on is in the `journal` directory and that you want to reference a page named `rant.html` that's also in that directory. In this case, you use only the name of the file, like this:

  ```
  <a href="rant.html">
  ```

- *Referencing a file in a subdirectory from the main directory*— This scenario is common because your home page (which is almost certainly in the main directory) is likely to have links to files in subdirectories. Suppose that you want to link to a page named `design.html` in the `articles` subdirectory of your home page. Your `<a>` tag takes the following form:

  ```
  <a href="articles/design.html">
  ```

- *Referencing a file in a subdirectory from a different subdirectory*—This scenario is the trickiest one. Suppose that you have a page in the `articles` subdirectory, and you want to link to a page named `poem.html` in the `journal` subdirectory. Here's the `<a>` tag:

  ```
  <a href="/journal/poem.html">
  ```

In the last example, the leading slash (/) tells the browser to first go up to the main directory and then go into the `journal` directory to find the `poem.html` file.

Lesson 16.2: *Linking to the Same Page*
Covers: In-page links

➡️ **Online:** wdpg.io/16-2-0

When a surfer clicks a standard link, the page loads, and the browser displays the top part of the page in the window. It's possible, however, to set up a special kind of link that forces the browser to display some other part of the page, such as a section in the middle.

When would you ever use such a link? Most of your HTML pages probably will be short and sweet, and the web surfers who drop by will have no trouble finding their way around. But for longer pages, you can set up links to various sections of the page, which enable a reader to jump directly to a section rather than scroll through the page to get there.

To create this kind of link, you must set up a special identifier that marks the spot to which you want to link. To understand how in-page links work, think of how you might mark a spot in a book you're reading. You might dog-ear the page, attach a sticky note, or place something (such as a bookmark) between the pages. An in-page link identifier performs the same function: It marks a particular spot in a web page, and you can use an a element to link directly to that spot.

To set up an identifier for an in-page link, you add an id attribute to a tag and supply it a value:

```
<h2 id="best-practices">Best Practices</h2>
```

The value you assign to the id attribute must meet the following criteria:

- It must be unique in the web page.

- It must start with a letter.

- The rest of the characters can be any combination of letters, digits (0–9), hyphens (-), underscores (_), colons (:), or periods (.).

How you set up your in-page link depends on whether it resides in the same page as the link or a different page. If the identifier and the link are in the same page, you link to it by using the id value, preceded by the hash symbol (#):

```
<a href="#best-practices">Go to the Best Practices section</a>
```

If the identifier is defined in a separate web page, your link's href value is the URL of that page, followed by the hash symbol (#) and the id value:

```
See my <a href="organization.html#best-practices">primer on best
practices</a>
```

The following example shows a few in-page links in action.

▶ Example

⇨ **Online:** wdpg.io/16-2-1

This example shows a page that uses some in-page links.

WEB PAGE

Organizing Your Web Page Text

Contents:

In-page links

Benefits
Workflow
Best Practices

All great documents have something in common: excellent organization. Content and formatting are important, but their effectiveness is diminished or even nullified if the document has a slipshod organization. However, even a page with only so-so content and negligible formatting can get its point across if it's organized coherently and sensibly.

In-page link address

`htmlcssplayground.com/results.html#best-practices`

HTML

```
<h1>Organizing Your Web Page Text</h1>          Link for Benefits
<h4>Contents:</h4>                               heading
<a href="#benefits">Benefits</a><br>
<a href="#workflow">Workflow</a><br>            Link for Workflow
<a href="#best-practices">Best Practices</a>     heading
<p>
                                                 Link for
All great documents have something in common: excellent
Best                                             organization. Content and formatting are important, but their
Practices                                        effectiveness is diminished or even nullified if the document
heading                                          has a slipshod organization. However, even a page with only so-so
content and negligible formatting can get its point across if it's
organized coherently and sensibly.              Identifier for Benefits
<h2 id="benefits">Benefits</h2>                  heading
There are many reasons to organize your web page text, but three
are the most important: narrative flow, accessibility, and search
engine optimization.
Narrative Flow</h3>
Research has shown &mdash; and poets and storytellers have known
for thousands of years &mdash; that humans have an innate hunger
for story. We learn better and take in data more effectively when
it's organized as a narrative.
<h3>Accessibility</h3>
Visually impaired visitors to your web page will often use special
screen readers to read aloud the page contents. These tools are
designed to look for and read web page headings so the user can
quickly get an overall sense of the page structure.
<h3>Search Engine Optimization</h3>
Most search engines include page headings as part of their
algorithms for determining where a page should rank in the
results. In general, text that resides higher up in the page
hierarchy is given more importance in the search results.
<h2 id="workflow">Workflow</h2>
<h2 id="best-practices">Best Practices</h2>
                                                 Identifier for
Identifier for Best Practices                    Workflow heading
heading
```

More HTML Elements for Web Designers

PLAY

Set up an external link to the following address: https://www.w3.org/TR/html5/text-level-semantics.html. *Set up an external in-page link to the identifier named* the-a-element *on the same page.* ⇨Online: wdpg.io/16-2-4

Inserting Special Characters

Your HTML and CSS files consist only of text, but that doesn't mean that they consist only of the letters, numbers, and other symbols that you can type with your keyboard. If your web text needs an em dash (—), a copyright symbol (©), or an e with an acute accent (é), you can add those elements to your page by using special codes called character entities. These entities are available in three flavors: hexadecimal code, decimal code, and entity name. The hex and decimal codes are numbers, and the entity names are friendlier symbols that describe (although often cryptically) the character you're trying to display. You can display the registered trademark symbol (™), for example, by using the hex code ™, the decimal code ™, or the entity name ™.

Note that all three references begin with an ampersand (&) and end with a semicolon (;). Don't forget either symbol when you use character entities in your own pages. Figure 16.2 shows a few common character entities.

REMEMBER

If you include the tag <meta charset="utf-8"> *in your page's header section, you can type characters such as the em dash (—) and copyright symbol (©) directly in your code. You type an em dash by pressing Alt+0151 in Windows or Option+Shift+- (hyphen) in macOS, for example.*

Character	Hex Code	Decimal Code	Entity Name
"	"	"	"
&	&	&	&
<	<	<	<
>	>	>	>
¢	¢	¢	¢
£	£	£	£
©	©	©	©
®	®	®	®
½	½	½	½
é	é	é	é
—	—	—	—

▶ Figure 16.2 Some HTML5 character entities and their codes

Using the HTML5 Entity Browser

HTML5 has nearly 1,500 defined character entities, so it's not surprising that two of the biggest frustrations associated with using character entities are knowing what characters are available and finding the character you want. Having been through this frustration many times myself, I decided to do something about it. To that end, I built the HTML5 Entity Browser, which organizes character entities by category (so you can easily see what's available) and offers a search feature (so you can find any character quickly). Here's how it works:

1   In the Web Design Playground (https://webdesignplayground.io), choose Menu > HTML5 Entity Browser.

2   Use the Category list to select the type of entity you're looking for.

    The app filters the list of entities to show only those in the category you selected, as shown in Figure 16.3.

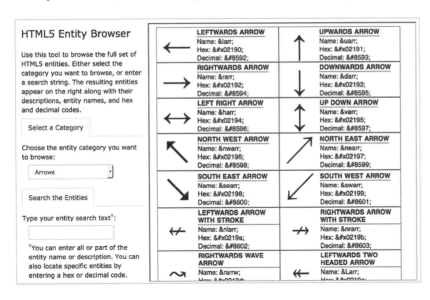

▶ Figure 16.3
With the HTML5 Entity Browser, choose a category to filter the list of entities, as shown here, or search the entities.

3   To search the list of entities, use the Search the Entities text box to enter all or part of the entity name or description.

    If you want to see a specific entity, you can enter that entity's hex or decimal code.

Adding Comments

A comment is a chunk of text that, although it resides in your HTML file, is skipped by the web browser, so it doesn't appear when your page is rendered. That behavior may strike you as odd, but comments have quite a few good uses:

- You can add notes to yourself in specific places of the page code. You can add a comment such as Here's where the logo goes when it's finished, for example.

- You can add explanatory text that describes parts of the page. If you have a section that comprises the header of your page, you can add a comment before the section such as This is the start of the header.

- You can skip problematic sections of your page. If you have a section that isn't working properly or a link that isn't set up yet, you can convert the text and tags to a comment so as not to cause problems for the browser or the user.

- You can add a copyright notice or other info for people who view your HTML source code.

BEWARE

Although comment text isn't displayed in the browser, it's easy for another person to see it by viewing the page source code. Therefore, don't put sensitive information inside a comment tag.

To turn any bit of text into a comment, surround it with the HTML comment tags. Specifically, you precede the comment with <!-- and follow it with -->, like this:

```
<!--This text is a comment-->
```

Summary

- If you're linking to a local file in the same directory, set the <a> tag's href attribute to the name of the file; otherwise, you need to precede the filename with the directory name.

- To create an in-page link, add the id attribute to the link location; then set your <a> tag's href attribute to the id value, preceded by a hash tag (#).

- To specify a special character, enter the character directly, if possible, or use the decimal code, hexadecimal code, or entity name, each of which begins with an ampersand (&) and ends with a semicolon (;).

- To add a comment to your code, surround the comment text with <!-- and -->.

Chapter 17

Adding a Splash of Color to Your Web Designs

Boldly be a pop of color in a black and white world. —Kate Smith

---

 This chapter covers

- Learning some color basics
- Understanding how CSS uses color
- Applying a color to an element
- Adding background colors
- Creating color gradients

CSS offers all the tools you need to add a dash of color to your headings, text, links, and backgrounds. You learn how to use those tools in this chapter, as well as how to wield a few special CSS tools for building color gradients that will raise the "wow" factor on your pages.

Understanding Colors

The good news about understanding colors for use in your web designs is that you don't need to understand much. Yes, entire books have been written on color theory, but you don't need to be versed in the physics of optics to create beautiful, eye-catching web pages. You need to know only two things: how to combine colors harmoniously and how colors are created. For the former, see "Choosing Harmonious Colors" later in this chapter; for the latter, read on.

> *Color is free on the web. While there's nothing wrong with black text on white, using different colors not only adds a bit of drama to the page, but also creates hierarchies for the content.* —Erik Spiekermann

MASTER

With 256 available values for each of the three colors, you have a palette of more than 16 million colors to choose among.

You can use two methods to create any color. The first method uses the fact that you can create any color in the spectrum by mixing the three main colors, which are red, green, and blue, so this method is sometimes called the *RGB method*. Painters do this mixing on a palette, but you're in the digital realm, so you mix your colors using numeric values, supplying a number between 0 and 255 (or a percentage between 0 and 100) for each of the three colors. A lower number means that the color is less intense, and a higher number means that the color is more intense.

Table 17.1 lists nine common colors and their respective red, green, and blue values.

▶ Table 17.1 The Red, Green, and Blue Values for Nine Common Colors

MASTER

Whenever the red, green, and blue values are equal, you get a grayscale color. Lower numbers produce darker grays, and higher numbers produce lighter grays.

Name	Red	Green	Blue	Color
Red	255	0	0	
Green	0	255	0	
Blue	0	0	255	
Yellow	255	255	0	
Magenta	255	0	255	
Cyan	0	255	255	
Black	0	0	0	
Gray	128	128	128	
White	255	255	255	

As you can see in Table 17.1, when only one color is specified (that is, has a value greater than 0), you get the pure color, but when two or more values are specified, you get a blend of those colors. To help you visualize this blending process, I've put together a short animation on the Web Design Playground. Choose Menu > RGB Visualizer (or surf directly to **wdpg.io/rgbvis**), and you'll see three circles—one red, one green, and one blue—slowly approach one another and then overlap. When the overlap occurs, as shown in Figure 17.1, notice four things:

- The overlap of red and blue produces magenta.
- The overlap of red and green produces yellow.
- The overlap of green and blue produces cyan.
- The overlap of all three colors produces white.

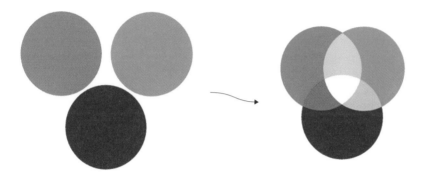

▶ Figure 17.1
On the Web Design Playground, choose Menu > RGB Visualizer to see an animation in which the three circles come together and the overlaps produce the blended colors shown here.

The second method of creating a color involves supplying numeric values for three attributes called hue, saturation, and luminance, so this technique is sometimes called the *HSL method*:

- *Hue*—This value (which is more or less equivalent to the term *color*) measures the position (in degrees) on the color wheel with values between 0 and 359, as shown in Figure 17.2. Lower numbers indicate a position near the red end (with red equal to 0 degrees), and higher numbers move through the yellow, green, blue, and violet parts of the spectrum.

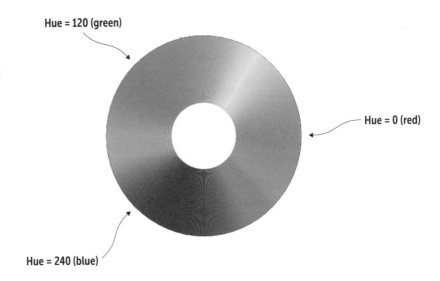

Hue = 120 (green)

Hue = 0 (red)

Hue = 240 (blue)

▶ Figure 17.2
Hue refers to the position on the color wheel, starting at 0 (red) and passing through 120 (green) and 240 (blue).

- *Saturation*—This value is a percentage and a measure of a given hue's purity. A saturation value of 100 means that the hue is a pure color. As shown in Figure 17.3, lower numbers indicate that more gray is mixed with the hue; at 0 percent, the color becomes part of the grayscale.

▶ Figure 17.3
Saturation is a measure of a color's purity or how much gray is mixed in. The color wheel in Figure 17.2 is set to 100 percent saturation. The lower the saturation percentage, the grayer the color appears.

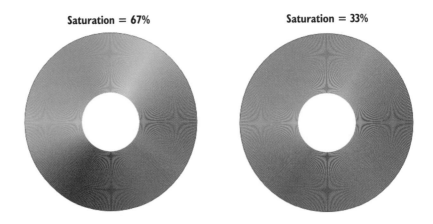

Saturation = 67%

Saturation = 33%

- *Luminance*—This value (also called *lightness* or *luminosity*) is also a percentage and a measure of how light or dark the color is. As you can see in Figure 17.4, lower percentages are darker (with 0 producing black), and higher percentages are lighter (with 100 creating white).

Luminance = 75%   **Luminance = 25%**

▶ Figure 17.4
Luminance measures the lightness of a color. The color wheel in Figure 17.3 is set to 50 percent luminance. Higher percentages produce lighter colors, and lower percentages produce darker colors.

Which method should you use? The answer depends on various factors. If you want to specify a single color, the RGB method is a bit more straightforward, but if you want to choose harmonious colors—such as colors that are complementary or analogous—the HSL method is best. Before you decide, you need to know the specifics of how you apply colors in CSS.

Adding Colors with CSS

It's a measure of the importance of color not only in the style sheet world, but also in web design, that CSS offers at least a half-dozen ways to define something as apparently simple as a color. Each method has its uses, so you're going to learn them all over the next few sections.

Lesson 17.1: **Specifying Red, Green, and Blue with the rgb() Function**
    Covers: The `rgb()` function

⇨ **Online:** wdpg.io/17-1-0

Earlier, you learned that you can define any of more than 16 million colors by specifying a value between 0 and 255 for each of the color's red, green, and blue components. One way to do this in CSS is to use the rgb() function, shown in Figure 17.5.

To use this function, replace *red-value* with a number between 0 and 255 to specify the red component; replace *green-value* with a number between 0 and 255 to specify the green component;

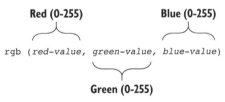

Red (0-255)   **Blue (0-255)**

rgb (*red-value, green-value, blue-value*)

Green (0-255)

▶ Figure 17.5
To specify a color's red, green, and blue components, you can use the `rgb()` function.

and replace *blue-value* with a number between 0 and 255 to specify the blue component. You can generate purple, for example, by using 128 for red, 0 for green, and 128 for blue. The following example shows how you'd use CSS to display all your h1 headings with purple text.

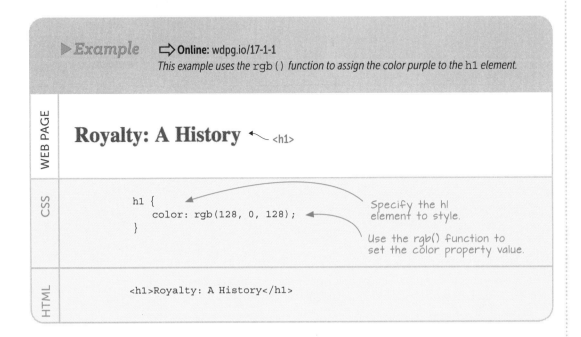

▶*Example* ⇨**Online:** wdpg.io/17-1-1
This example uses the rgb() *function to assign the color purple to the* h1 *element.*

WEB PAGE

Royalty: A History ← `<h1>`

CSS

```
h1 {
    color: rgb(128, 0, 128);
}
```

Specify the h1 element to style.

Use the rgb() function to set the color property value.

HTML

```
<h1>Royalty: A History</h1>
```

PLAY

How would you use the rgb() *function to apply the color red to an element?* ⇨**Online:** wdpg.io/17-1-2

You can also specify the rgb() function's *red-value*, *green-value*, and *blue-value* parameters by using percentages, with 100% specifying the full intensity of the color (equivalent to the 255 decimal value) and 0% specifying the lowest intensity of the color (so it's the same as 0 in the decimal notation). Table 17.2 is a repeat of Table 17.1 with the decimal values replaced by their percentage equivalents.

▶Table 17.2 The Red, Green, and Blue Percentages for Nine Common Colors

Name	Red	Green	Blue	Color
Red	100%	0	0	
Green	0	100%	0	
Blue	0	0	100%	
Yellow	100%	100%	0	

Name	Red	Green	Blue	Color
Magenta	100%	0	100%	
Cyan	0	100%	100%	
Black	0	0	0	
Gray	50%	50%	50%	
White	100%	100%	100%	

Here's the `color` definition for purple converted to percentages:

`color: rgb(50%, 0, 50%)`

PLAY

How would you use the `rgb()` *function to apply a light gray color to an element?* ⇨ **Online:** wdpg.io/17-1-3

Lesson 17.2: **Specifying Hue, Saturation, and Luminance with the hsl() Function**

Covers: The `hsl()` function

⇨ **Online:** wdpg.io/17-2-0

If you have a specific hue in mind, you may prefer to define your CSS color by specifying the color's hue, saturation, and luminance components. To do this in CSS, use the hsl() function, shown in Figure 17.6.

To use this function, replace *hue-value* with a number between 0 and 359 to specify the hue component; replace *sat-value* with a percentage between 0 and 100 to specify the saturation component; and replace *lum-value* with a percentage between 0 and 100 to specify the luminance component. Sticking with the purple h1 text example, the following shows how you'd use CSS to display all your h1 headings with purple text by using the hsl() function.

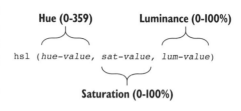

▶ Figure 17.6
To specify a color's hue, saturation, and luminance components, use the `hsl()` function.

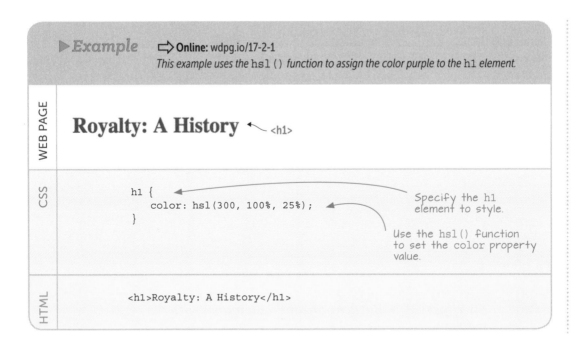

▶ *Example*   ⇨ **Online:** wdpg.io/17-2-1
This example uses the hsl() *function to assign the color purple to the* h1 *element.*

WEB PAGE

Royalty: A History ↖ <h1>

CSS

```
h1 {
    color: hsl(300, 100%, 25%);
}
```

Specify the h1 element to style.

Use the hsl() function to set the color property value.

HTML

```
<h1>Royalty: A History</h1>
```

PLAY

How would you use the hsl() *function to apply the color blue to an element?* ⇨ **Online:** wdpg.io/17-2-2

PLAY

How would you use the hsl() *function to apply the color white to an element?* ⇨ **Online:** wdpg.io/17-2-3

A Quick Note about Transparency

For the most part, you want your web page text to appear solid and readable. However, there will be times when, for the sake of adding visual interest to your page, you consciously decide to sacrifice a tiny bit of readability by making your text slightly transparent. This means that whatever is behind the text—it could be a solid color, an image, or even other text—shows through.

You control the transparency (also called the *opacity*) of your text by using variants of the rgb() and hsl() functions: rgba() and hsla().

You use these functions like rgb() and hsl(), respectively, except that you also specify a fourth parameter called the *alpha channel*. The *alpha channel* is a numeric value between 0.0 and 1.0, where 1.0 means that the text is completely opaque and 0.0 means that the text is completely transparent.

A Brief Detour into Hexadecimal Numbers

The next CSS color tool I'm going to tell you about uses *hexadecimal* numbers, which use base 16 instead of the base 10 used by regular decimal numbers. If you know about hexadecimal numbers, feel free to skip this section; otherwise, before moving on with CSS colors, you need to make a short but necessary detour into the hexadecimal realm.

Hexadecimal values are efficient because they use single-character symbols for everything from 0 to 15. Specifically, they use 0 through 9 for the first ten values, just as in decimal, but they use the letters A through F to represent the quantities 10 through 15. Figure 17.7 shows the decimal and hexadecimal equivalents for the quantities 0 through 15.

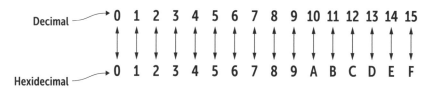

▶ Figure 17.7
Hexadecimal uses 0 through 9 the same as decimal, but it represents the quantities 10 through 15 with the letters A through F.

For two-digit values, a decimal number has two parts: a tens part on the left and a ones part on the right. The number 10 can be read as "one ten and zero ones," and 36 can be read as "three tens and six ones." A two-digit hex number also has two parts: a sixteens part on the left and a ones part on the right. The hex number 10 can be read as "one sixteen and zero ones" (making it the equivalent of 16 decimal), and 5C hex can be read as "five sixteens and C (twelve) ones," making it the equivalent of 92 decimal. Figure 17.8 shows a few examples.

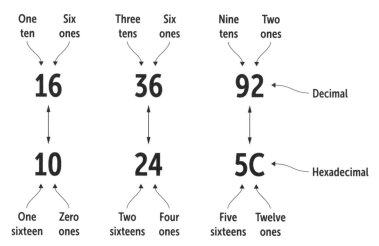

▶ Figure 17.8
In the same way that a two-digit decimal number consists of a tens place on the left and a ones place on the right, a two-digit hexadecimal number consists of a sixteens place on the left and a ones place on the right.

Lesson 17.3: *Using RGB Hex Codes*
Covers: RGB hexadecimal codes

> ⇨ **Online:** wdpg.io/17-3-0

Rather than using the rgb() function to specify a color's red, green, and blue components, you can use the CSS hexadecimal-based method, shown in Figure 17.9.

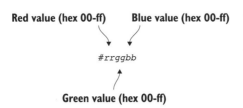

Red value (hex 00-ff)   **Blue value (hex 00-ff)**

`#rrggbb`

Green value (hex 00-ff)

These RGB hex codes always begin with the hash symbol (#), followed by the two-digit hex value for the red component, the two-digit hex value for the green component, and the two-digit hex value for the blue component. In each case, the allowed hex values range from 00 to ff. Because these codes consist of three hex values, they're often called *hex triplets*. Table 17.3 lists the RGB hex codes used for the nine common colors shown earlier in Tables 17.1 and 17.2.

▶ **Figure 17.9**
You can specify a color by using the code #rrggbb, where rr is the hex value for the red component, gg is the hex value for the green component, and bb is the hex value for the blue component.

▶ Table 17.3 The RGB Hex Codes for Nine Common Colors

Name	Red	Color
Red	#ff0000	
Green	#00ff00	
Blue	#0000ff	
Yellow	#ffff00	
Magenta	#ff00ff	
Cyan	#00ffff	
Black	#000000	
Gray	#808080	
White	#ffffff	

The following example shows how you'd use this method to apply purple to h1 text. The hex equivalent of decimal 128 is 80, so for the color value, the red component is hex 80, the green component is hex 00, and the blue component is hex 80.

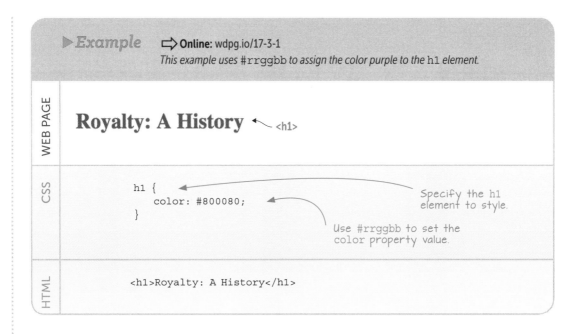

▶ *Example* ⇨ **Online:** wdpg.io/17-3-1

This example uses `#rrggbb` *to assign the color purple to the* `h1` *element.*

WEB PAGE

Royalty: A History ← `<h1>`

CSS

```
h1 {
    color: #800080;
}
```

Specify the h1 element to style.

Use #rrggbb to set the color property value.

HTML

```
<h1>Royalty: A History</h1>
```

You can use an even shorter code in certain circumstances. If each of the rr, gg, and bb values use repeated characters—such as 00, 66, or ff—you can use one of the repeated characters for each color. The following two codes are equivalent:

```
#3366cc
#36c
```

Working with the Color Chooser

Dealing in RGB codes, HSL values, and hexadecimals may be convenient for a computer, but the connection between those numbers and a particular color isn't intuitive for humans. Color keywords are more comprehensible, but they represent far too few of the available colors. To make it easier for you to view and ultimately choose a color to use on a web page, the Web Design Playground offers a tool called the Color Chooser. This tool offers a color palette control that lets you select a preset color or any combination of hue, saturation, luminosity, and transparency. The tool shows not only the resulting color, but also the `rgb()` function (both decimal and percentage), the `hsl()` function, the RGB hex triplet, the color keyword (if applicable), and the `r()` and `hsla()` functions if you set the transparency.

PLAY

What RGB code would you use to apply the color blue to an element?
⇨ Online: wdpg.io/17-3-2

PLAY

What RGB code would you use to apply the lightest possible gray to an element? ⇨ Online: wdpg.io/17-3-3

LEARN

To learn how to modify your colors with transparency, see the "Changing the Transparency" lesson on the Playground.
➡ Online: wdpg.io/17-7-0

Here how you use the Color Chooser tool:

1 In the Web Design Playground, choose Menu > Color Chooser (or go directly to wdpg.io/colorchooser).

2 Click the Color control to display the palette, as shown in Figure 17.10.

3 To choose a preset color, click one of the swatches on the left side of the control.

4 To specify a color, use the text box to enter an `rgb()` function, `hsl()` function, RGB hex triplet, color keyword, `rgba()` function, or `hsla()` function.

5 In the large color box, drag horizontally to set the saturation, or drag vertically to set the luminance.

6 Use the vertical box to set the hue and the horizontal box to set the transparency.

7 When you're done, click Close.

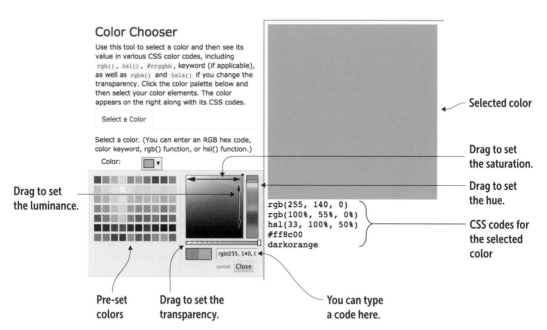

▶ Figure 17.10 Use the Web Design Playground's Color Chooser tool to select a color and see its various CSS codes.

Choosing Harmonious Colors

Now you know how to apply colors to your page elements, but that's only half the battle. Colors that are poorly matched or improperly applied can make a page look worse, not better. This section examines a few basics for effectively using colors in your page designs.

First, with so many colors available, the temptation is to go overboard and use a dozen hues on each page. Using too many colors, however, can confuse your users and even cause eye fatigue. Try to stick to two or three colors at most. If you must use more, try to use different shades of two or three hues.

When selecting colors, think about the psychological impact of your scheme on your users. Studies have shown that "cool" colors such as blue and gray evoke a sense of dependability and trust. Use these colors for a businesslike appearance. For pages that require a little more excitement, "warm" colors such as red, yellow, and orange can evoke a festive, fun atmosphere. For a safe, comfortable ambiance, try using brown and yellow. For an environmental touch, use green and brown.

Finally, you need to give some thought to how your colors work together. Some colors naturally clash and, when used together, will make your page look terrible. Fortunately, every hue has one or more colors that blend well with it, resulting in harmonious designs that are pleasing to your visitors' eyes. Note that harmonious doesn't mean boring! Depending on the colors you choose, the result can be anything from soothing to vibrant, so the color scheme you go with is a reflection of what you want your site to say.

Happily, you don't have to guess which colors will do the job. You can use the tricks described in the following list:

- *Choose complementary colors.* Complementary colors lie opposite each other on the color wheel. In terms of the `hsl()` function, complementary colors are those with hue values that are 180 degrees apart. Red—`hsl(0, 100%, 50%)`—is the complement of cyan—`hsl(180, 100%, 50%)`. As a rule, with any complementary color scheme, it's often best to use one color as the main hue on the page and the other color as an accent, particularly for elements you want the user to notice, such as Subscribe or Buy buttons and similar call-to-action objects. See "Color Scheme Gallery," later in this chapter, for an example web page that uses complementary colors.

- *Choose analogous colors. Analogous colors* lie adjacent to each other on the color wheel. In terms of the `hsl()` function, analogous colors are those with hue values that are plus or minus 30 degrees from the main color. Red—`hsl(0, 100%, 50%)`—is analogous to both `hsl(30, 100%, 50%)` and `hsl(330, 100%, 50%)`. If you prefer even less contrast (you want colors that are closer to each other), you can create an analogous scheme by using colors that are 15 degrees apart. If you go with a scheme that has more contrast, it's usually best to pick one color as the main hue for your page and to use the other two colors for buttons, borders, and other accents.

- *Choose triadic colors. Triadic colors* are three colors that lie an equal distance from one another on the color wheel. In terms of the `hsl()` function, triadic colors are those with hue values that are 120 degrees apart. Red—`hsl(0, 100%, 50%)`—is triadic to both `hsl(120, 100%, 50%)` and `hsl(240, 100%, 50%)`. Triadic colors tend to have a similar level of vibrancy, so they feel balanced and in harmony. Many sites that use a triadic scheme pick one color for the page background, another color for the page content and navigation, and the third color for borders and other accents.

- *Choose split complementary colors. A split complementary* color scheme is similar to a complementary color scheme except that instead of using the opposite hue on the color wheel, you use the two colors that lie 30 degrees to either side of that opposite color. Red—`hsl(0, 100%, 50%)`—is split complementary with both `hsl(150, 100%, 50%)` and `hsl(210, 100%, 50%)`. A good rule of thumb for implementing a split complementary color scheme is to use the original color as the page's main hue and use the other two colors for content, navigation, and accents.

Using the Color Scheme Calculator

If you know the color you want to use as the main hue on your page, calculating the rest of your color scheme is straightforward:

- *Complementary*—Add or subtract 180 degrees.
- *Analogous*—Add 30 degrees for one color and subtract 30 degrees for the other.

- *Triadic*—Add 120 degrees for one color and subtract 120 degrees for the other.

- *Split complementary*—Add 180 degrees to the hue; then subtract 30 degrees for one color and add 30 degrees for the other color.

The math is quite daunting if you know only the RGB code, however. Not to worry: I've put a Color Scheme Calculator on the Web Design Playground. Here's how you use it:

1 Choose Menu > Color Scheme Calculator (or navigate to wdpg.io/colorcalc).

2 On the Color Scheme Type tab, select the option for the color scheme type you want: Complementary, Analogous, Triadic, or Split Complementary.

   There's also a Monochrome scheme, which generates five colors with the same hue, but varying saturation and luminance values.

3 Use the color picker to select your initial color.

   You can click the color you want or use the text box to enter an RGB hex triplet or `rgb()` function. (You can also type a color keyword or `hsl()` function.) The calculator displays the color scheme and shows the RGB code, `rgb()` function, and `hsl()` function for each color, as shown in Figure 17.11.

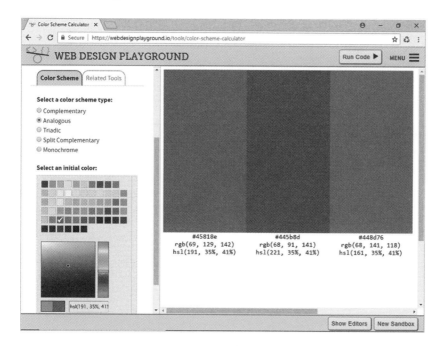

▶ Figure 17.11
Use the Web Design Playground's Color Scheme Calculator to generate a color scheme for a given RGB code.

Color Scheme Gallery

▶This web page uses two complementary colors to handle the bulk of its color load, proving that you don't need a dozen colors to create a striking design (http://www.upstruct. com/work/amandus-film-festival-2015).

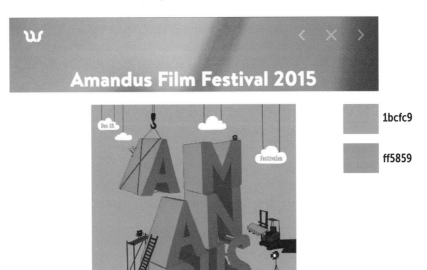

1bcfc9

ff5859

▶This site uses an analogous scheme to create a colorful, inviting landing page (http:// toriseye.quodis.com).

005931

ffa200

187816

▶This website uses its triadic color scheme for backgrounds and text (http://crayola.com).

af1c8d

ffa200

187816

▶An example of a site that uses a split complementary color scheme in which the darkest color provides the background and the brightest color provides the eye-grabbing accents (http://udoncampus.com).

f57b20

6c98b1

1b3148

Applying a Color Gradient

So far, all the colors you've worked with have been a single hue—sometimes lighter or darker or more transparent, true, but one hue nonetheless. It's possible, however, to style a single page element with multiple colors by using the concept of the gradient. A *gradient* is a combination of two or more colors in which one color gradually (or sometimes quickly) transitions into the next. When used sparingly, gradients can be effective ways to add visual interest and pizzazz to a web page.

Before you get started on the CSS, you need to know a few things:

- Gradients are images that the web browser creates automatically.

- Gradients can be applied only as backgrounds, although a wide range of elements supports background images.

- You can use two types of gradients: A *linear gradient* transitions from one color to the next along a straight line; a *radial* gradient transitions from one color to the next from a single point outward in the shape of an ellipse or circle.

In the next couple of lessons, you look at the CSS behind linear and radial gradients.

Lesson 17.4: **Creating a Linear Gradient**
Covers: The `linear-gradient` function

⇨ **Online:** wdpg.io/17-4-0

To specify a linear gradient, you apply the `linear-gradient()` function to the `background-image` property of whatever element you're styling. Figure 17.12 shows the general syntax to use.

▶ Figure 17.12
To define a linear gradient, use the `linear-gradient()` function to specify the angle and the color stops.

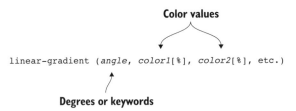

The *angle* value can be a number between 0 and 359 followed by the deg unit or the keyword to followed by the keyword for a horizontal direction (left or right), a vertical direction (top or bottom), or a diagonal direction (top left, top right, bottom left, or bottom right). The color values (*color1*, *color2*, and so on) can be any of the color values that you learned earlier in the chapter. The percentages specify the *color stops*, which are the transition positions where the previous color ends and the next color begins. The first default color stop is 0% (that is, starts at the beginning) and the last default color stop is 100% (that is, stops at the end), so you don't need to enter these values.

The following example shows an empty div element styled with a linear gradient.

PLAY

Create a linear gradient that runs at a 60-degree angle. For the first color, use hue 191 with full saturation and half luminance; for the second color, keep the same hue, but use one-quarter saturation and 15 percent luminance.
⇨ Online: wdpg.io/17-4-3

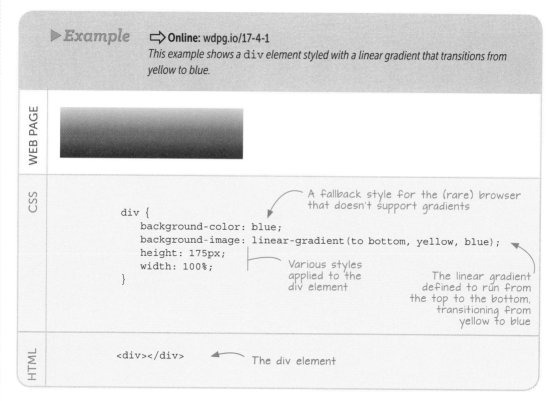

▶ *Example*   ⇨ **Online:** wdpg.io/17-4-1
This example shows a div element styled with a linear gradient that transitions from yellow to blue.

WEB PAGE

CSS

A fallback style for the (rare) browser that doesn't support gradients

```
div {
    background-color: blue;
    background-image: linear-gradient(to bottom, yellow, blue);
    height: 175px;
    width: 100%;
}
```

Various styles applied to the div element

The linear gradient defined to run from the top to the bottom, transitioning from yellow to blue

HTML

```
<div></div>
```

The div element

PLAY

Create a linear gradient that runs from the top-left corner to the bottom-right corner. Use #76a5af as the starting color and #073763 as the finishing color. ⇨ Online: wdpg .io/17-4-2

Adding a Splash of Color to Your Web Designs

PLAY

Determine the two colors that go with the color #674ea7 in an analogous color scheme. Create a linear gradient that uses all three colors and runs from bottom right to top left. ⇨ Online: wdpg.io/17-4-8

Notice in the example that I set the background color first and then applied the gradient. Adding a `background-color` declaration is a fallback for browsers that don't support gradients—mostly Internet Explorer 9 and earlier. Such browsers render the background color but ignore the gradient style. Fortunately, all modern browsers support gradients, so only the increasingly rare older versions of Internet Explorer require this fallback.

If you use three or more colors in your gradient, you need to give some thought as to where you want each color to stop and the next to begin. If you don't specify any stop locations, the browser does the work for you and assumes that the transition occurs halfway between the colors on either side. If you specify three colors, the middle color's transition position is at 50 percent, halfway between the first (0 percent) and third (100 percent) colors. The following example shows a linear gradient in which the second color kicks in a bit earlier.

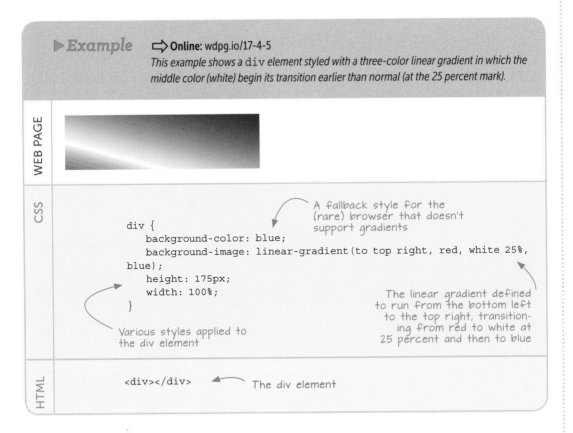

▶ *Example* ⇨ **Online:** wdpg.io/17-4-5

This example shows a `div` element styled with a three-color linear gradient in which the middle color (white) begin its transition earlier than normal (at the 25 percent mark).

WEB PAGE

CSS

```
div {
    background-color: blue;
    background-image: linear-gradient(to top right, red, white 25%,
blue);
    height: 175px;
    width: 100%;
}
```

A fallback style for the (rare) browser that doesn't support gradients

The linear gradient defined to run from the bottom left to the top right, transitioning from red to white at 25 percent and then to blue

Various styles applied to the div element

HTML

```
<div></div>
```

The div element

Lesson 17.5: *Creating a Radial Gradient*
Covers: The `radial-gradient` function

⇨ **Online:** wdpg.io/17-5-0

To specify a radial gradient, you apply the `radial-gradient()` function to the `background-image` property of an element. Figure 17.13 shows the general syntax.

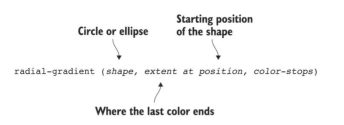

▶ Figure 17.13 Defining a radial gradient, using the `radial-gradient()` function to specify shape, extent, and color stops

The *shape* value can be `circle` (the default, so you can omit it) or `ellipse`. The *extent* value is a keyword pair that tells the browser the side or corner of the element where you want the last color to stop. The possible values are `closest-side`, `farthest-side`, `closest-corner`, and `farthest-corner`. The *position* value specifies the starting point for the shape; it can be a set of x-y points (e.g., `45px 100px`) or a keyword pair that combines a horizontal position (`left`, `center`, or `right`) with a vertical position (`top`, `center`, or `bottom`). The color values and stops are the same as for a linear gradient.

The default value for *extent* is `farthest-corner`, and the default value for *position* is `center center` (which can be shortened to `center`). The simplest possible rule for a radial gradient is `radial-gradient (color1, color2)`, which creates a centered circular gradient that transitions from *color1* to *color2* out to the furthest corner of the element.

The following example shows an empty `div` element styled with a radial gradient.

PLAY

Make attractive repeating background patterns using linear gradients and the CSS `background-size` *property.* ⇨ **Online:** wdpg.io/17-4-7

PLAY

Create a five-color linear gradient that runs from left to right. The five colors (and their stops) are #ffff00 *(0%);* #05c1ff *(20%);* #274e13 *(50%);* #05c1ff *(80%);* #ffff00 *(100%).*
⇨ **Online:** wdpg.io/17-4-6

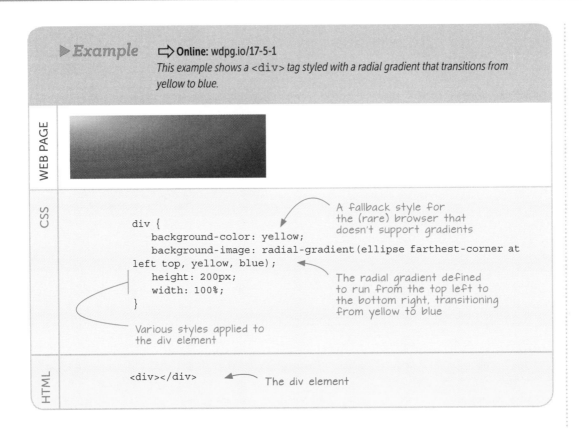

▶ *Example*   ⟹ **Online:** wdpg.io/17-5-1
This example shows a `<div>` tag styled with a radial gradient that transitions from yellow to blue.

WEB PAGE

CSS

```
div {
    background-color: yellow;
    background-image: radial-gradient(ellipse farthest-corner at
left top, yellow, blue);
    height: 200px;
    width: 100%;
}
```

A fallback style for the (rare) browser that doesn't support gradients

The radial gradient defined to run from the top left to the bottom right, transitioning from yellow to blue

Various styles applied to the div element

HTML

```
<div></div>
```

The div element

Lesson 17.6: *Gradients and Older Browsers*
Covers: Adding a gradient fallback color

⟹ **Online:** wdpg.io/17-6-0

The `linear-gradient` and `radial-gradient` properties are supported in all modern browsers, but not everyone uses a modern browser. The good news is that all the major browsers have fully supported gradients for a while now, so you don't need vendor prefixes. To be safe, however, you should include a *fallback color*, which is a default value for the `background-color` property.

Listing 17.1 shows the cross-browser code you should use for a linear gradient.

▶ Listing 17.1 Cross-Browser CSS for a Linear Gradient

The fallback color for browsers that don't support gradients

```
background-color: color;
background-image: linear-gradient(angle, color-stops);
```

The W3C standard syntax

The cross-browser code begins with the fallback color, in case your page is visited by someone who uses a browser that doesn't support gradients. The W3C standard code appears next so that it gets implemented by every browser that supports it. Here's an example:

```
background-color: cyan;
background-image: linear-gradient(to top left, red, cyan);
```

Listing 17.2 shows the cross-browser code you should use for a radial gradient.

▶ Listing 17.2 Cross-Browser CSS for a Radial Gradient

The fallback color for browsers that don't support gradients

```
background-color: color;
background-image: radial-gradient(shape, extent, direction, color-stops);
```

The W3C standard syntax

As with linear gradients, this cross-browser code consists of a fallback color to cover old browsers, followed by the W3C standard code. Here's an example:

```
background-color: #fff;
background-image: radial-gradient(ellipse farthest-corner at
center, #fff, #00f);
```

Using the Gradient Construction Kit

Gradients are among the most eye-catching CSS effects, but they're also some of the most laborious because of all the keywords, colors, and stops. To make implementing this important feature on your own pages easier for you, the Web Design Playground includes a Gradient Construction Kit that enables you to use a form to select all the elements of your gradient. As you build your gradient, you see exactly what the result looks like, and the CSS editor shows the cross-browser code that you can copy and paste into your project.

PLAY

Create a circular radial gradient with a center that starts 100 pixels from the top and 100 pixels from the left. Use the colors #c27ba0 and #3c78d8. ⇨ **Online: wdpg.io/17-5-2**

PLAY

What's the difference between the radial gradient keywords closest-corner *and* farthest-corner? *I've set up an exercise on the Web Design Playground to help you find out.* ⇨ **Online: wdpg.io/17-5-3**

Here's how you use the Gradient Construction Kit:

1. In the Web Design Playground, choose Menu > Gradient Construction Kit (or navigate directly to wdpg.io/kits/gradient).

2. Select the radio button for the type of Gradient you want to create: Linear or Radial.

   The controls in the Options tab change to reflect your choice.

3. Select the options for your linear or radial gradient.

4. In the Colors tab, select your colors and stops.

The Gradient Construction Kit displays the gradient and shows the cross-browser rules in the CSS editor, as shown in Figure 17.14.

▶ Figure 17.14
Use the Web Design Playground's Gradient Construction Kit to build a linear or radial gradient with a few mouse clicks.

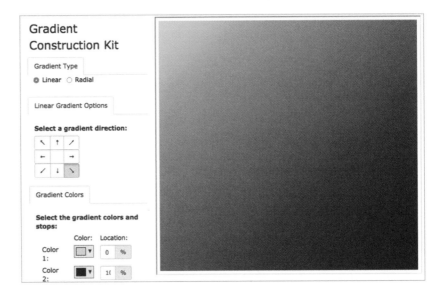

5. To choose a preset color, click one of the swatches on the left side of the control.

6. To specify a color, use the text box to enter an `rgb()` function, `hsl()` function, RGB hex triplet, color keyword, `rgba()` function, or `hsla()` function.

7. In the large color box, drag horizontally to set the saturation, or drag vertically to set the luminance.

8. Use the vertical box to set the hue and the horizontal box to set the transparency.

9. When you're done, click Close.

LEARN

To learn how to modify your colors with transparency, see the "Changing the Transparency" lesson on the Playground.
⇨ Online: wdpg.io/17-7-0

Summary

- Besides the color keywords you learned about in Chapter 4, you have five ways to specify a CSS color: the `rgb()` function, the `hsl()` function, an RGB hexadecimal code, the `rgba()` function, and the `hsla()` function.

- To color an element's text, use the `color` property.

- To color an element's background, use the `background-color` property.

- To apply a linear gradient to an element's background, use the `linear-gradient()` function; if you prefer a radial gradient background, use the `radial-gradient()` function.

Chapter 18

Enhancing Page Text with Typography

 90 percent of design is typography. —Jeffrey Zeldman

This chapter covers

- Setting the typeface
- Working with Google fonts
- Styling your web page words and paragraphs

Do you want to know the secret of great web design? Specifically, do you want to know the one design element common to almost all the best websites? The hidden-in-plain-sight design secret shared by nearly every outstanding website can be summed up in just two words:

Typography matters.

Typography—styles applied to enhance the legibility, readability, and appearance of text—is the web's secret sauce, its magic dust. When you come across a site that has aesthetic appeal, chances are that a big chunk of that appeal comes from the site's use of fonts, text sizes and styles, spacing, and other matters typographical. The site has text appeal.

If you want the same appeal on your own web pages, you need only remember those two all-important words: *Typography matters*. Typefaces matter. Type sizes and styles matter. Spacing, alignment, and indents matter. Fortunately, as you see in this chapter, CSS comes with a large set of typographical tools that you can wield to spruce up your text. No, you don't have the level of control that you get in a desktop page-layout program, but there are enough CSS properties and values to show the world that you care about your web page text.

Specifying the Typeface

To shift your typography into high gear, you need to go beyond the generic and system fonts that I talked about in Chapter 4 and embrace the powerful concepts of the font stack and web fonts.

Lesson 18.1: **Working with Font Stacks**
Covers: The `font-family` property

> ➡️ **Online:** wdpg.io/18-1-0

You may recall from Chapter 4 that when you use the `font-family` property, you can use multiple font families as long as you separate them with commas in what is known as a *font stack*.

Why would you specify more than one font family? With few exceptions, you can't be certain that a system font is installed on the user's device. Although the sans-serif font Helvetica is installed on 100 percent of Macs, for example, it's installed on a mere 7 percent of Windows PCs. Similarly, the serif font Cambria is installed on more than 83 percent of Windows PCs but available on only about 35 percent of Macs. When you specify a font stack, the browser checks the first family to see whether it's installed. If not, the browser tries the next font family in the list, and the process continues until the browser finds an installed system font. If none is found, it's always good practice to include a similar generic font family at the end of the font stack. If your system fonts are serifs, for example, include the `serif` generic font at the end of the stack.

Besides the generic font, are there any other sure bets that you can include in your font stack? Alas, not really, although some fonts are installed on at least 90 percent of both Macs and Windows PCs. The sans-serif fonts are Arial, Arial Black, Tahoma, Trebuchet MS, and Verdana. The serif fonts are Georgia and Times New Roman. The monospace font is Courier New.

LEARN

To get the installation percentages for many popular system fonts, as well as suggested stacks for each font, see the CSS Font Stack at https:// www.cssfontstack.com.

Another font stack strategy is to include the font families in the following order:

- Your preferred font

- A close facsimile of the preferred font

- A similar font that's nearly universal in both Mac and Windows

- The generic font from the same style

Here's an example:

```
font-family: "League Spartan", Futura, Tahoma, sans-serif;
```

The following example creates two font stacks: one for the h3 element and one for the p and li elements.

▶ *Example*   ➪ **Online:** wdpg.io/18-1-1

This example shows a serif-based font stack applied to the h3 *element, as well as a sans-serif-based font stack applied to the* p *and* li *elements.*

WEB PAGE

─── The h3 element   ─── The p element

People of Collar ←

The adjectives *white-collar* and *blue-collar* are familiar to most of us, but there are a few more whimsical variants that you might not have heard of:

The li elements ─

- Black-and-blue-collar: Football players
- Grey-collar: Employees who perform both white- and blue-collar tasks
- Green-collar: Environmentalists
- Open-collar: People who work at home
- Steel-collar: Robots

CSS

The h3 element gets a serif-based font stack.

```
h3 {
    font-family: "Lucida Bright", Georgia, serif;
}
p, li {
    font-family: Tahoma, Helvetica, Arial, sans-serif;
}
```

The p and li elements get a sans-serif-based font stack.

continued

HTML

```html
<h3>People of Collar</h3>
<p>The adjectives <i>white-collar</i> and <i>blue-collar</i> are
familiar to most of us, but here are a few more whimsical variants
that you might not have heard of:</p>
<ul>
    <li>Black-and-blue-collar: Football players</li>
    <li>Green-collar: Environmentalists</li>
    <li>Grey-collar: Employees who perform both white- and blue-
collar tasks</li>
    <li>Open-collar: People who work at home</li>
    <li>Steel-collar: Robots</li>
</ul>
```

Here are a few pointers to bear in mind when you build a font stack for your web design:

- If you have a less popular system font you want to try, put it at the beginning of the stack. If you put it after a font that's installed on, say, 99 percent of devices, the less-popular font will rarely be used.

- If possible, try to match font characteristics within the stack. Don't include in the same stack both a narrow font such as Arial and a relatively thick font such as Verdana, for example.

- Always end the font stack with a generic font from the same style.

Specifying Web Fonts

Relying on system fonts is a straightforward way to bump up your typography a notch from the browser's default fonts. But system fonts suffer from two glaring problems: A limited number of system fonts is available, and you can't be sure that a given system font is installed on the user's computer. The latter is a big problem because it means that you can't know with any certainty how your web page will appear to every user. If you believe that typography matters (and you should), this uncertainty is a major design hurdle.

Fortunately, you can leap gazellelike over that hurdle by implementing web fonts on your pages. *Web fonts* are font files that are hosted on the web and referenced by a special CSS directive named @font-face. The web browser uses that directive to load the font files, thus ensuring that every user sees the same fonts.

You have two ways to host web fonts:

- Use a third-party host.

- Host the font files on your own site.

The next two lessons provide the details as well as the pros and cons associated with each method.

Lesson 18.2: **Using Third-Party Hosted Fonts**
Covers: The `link` element

⇨ **Online:** wdpg.io/18-2-0

By far the easiest way to implement web fonts is to link to the fonts hosted on a third-party site. Many font-hosting services are available, including Fonts. com (**https://www.fonts.com**) and Adobe Typekit (**https://typekit.com**). In most cases, you can purchase a font outright or pay a monthly fee, which gives you access to a wide variety of fonts. Most new web designers, however, use Google Fonts (**https://fonts.google.com**), which offers hundreds of free web fonts.

The main advantage of using a third party is that all rights to use the web fonts have been cleared. Fonts are intellectual property, so you need permission from the creator to use them, particularly on a website. Font hosts have already obtained the necessary licenses, so their fonts are hassle- and guilt-free.

❝ *Web font services . . . handle the bulk of the licensing and hosting work, leaving you to do what you do best— build amazing and beautiful websites.* —Dan Eden

The main disadvantage of using a third party is that the font files reside on a remote server, so it can sometimes take a bit of extra time for your fonts to load. The more fonts you link to, the slower the load time. Most big-time font-hosting services have optimized delivery mechanisms, however, so this font lag usually isn't a big problem.

The method by which you specify which fonts you want to use varies depending on the service, but the general procedure usually goes something like this:

1 On the font host's website, locate and select the typeface you want to use.

2 Customize the typeface by adding extra fonts such as italic, bold, and possibly bold italic.

3 Copy the `<link>` tag generated by the font host and paste the tag into the head section of your web page (that is, between the `<head>` and `</head>` tags).

This tag loads from the host a CSS file that includes the required font code. Here's the `<link>` tag generated by Google Fonts for the Lato

BEWARE

Remember that the more fonts you add, the slower your web pages will load. Link only to fonts you absolutely need. Besides the regular font, most web pages need only italic and bold.

FAQ

What do numbers such as 400 and 700 refer to? *They refer to the weight of the font, where 400 designates a regular font and 700 designates a bold font. See Chapter 4.*

typeface (where `400` refers to the regular font, `400i` refers to regular italic, and `700` refers to bold):

```
<link href="https://fonts.googleapis.com/
css?family=Lato:400,400i,700" rel="stylesheet">
```

4   Add the font to your styles.

The following property tells the web browser to use the Lato font family for all paragraph text (with the addition of a generic font name to display in case the third-party font file can't be loaded):

```
p {
    font-family: Lato, sans-serif;
}
```

▶ *Example*   ⇨ **Online:** wdpg.io/18-2-1

This example shows two snippets of text. The first doesn't appear within a <p> tag, so it uses the browser's default font, and the second appears within a <p> tag, so it uses the font family specified by the property shown in the CSS section.

WEB PAGE

This text just uses the browser's default font.

This text resides within an HTML paragraph, so it uses the font specified in the style definition for the p tag.

CSS

```
p {
    font-family: Lato, sans-serif;
}
```

The p element uses the Lato font family.

HTML

Tells the browser to down-load the font from Google

```
<link href="https://fonts.googleapis.com/
css?family=Lato:400,400i,700" rel="stylesheet">

This text just uses the browser's default font.

<p>
This text resides within an HTML paragraph, so it uses the font
specified in the style definition for the p tag.
</p>
```

No p element is specified, so the default font is used.

This text is within a p element, so it's formatted with the Lato font.

Lesson 18.3: **Hosting Your Own Fonts**
Covers: The `@font-face` at-rule

⇨ **Online:** wdpg.io/18-3-0

Using a third-party font host is the easiest way to get out of the default-font rut and make your pages shine with an interesting typeface or two. Some web designers, however, dislike having the look of their pages at the mercy of some remote server, which might work slowly or not at all. In such cases, designers go the host-it-yourself route, in which the actual font files reside on the same server as the web page.

Unfortunately, you have a price to pay for the inherent speed and reliability of hosting your own fonts: complexity. Whereas using third-party-hosted fonts is a straightforward matter of generating and using a `<link>` tag for a remote stylesheet, hosting your own fonts has two major factors that raise the complexity level.

The first complicating factor is font licensing. Most commercial fonts come with a license that prevents them from being used on the web. Before you can host a font yourself, you must purchase a license to use the font on the web (assuming such a license is offered), or you can look for an open-source font that allows web use.

For the latter, here are a few font collections to try:

- Font Squirrel (https://www.fontsquirrel.com)
- Fontspring (https://www.fontspring.com)
- Fontex (www.fontex.org)
- Open Font Library (https://fontlibrary.org)

The second complicating factor is the mess that's otherwise known as font file formats. You might think that you need to upload a single font file to your server, but the state of the font art isn't so simple. There are, in fact, three file formats:

- *EOT (Embedded Open Type)*—Supported by Internet Explorer and the only font file format supported by Internet Explorer before version 9.

- *WOFF (Web Open Font Format)*—Supported by Internet Explorer 9 and later, Mozilla Firefox 3.6 and later, and Google Chrome 6 and later. A newer version called WOFF 2.0 (or WOFF2) is supported by Microsoft Edge 14 and later; Chrome 36 and later; Firefox 39 and later; Opera 23 and later; Safari 12, and later, iOS Safari 10.2, and later; and Android 62, and later.

- *TTF/OTF (TrueType Font/OpenType Font)*—Supported by all browsers except Internet Explorer 8 and earlier.

PLAY

Use Google Fonts to generate a `<link>` *tag for a stylesheet that defines just the regular font of the Merriweather typeface. Set up a style that applies the regular font to all page text and includes a generic font name as a fallback.*
⇨ Online: wdpg.io/18-2-2

FAQ

Is a local font file always faster than a remote font file? *Not necessarily. Many font providers use content delivery networks (CDNs) that are very fast, so the lag can often be less than with a local file.*

BEWARE

Fonts are intellectual property and should be treated as such. Before hosting any font on your site, make sure that you have a license to use the font for personal and/or commercial use (depending on the nature of your site).

The good news indeed is that you no longer need most of these formats. EOT is out because few people still use Internet Explorer 8 or earlier, and TTF/OTF are redundant because they're contained in the WOFF and WOFF2 formats. (A fourth format, called SVG, is now considered to be obsolete.) In short, you need to worry about only two font file formats: WOFF and WOFF2. Not bad!

Theoretically, the idea is that you download your licensed font file, which may be in the TTF file format, and then you somehow use that file to generate the other formats. Practically, that's difficult to do, so most folks use a Font Squirrel service called the Webfont Generator (**https://www.fontsquirrel.com/tools/webfont-generator**), which takes your downloaded font file and automatically creates a package that includes the other file formats.

Even better, the Webfont Generator package includes the necessary CSS code to use the fonts on your site. This code uses the `@font-face` at-rule, and the generic syntax looks like this:

```
@font-face {
    font-family: 'Font Name';
    src: url('font_filename.woff2') format('woff2'),
         url('font_filename.woff') format('woff');
}
```

Font names with spaces must be enclosed in quotation marks.

To apply the `@font-face` rule, use its `font-family` value as the `font-family` property of the element you want to style.

▶ *Example*   ⇨ **Online: wdpg.io/18-3-1**
This example sets up an `@font-face` *rule for the Bree Serif font and applies it to the* `ul` *element.*

WEB PAGE

Prefer to get your word origins on the web? Looking to kill some time at work? Wondering when this incessant questioning will end? Here are some fun websites that'll give your clicking finger a workout:

<ul> text

- Online Etymology Dictionary (www.etymonline.com)
- Oxford English Dictionary (www.oed.com)
- The Phrase Finder (www.phrases.org.uk)
- The Word Detective (www.word-detective.com)
- Word Spy (www.wordspy.com)
- World Wide Words (www.worldwidewords.org)

CSS

```
@font-face {
    font-family: 'Bree Serif';
    src: url('/fonts/breeserif.woff2') format('woff2'),
        url('/fonts/breeserif.woff') format('woff');
}
ul {
    font-family: 'Bree Serif';
}
```

The font-family name is used to apply the font to the element.

HTML

```
<p>
Prefer to get your word origins on the web? Looking to kill some
time at work? Wondering when this incessant questioning will end?
Here are some fun websites that'll give your clicking finger a
workout:
<p>
<ul>
    <li>Online Etymology Dictionary (www.etymonline.com)</li>
    <li>Oxford English Dictionary (www.oed.com)</li>
    <li>The Phrase Finder (www.phrases.org.uk)</li>
    <li>The Word Detective (www.word-detective.com</li>
    <li>Word Spy (www.wordspy.com)</li>
    <li>World Wide Words (www.worldwidewords.org)</li>
</ul>
```

Here are some notes to bear in mind when using directories with the @font-face rule filenames:

- If the font files reside in the same directory as the CSS file (or the HTML file that contains the CSS code), no directory is required:

```
url('breeserif.woff2')
```

- If the font files reside in a subdirectory of the location where the CSS (or HTML) file is stored, precede the filename with the directory name and a backslash (/):

```
url('fonts/breeserif.woff2')
```

- If the font files reside in a subdirectory of the site's root directory, precede the filename with a backslash (/), the directory name, and then another backslash (/):

```
url('/fonts/breeserif.woff2')
```

MASTER

Mirroring the current font file format reality, the Webfont Generator only generates WOFF and WOFF2 fonts by default. If you need other font file formats, be sure to activate the Expert radio button; then use the check boxes to choose the formats you want.

REMEMBER

For best cross-browser results, set up the @font-face rule so that the WOFF2 font format appears before the WOFF format. The Webfont Generator should do this automatically.

Working with Text Styles

When you have your typeface (or typefaces) picked out and can format them with different type sizes, you're well on your way to making typographically pleasing web pages. But to make your pages stand out from the herd, you need to know a few more CSS properties related to styling text.

Lesson 18.4: **Styling Small Caps**

Covers: The `font-variant` property

USE IT

Small caps are also often used to make all-uppercase text (such as acronyms) blend in a bit better with the surrounding text.

⇨ **Online:** wdpg.io/18-4-0

When you want some page text to be noticed, most of the time you'll turn to bold or italics to get the job done. For something a bit different, however, try small caps. Small caps are an all-uppercase style of text in which lowercase letters are converted to uppercase equivalents that are slightly smaller than normal uppercase letters. (Original uppercase text is left unchanged.)

You style text as small caps by using the `font-variant` property and setting its value to `small-caps`.

▶ *Example*   ⇨ **Online:** wdpg.io/18-4-1

This example uses the `font-variant` *property set to* `small-caps` *to style the names in the text as small caps.*

WEB PAGE	Movable type was invented by JOHANNES GUTENBERG in the mid-fifteenth century. The first printing press in England was set up by WILLIAM CAXTON in 1476.
CSS	```span {\n font-variant: small-caps;\n}``` — This styles the span element to use small caps.
HTML	```Movable type was invented by <span>Johannes Gutenberg</span> in the mid-fifteenth century. The first printing press in England was set up by <span>William Caxton</span> in 1876.``` The names within the span elements are rendered using small caps.

Lesson 18.5: **Setting the Line Height**

Covers: The `line-height` property

⇨ **Online:** wdpg.io/18-5-0

The last major factor in making your web page text look typographically solid is the *line height*, which is the distance between the baselines of two adjacent lines of text. For a given line of text, the *baseline* is the invisible line upon which lowercase characters such as *o* and *x* appear to sit.

You set the line height by using the CSS property named `line-height`. The types of values you can assign to this property are outlined in Table 18.1.

▶ Table 18.1 Values You Can Apply to the `line-height` Property

Value	Description
`number`	A numeric value entered without a unit. The computed line height is the current type size multiplied by the number.
`length`	A numeric value entered with a unit, such as `em`
`percentage`	A percentage value. The computed line height is the current type size multiplied by the percentage.
`normal`	A keyword that tells the browser to set the line height automatically based on the current type size.

The line height is crucial for readable text, as you can see in Figure 18.1. The text on the left is set with `line-height` equal to 0.75, which results in the lines being unreadably close together. The text on the right is set with `line-height` equal to 2, which results in the lines being too far apart for comfortable reading. The text in the middle has its `line-height` set to 1.2, which looks just right.

❝ *Typography is two-dimensional architecture, based on experience and imagination, and guided by rules and readability.* —Hermann Zapf

MASTER

Another way to manipulate the case of text is with the `text-transform` *property. Set this property to* `lowercase` *to convert the text to lowercase letters or* `uppercase` *to convert the text to uppercase. You can also use* `capitalize` *to apply uppercase to only the first letter of each word.*

▶Figure 18.1
When the line height is too small (left) or too large (right), the text is difficult to read.

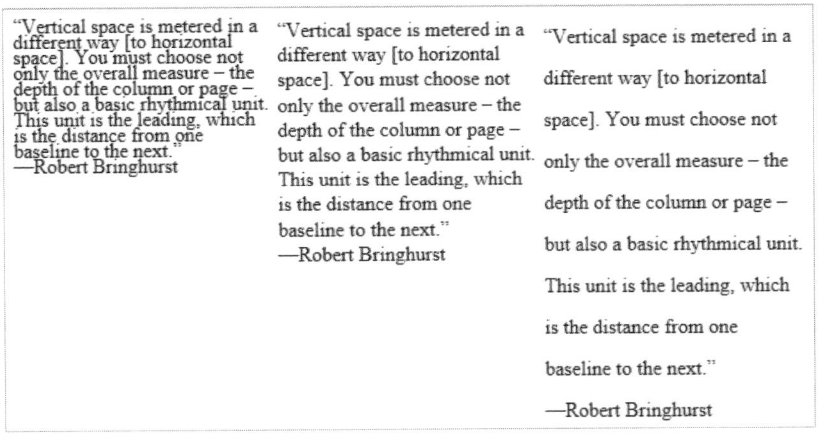

"Vertical space is metered in a different way [to horizontal space]. You must choose not only the overall measure – the depth of the column or page – but also a basic rhythmical unit. This unit is the leading, which is the distance from one baseline to the next."
—Robert Bringhurst

"Vertical space is metered in a different way [to horizontal space]. You must choose not only the overall measure – the depth of the column or page – but also a basic rhythmical unit. This unit is the leading, which is the distance from one baseline to the next."
—Robert Bringhurst

"Vertical space is metered in a different way [to horizontal space]. You must choose not only the overall measure – the depth of the column or page – but also a basic rhythmical unit. This unit is the leading, which is the distance from one baseline to the next."
—Robert Bringhurst

▶*Try This*   ⇨ **Online: wdpg.io/18-5-2**
This example sets the `line-height` property of the p element to 0.9, which results in so-called *tight leading*. Try a *normal leading* value of around 1.2, as well as a *loose leading* value of 1.5 or higher.

WEB PAGE

The name *line height* is often used synonymously with *leading* (it's pronounced *ledding*). This term comes from the movable type profession, where typesetters often use a strip of lead to set the amount of space between two lines of text.

CSS

```
p {
    font-size: 1.5em;
    line-height: 0.9;
}
```

Adjust the p element's line-height value to create tight, normal, and loose leading.

HTML

```
<p>
The name <i>line height</i> is often used synonymously with
<i>leading</i> (it's pronounced <i>ledding</i>). This term comes
from the movable type profession, where typesetters often use a
strip of lead to set the amount of space between two lines of text.
</p>.
```

Lesson 18.6: **Using the Shorthand Font Property**
Covers: The `font` property

⇨ **Online:** wdpg.io/18-6-0

As you've seen so far in this book, there are six main font-related components for CSS typography: typeface, type size, bolding, italics, small caps, and line height. These components are represented, respectively, by the CSS properties `font-family`, `font-size`, `font-weight`, `font-style`, `font-variant`, and `line-height`. Handily, you can apply any or all of these properties with a single statement by using the `font` shorthand property, which takes the syntax shown in Figure 18.2.

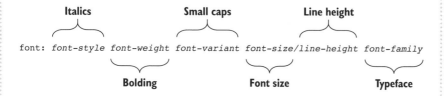

▶ Figure 18.2
You can apply up to six font properties at the same time by using the `font` property.

This syntax is a straightforward repetition of everything you've learned so far, although you need to keep the following notes in mind:

- You can use some or all of the values, but at minimum, you must provide the *font-size* and the *font-family* values, in that order.

- You can add the *font-style*, *font-weight*, and *font-variant* values in any order, as long as they all come before the *font-size* value.

- You've no doubt noticed, and are more than a little curious about, the *font-size/line-height* part of the syntax. That slash is borrowed from traditional print typography, in which as shorthand, one might say that text was "set 12/18," meaning that it uses 12-point type and an 18-point line height.

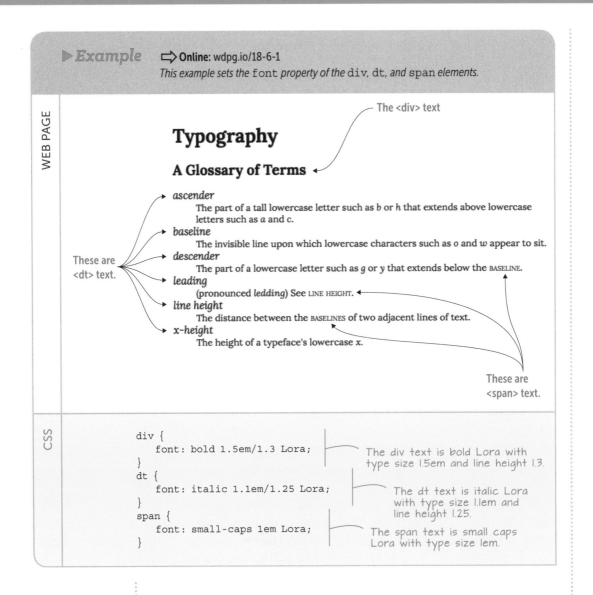

▶ *Example* ⇨ **Online:** wdpg.io/18-6-1
This example sets the `font` *property of the* div, dt, *and* span *elements.*

WEB PAGE

The <div> text

Typography

A Glossary of Terms

These are <dt> text.

ascender
The part of a tall lowercase letter such as b or h that extends above lowercase letters such as a and c.

baseline
The invisible line upon which lowercase characters such as o and w appear to sit.

descender
The part of a lowercase letter such as g or y that extends below the BASELINE.

leading
(pronounced *ledding*) See LINE HEIGHT.

line height
The distance between the BASELINES of two adjacent lines of text.

x-height
The height of a typeface's lowercase x.

These are <span> text.

CSS

```
div {
    font: bold 1.5em/1.3 Lora;
}
dt {
    font: italic 1.1em/1.25 Lora;
}
span {
    font: small-caps 1em Lora;
}
```

The div text is bold Lora with type size 1.5em and line height 1.3.

The dt text is italic Lora with type size 1.1em and line height 1.25.

The span text is small caps Lora with type size 1em.

HTML

This element embeds the Lora typeface from Google Fonts.

```html
<link href="https://fonts.googleapis.com/
css?family=Lora:400,400i,700,700i" rel="stylesheet">

<h1>Typography</h1>
<div>A Glossary of Terms</div>
<dl>
<dt>ascender</dt>
<dd>The part of a tall lowercase letter such as <i>b</i> or <i>h</i> that extends above lowercase letters such as <i>a</i> and <i>c</i>.
<dt>baseline</dt>
<dd>The invisible line upon which lowercase characters such as <i>o</i> and <i>w</i> appear to sit.</dd>
<dt>descender</dt>
<dd>The part of a lowercase letter such as <i>g</i> or <i>y</i> that extends below the <span>baseline</span>.
<dt>leading</dt>
<dd>(pronounced <i>ledding</i>) See <span>line height</span>.</dd>
<dt>line height</dt>
<dd>The distance between the <span>baselines</span> of two adjacent lines of text.</dd><dt>x-height</dt>
<dd>The height of a typeface's lowercase <i>x</i>.</dd>
</dl>
```

Web Typography Gallery

▶ The Anchor & Orbit site (www.anchorandorbit.com) uses a combination of three typefaces: P22 Underground for the headers, Caslon for the body text, and Cotoris for the logo.

P22 Underground

Cotoris

Caslon

▶ The Scytale site (https://scytale.pt) uses Flama Medium for the headers and Adelle Light for the body text.

SCYTALE

Scytale is a web development & design studio specialised in producing intelligent applications, delivering engaging products that improve life, work and play. From interaction to visual design, we solve problems, explore solutions, and think that every detail matters.

Adelle Light

WE BLEND DESIGN & TECHNOLOGY TO CREATE EXPERIENCES

Flama Medium

OUR EXPERTISE

▶The website of designer Kait Bos (**www.kaitbos.com**) uses the Capriola typeface for the navigation and the body text, and the Archer Light Pro typeface for the main heading.

▶The website for the Rule of Three copywriting studio (**https://rule-of-three.co.uk**) uses a single typeface, Sorts Mill Goudy, at various type sizes.

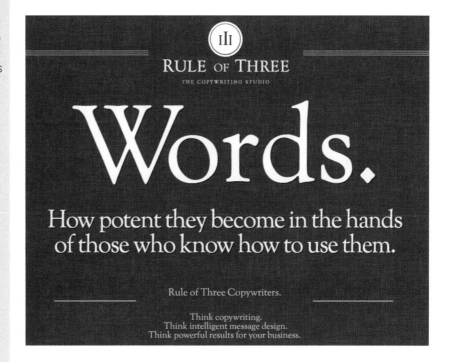

Summary

- Use hosted or local font files rather than rely on system fonts.
- Choose a typeface that suits your text and your overall message.
- Use `font-variant: small-caps` as an alternative way to emphasize or highlight text.
- Give your text blocks room (but not too much room) between the lines by setting the `line-height` property.
- Save time by using the `font` property as shorthand.

Chapter 19

Learning Advanced CSS Selectors

HTML elements enable web page designers to mark up a document's structure, but beyond trust and hope, you don't have any control over your text's appearance. CSS changes that. CSS puts the designer in the driver's seat. — Håkon Wium Lie

This chapter covers

- Learning the powerful ID and universal selectors
- Leveling your style game with the descendant, child, and sibling selectors
- Targeting your styles by combining two or more selectors
- Becoming a style master by understanding CSS inheritance, cascading, and specificity

On the surface, CSS seems like a simple topic: You apply values to some properties, combine them into a rule, and then apply that rule to a page element. Repeat a few more times, and voilà: your page is beautiful. But the apparent simplicity of CSS is only skin-deep. Underneath the straightforward implementation of declarations and rules are obscure caves of complexity and unfathomed depths of dynamism. This chapter serves as an introduction to this hidden world, which is home to some of the most powerful and practical CSS concepts.

Working with ID Selectors

LEARN

My WebDev Workshop includes a complete rundown of all the CSS selectors, with examples. Check it out: https:// webdev.mcfedries. com/code/selector-reference/.

In Chapter 7, I introduced you to CSS selectors, which enable you to specify the page object you want to style:

```
selector {
    property1: value1;
    property2: value2;
    ...
}
```

So far, you've learned that the `selector` part of this CSS rule can be the name of an HTML tag (a *type selector*) or the name of a CSS class (a *class selector*). A rather large collection of CSS selectors exists, however. Many of these selectors are rather obscure, but the more common ones are powerful tools indeed. The lessons in this chapter introduce five of these selectors, beginning with the ID selector.

Lesson 19.1: *Using ID Selectors*
Covers: The #id selector

BEWARE

Again, like class names, id values are case-sensitive.

REMEMBER

As with class names, your id value must begin with a letter and can include any combination of letters, numbers, hyphens (-), underscores (_).

⇨ **Online:** wdpg.io/19-1-0

Back in Chapter 16, you learned that you can link to a specific element in a web page by adding the id attribute to that element and then including the id value in your link address. You can also use an element's id value to apply CSS styling to that element. To do this in an internal or external style sheet, you type the id value preceded by a hash symbol (#) to create the selector:

```
#id-value {
    property1: value1;
    property2: value2;
    ...
}
```

The following example shows ID selectors in action.

Online: wdpg.io/19-1-1

▶ *Example*

This example adds an ID to each of two `<div>` tags—`section-quote` and `section-summary`—and then uses the corresponding ID selectors to apply rules to each `div` element.

WEB PAGE

Metaphors for New Words

"Because in our brief lives we catch so little of the vastness of history, we tend too much to think of language as being solid as a dictionary, with a granite-like permanence, rather than as the rampant restless sea of metaphor which it is."
—Julian Jaynes

} id= "section-quote"

We make metaphors for many things, but when we make many metaphors for one thing, it says that thing is important to us. We make metaphors for new words almost as readily as we make new words.

} id= "section-summary"

CSS

```css
#section-quote {
    color: darkgray;
    font-size: 1.25em;
    font-style: italic;
    text-align: right;
}
#section-summary {
    color: dimgray;
    font-size: 1.5em;
    font-weight: bold;
    text-align: center;
}
```

Rule for the
section-quote id

Rule for the
section-summary id

HTML

```html
<h1>
    Metaphors for New Words
</h1>
<div id="section-quote">
"Because in our brief lives we catch so little of the vastness of
history, we tend too much to think of language as being solid as
a dictionary, with a granite-like permanence, rather than as the
rampant restless sea of metaphor which it is."<br>-Julian Jaynes
</div>
<div id="section-summary">
We make metaphors for many things, but when we make many metaphors
for one thing, it says that thing is important to us. We make
metaphors for new words almost as readily as we make new words.
</div>
```

The section-quote id
assigned to a div element

The section-summary id
assigned to a div element

BEWARE

ID selectors, because they apply to a single element, make your CSS code harder to maintain and troubleshoot. You'll understand why when I talk about specificity later in this chapter. Therefore, the true best practice when it comes to ID selectors is to never use them.

Best Practices: Classes Versus IDs

When should you use an ID selector versus a class selector? Ask yourself the following questions:

- Will the styles I want to use be applied to one and only one element?

  If so, use an ID selector on that element.

- Will the styles I want to use be applied to multiple elements?

  If so, use a class selector on each of those elements.

- Will the styles I want to use be applied to only one element now but could be applied to other elements in the future?

  If so, use a class selector on that one element now. You can always apply the class selector to other elements as needed down the road.

Web Page Genealogy: Parents, Descendants, and Siblings

Before continuing with the selectors, you need to take a mercifully brief detour into the hierarchical structure of a web page so that you can learn a few key concepts. Figure 19.1 shows the hierarchy of a typical web page.

Now traverse this (upside-down) tree structure:

- The `html` element is the root of the structure.
- The `html` element has two main branches: `head` and `body`.
- The `head` element has two branches: `title` and `style`.
- The `body` element has three branches: an `h1` element and two `p` elements.
- The first of the `p` elements has a `div` branch.
- That `div` branch has two `p` branches.
- The second of those `p` branches has a `section` branch.
- The `section` branch has two `p` branches.

Given this hierarchy, I can define a few useful terms that you'll need to understand the CSS selectors that follow:

- *Parent*—An element that contains one or more other elements. In Figure 19.1, `html` is the parent of the `head` and `body` elements, and the `div` element is the parent of the two `p` elements.

- *Grandparent*—An element that contains a second level of elements. In Figure 19.1, `html` is the grandparent of (among others) the `title` and `h1` elements, and the `div` element is the grandparent of the `section` element.

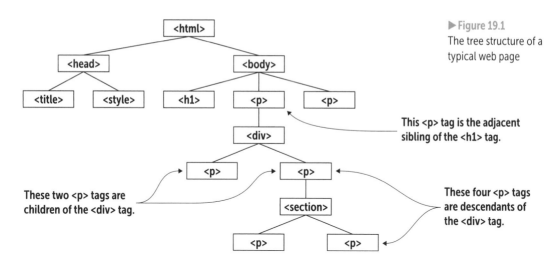

The tree structure of a typical web page

- *Ancestor*—An element that contains one or more levels of elements. In Figure 19.1, html is an ancestor of every other element, and the body element is an ancestor of the div element and every element contained within the div element.

- *Child*—An element that's contained within an element that lies one level above it in the hierarchy. That is, the element has a parent in the structure. In Figure 19.1, title is a child of head, and the div is a child of its containing p element.

- *Descendant*—An element that's contained within an element that lies one or more levels above it in the hierarchy. That is, the element has an ancestor in the structure. In Figure 19.1, title is a descendant of html, and the four p elements are all descendants of their containing div element.

- *Sibling*—An element that lies on the same level as another element. In Figure 19.1, the three child elements of the body element—that is, the h1 and the two p elements—are all siblings. Note in particular that a sibling that comes right after another sibling is called an *adjacent sibling*.

Working with Contextual Selectors

With the terms from the preceding section in mind, I want now to talk about how you use the web page hierarchy to construct some powerful CSS rules by using three *contextual selectors* (so-named because they define an element's context within the web page).

Lesson 19.2: **The Descendant Selector**

Covers: The x y selector

➡️ Online: wdpg.io/19-2-0

REMEMBER

In CSS lingo, the character that you place between two elements to form a selector (such as the space used in the descendant selector) is called a combinator.

MASTER

Yep, a space is a head-scratching character choice to define a CSS selector, but the latest CSS specs introduce an explicit descendant combinator: the double greater-than sign (div >> p instead of div p). No browsers support this yet, but all will in the future.

BEWARE

The descendant selector is powerful because it targets every descendant of an ancestor, no matter how far down the hierarchy those descendants reside. To avoid unexpected results, if you want to target a descendant one level below an ancestor, you should use the child selector (discussed in Lesson 19.3).

One common CSS scenario is applying a style rule to all the elements contained within (that is, are descendants of) some other element (the ancestor). To do that, use the *descendant selector*, which separates the ancestor and descendant elements with a space, as shown in the following syntax:

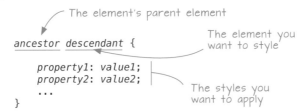

```
                    The element's parent element

ancestor descendant {                The element you
                                     want to style
    property1: value1;
    property2: value2;               The styles you
    ...                              want to apply
}
```

Your page may have a couple of p elements at the beginning that serve as a summary of the page and quite a few more p elements that hold the body text. Assuming you want to style the summary text differently from the body text, a generic p selector won't work. If, instead, you enclose all the body text p elements in a div element, you can target all the p elements with the following selector:

```
div p
```

The following example uses the descendant selector to style a page's body text.

▶ *Example*   ⇨ **Online:** wdpg.io/19-2-1

This example uses the descendant selector `div p` *to target only those* `p` *elements that are contained within the* `div` *element.*

WEB PAGE

Weird Word Origins

Welcome to the always wonderful, sometimes weird, and often downright wacky world of word histories

> This <p> tag is not a descendant of a <div>.

Never thought you'd hear adjectives such as *wacky* and *weird* associated with the history of words? Think again, oh soon-to-be-even-wiser-than-you-are-now reader! The study of word origins isn't about memorizing technical terms or resurrecting dead languages or puzzling over parts of speech. Instead, it's all about telling stories.

The history of a word is a narrative, plain and simple: where the word began, how it changed over time, and how it got where it is today. Delightfully, these narratives are often full of plot twists, turning points, heroes and villains, and surprise endings.

> These <p> tags are descendants of a <div>.

CSS

```
body {
    color: blue;
    font-family: Verdana, sans-serif;
    font-size: 1.2em;
}
div p {
    color: #444;
    font-family: Georgia, serif;
    font-size: 0.75em;
}
```

> Styles applied to all text

> Styles applied only to p elements that are descendants of a div element

HTML

```
<h2>Weird Word Origins</h2>
<p>Welcome to the always wonderful, sometimes weird, and often
downright wacky world of word histories</p>
<div>
    <p>Never thought you'd hear adjectives such as <i>wacky</
i> and <i>weird</i> associated with the history of words? Think
again, oh soon-to-be-even-wiser-than-you-are-now reader! The
study of word origins isn't about memorizing technical terms or
resurrecting dead languages or puzzling over parts of speech.
Instead, it's all about telling stories.</p>
    <p>The history of a word is a narrative, plain and simple:
where the word began, how it changed over time, and how it got
where it is today. Delightfully, these narratives are often full
of plot twists, turning points, heroes and villains, and surprise
endings.</p>
</div>
```

Lesson 19.3: **The Child Selector**
Covers: The x > y selector

⇨ **Online:** wdpg.io/19-3-0

Rather than select every descendant of a specified element, you often need to target only its children. To do that, use the *child selector*, which separates the parent and child elements with a greater-than sign (>), as shown in the following syntax:

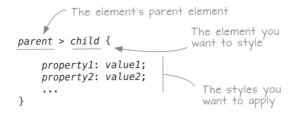

Referring to Figure 19.1, you can style the div element's two p children with the following selector:

```
div > p
```

The following example uses the child selector to style those p elements that are children of a div element.

PLAY

Create a rule that applies a green color and a font size of 1.2em to any <code> tag that is a descendant of a <div> tag. ⇨ **Online:** wdpg.io/19-2-2

MASTER

To select an element that's the first child of its parent, use the element:first-child *pseudo-class. Similarly, to select an element that's the last child of its parent, use the* element:last-child *pseudo-class.* ⇨ **Online:** wdpg.io/19-3-4

MASTER

Another powerful child pseudo-class is :nth-child(n), *where n specifies which children you want to select. Use* :nth-child(odd) *to select the odd (first, third, and so on) children, or* :nth-child(even) *to select the even (second, fourth, and so on) elements.* ⇨ **Online:** wdpg.io/19-3-5

▶ *Example*   ⇨ **Online:** wdpg.io/19-3-1

This example uses the div > p *child selector to set a font size of 1.25em and a color of dark green to only those* p *elements that are direct children of a* div *element.*

WEB PAGE

Contextual Selectors

The Descendant Selector

The Child Selector

The First Child Selector

The Last Child Selector

The Nth Child Selector

The Sibling Selector

These <p> tags are children of a <div>.

These <p> tags are not children of a <div>.

CSS

```css
p {
    color: darkblue;
    font-size: 1em;
    font-weight: bold;
}
div > p {
    font-size: 1.25em;
    color: darkgreen;
}
```

Styles for all p text

Styles for p elements that are children of div elements

HTML

```html
<h1>Contextual Selectors</h1>
<div>
    <p>The Descendant Selector</p>
    <p>The Child Selector</p>
        <section>
            <p>The First Child Selector</p>
            <p>The Last Child Selector</p>
            <p>The Nth Child Selector</p>
        </section>
    <p>The Sibling Selector</p>
</div>
```

The child p elements

Lesson 19.4: *The Sibling Selector*
Covers: The x ~ y selector

PLAY

Given a numbered list that's nested within another numbered list, use the child selector to create a rule that styles the nested list to use lowercase letters instead of numbers. ⇨Online: wdpg.io/19-3-2

⇨ **Online:** wdpg.io/19-4-0

Instead of selecting an element's children or descendants, you might need to target its siblings. To do that, use the *sibling selector*, which separates the reference element and the sibling element with a tilde (~), as shown in the following syntax:

```
element ~ sibling {
    property1: value1;
    property2: value2;
    ...
}
```

The reference element

The element you want to style

The styles you want to apply

In Figure 19.1, you can style the two p elements that are the siblings of the h1 element with the following selector:

```
h1 ~ p
```

The following example shows the sibling selector in action.

▶ *Example*   ⇨**Online:** wdpg.io/19-4-1
This example uses the h1 ~ div sibling selector to set a sans-serif font stack and a bold font weight to only those div elements that are siblings of the h1 element.

WEB PAGE

A Smart Vocabulary—Contents

The <h1> tag

Chapter 1: Names of Things You Didn't Know Had Names
From the indentation on your upper lip to the indentation on the bottom of a wine bottle.
Chapter 2: Making Word Whoopee
Codswallop, nincompoop, willy-nilly, and other words that will bring a smile to your face.

These <div> tags are siblings of the <h1>.

These <div> tags are not siblings of the <h1>.

CSS

```
div {
    font-family: Georgia, serif;
    font-weight: normal;
}
h1 ~ div {
    font-family: Verdana, sans-serif;
    font-weight: bold;
}
```

Styles for all div text

Styles for div elements that are siblings of h1

```
HTML
        <h1>
            A Smart Vocabulary—Contents
        </h1>
        <div>
            Chapter 1: Names of Things You Didn't Know Had Names
            <div>From the indentation on your upper lip to the indentation
        on the bottom of a wine bottle.</div>
        </div>
        <div>
            Chapter 2:  Making Word Whoopee
            <div>Codswallop, nincompoop, willy-nilly, and other words that
        will bring a smile to your face.</div>
        </div>
```

The sibling div elements

Taking Things up a Notch by Combining Selectors

CSS selectors are useful tools because they enable you to target areas of your web page that you want styled. By specifying a particular class or an element's descendants, you gain much more control of your page presentation. But what if instead of needing to use either the class selector or the descendant selector, you need to use both? That is, what if you want to target not the element that has been assigned a particular class, but its descendants? Table 19.1 demonstrates a few ways to combine CSS selectors.

MASTER

To select only the adjacent sibling of an element, change the tilde to a plus sign: `element + sibling` *(as in* h1 + p*).* ⇨ **Online:** wdpg .io/19-4-4

▶ Table 19.1 Some Ways to Combine Selectors

Example	Description
`<div class="sidebar alert">`	Applies both the class named `sidebar` and the class named `alert` to the `div` element
`p.footnote {styles}`	Applies a rule to those `p` elements that have been assigned the class named `footnote`
`p.footnote > a {styles}`	Applies a rule to a elements that are the children of those `p` elements that have been assigned the class named `footnote`
`p.footnote  a.external {styles}`	Applies a rule to a elements that have been assigned the class named `external` and that are the descendants of those `p` elements that have been assigned the class named `footnote`
`#payables-table li:nth-child(even) {styles}`	Applies a rule to the even numbered `li` elements in the list that has been assigned the ID `payables-table`

While I'm on the topic of combining things, I should mention that it's perfectly valid CSS to apply a single style rule to two or more selectors. You do that by separating the selectors with commas, like so:

```
selectorA,
selectorB {
    property1: value1;
    property2: value2;
    ...
}
```

Suppose that you have a class named `pullquote` that you use to style the pull quotes in your website's news articles and a class named `sidebar` that you use for the sidebars in your website's tutorial pages. If these two classes use the same rule, you can combine them:

```
.pullquote,
.sidebar {
    color: #444;
    background-color: #ccc;
}
```

Lesson 19.5: **The ::before and ::after Pseudo-elements**

Covers: `::before` and `::after`

REMEMBER

To insert a special character as the custom content, use the character's hexadecimal code, preceded by a backslash (\\). The declaration content: '\0266f'; , *for example, specifies the musical sharp sign (♯) as the custom content. Use the HTML5 Entity Browser (**wdpg.io/charent**) to look up a character's hex code.*

⇨ **Online:** wdpg.io/19-5-0

In CSS, you can create web page objects that aren't officially part of the page hierarchy, and these objects are known as *pseudo-elements*. Two common examples are `::before` and `::after`, which you use to insert content before and after, respectively, the content of whatever element you specify. In CSS, this content is called *generated content* because you don't type the content yourself; it's created by the browser automatically. Here's the syntax:

```
                          The web page element
                ⌐
                              Where you want the
element::before|after {       content added
                          ◄
    content: value;     ◄     The content you
    content_styles;     ◄     want to insert
}
                              Optional styles applied to
                              the inserted content
```

You'll occasionally see the single-colon variants `:before` and `:after`. Sites use this older syntax to provide support for Internet Explorer 8. Because that browser now stands at around one-tenth of 1 percent global use (and shrinking), the world has moved on to the double-colon standard that you see in this book.

You can use the following rule to automatically add a pilcrow (¶), also called a paragraph mark, after each paragraph:

```
p::after {
    content: '¶';
}
```

One of the most common uses for the `::before` pseudo-element is to replace the default bullets in an unordered list with custom bullets. The following example shows how.

▶ *Example*   ⇨ **Online:** wdpg.io/19-5-1

This example uses `list-style-type` *to remove the bullets from the* `ul` *element and then uses* `li::before` *to add a custom bullet character—a pointing finger (hex code 261e)—and a nonbreaking space (hex 00a0).*

WEB PAGE

Here are some interesting characters to use in place of the standard bullets:

☞ Circled bullet: ◉

☞ Circled white bullet: ◎

☞ Rightwards arrow with loop: ↬

☞ Black star: ★

☞ White star: ☆

☞ Triangle bullet: ▸

└── Pointing finger character as a custom bullet

CSS

```
ul {
    list-style-type: none;          ── Removes the default bullet
    margin-left: 0;
    padding-left: 1em;              ── Ensures that bullet text
    text-indent: -1em;                 wraps correctly
}

li::before {
    content:'\261e\00a0';           ── Adds a pointing finger
    color: red;                        and space
    font-size: 1.1em;
}                                   ── Styles the
                                       custom bullet
```

continued

```
HTML
        <div>
            Here are some interesting characters to use in place of the
        standard bullets:
        </div>
        <ul>
            <li>Circled bullet: &#x029bf;</li>
            <li>Circled white bullet: &#x029be;</li>
            <li>Rightwards arrow with loop: &#x021ac;</li>
            <li>Black star: &#x02605;</li>
            <li>White star: &#x02606;</li>
            <li>Triangle bullet: &#x2023;</li>
        </ul>
```

PLAY

An external link is one that points to a resource on a different site. Create a CSS rule that automatically adds an icon to denote external links, the way that Wikipedia does (see Figure 19.2). ⇨ Online: wdpg.io/19-5-3

PLAY

CSS offers the `counter-increment` *property that lets you set up a counter for a numbered list. If you set the* ol *element's* `list-style-type` *property to* none*, you can use* `ol::before` *to create custom numbers for a list.* ⇨ Online: wdpg .io/19-5-2

External links

- Official website ⎘
- CSS⎘ at DMOZ

▶ Figure 19.2
Wikipedia marks external links with an icon.

While I'm talking about pseudo-elements, it's worth mentioning that you can use the `::first-letter` pseudo-element to apply one or more styles to the first letter of a text block. `div::first-letter {font-size: 1.5em; color: red;}`, for example, styles the first letter of each `div` element to have size 1em and color red. To style the entire first line of a text block, use the `::first-line` pseudo-element.

Resetting CSS with the Universal Selector

The *universal selector* (*) applies to every element on the web page, which may seem to be an odd way of approaching styles. After all, how often would a particular set of styles apply to every element on a page? Almost never. The universal selector is useful, however, when it comes to a *CSS reset*—a way of removing the web browser's default styles so that you can apply your own without having to worry about conflicts with the browser. Here's a basic CSS reset:

```
* {
    font-size: 100%;
    margin: 0;
    padding: 0;
}
```

This reset defines the default font size and removes the browser's default margins and padding (both of which you learned about in Chapter 9).

Styles: What a Tangled Web Page They Weave

Most of the style declarations and rules you've worked with so far have operated in splendid isolation. You style an h1 element with a font size and a p element with an alignment, and the web browser applies these two rules independently of each other. However, in the real world of web design, such simplicity is rare. I'm talking hen's-teeth rare. For all but the most basic web pages, it's a certainty that your styles are fraternizing and sometimes even fighting with one another. It's mayhem, but you can restore some semblance of order by understanding three key CSS mechanisms: inheritance, the cascade, and specificity.

MASTER

Here are some other common CSS reset declarations:
```
border: 0;
font-family:
inherit;
font-style:
inherit;
font-weight:
inherit;
vertical-align:
baseline;
```

Lesson 19.6: ***Understanding Inheritance***
Covers: CSS inheritance

⇨ **Online:** wdpg.io/19-6-0

With all that talk earlier in the chapter about ancestors, parents, children, and descendants, you won't be surprised to learn that CSS comes with a method for passing traits along from one "generation" to the next. This method is called, appropriately enough, *inheritance*, and it means that for certain CSS properties, if a parent element is styled with that property, its child and descendant elements are automatically styled the same way.

In the following example, a div element is assigned the class intro, which styles the element with 1.1em brown text. Notice that the div element's children—the em, sup, and code elements, as well as the nested div element—are styled the same way because in each case, they've inherited those styles from the parent div.

What did I mean when I said that only certain properties are inherited? Although many CSS properties are inherited by descendant elements, not all of them are. If you were to apply a border around the parent div element in the preceding example, that same border style wouldn't be applied to any of its descendants, because it would look odd to have, say, a border around an em or a sup element.

PLAY

The a element inherits style properties such as color, *but you don't see this inheritance; the browser overrides the inheritance so that your links stand out from the regular page text. Can you think of a way to force the text of child a elements to use the same color as their parent?*
⇨ Online: wdpg.io/19-6-2

Learning Advanced CSS Selectors

► Example   **⇨ Online:** wdpg.io/19-6-1

This example demonstrates inheritance by showing how the styles of the parent div *element get passed down to child elements such as* em, code, *and the nested* div.

WEB PAGE

A child <em>

The parent <div>

Why don't *all* CSS properties inherit their parent's styles?[*] Because in some cases it would lead to weird or nonsensical results. For example, if you apply a border around, say, a div element, it would look odd indeed to apply the same border to a child span or strong element. Similarly, applying, say, a p element's width value to a child em element doesn't make sense.

A child <code>

[*] See www.w3.org/TR/REC-CSS2/propidx.html

A child <div>

CSS

```
.intro {
    color: saddlebrown;
    font-size: 1.1em;
    line-height: 1.4;
}
```

Styles for the intro class

HTML

The parent div element

A child em element

```
<div class="intro">
Why don't <em>all</em> CSS properties inherit their parent's
styles?<sup>*</sup> Because in some cases it would lead to weird
or nonsensical results. For example, if you apply a border around,
say, a <code>div</code> element, it would look odd indeed to apply
the same border to a child <code>span</code> or <code>strong</
code> element. Similarly, applying, say, a <code>p</code>
element's <code>width</code> value to a child <code>em</code>
element doesn't make sense.

    <div>
        <sup>*</sup> See www.w3.org/TR/REC-CSS2/propidx.html
    </div>
</div>
```

A child code element

A child div element

Lesson 19.7: *Learning About the Cascade*
Covers: CSS cascade

➡ **Online:** wdpg.io/19-7-0

Besides the fact that styles get passed down from parent elements to descendant elements though inheritance, CSS also defines the way that the styles get propagated. This definition is called the *cascade*, and if inheritance is the "what" of style propagation, the cascade is the "how." (Before continuing, let me answer the question that's no doubt on your mind: Yes, the cascade is the reason why collections of styles are called *cascading* style sheets.) To see how the cascade works, consider the following code:

```
<style>
    div {
        color: red;                    Internal style sheet
    }
</style>

<div style="color: blue;">            Inline style
    What is the color of this text?
</div>
```

Here, an internal style sheet tells the `div` element to use red text, and an inline style colors the `<div>` tag's text blue. What color is the text between the `<div>` and `</div>` tags? That is, how will the browser resolve the conflict between the internal style sheet and the inline style?

To answer both questions, you need to know how the cascade does its job. First, you already know that there are three main ways to specify CSS: inline styles, internal style sheets, and external style sheets. Together, these methods constitute what the W3C calls *author style sheets* (because they're created by the person who wrote the web page; that's you). But two other style sheets get applied when a web page loads: the browser's default styles (called the *user agent style sheet*), and the browser user's custom styles (called the *user style sheet*).

The cascade organizes these five sources of style data into the following hierarchy:

- User agent style sheet
- User style sheet
- External style sheets
- Internal style sheets
- Inline styles

LEARN

The World Wide Web Consortium (W3C) maintains a complete list of CSS properties. Among other tidbits, that list helpfully specifies whether each property is inherited. See https://www.w3.org/TR/REC-CSS2/propidx.html.

REMEMBER

Speaking generally, the closer a style declaration is to the actual element that it's styling, the greater its weight.

These sources are listed in *ascending* order of importance (*weight*, in CSS lingo). If the browser sees that a particular style rule is defined in two or more of these sources, it resolves the conflict by applying the style from the source that has the greatest weight. For the code example I showed earlier, you can see that an inline style trumps an internal style sheet, so the text between the <div> and </div> tags will display as blue, as shown in the following example.

▶ *Example*   ⟹ **Online:** wdpg.io/19-7-1

This example demonstrates the CSS cascade, where the div element's inline style gets rendered because it carries more weight than the div type selector from the internal style sheet.

WEB PAGE

What is the color of this text? ← The <div> tag

HTML

```
<style>
    div {
        color: red;                 Internal style
    }                               sheet
</style>

<div style="color: blue;">          Inline style
    What is the color of this text?
</div>
```

Lesson 19.8: **Introducing Specificity**
Covers: CSS specificity

MASTER

There's a sixth style source you need to know: adding the !important *keyword to the end of any style declaration. This keyword carries the greatest possible CSS weight, so it overrides any other source.*
⟹ **Online:** wdpg.io/19-7-2

⟹ **Online:** wdpg.io/19-8-0

You may be wondering what happens to the CSS cascade when two styles that target the same element come from the same source. Consider the following code:

```
<style>
    p.colored-text {
        color: purple;
    }
    .colored-text {
```

```
          color: blue;
     }
     div p {
          color: green;
     }
     p {
          color: red;
     }
</style>

<div>
     <p class="colored-text">What is the color of this text?</p>
</div>
```

Descendant selector

Type selector

The style sheet contains four rules, all of which target the p element. The first rule selects all p elements that use the colored-text class; the second rule selects all elements that use the colored-text class; the third rule selects p elements that are descendants of a div element; and the fourth rule selects all p elements. What color will the browser render the text between the <p> and </p> tags? The cascade alone doesn't answer this question because all the rules come from an internal style sheet and therefore are given equal weight.

To figure out the winner in this CSS fight, you need to know a bit about a concept called *specificity*. Specificity is one of the most complex ideas in all of CSS, but for purposes of this chapter, I can say this about it: The more specifically a particular selector targets something on a web page, the greater weight it's given when the browser is calculating which rules to apply. You can judge how specifically a selector targets something by applying the following recipe to the selector:

1 Count the number of elements (such as p or div) and pseudo-elements (such as ::before), and assign 1 point to each.

2 Count the number of classes and pseudo-classes (such as :hover), and assign 10 points to each.

3 Count the number of IDs, and assign 100 points to each.

4 If the selector is part of an inline style sheet, assign 1,000 points.

The points assigned are indicative of the weight each selector carries. Returning to the example, count the points:

- p.colored-text—This selector contains one element and one class, for a total of 11 points.

- .colored-text—This selector contains one class, for a total of 10 points.

- div p—This selector contains two elements, for a total of 2 points.

- p—This selector contains one element, for a total of 1 point.

You can see that the `p.colored-text` selector has the most points, so the text between the `<p>` and `</p>` tags gets rendered as purple, as shown in the following example.

▶ *Example* ⇨ **Online:** wdpg.io/19-8-1

This example demonstrates CSS specificity, where the selector `p.colored-text` is more specific that the other selectors, so the browser renders the text as purple.

WEB PAGE

What is the color of this text? — The `<p>` tag

HTML

```
<style>
    p.colored-text {            ← Specificity = 11 points
        color: purple;
    }
    .colored-text {             ← Specificity = 10 points
        color: blue;
    }
    div p {            Specificity = 2 points
        color: green;
    }
    p {            Specificity = 1 point
        color: red;
    }
</style>
<div>
    <p class="colored-text">What is the color of this text?</p>
</div>
```

❝❝ *The different weight of selectors is usually the reason why your CSS rules don't apply to some elements, although you think they should. To minimize the time you spend bug hunting, you need to understand how browsers interpret your code. And to understand that, you need to have a firm understanding of how specificity works.* —Vitaly Friedman

Summary

- An *ID selector* applies CSS rules to any element that uses the specified ID value.

- To target all the elements contained within a parent element, use the *descendant selector*, which is the parent and descendant element names separated by a space.

- To target all the child elements contained within a parent element, use the *child selector*, which is the parent and child element names separated by a greater-than sign (>).

- To target all the elements that are siblings of some other element, use the *sibling selector*, which is the names of the two elements separated by a tilde (~).

- Append `::before` or `::after` to a selector to insert generated content before or after the element's content.

- Many CSS properties are inherited from the element's parent.

- Inheritance occurs via the cascade, which assigns greater importance to declarations whose sources are closer to the element. In ascending order, these sources are browser default styles, user custom styles, external style sheets, internal style sheets, and inline styles.

- For declarations from the same source, specificity tells the browser to render the styles from the more specific of the selectors. In ascending order, these selectors are elements and pseudo-elements, classes and pseudo-classes, IDs, inline styles, and the `!important` keyword.

Chapter 20

PROJECT: Creating a Portfolio Page

> " *An online portfolio is a great branding tool that every job seeker should have. It is a great way for candidates to differentiate themselves, offer insight into their personalities, and showcase their talents.* —Alexandra Janvey

---

 This chapter covers

- Planning and sketching your portfolio page
- Choosing typefaces and colors for your page
- Adding the page text and images
- Adding contact information

If you do creative work—illustration, writing, music, fine art, or even web design—you owe it to yourself and your career to put yourself out there and tell the world how talented you are. How do you do that? Social media is the standard way of blowing your own horn these days. That's fine, but when you use someone else's platform to talk yourself up, you're giving up lots of control over how you present yourself. It's always better to control your own message, and the best way to do that is to build your own online presence. For creative types, that online stake in the ground should include a portfolio page that showcases your best or your most recent work.

This chapter takes you through the process of putting together a simple portfolio page. I'll be concentrating on many of the techniques you learned here in Part 4 (such as in-page links, typography, and colors), but by the end, you'll see how to build a sophisticated portfolio page that'll put your best creative foot forward.

What You'll Be Building

This project is a basic portfolio page, which refers to a page that's designed to show off some of (or even all) your creative work. It's the online equivalent of a hard-copy portfolio that starving artists have been lugging around from patron to patron and employer to employer for decades. The main idea of a portfolio page is to show off your creative work to people who may want to buy it or may want to hire you to do your creative thing. If your creative work is a hobby, by all means use your portfolio page to show off your side projects to anyone you can persuade to stop by.

Sketching the Layout

You've been through several of this book's projects by now, so you know the drill: Begin by using a pen or pencil to draw the basic layout on a piece of paper. This drawing gives you a kind of blueprint to use when you start throwing around HTML tags and CSS properties.

Figure 20.1 shows the example that I'm going to use for my portfolio page. This page is a variation on a layout that's sometimes called *five boxes*: one large box that serves as your introduction followed by four smaller boxes that you populate with your portfolio images.

Figure 20.1 shows the layout of a page with the following six sections:

- A page header that includes a logo, a page title, and a few links to other page sections
- A short introduction to the portfolio
- The portfolio with four examples of my work
- A section that tells the page visitor about me and my work
- A section that enables the reader to contact me
- A page footer with a copyright notice and links to social media

The first task on your portfolio to-do list is to choose the typeface or typefaces you want to use for your page.

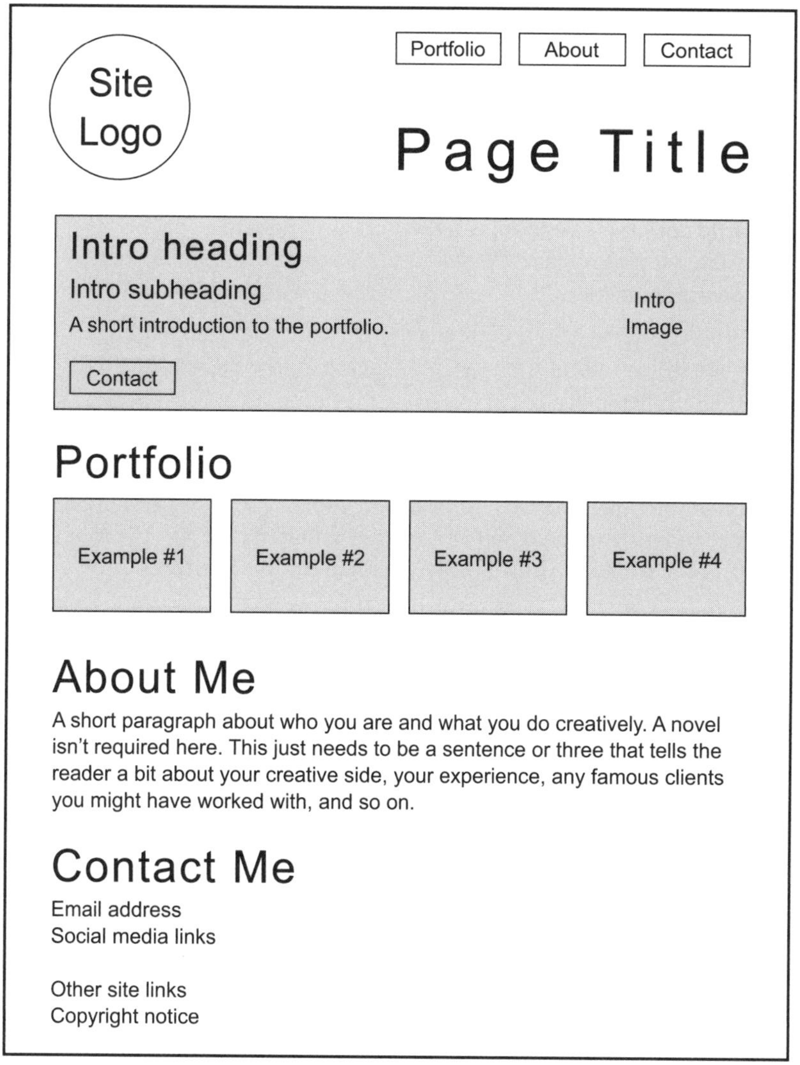

| Portfolio | About | Contact |

Site Logo

Page Title

Intro heading
Intro subheading

A short introduction to the portfolio.

Intro Image

| Contact |

Portfolio

| Example #1 | Example #2 | Example #3 | Example #4 |

About Me

A short paragraph about who you are and what you do creatively. A novel isn't required here. This just needs to be a sentence or three that tells the reader a bit about your creative side, your experience, any famous clients you might have worked with, and so on.

Contact Me

Email address
Social media links

Other site links
Copyright notice

▶ **Figure 20.1**
Before you start slinging HTML and CSS, draw up a quick sketch of the page layout and content.

Choosing Typefaces

Although the portfolio itself consists of images, your portfolio page contains a decent amount of text, including headings and *body text*—the large blocks of nonheading text that comprises the bulk of your portfolio's words. Because a good chunk of your audience will be reading your page on the screens of laptops, tablets, and smartphones, it's important to take a bit of time up front to choose typefaces that will be legible and readable on these smaller screens.

MASTER

You can visit Google Fonts (https://fonts.google.com), view a typeface, type some text, and then eyeball the result to see how good it looks and how easy it is to read. But if you want to be a bit more methodical, certain criteria are common to typefaces that render well on small screens. Here are four things to look for when you're auditioning type on Google Fonts (or whichever font provider you use), each of which is demonstrated in Figure 20.2:

- *Large counters*—A *counter* is the enclosed negative space inside letters such as *A, R, d,* and *g.* A large counter enhances character legibility.

- *Large apertures*—An *aperture* is the partially enclosed negative space inside letters such as *C, S, a,* and *e.* A large aperture also enhances legibility.

- *Medium to large x-height*—The *x-height* is the distance from the baseline to the top of lowercase letters such as *x* and *o,* or to the top of the bowl in letters that have ascenders (such as *d* and *h*) or descenders (such as *g* and *y*). A decent x-height (say, half the font size or more) usually leads to large counters and apertures.

- *Low to medium stroke contrast*—Extremely thin strokes can get lost on a small screen, making text difficult to read. Look for typefaces that have a minimal difference between the thinnest and thickest strokes.

You could build your page with a single typeface, but mixing two typefaces—one for headings and the other for body text—adds dynamism and contrast to the page. My preferred use is a sans-serif typeface for headings and a serif typeface for body text, but I'm going to reverse these preferences for my version of the project. For your own portfolio page, feel free to use two serif or two sans-serif fonts. The only criterion to look for is that the two typefaces work in harmony, which means that they have similar legibility characteristics: counters, apertures, x-height, and stroke contrast. Finally, make sure that each typeface you choose comes with the fonts you require, which at minimum usually means regular, italic, and bold fonts.

▶ Figure 20.2
When deciding on a typeface that will render well even on small displays, look for larger counters and apertures, good x-height, and low stroke contrast.

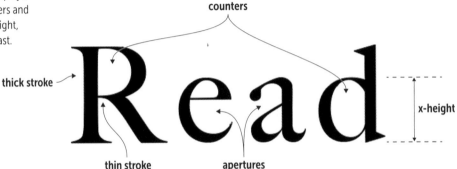

Google Fonts offers hundreds of typefaces and dozens that work well on even the smallest screens. How do you choose? It's certainly fun to play around on the site, but if you prefer a starting point, Table 20.1 lists a half-dozen body and heading typeface pairings that work well (and an alternative sans-serif font for headings).

▶ Table 20.1 Recommended Google Fonts Pairings for Headings and Body Text

Headings	Body	Body (Alternative)
Playfair Display	Open Sans	Raleway
Merriweather	Fira Sans	Merriweather Sans
Source Serif Pro	Source Sans Pro	Lato
Domine	Roboto	Open Sans
Lora	Varela Round	Lato
Roboto Slab	Roboto	Raleway

For this project's headings, I'm going to use one of my favorite text typefaces: Playfair Display. This is a gorgeous font that offers nice big counters and a generous x-height. It has a high stroke contrast, but that shouldn't be much of a problem for the larger heading sizes I'll be using. Playfair Display comes in six fonts, so it has a style for every occasion. For the body text, I'm going to use Open Sans, one of the most popular sans serifs on the web. It's a sturdy typeface that features large counters and x-height, as well as minimal stroke contrast. A less-popular but still excellent alternative is Merriweather Sans, the sans-serif companion to Merriweather.

To use Google Fonts to link to Playfair Display's bold and bold italic fonts, and to Open Sans' regular, italic, and bold fonts, I'll use the following `<link>` tag:

```
<link href="https://fonts.googleapis.com/
css?family=Playfair+Display:700,700i|Open+Sans:400,400i,700"
rel="stylesheet">
```

In my CSS, I'll use the following declarations to specify these families:

```
font-family: "Playfair Display", Georgia, serif;
font-family: "Open Sans", Verdana, sans-serif;
```

With the page layout in place and your typefaces chosen, your next job is to pick out a color scheme.

Choosing a Color Scheme

The colors you choose depend on the type of portfolio you're highlighting and the overall image you want to project. The example I'm going to use is for a book restoration and repair service (which is, alas, hypothetical). I want to use colors that exude warmth (because people who love old books enough to want them restored tend to be warm, gentle folk) and security (because

REMEMBER

Although it's unlikely that Google would fail to deliver your linked fonts, there could be a lag before the fonts show up. To ensure the browser doesn't display the default serif or sans-serif while it waits, add a system font to your stack. Georgia (for serifs) and Verdana (for sans serifs) are installed on almost all new computers.

those same people don't want to give their precious books to just anyone). Rich brown colors can set both emotional tones quite effectively. Using the Web Design Playground's Color Scheme Calculator (see **wdpg.io/colorcalc**), I chose a monochrome color scheme based on the color value #77613c, as shown in Figure 20.3.

▶ **Figure 20.3**
A monochrome color scheme based on the hex color value **#77613c**

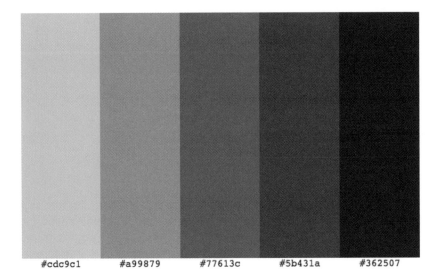

| #cdc9c1 | #a99879 | #77613c | #5b431a | #362507 |

With the page layout in place and your typefaces and colors chosen, it's time to translate this rough sketch into precise HTML and CSS code.

Building the Page

To build out your portfolio page, start with the skeleton code that I introduced you to in Chapter 2. From there, go section by section, adding text, tags, and properties.

The Initial Structure

To start, take the basic page structure from Chapter 2 and add the portfolio layout, using the HTML5 semantic page layout tags:

- The page header section uses the `header` element, and it consists of three items: an `img` element for the site logo, a navigation area that uses the `nav` element and consists of an unordered list of links to other items on the page, and an `h1` element for the page title.

- The main section uses the `main` element, and it consists of several `section` elements, each of which is a container for a different section of the page.

- The page footer section uses the `footer` element, and it consists of a copyright notice and links to several social media sites.

▶ *Try This*   ⇨ **Online:** wdpg.io/projects/portfolio-page/01
Here are the elements that make up the portfolio page's initial HTML structure.

WEB PAGE

YOUR
LOGO
HERE

Portfolio
About
Contact
Page Title
Portfolio

Header section ⎬

| 150 x 150 | 150 x 150 | 150 x 150 | 150 x 150 |

⎬ Main section

About Me
Contact Me
Copyright and social media links ◀ —— Footer section

HTML

The header section ⌇

```
<header>
    <img src="/images/your-logo-here.tif" alt="My logo">
    <nav>
        <ul>
            <li>Portfolio</li>
            <li>About</li>
            <li>Contact</li>
        </ul>
        <h1>Page Title</h1>
    </nav>
</header>
<main>>
    <section>>
        <h1>Portfolio</h1>>
        <img src="http://placehold.it/150x150" alt="">>
        <img src="http://placehold.it/150x150" alt="">>
        <img src="http://placehold.it/150x150" alt="">>
        <img src="http://placehold.it/150x150" alt="">>
    </section>>
    <section>>
        <h1>About Me</h1>>
    </section>>
    <section>>
        <h1>Contact Me</h1>>
    </section>>
</main>
<footer>
    <p>Copyright and social media links</p>
</footer>
```

The main section ⌇

The footer section ⌇

The portfolio page is about as bare-bones as pages come right now, but it won't stay that way for long. I'll turn now to structuring the page's overall layout.

The Overall Layout

As you might imagine, putting together a layout nicknamed five boxes simply cries out for a flexbox-based structure, and that's what you'll add here. You want the content to be centered in the middle of the browser window. To accomplish this task, use two main flexbox containers for the overall structure:

- The initial flexbox container will be the body element. By configuring this element with flex-direction: row and justify-content: center, you create a single-row container in which all content gets centered horizontally.

- For the content itself, nest a div element inside the body element. That div is a flexbox container with flex-direction: column and justify-content: flex-start, which gives you a single-column container with the content aligned with the top of the container.

The following example shows you how to set everything up.

▶ *Try This*   ⇨ **Online:** wdpg.io/projects/portfolio-page/02
This example shows you how to configure the body element and a nested div as flexbox containers for the entire page.

CSS

```
body {
    display: flex;
    flex-direction: row;
    justify-content: center;
    min-height: 100vh;
    margin-top: 1rem;
    font-family: "Open Sans", Verdana, sans-serif; >
    background-color: #cdc9c1; >
    background-image: radial-gradient(circle farthest-side at
center top, hsl(0, 0%, 100%) 0%, #cdc9c1 100%);>
    color: #362507;
}
.container {
    display: flex;
    flex-direction: column;
    justify-content: flex-start;
    max-width: 60rem;
}
```

Set up the main flexbox container.

Apply a font stack and the background and text colors.

Set up the nested flexbox container for the content.

Set a maximum width for the content.

```
<body>
    <div class="container">
    </div>
</body>
```

HTML

The Header Section

The header section consists of a `header` element that contains three items: an `img` element for the page logo, a `nav` element for the navigation links, and an `h1` element for the page title. I also want the header to have the following features:

- The page logo should be aligned with the left side of the content container, and the navigation and title should be aligned with the right side of the content container.

- All the header content should be centered vertically within the header.

The easiest method is to use flexbox, so configure the `header` element as a flexbox container with a horizontal main axis and `align-items` set to `center`. For horizontal alignments, separate the header into left and right sections by using `div` elements.

The following example shows the HTML and CSS that I used to accomplish these goals and to style the rest of the header layout.

REMEMBER

*Flexbox now enjoys near-universal browser support, so to keep things simple and uncluttered, the code you see here and on the Playground doesn't include any vendor prefixes. If you need to support old browsers, use Autoprefixer (*https://autoprefixer.github.io*) to generate the prefixes.*

▶ *Try This*   ⇨ **Online:** wdpg.io/projects/portfolio-page/03
This example adds the HTML code for the header and the CSS for the header structure.

WEB PAGE

- Portfolio**This Old Book**
- About
- Contact

continued

CSS

```css
header {
    display: flex;
    justify-content: center;
    align-items: center;
    padding: .5rem 0;
    width: 100%;
}
.header-left {
    flex: 1 0 33%;
    text-align: left;
}
.header-right {
    flex: 2 0 67%;
    display: flex;
    flex-wrap: wrap;
    justify-content: flex-end;
}
```

The header is a flexbox container.

The left header gets one-third of the width; the right gets two-thirds.

The right header is a flexbox container.

HTML

```html
<header>
    <div class="header-left">
        <img src="/images/portfolio-logo.tif"
alt="This Old Book logo">
    </div>
    <div class="header-right">
        <nav>
            <ul>
                <li><a href="#portfolio" class="btn">Portfolio</a></li>
                <li><a href="#about" class="btn">About</a></li>
                <li><a href="#contact" class="btn">Contact</a></li>
            </ul>
        </nav>
        <h1>This Old Book</h1>
    </div>
</header>
```

The left side of the header

The right side of the header

With the header structure set up, you can tend to the styling of the header elements. The logo is fine as is, but you need to turn the navigation links into proper buttons and to style the page title. The following example shows the HTML and CSS that I used.

▶ **Try This** ⇨ **Online:** wdpg.io/projects/portfolio-page/04
This example styles the header elements.

WEB PAGE

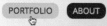

PORTFOLIO   ABOUT   CONTACT

This Old Book

CSS

```css
h1 {
    padding-top: 1rem;
}
.btn {
    background-color: #362507;
    padding: .25rem .75rem;
    border-radius: .75rem;
    font-size: 1rem;
    color: #cdc9c1;
    text-transform: uppercase;
}
nav ul {
    display: flex;
    list-style-type: none;
}
nav li {
    padding-left: 1rem;
}
a {
    text-decoration: none;
}
a:hover {
    color: #362507;
    background-color: #cdc9c1;
}
h1 {
    font-size: 4rem;
    font-weight: bold;
    font-family: "Playfair Display", Georgia, serif;
}
```

The h1 element is given some padding.

This class turns the navigation items into proper buttons.

This CSS styles the list of navigation items.

This CSS styles the links (regular and hover).

This CSS styles the page title.

MASTER

The border-radius
*property rounds the
corners of an element.
You can specify a
measurement value (the
higher the value, the
more the corners are
rounded), or you can
enter a percentage (a
value of 50% rounds the
borders into a circle, for
example).*

Of special note here is the btn class, which you saw earlier applied to the
<a> tags in the nav section. Each a element is a bulleted-list item, and the
purpose of the btn class is to turn the content of each li element (the link
text) into a proper button. Here's what the btn class does:

- It adds a background color.

- It adds padding around the text.

- It uses the border-radius property to round the corners.

- It sets the font size and color, and converts the text to
  uppercase.

The Portfolio Introduction

The portfolio introduction serves to bring the reader into your page by
offering a quick overview of what you do creatively. It should have a title
and perhaps a subtitle, a short paragraph, and another link to your contact
section.

In the following example, I've styled my page introduction with dark
brown text (#362507), an h2 title, an h3 subtitle, a clickable button, and a
related image for visual interest. To keep everything nice and neat, I set up
the introduction (using a class named intro) as a flexbox container.

▶ *Try This*   ⇨ **Online:** wdpg.io/projects/portfolio-page/05
This example adds the introduction to the portfolio page.

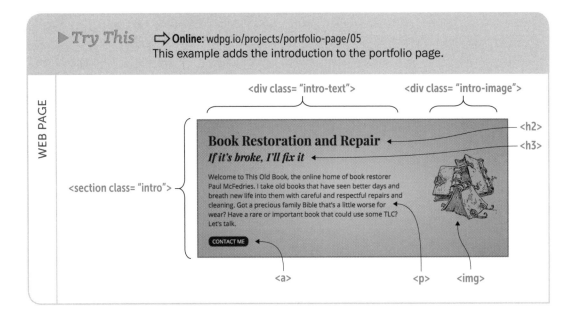

CSS

The CSS for the
intro class

```css
.intro {
    display: flex;
    align-items: center;
    margin: 2rem 0;
    width: 100%;
    border: 3px solid #77613c;
    color: #362507;
    font-size: 1.25rem;
    background-color: #a99879;
    background-image: radial-gradient(ellipse closest-corner at
center,
#cdc9c1 0%, #a99879 100%);
}
.intro-text {
    flex: 2 0 67%;
    padding: 2rem 0 2rem 2rem;
}
.intro-text p {
    margin: 1.5rem 0;
}
.intro-image {
    flex: 1 0 33%;
    padding-right: 2rem;
    text-align: right;
}
h2 {
  font-size: 2.5rem;
}
h3 {
  font-size: 2rem;
  font-style: italic;
}
h2, h3 {
  font-family: "Playfair Display", Georgia, serif;
}
```

The CSS for the
intro-text class

The CSS for the
intro-image class

The CSS
for the
headings

continued

HTML

```
<main>
    <section class="intro">
        <div class="intro-text">
            <h2>Book Restoration and Repair</h2>
            <h3>If it's broke, I'll fix it</h3>
            <p>Welcome to This Old Book, the online home of book
restorer Paul McFedries. I take old books that have seen better
days and breath new life into them with careful and respectful
repairs and cleaning. Got a precious family Bible that's a little
worse for wear? Have a rare or important book that could use some
TLC? Let's talk.
            </p>
            <div>
                <a href="#contact" class="btn">Contact Me</a>
            </div>
        </div>
        <div class="intro-image">
            <img src="/images/portfolio-intro.tif"
alt="Illustration showing several old books">
        </div>
    </section>
</main>
```

The Portfolio

Next is the real meat of the page, which is the portfolio itself—a series of images that show off your work. When deciding how much to show, you have three choices:

- *Show all your work.* This option is the way to go if your portfolio is small. If you have a big portfolio, you can show it, but it may be better to show just a subset and then link to a second page that shows everything.

- *Show your most recent work.* This option is a good one if you think that your newest stuff is particularly good, if your style has changed recently, or if you've landed some high-profile clients.

- *Show your best work.* This route is the one to take if you want to really show people what you can do.

A typical portfolio has one to three rows, with two to four images per row. You'll want to precede the portfolio with a heading and perhaps a sentence or two as a lead-in. The portfolio itself should be configured as a flexbox container to make everything look tidy. The following example shows how I did all this on my portfolio page.

WEB PAGE

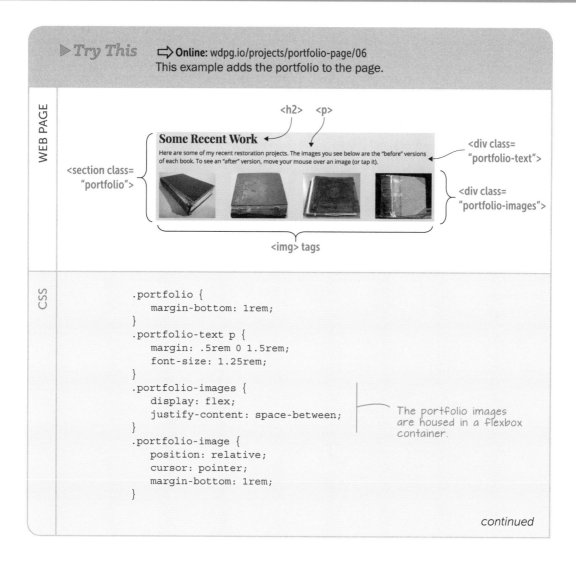

`<h2>` `<p>`

Some Recent Work ◄

Here are some of my recent restoration projects. The images you see below are the "before" versions of each book. To see an "after" version, move your mouse over an image (or tap it).

`<section class= "portfolio">`

`<div class= "portfolio-text">`

`<div class= "portfolio-images">`

`<img> tags`

CSS

```css
.portfolio {
    margin-bottom: 1rem;
}
.portfolio-text p {
    margin: .5rem 0 1.5rem;
    font-size: 1.25rem;
}
.portfolio-images {
    display: flex;
    justify-content: space-between;
}
.portfolio-image {
    position: relative;
    cursor: pointer;
    margin-bottom: 1rem;
}
```

The portfolio images are housed in a flexbox container.

continued

HTML

The portfolio text container is a div element with class portfolio-text.

The portfolio container is a section element with class and id portfolio.

```
<section class="portfolio" id="portfolio">
    <div class="portfolio-text">
        <h2>Some Recent Work</h2>
        <p>Here are some of my recent restoration projects. The
images you see below are the "before" versions of each book. To
see an "after" version, move your mouse over an image (or tap
it).</p>
    </div>
    <div class="portfolio-images">
        <div class="portfolio-image">
            <img src="/images/portfolio-book1-before.tif">
            <img class="image-overlay" src="/images/portfolio-
book1-after.tif">
        </div>
        <div class="portfolio-image">
            <img src="/images/portfolio-book2-before.tif">
            <img class="image-overlay" src="/images/portfolio-
book2-after.tif">
        </div>
        <div class="portfolio-image">
            <img src="/images/portfolio-book3-before.tif">
            <img class="image-overlay" src="/images/portfolio-
book3-after.tif">
        </div>
        <div class="portfolio-image">
            <img src="/images/portfolio-book4-before.tif">
            <img class="image-overlay" src="/images/portfolio-
book4-after.tif">
        </div>
    </div>
</section>
```

The portfolio images container is a div element with class portfolio-images.

The portfolio content resides in a section tag to which I've assigned the portfolio class. Note, too, that I assigned the id portfolio, which sets up this section element as a target for the header's Portfolio navigation link you saw earlier.

The portfolio text resides in a div with class portfolio-text. It consists of an h2 heading and a p element for the lead-in sentence.

The portfolio images reside in a `div` with class `portfolio-images`. It consists of several `div` elements (with class `portfolio-image`). For most portfolios, you need only include an `img` element within each of these `div` elements. In my project, however, I wanted to present before and after images, with the latter appearing when the user hovers the mouse over an image (or taps an image on a portable device). To do that, I added a second `img` element with class `image-overlay`. Here's the CSS for that class:

```
.image-overlay {
  position: absolute;
  left: 0;
  top: 0;
  width: 200px;
  height: 156px;
  z-index: 1;
  opacity: 0;
  transition: opacity 1.5s ease;
}
.image-overlay:hover {
  opacity: 1;
}
```

USE IT

The idea of having before and after images in your portfolio is useful for many creative pursuits, including furniture repair, art restoration, fitness training, hair styling, and interior decoration.

The overlay uses the same dimensions as the before image, and it's positioned absolutely at the top-left corner of the `div` element with class `portfolio-image` (which uses relative positioning to set a positioning context for the after image). The overlay is given a `z-index` value of `1` to make sure it appears on top of the before image, and it's given an `opacity` value of `0` to prevent it from appearing when the page first loads. Then the `hover` event changes the `opacity` value to `1` to make the image appear. The `transition` property in the `image-overlay` class animates the appearance of the overlay.

The About Section

The next element of the portfolio page is the About section, which you can use to toot your own horn in whatever way you feel comfortable. You can talk up your education, your work experience, your appointments, your awards, and so on. Use whatever works to supply your portfolio the bona fides required to persuade potential clients, employers, or sponsors that you have the creative chops they're looking for.

The About section is simple: a heading followed by a paragraph of self-aggrandizing text. The following shows an example.

Project: Creating a Portfolio Page

▶ *Try This* ⇨ **Online:** wdpg.io/projects/portfolio-page/07
This example adds the About section to the portfolio page.

WEB PAGE

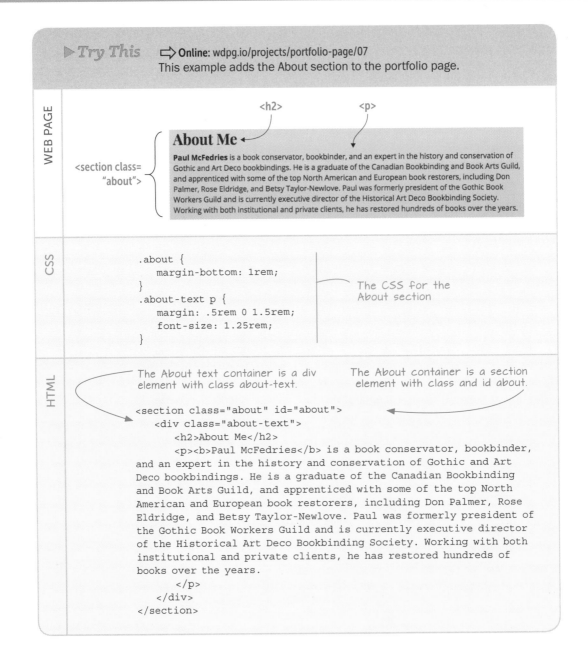

`<h2>` `<p>`

About Me ←

`<section class="about">`

Paul McFedries is a book conservator, bookbinder, and an expert in the history and conservation of Gothic and Art Deco bookbindings. He is a graduate of the Canadian Bookbinding and Book Arts Guild, and apprenticed with some of the top North American and European book restorers, including Don Palmer, Rose Eldridge, and Betsy Taylor-Newlove. Paul was formerly president of the Gothic Book Workers Guild and is currently executive director of the Historical Art Deco Bookbinding Society. Working with both institutional and private clients, he has restored hundreds of books over the years.

CSS

```css
.about {
    margin-bottom: 1rem;
}
.about-text p {
    margin: .5rem 0 1.5rem;
    font-size: 1.25rem;
}
```

The CSS for the About section

HTML

The About text container is a div element with class about-text.

The About container is a section element with class and id about.

```html
<section class="about" id="about">
    <div class="about-text">
        <h2>About Me</h2>
        <p><b>Paul McFedries</b> is a book conservator, bookbinder,
and an expert in the history and conservation of Gothic and Art
Deco bookbindings. He is a graduate of the Canadian Bookbinding
and Book Arts Guild, and apprenticed with some of the top North
American and European book restorers, including Don Palmer, Rose
Eldridge, and Betsy Taylor-Newlove. Paul was formerly president of
the Gothic Book Workers Guild and is currently executive director
of the Historical Art Deco Bookbinding Society. Working with both
institutional and private clients, he has restored hundreds of
books over the years.
        </p>
    </div>
</section>
```

The About content uses a `section` element with the about class. I also assigned the id `about`, which sets up this element as a target for the About navigation link in the header.

The Contact Section

The final element of the main section of the portfolio page is the all-important Contact section, which is where you give interested visitors one or more ways to get in touch with you. At minimum, you should supply an email address, but you'll almost always want to include one or more links to your social networking profiles.

The Contact section is straightforward: a heading, a lead-in paragraph, and your email address and social network links. The following shows an example.

FAQ

Can I have people contact me using a form? *A form is a great way to get a message, but it's not ideal for most new web designers because it requires a script to process the form data. However, some services on the web not only enable you to build a form, but also process the data for you. Check out TypeForm (*https://www.typeform.com*) and Wufoo (*https://www.wufoo.com*).*

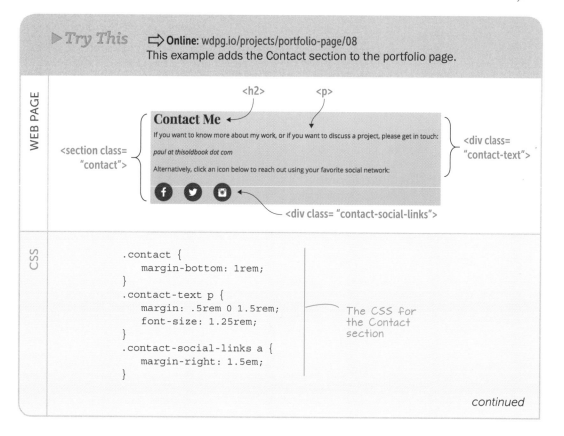

▶ *Try This* ⇨ **Online:** wdpg.io/projects/portfolio-page/08
This example adds the Contact section to the portfolio page.

WEB PAGE

`<h2>` `<p>`

Contact Me

`<section class= "contact">`

If you want to know more about my work, or if you want to discuss a project, please get in touch:

paul at thisoldbook dot com

Alternatively, click an icon below to reach out using your favorite social network:

`<div class= "contact-text">`

`<div class= "contact-social-links">`

CSS

```css
.contact {
    margin-bottom: 1rem;
}
.contact-text p {
    margin: .5rem 0 1.5rem;
    font-size: 1.25rem;
}
.contact-social-links a {
    margin-right: 1.5em;
}
```

The CSS for the Contact section

continued

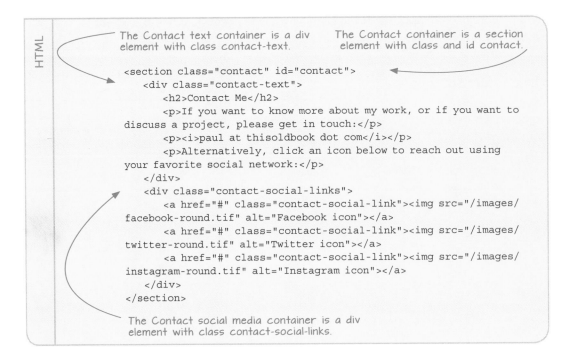

HTML

The Contact text container is a div element with class contact-text.

The Contact container is a section element with class and id contact.

```html
<section class="contact" id="contact">
    <div class="contact-text">
        <h2>Contact Me</h2>
        <p>If you want to know more about my work, or if you want to
discuss a project, please get in touch:</p>
        <p><i>paul at thisoldbook dot com</i></p>
        <p>Alternatively, click an icon below to reach out using
your favorite social network:</p>
    </div>
    <div class="contact-social-links">
        <a href="#" class="contact-social-link"><img src="/images/
facebook-round.tif" alt="Facebook icon"></a>
        <a href="#" class="contact-social-link"><img src="/images/
twitter-round.tif" alt="Twitter icon"></a>
        <a href="#" class="contact-social-link"><img src="/images/
instagram-round.tif" alt="Instagram icon"></a>
    </div>
</section>
```

The Contact social media container is a div element with class contact-social-links.

REMEMBER

When you add your email address to the Contact section, make sure that you don't display the address in plain text so that the address isn't harvested by spammers. Instead, obfuscate the address in a way that fools the spammers' bots but is still straightforward for a human to decode.

The Contact content uses a `section` tag with the `contact` class and an id value set to `contact`, which enables this element to act as an anchor for the Contact button in the header and the Contact Me button in the portfolio introduction.

The Page Footer

The final element of the portfolio page is the page footer. As you can see in the following example, I used the footer to display a copyright notice and some links to other sections of the site.

▶ *Try This* ⇨ **Online:** wdpg.io/projects/portfolio-page/09
This example adds the footer to the portfolio page.

WEB PAGE

```
<div class= "footer-copyright">
```

<footer> →   *Copyright 2019 This Old Book* ◄   → Home FAQ Site Map Privacy

```
<div class= "footer-links">
```

CSS

```css
footer {
    display: flex;
    padding: 1em 0;
    border-top: 1px solid #a99879;
}
.footer-copyright {
    flex: 1 0 50%;
    text-align: left;
    font-style: italic;
    font-size: 1.25em;
}
.footer-links {
    flex: 1 0 50%;
    text-align: right;
    font-size: 1.25em;
}
.footer-links a {
    color: #362507;
    margin-left: 1em;
}
```

The footer is set
up as a flexbox
container.

HTML

```html
<footer>
    <div class="footer-copyright">
        Copyright 2019 This Old Book
    </div>
    <div class="footer-links">
        <a href="#">Home</a>
        <a href="#">FAQ</a>
        <a href="#">Site Map</a>
        <a href="#">Privacy</a>
    </div>
</footer>
```

The footer copyright notice
is a div element with class
footer-copyright.

The footer site links container
is a div element with class
footer-links.

The footer content uses a `footer` element that's configured as a flexbox container. The copyright notice (with class `footer-copyright`) is a flexbox item aligned to the left, and the site links (with class `footer-links`) is a flexbox item aligned to the right.

From Here

The final version of the portfolio page (mine is shown in Figure 20.4) offers a solid start for getting the word out about your creative work.

▶ Figure 20.4
A portfolio page, ready for the web

The biggest thing missing from the portfolio page is responsiveness. The page looks good in desktop web browsers and even on some tablets in landscape mode, but the design breaks on smaller screens. I'll leave you the exercise to add media query breakpoints (see Chapter 13) that help the page look good all the way down to a smartphone.

This is the last chapter of the book, but that doesn't mean it's the last chapter of your web-design education. Far from it. Be sure to pay a visit to the Web Design Playground (https://webdesignplayground.io/) for lots of examples, exercises, and tutorials that will help you sharpen your skills and expand your knowledge. See you there!

Summary

- Sketch out the page you want to build.
- Choose the typefaces for the headings and body text.
- Choose a color scheme.
- Build the initial page structure: the barebones HTML tags and the global CSS properties applied to the `body` element.
- Set up your main flexbox containers.
- Fill in and style each section one by one: the header, the portfolio introduction, the portfolio itself, the About section, the Contact section, and the footer.

From Playground to Web: Getting Your Pages Online

When something is such a creative medium as the web, the limits to it are our imaginations. —Tim Berners-Lee

---

 This appendix covers

- Downloading page files from the Web Design Playground
- Validating HTML and CSS syntax
- Understanding and selecting a web hosting service
- Uploading page files to your web host

You've covered much ground in this book, and no doubt worked your fingers to the bone applying the electronic equivalent of spit and polish to buff your website's pages to an impressive sheen. But you need to perform a couple of related tasks before you can cross "Make website" off the to-do list: Find a web home for your site, and move your website files to that new home. This appendix helps take care of both tasks. You first learn how to look for and choose a spot on the web where friends, family, and even total strangers from far-flung corners of the world can eyeball your creation. Then you learn how to emigrate your web pages from their native land (the Web Design Playground or your hard disk) to the New World (the web). You'll learn how to best prepare your pages for the journey, select a mode of transportation, and settle the pages in when they've arrived.

From There to Here: Saving Your Playground Work

If you've been using the Web Design Playground to try some experiments and even build a few sandboxes (the name I use to describe projects on the Playground), the next step is getting your code from the Playground to your computer. You have two ways to go about this: copying code and downloading code. To begin, I'll show you how to copy code from the Playground.

Copying Playground Code

The Web Design Playground is chock full of HTML and CSS code: It's in the lesson pages, it's in the HTML Editor, and it's in the CSS Editor. One way of getting code to your computer is to copy it from one of these Playground locations. When you've done that, you can paste the code into an existing file, using your favorite text editor.

The Web Design Playground offers three ways to copy code:

- *In a lesson*—When a lesson page offers an HTML or CSS code snippet, you see a Copy to Clipboard button below the code, as shown in Figure A.1. Click that button to copy the code to your computer's clipboard (the memory area used to store the most recently copied or cut data).

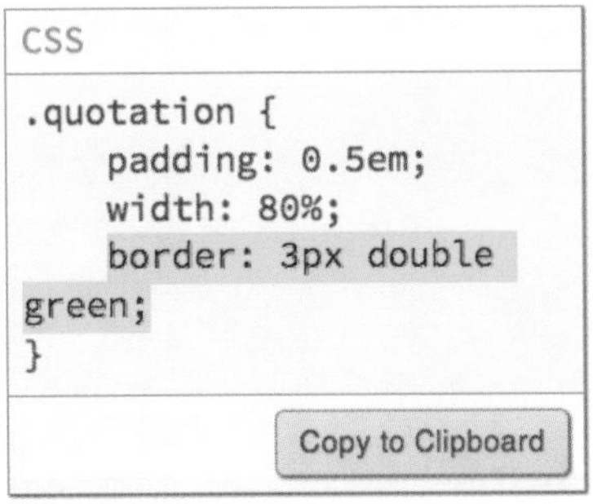

```css
CSS

.quotation {
    padding: 0.5em;
    width: 80%;
    border: 3px double
green;
}

                    Copy to Clipboard
```

▶ Figure A.1
To copy code from an HTML or CSS snippet in a Playground lesson, click the Copy to Clipboard button.

- *In the HTML Editor*—The HTML Editor contains the current lesson's HTML code, existing HTML code that you've modified, or custom HTML code that you've added to a sandbox. Whatever the source, you can grab the HTML code by clicking the menu icon in the top-left corner of the HTML Editor and then clicking Copy to Clipboard, as shown in Figure A.2. This step copies the full HTML code to your computer's clipboard.

▶Figure A.2
To copy code from the HTML Editor, click the Editor's menu icon and then click Copy to Clipboard.

- *In the CSS Editor*—The CSS Editor contains the current lesson's CSS code, existing CSS code that you've modified, or custom CSS code that you've added to a sandbox. To place that CSS code in your computer's memory, click the menu icon in the top-left corner of the CSS Editor and then click Copy to Clipboard, as shown in Figure A.3. This step copies the full CSS code to your computer's clipboard.

▶Figure A.3
To copy code from the CSS Editor, click the Editor's menu icon and then click Copy to Clipboard.

When you've run the Copy to Clipboard command, open your HTML or CSS file in a text editor, position the insertion point where you want the copied code to appear, and then run the text editor's command for pasting clipboard data. In the vast majority of editors, you do this by choosing Edit > Paste or by pressing Ctrl+V (Windows) or Cmd+V (Mac).

Downloading Playground Code

Rather than copy and paste bits of HTML or CSS code, you may prefer to get the entire contents of both the HTML and CSS editors. This is the way to go if you want all the code from a particular lesson, or if you've created a sandbox and have been populating it with custom HTML and CSS code.

Here are the steps to follow:

1 In the Web Design Playground, open the lesson that has the code you want, or create a sandbox with your custom code.
2 Choose Menu > Download Code.

   The Playground gathers the code into a zip archive file and tells your web browser to download the file.

3 Locate the downloaded file, which is named webdesign.zip.

4 Double-click the webdesign.zip archive to open it.

In the folder that appears, you see two files:

- `index.html`—This file contains a basic HTML page structure with the contents of the HTML Editor inserted between the `<body>` and `</body>` tags. It also includes a `link` element in the `<head>` section that references the `styles.css` file.

- `styles.css`—This file contains the contents of the CSS Editor.

5 Copy or move these files to the folder where you store the rest of your web -page files (such as the page image files).

Now that you have your Playground code safely stashed on your Mac or PC, you're about ready to get that code onto the web. Before you can do that, however, you need to perform a few more chores to get your files web-ready. First on this to-do list is setting up your web page folders on your computer.

Setting Up Your Folders

When you sign up for a home to store your web page files (see "Getting a Web Host" later in this appendix), you're given your own folder to store files on the server. That folder is called your website's *root* folder. The question you need to ask yourself now is an apparently simple one: Do I need to create one or more subfolders within the root folder?

I use the word *apparently* here because it's not always clear whether you need subfolders. Examine the possible scenarios:

- *One web project consisting of a single file*—The simplest possible web project is one that consists of a single HTML file. That file contains only text, HTML tags, CSS styles inserted inline or in an internal style sheet (that is, between the `<style>` and `</style>` tags), and media (such as images) that use remote references (that is, references to files that reside on other websites). In this case, you can store that file in the root folder and you don't need any subfolders.

- *One web project consisting of a small number of files*—Most simple or beginning web projects consist of a few files: an HTML file, a CSS file, and one or more image files. In this case, it's almost certainly overkill to use subfolders, so you should store all the files in the root folder.

- *One web project consisting of a large number of files*—It's not unusual for a large project to have multiple HTML files, several CSS files, and lots of media files, particularly images. In this scenario, it's fine to place all your HTML files in the root folder, but to keep things organized, you should create separate subfolders for each of the other types of files: CSS, images, and so on.

- *Multiple web projects*—If you get into web design even a little, you'll find that you can't create only one project. Multiple projects are the norm, and in this case, you should keep the projects separate by storing each one in its own subfolder. If a particular project is large, you'll want to create sub-subfolders to store the project's various file types (CSS, images, media, and so on).

Why worry about all this now? You'll make your web design life immeasurably easier and more efficient if you set up your computer's local folder structure to mirror what you want to set up remotely after you sign up with a web host:

1 Begin by designating a local folder as the main storage area for your web files.

This folder will be your local equivalent of your root folder on the web host.

2 If you'll be working on multiple web projects, set up a subfolder for each project.

3 If a project is large enough to require subfolders for certain file types, create these subfolders within the project folder.

4 When you download files from the Playground (as described in the preceding section), or when you create your own HTML, CSS, or image files and save them for the first time, be sure to store them in the appropriate folder.

With all that done, your next task is making sure that your code passes muster by getting it validated.

Validating Your Code

You've seen in this book that although HTML tags and CSS properties aren't complex, they can be finicky. If you forget a closing tag or brace, leave out a quotation mark or comma, or spell a tag or property name incorrectly, there's a good chance that your web page won't render properly. In some cases, the error is a glaring one (such as the page's failing to show anything), but all too often, the error is subtle and hard to notice.

Either way, you don't want to foist an error-filled page on the web public, so besides going over your HTML and CSS code with a careful eye, you can get some help online by submitting your code to one of the available validation services.

From Playground to Web: Getting Your Pages Online

REMEMBER

Another way to run the validation is to copy your HTML code from your text editor, select the Validate by Direct Input tab, paste your HTML code into the text box, and then click Check.

Validating HTML

The World Wide Web Consortium (W3C) hosts a Markup Validation Service that can examine your HTML code and let you know whether it contains any errors or warnings. Here's how you use it:

1 Use a web browser to surf to https://validator.w3.org.

2 Click the Validate by File Upload tab.

3 Click Browse (Windows) or Choose File (Mac).

   The site prompts you to select the file you want to validate.

4 Locate and select the HTML file you want to check; then click Open.

   The site uploads the file.

5 Click Check.

   The Markup Validation Service checks the HTML code and displays the results.

Ideally, you'll see the `No errors or warnings to show` message, as shown in Figure A.4.

▶ Figure A.4
HTML validation bliss: **No errors or warnings to show**.

If your HTML file didn't validate, you'll see one or more error or warning messages, as shown in Figure A.5.

▶ Figure A.5
HTML validation misery: **There were errors**.

Validating CSS

The W3C also offers the CSS Validation Service, which can peruse your CSS code and alert you to any errors or warnings. Here's how to use it:

1 Use a web browser to surf to https://jigsaw.w3.org/css-validator.

2 Click the By File Upload tab.

3 Click Browse (Windows) or Choose File (Mac).

The site prompts you to select the file you want to validate.

4 Locate and select the CSS file you want to check; then click Open.

The site uploads the file.

5 Click Check.

The CSS Validation Service checks the CSS code and displays the results.

Ideally, you'll see the No Error Found message, shown in Figure A.6.

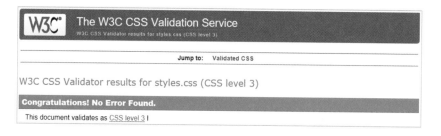

▶ Figure A.6
CSS validation joy:
`Congratulations!`
`No Error Found.`

If your CSS file contains invalid data, however, the service returns one or more errors or warnings, as shown in Figure A.7.

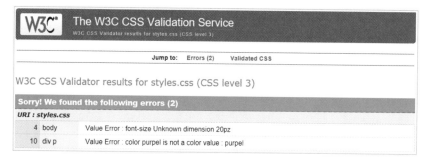

▶ Figure A.7
CSS validation sorrow:
`We found the`
`following errors.`

When you've fixed all the errors in your code, your HTML and CSS files are ready for the primetime of the web. First, though, you need to secure a place to put those files. You need, in short, to find a web host.

REMEMBER

An alternative CSS validation method is to copy your CSS code from your text editor, select the By Direct Input tab, paste your CSS code into the text box, and then click Check.

Getting a Web Host

Back in Chapter 1, you learned that a web page is stored on a special computer called a *web server*, which accepts and responds to web browser requests for the page and its associated files. Before anyone else can view your web project, you need to get its files on a web server. To do that, you need to sign up with a service that offers space on its server. Because the service in effect plays host to your files, such a service is called a *web hosting provider*, or *web host* for short.

When you evaluate a web host, what criteria should you use? The answer depends on the type of website you want to set up, but the following criteria are the most common:

- *Maximum bandwidth*—The maximum amount of your data per month that the host will transfer to web browsers. In most cases, you pay extra for data that exceeds your monthly maximum. Some web hosts offer unlimited bandwidth.

- *Total disk space*—The amount of hard disk storage space you get on the web server. At a minimum, total disk space usually is a few hundred megabytes, which is more than enough for a simple site.

- *Number of websites*—The number of root folders you can set up.

- *Number of email addresses*—The number of email addresses that are included with the hosting service.

- *Domain name hosting*—Whether the web host also hosts domain names that you've previously purchased from a domain name registrar. Some hosts sell domain names, and others offer free subdomain names of the form *yourdomain.webhostdomain*.com.

- *FTP support*—Support for the File Transfer Protocol, which is the internet service you use to transfer your files to the web host. Almost all web hosts support FTP, but some offer only proprietary file transfer services.

As a rule, the cheaper the web host, the fewer of these features you get. Before you start looking for a web host, make a list of these features and decide what you need and what's optional. That might be difficult right now for something like maximum bandwidth, because bandwidth is determined in part by how popular your site becomes, but make your best stabs at each one for now.

When you're looking for a web host, you have three main choices:

- *Your Internet service provider (ISP)*—The company or institution you use to access the internet may also offer a web hosting service. Many ISPs offer free web hosting for simple personal websites, and some organization networks include a web server that you can use. In most cases, the hosting includes features such as bandwidth and disk space at the lower end of the scale.

- *A free web hosting provider*—Many services will host your web pages without charge. The catch is that you usually have fairly severe restrictions on most hosting features, particularly bandwidth and disk space, and you almost always get only a single website. Some free web hosts also display ads, although that's becoming rare these days.

- *A commercial web hosting provider*—If you want to get a reasonable set of features for your web presence, you need to shell out money to rent space with a commercial web hosting provider. Note that I'm not talking about big bucks. Popular providers such as Bluehost (https://www.bluehost.com), GoDaddy (https://www.godaddy.com), and HostGator (http://www.hostgator.com) offer feature-packed hosting usually for less than $5 dollars per month. If you think you'll be getting into web design beyond the creation of a basic home page, you should definitely consider a commercial web host.

When you've signed up with a web host, it usually takes anywhere from a few minutes to a few hours before everything is ready. When your hosting service is good to go, then it's time to get your stuff online.

Uploading Your Files

With your HTML and CSS files coded and validated, your support files (such as images) in place, your folders set up, and your web host ready to serve your stuff to a waiting world, all that remains is to send your files from your computer to the web host's server—a process known as *uploading*.

How you go about uploading your files depends on the web host, but the following three methods are by far the most common:

- *FTP*—Most hosts offer support for FTP uploads. First, you need to get yourself an *FTP client*, which is a software program that connects to your web host's FTP server and offers an interface for basic file chores, such as navigating and creating folders, uploading the files, and deleting and renaming files. Popular Windows clients are CuteFTP (https://www.globalscape.com/cuteftp) and CyberDuck (https://cyberduck.io). For the Mac, try Transmit (https://panic.com/transmit) or FileZilla (https://filezilla-project.org). When you've downloaded the software, check your web host's support pages for information on how to connect to the host's FTP server.

- *cPanel*—Many web hosts offer an administration tool called cPanel that presents a simple interface for hosting tasks such as email and domain management. cPanel also offers a File Manager component that you can use to upload files and perform other file management chores.

- *Proprietary*—Some web hosts offer their own interface for uploading and working with files. See your host's support page for instructions.

Whatever method is available, upload all your website files and folders to your root folder on your host. Then load your site into your favorite web browser to make sure that everything's working okay. It wouldn't hurt to try your site in a few different browsers and on a few different devices to make sure thate it works properly for a wide variety of users. Welcome to the web!

Selecting a Text Editor

You can use the Web Design Playground to experiment and play with HTML and CSS, but when it's time to get serious about your code, you'll want to edit it on your computer. To do that, you need a text editor, preferably one that was designed with web coding in mind. Such an editor comes with features such as syntax highlighting (which color-codes certain syntax elements for easier reading), line numbers, code completion (when you start typing something, the editor displays a list of possible code items that complete your typing), and text processing (such as automatic indentation of code blocks, converting tabs to spaces and vice versa, shifting chunks of code right or left, removing unneeded spaces at the end of lines, and hiding blocks of code).

Here, in alphabetical order, are a few editors that offer all these features (and usually quite a few more):

- *Atom*—Available for Windows and Mac. Free! https://atom.io

- *Brackets*—Available for Windows and Mac. Also free! http://brackets.io

- *Coda*—Available for Mac for $99, but a free trial is available. www.panic.com/coda

- *Notepad++*—Available for Windows only. Another freebie. https://notepad-plus-plus.org

- *Sublime Text*—Available for both Windows and Mac for $80, but a free trial is available. www.sublimeext.com

- *TextMate*—Available for Mac only for €48.75 (about $57), but a free trial is available. http://macromates.com

Summary

- Get your code from the Web Design Playground to your computer either by copying and pasting the code, or by downloading the contents of the HTML and CSS Editors.

- Set up your website folders on your computer.

- Use the W3C's online validation services to look for errors in your HTML and CSS code.

- Sign up for a web hosting provider.

- Upload your website files to your web host.

Index

A

`<abbr>` tag   290
absolute positioning   134–136
absolute values   120
adaptive layouts   240–244
adjacent sibling   353
Adobe Typekit   335
::after pseudo-element   360–362
`align-content` property   279
aligning
  images   92–93
  overriding item alignment in flexbox
    218–219
  paragraphs horizontally   60
  text   92–93
`align-items` property   210, 279
alpha channel   312
alt attribute   86
analogous colors   318
`ancestor` element   353
anchors   35
Andersson-Wise site   264
apertures   374
`article` element   240
`<article>` tag   188
`aside` element   240, 254
`<aside>` tag   189
attributes   15
audio
  adding to page   100–108
  embedding in web pages   105–108
  web audio formats   101
Authentic Jobs site   266
author stylesheets   365
auto keyword   149
Autoprefixer   219, 275

B

`background-attachment` property   162
`background-color` property   66

`background-image` property   94
background images   94–99
  adding hero images   97
  `background` shorthand properties   99
  controlling background repeat   95
  hero background images   161–162
  setting background positions   96
backgrounds
  applying colors to   66–68
  controlling repeat   95
  setting background position   96
`background` shorthand properties   99
`background-size` property   325
banded content   156
::before pseudo-element   360–362
`block-level` elements   42, 124
`blockquote` element   31
blocks, adding visual breaks between   43–44
Bluehost   403
`body` tag   23
body text   71
bold text   57–58
Bootstrap   186
borders   139–153
box model   140–141
breakpoints. *See* media query breakpoints
breaks. *See also* line breaks
  overview   245
  visual, adding between blocks   43–44
`br` element   40
bulleted lists   45, 47–49, 91

C

Calibri typeface   58
call-to-action buttons   161, 164–165
captions   271, 283–285
cascade   365–366
Cascading Style Sheets. *See* CSS
CDNs (content delivery networks)   337
centering. *See* dead-centering elements
character entities   302

child selectors   356
cite attribute   31
`<cite>` tag   291
class selectors
    overview   117–118
    versus ID selectors   352
`clear` property   124
code
    for Web Design Playground
        copying   396–397
        downloading   397–398
        validating   399–401
        CSS   401
        HTML   400
`<code>` tag   291
collapsing
    containers   125–127
    margins   152–153
colon character   17
Color Chooser tool   315–328
color property   65
colors   305–329
    adding with CSS   309–316
        Color Chooser tool   315–316
        hexadecimal numbers   312–313
        hsl( ) function   311
        RBG hex codes   314–315
        rgb( ) function   309–311
        transparency   312
    applying color gradient   322–329
        creating linear gradients   322–324
        creating radial gradients   325
        gradients and older browsers   326–327
        using Gradient Construction Kit   327–329
    applying to backgrounds   66–68
    applying to text   65
    choosing color scheme
        for home pages   71–72
        for landing pages   158
        for photo galleries   272
        for portfolio pages   375–376
    Color Scheme calculator   318–319
    harmonious, choosing   317–318
    overview of   64–68, 306–309
Color Scheme calculator   318–319

comments   75, 304
complementary colors   317
containers. *See also* inline containers
    in flexbox   205–212
        arranging items along cross axis   208–209
        arranging items along main axis   208
        arranging multiple lines along cross axis   211–212
        direction of container items   206–207
        wrapping items   210–211
    preventing collapse   125–127
content bands   166–168
content delivery networks (CDNs)   337
contextual selectors, in CSS   353–358
    child selectors   356
    descendant selectors   354
    sibling selectors   358
copyright symbol   81, 281
counter-increment property   362
counters   374
cPanel   404
cross axis
    arranging items along   208–209
    arranging multiple lines along   211–212
CSS (Cascading Style Sheets)   3–20, 349–369
    adding colors with   309–316
        Color Chooser tool   315–316
        hexadecimal numbers   312–313
        hsl( ) function   311
        RBG hex codes   314–315
        rgb( ) function   309–311
        transparency   312
    ::after pseudo-element   360–362
    ::before pseudo-element   360–362
    combining selectors   359–360
    contextual selectors   353–358
        child selectors   356
        descendant selectors   353–354
        parent selectors   352–353
        sibling selectors   353–358
    creating web with   10–11
    example of   8–9
    ID selectors   350–352
    in Web Design Playground   12

limitations of   10
overview of   7–9
properties   16
resetting with universal selectors   362
separating structure and presentation   8
styles   363–369
  cascade   365–366
  inheritance   363
  specificity   366–369
units of measurement in   119–120
uses for   8
validating   401
CSS Editor   397
cursive typefaces   53, 271
CuteFTP   403
CyberDuck   403

D

darkgray keyword   64
dead-centering elements   212–213
declaration block   16, 113
descendant element   353
descendant selectors   353–354
description list   45
<dfn> tag   292
direction of container items   206–207
div element   41
drop caps   128
dynamic captions   283–285

E

elements. *See also* semantic
        page elements
  ::after pseudo-element   360, 362
  ::before pseudo-element   360–362
  dead-centering with flexbox   212–213
  floating   121–137
    clearing floated elements   124–125
    default page flow   122
    floating drop caps   128
    floating pull quotes   129–131
    preventing container collapse   125–127
  positioning   121–137
    absolute positioning   134–136

default page flow   122
    fixed positioning   136–137
    relative positioning   132–133
Embedded Open Type (EOT)   337
embedded style sheet   112
embedding
  audio in web pages   105–108
  video in web pages   102–104
emphasizing text   29–30
empty string   86
em tag   14
EOT (Embedded Open Type)   337
external link   362
external style sheets   115–117

F

fallback color   326
fantasy typefaces   53
faux-column effect   195, 242
feet   53
figcaption element   89, 284
figure element   89
file formats   87
files
  local, linking to   298–299
  uploading   403–404
File Transfer Protocol (FTP)   402
FileZilla   403
fixed footers   281
fixed positioning   136–137
fixed-width layouts   53, 232–249
flex-basis property   216, 239
flexbox
  browser support   219–220
  containers   205–212
    arranging items along cross axis   208–209
    arranging items along main axis   208
    arranging multiple lines along cross
        axis   211–212
    direction of container items   206–207
    wrapping items   210–211
  creating holy-grail layouts with   222–227
  creating page layouts with
    creating thumbnail lists   220
  overview   203

Index

dead-centering elements with 212–213
flexbox items 213–219
    changing order of items 217
    flex shorthand property 217
    growing items 214
    overriding item alignment 218–219
    shrinking items 215
    suggesting initial sizes for items 216–217
overview of 204–205
flex-direction property 206, 216, 283
flex-grow property 214, 238, 280
flexible layouts 237–240
flex shorthand property 217
flex-shrink property 215, 238
flex-start value 208
flex-wrap property 238
flex-wrap values 211
floating
    drop caps 128
    elements 121–137
        clearing floated elements 124–125
        default page flow 122
        preventing container collapse 125–127
    pull quotes 129–131
float property
    creating holy-grail layouts with 191–196
    creating page layouts with 191–196
    overview 185
flow. See page flow
flush 63
folders 398–399
Fontex 337
@font-face directive 334
font-family property 53, 78, 158, 332
fonts
    font stacks 332–334
    generic 53–54
    hosting 337–339
    responsive font sizes 259
    shorthand properties 343–348
    specifying web fonts 334
    system 54–55
    third-party hosted fonts 335–336
font-size property 56, 75, 258
Fontspring 337

Font Squirrel 337
font-variant property 340
footer element 195, 225
footer sections 279–280
<footer> tag 189
footers, fixed 281. See also page footers
FTP (File Transfer Protocol) 402

G

generated content 360
Georgia typeface 79
GIF (Graphics Interchange Format) 88
GoDaddy 403
Google Fonts 335, 374
gradient
    applying 322–329
    creating linear gradients 322–324
    creating radial gradients 325
    older browsers and 326–327
    using Gradient Construction Kit 327–329
Gradient Construction Kit 327–329
grandparent element 352
Graphics Interchange Format (GIF) 88
grayscale keyword 64

H

h1 through h6 tags 14
hanging indent 63
hash symbol 300, 314
<header> tag 187
headers 160–161
headings 33–34
head tag 23
height, setting
    of lines 341
    overview 142–143
hero images
    adding 97
    background images 161–162
hexadecimal numbers 312–313
hex triplets 314
Hicks Design 263
holy-grail layouts 190
    creating with flexbox 222–227

creating with floats   191–196
creating with inline blocks   197–201
overview   184–185
horizontal alignment of paragraphs   60
horizontal measures   261
horizontal navigation   145
horizontal rule   43
HostGator   403
house styles   7
href attribute   16, 35
hr element   43
hsl( ) function   311
HSL (hue, saturation, and luminance)   307, 311
HTML5 (Hypertext Markup Language)
   entity browser   303
   inserting figures   89
   semantic page elements   186–190
      <article> tags   188
      <aside> tags   189
      <footer> tags   189
      <header> tags   187
      <main> tags   187
      <nav> tags   187
      <section> tags   188
HTML Editor   396
HTML (Hypertext Markup Language)
   <abbr> tag   290
   adding comments   304
   adding tag attributes   15–16
   <cite> tag   291
   <code> tag   291
   creating web with   10–11
   <dfn> tag   292
   elements   289–304
   example of   5–6
   for page structure   38–44
      adding visual breaks between blocks
         43–44
      creating inline containers   42
      dividing web page text   41
      inserting line breaks   40
      paragraphs   38
   HTML5 entity browser   303
   inserting special characters   302
   in Web Design Playground   12

<kbd> tag   292
limitations of   10
links   298–300
   linking to local files   298–299
   linking to same page   300
<mark> tag   292
overview of   4–6
<pre> tag   293
<samp> tag   294
<small> tag   294
<s> tag   294
<sub> tag   295
<sup> tag   295
tags   14–15
<time> tag   296
uses for   4–5
<u> tag   297
validating   400
<var> tag   298
html tag   23
hue, saturation, and luminance (HSL)   307, 311
hypertext reference   16, 35

I

ID selectors
   in CSS   350–352
   versus class selectors   352
images   86–93
   aligning   92–93
   as custom bullets   91
   background images   94–99
      adding hero images   97
      background shorthand properties   99
      controlling background repeat   95
      setting background positions   96
   creating fluid images   252–254
   delivering responsively   255–256
   getting graphics   88–89
   image file formats   87
   inserting HTML5 figures   89
   optimizing   99–100
   responsive   252–256
   setting up as links   90
img element   15, 86

!important keyword   367
indenting text   62
indent styles   63
inheritance   258, 363
inline blocks
    creating holy-grail layout with   197–201
    creating page layouts with   196–201
inline-block technique   237
inline containers   42
inline elements   42
inline styles   110–112
internal style sheets   112–115
ISP (internet service provider), web hosting
        by   402
italicizing text   59

J

JPEG (Joint Photographic Experts Group)   88
justification axis   210
justify-content property   208

K

<kbd> tag   292
keyphrase   28
keywords   28–29

L

landing pages   155–180
    building   159–178
        call-to-action buttons   164–165
        headers   160–161
        hero background image   161–162
        initial structure   159–160
        page footers   177–178
        pricing tables   170–174
        product descriptions   165
        product images   162–163
        product info   163–164
        product testimonials   169–170
        setting up content bands   166–168
        social media links   176–177
    choosing color schemes   158
    choosing typefaces   157–158
    overview of   156
    sketching layout of   156–157

layouts *See also* holy-grail layouts; page layouts
    creating   233–249
        adaptive layouts   240–244
        flexible layouts   237–240
        mobile-first layouts   246–248
    identifying   248–249
    liquid layouts   233–237
    media query breakpoints   245
lightness   308
linear gradients   322, 322–324
line breaks   40
line-height property   76
lines
    arranging multiple along cross axis   211–212
    setting height of   341
links   298–300
    overview   4, 35–36
    setting up images as   90
    to local files   298–299
    to same page   300
    to social media   77, 176–177
liquid layouts
    creating   233–235
    with viewport units   236–237
lists
    bulleted lists, adding   47–49
    numbered lists, adding   45–46
    organizing text into   44–49
    thumbnail lists, creating   220
list-style-image property   91
list-style-type CSS property   46, 48
list-style-type property   276
li tag   45
local font file   337
lossless compression   88
luminance
    overview   308
    specifying with hsl() function   311

M

main axis   208
main sections   278
<main> tag   187
margins   139–153
    collapsing   152–153
    controlling   149–151

`margin-top` property 153
margin values 149
`<mark>` tag 292
markup 4
`max-width` property 234, 245
measurement
  responsive 260–267
  units of 119–120
media query breakpoints 245
`@media` rule 241
`meta` tag 23
`min-width` property 144, 245
mobile-first layouts 246–248
monospace typeface 53
MPEG-4 container 101

N

nav bars 282–283
`<nav>` tag 187
negative indent 63
negative margin values 149
negative order values 218
nested `div` element 167
nowrap value 211
numbered lists 45–46

O

Ogg container 101
ol tag 45
opacity 312
Open Font Library 337
ordered list 45
order values 218
outdent 63
outer `div` element 167
`outline` property 148
`overflow` property 143

P

padding 144–145
`padding-bottom` property 281
`padding-right` property 129, 146
padding-top declaration 129
page flow 122

page footers
  of home pages 80
  of landing page 177–178
  of portfolio pages 390–392
page layouts 183–201
  creating 274
    adaptive layouts 240–244
    flexible layouts 237–240
    mobile-first layouts 246–248
    with floats 191–196
    with inline blocks 196–201
  creating with flexbox 203
    creating holy-grail layouts with
      flexbox 222–227
    creating thumbnail lists 220
    dead-centering elements 212–213
    flexbox browser support 219–220
    flexbox containers 205–212
    flexbox items 213–219
    overview 204–205
  fixed-width layouts 232–249
  holy-grail layouts 185–190
  HTML5 semantic page elements
    186–190
    `<article>` tags 188
    `<aside>` tags 189
    `<footer>` tags 189
    `<header>` tags 187
    `<main>` tags 187
    `<nav>` tags 187
    `<section>` tags 188
  liquid layouts
    creating 233–235
    with viewport units 236–237
  methods 185–186
  of portfolio pages 378
  sketching
    of home pages 70–71
    of landing pages 156–157
    of photo gallery 270
    of portfolio pages 372
page structure 37–49
  HTML elements for 38–44
    adding visual breaks between blocks
      43–44
    creating inline containers 42

dividing web page text   41
inserting line breaks   40
paragraphs   38
of landing pages   159–160
of photo galleries   273–274
organizing text into lists   44–49
adding bulleted lists   47–49
adding numbered lists   45–46
overview   22–23
Palettable   158
paragraphs   60–62
aligning horizontally   60
indenting text   62
overview   38
parent element   352
parent selectors   352–353
percentages   233
photo galleries, creating   281–285
adding dynamic captions   283–285
choosing colors   272
choosing typefaces   271
fixed footers   281
footer sections   279–280
header sections   275
initial structure of   273–274
main sections   278
navigation sections   276–277
overall layout of   274
overview   269–272
preparing photos   270
sketching layouts   270
sticky nav bars   282–283
pixels   93
Playfair Display   375
playground. See Web Design Playground
PNG (Portable Network Graphics)   88
portfolio pages   371–393
building   376–392
about section   387–389
contact section   389–390
header sections   379–382
initial structure of   376–378
overall layout of   378
page footers   390–392

portfolio introduction   382
portfolios   384–387
choosing color schemes   375–376
choosing typefaces   373–375
overview of   372
sketching layout of   372
positioning
absolute positioning   134–136
elements   121–137, 131–137
fixed positioning   136–137
relative positioning   132–133
position property   132
positive indent   63
positive margin values   149
<pre> tag   293
preformatted text   293
pricing tables   170–174
products
descriptions of   165
images of   162–163
info   163–164
testimonials   169–170
pseudo-elements
::after   360–362
::before   360–362
p tag   38
pull quotes   129–131, 147, 360

Q
quotations   31–32, 54, 248

R
radial gradients   322, 325
RBG (Red, Green, and Blue) hex codes   314–315
referencing external style sheets   115–117
relative positioning   132–133
relative values   120
remote font file   337
repeat, background   95
resetting CSS with universal selectors   362
responsive
images   252–256
creating fluid images   252–254
delivering images responsively   255–256

layouts
    creating   233–249
    creating adaptive layouts   240–244
    creating flexible layouts   237–240
    creating mobile-first layouts   246–248
    identifying   248–249
    liquid layouts   233–237
    media query breakpoints   245
    responsive font sizes   259
    responsive measurements   260–267
    typography   251–267, 257–267
rgb( ) function   309–311
RGB method   306
root element   120, 258
row value   207

S

<s> tag   294
<samp> tag   294
sans-serif typeface   53, 71
saturation
    overview   308
    specifying with hsl( ) function   311
Scalable Vector Graphics (SVG)   88
<section> tags   188
selectors
    child   356
    combining   359–360
    contextual   353–358
    descendant   353–354
    ID selectors   350–352
    parent   352–353
    sibling   353–358
    universal   362
self-closing tags   14
semantic page elements. See HTML5 semantic
        page elements
serif typeface   53
shorthand. See background shorthand
        properties
shorthand font properties   343–348
shrinking items   215
sibling selectors   353–358
sizes
    height, setting   142–143

of type, setting   56
    styling   139–153
    suggesting for items in flexbox   216–217
    width, setting   142–143
sizes attribute   255
sketching layouts
    of home pages   70–71
    of landing pages   156–157
    of photo gallery   270
    of portfolio pages   372
small caps   340
<small> tag   294
space-around value   208, 212
span element   42
special characters   302
specificity   366–369
split complementary colors   318
src attribute   86, 103, 255
srcset attribute   255
sticky value   282
stretch value   208
strong element   27, 30
strong tag   57
structure. See page structure
style attribute   7, 110
style rules   17, 113
styles
    adding internal style sheets   112–115
    adding to pages   110–118
    inserting inline styles   110–112
    referencing external style sheets   115–117
    using class selectors   117–118
style tag   23
<sub> tag   295
<sup> tag   295
SVG (Scalable Vector Graphics)   88

T

tables, pricing   170–174
tags
    adding tag attributes   15–16
    in HTML   14–15
    overview   4
text
    adding   25–26

aligning   92–93
alternative, formatting   30–31
applying colors to   65
bold   57–58
dividing web page text   41
emphasizing   29–30
important, marking   27
indenting   62
italics   59
of body   78–80
organizing into lists   44–49
   adding bulleted lists   47–49
   adding numbered lists   45–46
setting type size   56
specifying generic font   53–54
specifying system font   54–55
styles   57–59
styling typeface   52–53
`text-align-last` property   62
`text-align` property   60
text editors   404–405
text elements   26–32
   emphasizing text   29–30
   formatting alternative text   30–31
   formatting keywords   28–29
   marking important text   27
   quotations   31–32
`text-indent` property   62
text styles   340–348
   setting line height   341
   shorthand `font` properties   343–348
   styling small caps   340
thumbnail lists   220, 270
tiling background   95
`<time>` tag   296
title attribute   290
titles
   adding   23–24
   of pages   75
trademark symbol   302
Transmit   403
transparency   312
triadic colors   318
TTF/OTF (TrueType Font/OpenType Font)   337

typefaces
   choosing
      for home pages   71
      for landing pages   157–158
      for photo galleries   271
      for portfolio pages   373–375
   font stacks   332–334
   hosting fonts   337–339
   specifying   332–339
   specifying web fonts   334
   styling   52–53
   third-party hosted fonts   335–336
type selector   117

U

`<u>` tag   297
`ul` tag   47
Uniform Resource Locator (URL)   35
units of measurement   119–120
universal selectors   142, 362, 367
unordered list   45
uploading files   403–404
URL (Uniform Resource Locator)   35
user agent style sheet   365

V

`<var>` tag   298
validating code   399–401
`vertical-align` property   92
vertical-bar symbol   77
vertical measures   261
video
   adding to page   100–108
   embedding in web pages   102–104
   web video formats   101
viewport height unit   236
viewport maximum unit   237
viewport minimum unit   237
visual breaks   43–44

W

W3C (World Wide Web Consortium)
   297, 365, 400

web audio formats   101
Web Design Playground   11–20
  copying code   396–397
  CSS in   12
  downloading code   397–398
  HTML in   12
  loading lesson files   12–13
  saving work in   13, 396–398
Webfont Generator package   338
web hosting provider   10, 402
WebM container   101
Web Open Font Format (WOFF)   337
Web Page Markup Language (WPML)   4
web pages

  initial structure of   72–75
  page introduction   76
web video formats   101
whitespace   26, 136
width, setting   142–143
WOFF (Web Open Font Format)   337
World Wide Web Consortium (W3C)
        297, 365, 400
wrapping items, in flexbox   210–211

Z

Zapf Dingbats typeface   158
z-index property   132, 136